WITHDRAWN

The Religious Imagination of American Women

MARY FARRELL BEDNAROWSKI

Indiana
University
Press

BLOOMINGTON AND INDIANAPOLIS

This book is a publication of
Indiana University Press
601 North Morton Street
Bloomington, Indiana 47404-3797 USA
www.indiana.edu/~iupress

Telephone orders 800-842-6796
Fax orders 812-855-7931
Orders by e-mail iuporder@indiana.edu

The paper used in this publication meets the minimum
requirements of American National Standard for Information
Sciences—Permanence of Paper for Printed Library
Materials, ANSI Z39.48-1984.

MANUFACTURED IN THE UNITED STATES OF AMERICA

Library of Congress Cataloging-in-Publication Data

Bednarowski, Mary Farrell.
    The religious imagination of American women / by Mary Farrell
Bednarowski.
        p.   cm. — (Religion in North America)
    Includes bibliographical references and index.
    ISBN 0-253-33594-9 (alk. paper). — ISBN 0-253-21338-X (pbk. :
alk. paper)
    1. Women—Religious life—United States. 2. Religious thought—
United States—20th century. 3. Feminist theology. 4. United
States—Religion—1965– I. Title. II. Series.
BL625.7.B425 1999
200′.82′0973—dc21   99-23096

1 2 3 4 5   04 03 02 01 00 99

For Keith, Betsy and Jason, and Paul
and
Irene Smith Bednarowski, Queen of Mothers-in-Law

RELIGION

for Anne E. Patrick, SNJM

I grew up in this house.
It is heavy and dark.
The ground on which it stands
is beginning to cave in.

When it rains
the foundation leaks.
I watch and pray for a rainbow.

Once the walls were familiar,
comforting. But now the rooms
feel small and cramped,
moldy and gray.

It's been remodeled time
and again, but the basic structure
remains the same.
Old materials, still functional,
beautiful . . . but I want something spacious
with warmth and light.

I am drawn to houses in the East,

but I live here, the hallways of its history
lined with age old manuscripts
full of architectural plans.
I rip them apart page by page
searching for a house
without walls.

Pam Wynn

Contents

Foreword

Mary Farrell Bednarowski's new book represents scholarship come of age. Women's studies, feminist studies, and gender studies have all interwoven themselves with contemporary interests in American religion and spirituality to produce a series of specialized studies of women and religion. Building on that work and inflecting it with her own particular concerns and approach, Bednarowski here offers an authoritative synthesis not of women's religious *experience*, as many would be tempted to do, but of women's religious *thought* in the American context. Her period is the extended present—public expressions of American women thinking religiously from 1985 onward, with special attention to the 1990s. And her focus is on the comparative task, cutting across different traditions in terms of the five themes that frame her interpretive vision.

First and above all, Bednarowski argues, these women's religious thought is ambivalent, for it is the product of people who are both insiders and outsiders in their traditions and who therefore stand in a place of creative tension that is positive. Second, Bednarowski tells us, women's religious thought is characterized by a sense of the immanence of the divine or sacred world, with a strongly persistent habit of bringing religion down to earth. Third, says Bednarowski, if women favor religion on the ground, they also celebrate the revelatory power of the ordinary, and their claim that the ordinary is sacred is important for its capacity to generate a certain kind of religious thought. Fourth, she says, women's religious thought is characterized prominently by themes of relationship and relatedness, important again here for their ability to yield fruit in religious thought. Finally, in Bednarowski's reading, American women's religious thought is pervaded by the theme of healing, a healing that is conceptualized in ever more expansive ways to encompass well nigh the whole of life.

In positing and describing all of this, Bednarowski treads ground that is laced with scholarly land mines. Is she trying to claim that there is something unique about women as women when they are being religious? And should she be? Are the themes she uncovers so general as to be simply descriptions of the human? Or are they merely truisms about women conveyed ubiquitously by American vernacular culture? What role do history and lived experience play in thought? Do all women in America fit into the same or similar religious molds? Can Bednarowski talk about thought at all except in the context of an ongoing and lengthy tradition of self-conscious theology directed by seminary schools and professors? And what relationship does thought have, anyway, to issues of women's spirituality, which are everywhere seemingly à la mode?

As readers will find here, Bednarowski is an astute guide through and past the land mines. She is unwilling to say that women's religious thought in the land of the free is totally distinctive, a separate species of religionizing from that of the male chorus. Neither is she willing to write it off as being just like the theological expressions of men. She understands the banality that some of the themes and claims come trailing, but she is also a depth reader who can move past surface to recover a substantive dimension beneath the truisms. She takes history seriously; but she takes gendered experience as seriously. She reads feminist theologians carefully, but she also reads op-ed pieces and more ephemeral literature. She finds women's thought inevitably tied to experience and action, so that her work leads her into the realm of women's spirituality that in one sense she has consciously eschewed in her decision to focus on "thought." And she writes with an ease and a grace that bring the reader in close touch with her material.

In this context, two abilities most distinguish Bednarowski's contribution in these pages. First, Bednarowski brings to her subject a long background in studying new religious movements in the United States *and* as long a background of involvement with mainstream Christianity, through both her teaching situation and her personal religious history. Thus, she represents a balanced voice—not just a student of the New Age who can explore Goddess spirituality, Wiccan practice, feminist eco-theology, and the like, not just a liberal or progressive Christian scholar who can tell us all about the church and, in a few cases, the synagogue. Moreover, although liberal Christian feminist thought forms the center of Bednarowski's volume, balance opens into a catholicity of vision that is able to encompass not merely the Goddess and the church, but also an even more extended sampling of the intense religious pluralism that characterizes America at the turn of the millennium. African-American, Latina, and Native American women all have found their voices on her pages. So have Buddhists and Muslims and assorted others.

Second, and perhaps most exciting, what Bednarowski is able to do—and to do so well—in her study is to construct a theology in ways appropriate to a scholar of American religious history in postmodern times. By naming the characteristics of women's religious thought, by linking themes with other themes—ambivalence toward at-homeness linked with the ordinary, commitment to healing linked with the primacy of relatedness, comfort with immanence linked with an embodied and "material" spirituality, for example— Bednarowski is engaged in declarative practice that will shape what others see and say about her subject. By pointing the way for readers to see what she says is there, she also points the way in defining a theology. This particular religious landscape will look different to readers after they encounter Bednarowski's work.

In sum, Bednarowski's exploration of ambivalence and related themes is hardly ambivalent itself in its facility with its subject and in its definitiveness. Mary Farrell Bednarowski's work is a landmark volume in the Religion in North America series, and it promises to lead the conversation regarding the religious thought of American women well into the next millennium.

Catherine L. Albanese
Stephen J. Stein, Series Editors

Acknowledgments

Like many academic women of my generation, I began graduate school in the 1960s with a set of experiences of myself as a woman in American culture and religion, and women in general, that were mostly uninterpreted in light of any broader patterns. By the time I finished my work in American Studies in 1973, I was aware that my scholarly work would most likely always be concerned to some extent with issues of gender. What I did not know was that I would do most of that work in a Protestant theological seminary—not something a Roman Catholic woman might have predicted. It is to that institution, United Theological Seminary of the Twin Cities, with its history of commitment to women's full participation in their religious communities, and to my colleagues there that I want to express particular gratitude in relation to this book: for sabbatical time, for support, for encouragement to shape the implications of my interest in religious ideas in my own way—not as a theologian but as a student of American religion and culture. We are a small faculty, and there is no one who did not help me in one way or another. Everyone read at least one chapter, and several people read more than one: Christie Neuger, Clyde Steckel, Wilson Yates. Sue Ebbers edited the first draft of the entire manuscript with grace and vigor. The time they took to write comments, make suggestions, and talk things over has been a great gift to me. Dale Dobias, our reference librarian, found things I asked for and brought me things I hadn't known about. Many thanks, also, to my former and much-missed colleague, Mary Potter Engel, for her careful and creative reading; to UTS graduate Deborah Adele for research assistance on Chapters 5 and 6; to Patrick Henry of the Ecumenical Institute in Collegeville, Minnesota, for his encouraging reading of the first two chapters; and to Catherine Albanese and Stephen Stein for their rigorous and detailed response to the first draft. For the perfect place to write about women and religion, my gratitude to the Benedictine Sisters of St. Joseph, Minnesota, and their Studium community, especially Janice Wedl, Merle Nolde, Linda Kulzer, Dolores Super, and Shaun O'Meara. For conversations about particular aspects of the manuscript, my gratitude, as well, to Mary Ellen Dumas and Rabbi Marcia Zimmerman. And my appreciation to Pam Wynn for permission to use her poem, "Religion." For the kind of friendship that includes talking not just about book manuscripts but also a million other things, my profound thanks to Roberta Gladowski, Sally Hill, Pamela Carter Joern, Amanda Porterfield, Kim Power, Jean Ward, Catherine Wessinger, and Gayle Graham Yates. And for the perspective and grounding that only life in a family can offer, my love and thanks to my husband, Keith, my daughter, Betsy, my son, Paul, and my son-in-law, Jason.

The Religious Imagination of American Women

1

American Women as Religious Thinkers

Dissenting Participants

This is a book about American women's religious thought at the end of the twentieth century and about women as self-conscious, theologically creative participants in their own particular religious communities. Its most basic question is this: when women write and speak publicly about religious ideas, what do they have to say? The heart of the book is an exploration of five themes or ideas that pervade the religious writings of women across a variety of communities and that function as catalysts to the theological imaginations of women: (1) an ongoing, creative, and, increasingly, cultivated ambivalence toward their religious communities; (2) an emphasis on the immanence—that is, the in-dwelling—of the sacred; (3) a regard for the ordinary as revelatory of the sacred; (4) a view of ultimate reality as relational; and (5) an interpretation of healing, both physical and spiritual, as a primary rather than a secondary function of religion.

Taken altogether, these ideas give rise to a broad interpretive framework that shapes women's analyses of gender issues in their various communities and also their approaches to theological innovation, conservation, reform, and transformation in those communities. Within this wider framework of general themes, women retain the symbols, rituals, teachings, and much of the language of their particular communities. A manifestation of common themes, as it turns out, does not obliterate or diminish specificity in women's religious thought. In fact, it is my strong conviction that the elaboration of these five themes within particular communities enhances distinctiveness of expression as women work to illuminate what is at stake in the realm of religious ideas, not only for themselves but for their whole communities and for society.

Although I certainly want to say that women across many communities embrace these ideas, I want to do so without pushing for a pan-woman spirituality and a unanimity of purpose and experience among women that can't be supported. I don't think that the traditional concept of piety, meaning primarily a set of religious affections, or the more contemporary term, "spirituality," quite captures what I'm trying to convey. Both these terms suggest a togetherness, a cohesiveness, that from my perspective goes too far, particularly at a time when women in many communities are emphasizing the particularity of their experiences. And yet I consider it both possible and useful to think of these ideas as constituting at least the broad outlines of a worldview, or, perhaps better said, an interpretive orientation toward reality: one that is ambivalent, immanentist, earth-oriented, pluralistic, and pragmatic. It is an orientation toward reality that functions as a stimulus not to one but to multiple pieties and spiritualities.[1] Whether it is equally possible and useful to go so far as to call this constellation of ideas "women's religion," or "women's spirituality," is another question, one that I will take up with more specificity in the Epilogue after the voices of many women have been heard and there is more to go on.

I belabor this issue of how most fruitfully to refer in the aggregate to the ideas under consideration because it is part of another dimension of inquiry that undergirds this study. Where do these ideas fit within broader patterns of American religious thought? Or, to put this a little differently, how is consciousness of gender affecting American religious thought?

To return to the five themes themselves, I do not consider any of them exclusive to the religious thought of women; what I'm getting at is, rather, a matter of emphasis and elaboration. These themes show up over and over again in many religious traditions and in the writings of men as well as women. It is not my intention to argue that these themes cannot be found in the theological work of men. This is a book about what women *do* have to say, not about what men *do not* have to say. Nor do I hold that women are in total agreement about what these ideas mean. Each poses theoretical and practical difficulties, and those who cite the ideas so extensively do not all agree on their meanings and implications. I cannot claim that there is anything original about the ideas, and, taken separately, they are not even very startling. In fact, one could say that these ideas appear so frequently in women's religious thought that they threaten, on the surface, to become empty of meaning. The philosopher Nancy Frankenberry has suggested about "relationality," for example, that "[i]ndeed, if there is currently one term in feminist theology and critical theory in general that ought to be paid overtime, as Humpty Dumpty said, because it does so much work, it is 'relations.' By now the literature verges on becoming a pastiche about the power of 'relations.'"[2]

It is difficult to deny the cogency of Frankenberry's comment, at least up to a point. One could say the same thing about "immanence" and "the sacred-ness of the ordinary" and "healing." But if these ideas are cited so frequently as to become platitudinous and even incantatory at times, they are nonetheless immensely powerful—precisely, I think, because they are used so frequently. This study is an exploration of where their power lies. My interest is in demonstrating *that* they are used by women of very different religious traditions, but even more in looking at *how* they have served women and why they are so compelling and fruitful. If one looks at how the concept of "relationship" has fostered new understandings of the sacred and ultimate reality, of human nature and agency, and the workings of the world, then the term no longer appears over-used and under-defined, but dense and complicated with insights and meanings from many traditions. That complexifying and intensifying of ideas—the realm of theological creativity—is what this book is about.

I am convinced, then, that the power of these ideas and their importance in women's thought derives not from their esoteric nature, their singleness of meaning, or their uniqueness to women's religious thought, but from other factors. They are, first of all, versatile ideas, and therefore they are useful to women of many communities. They are not specifically or relentlessly theological ideas peculiar to one community, but they draw on reserves of meaning already present to one extent or another in most religious worldviews. The concept of immanence, for example, is compatible with many different models of the divine as well as with nontheistic and polytheistic understandings of ultimate reality. They are ideas that are much more evocative than propositional; they tend to open up the need for further exploration rather than close it down. Therefore they are more likely to function at the level of inspiration rather than prescription. These ideas also offer potential both for critique of existing systems of thought and for the construction of alternative visions, as I will work to demonstrate in each chapter. They are accessible at different levels of depth and sophistication and often help to bridge, rather than create, gaps between women who are theologically educated and those who are not. Concepts such as "immanence" or "relational justice" can be "problematized" endlessly—theologically, philosophically, psychologically—but they can also be grasped more immediately and with less complexity. In other words, these are not ideas available only to the theologically and particularly initiated. They are clearly useful to women inside and outside established religious traditions, and they make sense as well to women who distinguish between "spirituality" and "religion" and favor the former.

Context of the Study

This study takes place at a particular time in what is called feminism's second wave in America (the first having occurred in the nineteenth century), a movement that is by now nearly forty years old. I take for granted as background a set of assumptions on the part of women, all of them powerful in their impli-cation for women's religious thought—assumptions sometimes more aptly per-ceived as a series of discoveries, because they appear now to be discoveries of what in retrospect seems obvious. Once articulated and expanded, they have taken on the power of the familiar made new and namable. Some of these discoveries, particularly early on, have led to an awareness of the importance of historical knowledge about women as one foundation for creative theol-ogy. Others are concerned with relationships among various communities of women. Some have to do with the general intellectual climate and trends in theology and religious studies at the end of the twentieth century. All of them are related to the broad insight that, for a variety of reasons and for good and for ill, women have experienced religion differently from men—and that this reality has implications for theology. And thus, in turn, all of them are serving as catalysts for women's religious thought. I present them in loose and overlap-ping chronological order.

1. The early, startling, and continually expanding discovery of the extent to which women have been excluded from the histories of their traditions and from having a voice in the theological formation of their traditions.

2. The continually growing recognition that, if women have been mostly absent from the public practices of their religious communities, they have been present in other, more private ways that have been unacknowledged and undervalued and must be recovered.

3. The realization that not only have women been excluded from full par-ticipation in their religious communities, but the exclusion has been based on a theological rendering of women as differently human or less fully human than men—a different species, somehow, who could and should not speak for themselves but needed to be spoken to and about.

These first three discoveries have obviously promoted a great deal of work in American religious history and in theology. They have motivated women to ask both what prevailing religious ideas are responsible for historical patterns of exclusion and inclusion and what kinds of religious ideas are more condu-cive to women's full participation.

4. The increasing theological authority of what has come to be called "women's experience"—that is, the conviction that whatever women have learned about themselves from society and from their religious communities, "life" has taught them something else that calls into question what they had previously accepted.

5. Accusations by women of color that religious feminism is primarily a product of the white middle class and so irrelevant and even destructive to their more pressing issues of survival.

6. The growing reluctance to make universal claims about women's expe-rience or women's nature, a reluctance that has come to be called "anti-essen-tialism." As a result, "women's experience" has become an enormously com-plicated category of inquiry as women from many communities have begun to

articulate their own particular experiences of being women. If this has led to strife among women, it has also fostered the increasingly distinctive articulation of their experiences by women of particular communities. This development has contributed to a caution about making universal claims, but also to a greater proliferation of ideas about what it means to be a woman in any given community.

7. The emergence of new kinds of women's theologies—womanist, *mujerista*, goddess—in other words, a particularizing not just of women's voices but of many different communities of women.[3]

8. The emerging concern that women's insistence on their differences may diminish the moral force of claims for justice made on behalf of all women and the accompanying search for creative ways to retain the highly contextual nature of women's religious thought without losing the capacity to make broad-based ethical demands.

9. An ever-increasing number of women pursuing theological educations and entry into ordained ministry and religious leadership and scholarship, and thus the ongoing growth of a multi-generational body of women working in religion and theology.

10. The pressing insights of deconstructionism and a postmodern worldview that insist on the impossibility of uncovering or even pointing to a metaphysically stable reality that lies behind or beneath verbal interpretations; and the realization, also, of the "constructive" nature of religious thought—that the task of the religious thinker is to keep religious ideas and symbols vital rather than to protect and maintain them as static entities.

11. Acceptance of the reality that insights about the exclusion of women in particular traditions and religion in general do not lead to sudden drastic changes—in other words, slow progress and a turning to discussions of the need for "systemic change" or "transformation" of religious traditions rather than simply changes in liturgical language or ordination to clerical status.[4] Accompanying this realization has been the development of terms like "patriarchy," which have become hermeneutically and heuristically indispensable, although not uncontroversial, in many women's theologies. It has also led to an emphasis on the need for transformation of theology and religious ideas. "The right question is theological," according to Judith Plaskow, a Jewish feminist theologian.[5] This is Plaskow's way of insisting that women's exclusion from full participation in their communities is not caused merely by social arrangements; it is embedded in traditions' theological understandings of how the universe operates.

12. A recognition among women that theology and religious thought are arenas of human creativity. One detects in women's religious thought a growing confidence and delight in the play of religious ideas combined with the conviction that there is a great deal at stake in this enterprise for women and men both, for the world and for the planet. As more and more women enter the fields of religion and theology, there is a reinforcing of the experience

that theology, particularly, is a discipline like any other—that it is accessible to those who study it, and that it is also an art form, one devoted to the constructing of worldviews, that invites playing with ideas and conventions. As with any art form, part of the challenge and the joy is to work at discovering how far one can go before one is past the boundaries to such an extent that the enterprise becomes meaningless to a particular community. As we shall see, this play with ideas has both aesthetic and ethical implications; the verdict as to whether or not the new forms are compelling emerges as it becomes clear whether they are considered authentic and powerful by the communities to whom they are offered. Not every new idea, as many have pointed out, survives within any given community; not every bit of knowledge recovered about women's history in a tradition will be incorporated into the ongoing tradition. Thus, there is not only a prophetic tone to women's religious thought, a crying out against injustice, but a highly speculative and creative quality as well.

13. An amelioration of some of the more polarizing choices women experienced in regard to their traditions in the early stages of their participation in the creation of religious thought: be silent or get out; give up or get out; work from within or get out; be a radical (which meant getting out, usually) or a reformer (which meant staying in). As will become apparent in Chapter 2, there are more subtle ways both to stay in and to get out than had previously been supposed. And one of the decisive issues for many women is whether they have a community that supports them. Where can they do theological work and for whom are they doing it?

14. A sense that we may be at a turning point in this feminist movement, and a recognition that this is not the first time in history that women have recognized the extent of their exclusion. This latter awareness raises significant questions about what comes next. Historical patterns do not offer much reason for optimism about the persistence of gains for women over time, and women with any knowledge of previous feminist movements are well aware of how quickly they can fade away. Gerda Lerner calls this the failure to develop a feminist consciousness. This failure in previous centuries motivates contemporary concerns of how to keep feminism alive into the next century and into future generations.[6]

15. Women's demonstration that their theological work is not exclusive to matters of gender but also necessarily involved with contemporary issues of religion that are inevitable concerns at the end of the twentieth century. Given what we know of the limitations of religious systems, what does it now mean to be a religiously committed person or a member of a religious community? How do we, women or men, speak cogently about ultimate reality or the sacred at the end of the twentieth century? In light of what we are discovering about the unstable and power-driven nature of religious texts, language, and authority, in what do we place our trust?—and for what reasons? In a culture that must take religious pluralism for granted, who are we as members of particular

religious communities in relation to other religious communities? At a time in history when religion is perceived as one among many human institutions, what is its distinctive role in contributing to the common good?

The five themes on which I elaborate in the following chapters not only demonstrate women's consciousness of the significance of gender for the construction of religious ideas and worldviews, but have insights to offer, as well, from the perspectives of women about these broader questions. The subject of ambivalence is closely related to issues of religious commitment and women's persistent efforts to offer both devotion and challenge to their communities. An emphasis on immanence is concerned with how the sacred, however defined, is experienced and articulated—and on whose authority. Claiming the sacredness of the ordinary opens up some of the theological implications of immanental worldviews and fosters questions, as well, about what kind of content, even what level of personal detail, is appropriate for the religious thought of a community. An insistence on the relational nature of reality points to the complexities of the moral life in a plural culture. And an inclination to perceive healing as a primary task of religion motivates questions about the overall function of religion: what is it for?

Circumscription of the Topic

My focus in this study is the religious thought of American women that has emerged since about 1985, but particularly in the 1990s through 1997.[7] I have used two principles of selection in order to adequately represent multiple voices; both require difficult choices. The first is variety. It is simply not possible at this historical moment to write about American women's religious thought without including voices from many different communities of women, and thus I have searched in many different arenas for perspectives on the themes under consideration in this book.[8] But "variety" in any work has its limits. This volume is by no means an exhaustive survey of women's religious thinking in America, although I do my best to draw from sufficiently diverse examples and to cast a wide net in gathering those examples. It is not, either, meant to be primarily an investigation of the thought of prominent feminist theologians, however much I make use of their work, particularly some who have been well known since the late 1960s and 1970s. These are women who have been active participants through much of the history of recent women's thought and who have had enough time and critical response to reconsider earlier claims and address a variety of theological issues. I have felt an obligation to give some indication of the extent to which their influence has shaped contemporary women's religious thought. In this, I concur with American religious historian Ann Braude's contention that "[n]ames like Rosemary Radford Ruether and Elisabeth Schüssler Fiorenza have become household words among American church women who may not be able to name a single male theologian."[9] One could add a long list of other names as well, among them Marjorie Suchocki, Sallie McFague, Judith Plaskow, Rita Gross, Elizabeth Johnson, Beverly Wildung Harrison, Riffat Hassan.

At the same time, because I want this study to illustrate the widespread and fruitful nature of the five ideas under consideration—disagreements, nuances, qualifications, amplifications—I have looked for women's voices in works that are more popular than academic, in newsletters as well as theological texts, in the writings of women who are less well known, or, perhaps better said, known primarily to particular communities rather than nationally or internationally. I have also included references to several historical figures, usually in order to illustrate points of continuity and divergence between contemporary women and women of previous generations.

In terms of what I define as a "tradition" or a "community," I have worked to include the traditional triad of Protestants, Catholics, and Jews; more recent and growing communities such as Muslims and Buddhists; indigenous and likewise growing movements such as Mormons. Given the demographics of American society, these communities do not, though, receive attention in equal measure. Nor is a designation like "Protestant" or "Catholic" in any sense monolithic, and there are times in this study when it is illuminating to distinguish among various denominations of Protestants or the ethnic derivations of Catholics and Jews. I have considered it important, as well, to pay attention to the theological work of women in communities of color and to point out that the categorization "communities of color" brings with it its own complexities. For example, the religious ideas of African-American women are mediated not just through the black experience in America but through particular religious traditions. Or another example from a group more recently arrived in America: Korean-American women who are Christian, and more specifically Protestant, experience religion differently from those who are Confucian, but as Korean-American religious studies scholar Jung Ha Kim explains, "Confucianism has sunk such deep roots into Korean-American women's souls and ethos that very few are able to make distinctions among being a Confucian, a Confucianized Christian, a Christianized Confucian or a Korean."[10] It is obvious that a book such as this one cannot take into account all the theological and cultural complexities that make up the lives of so many different communities of American women. Yet their realities stir beneath the surface of any generalization I make.

I have also thought it a good idea to seek out the voices of women who are participating in new religious movements—women who have moved away from established religious traditions and either have joined existing groups such as Goddess religions, contemporary New Thought religions, and New Age spiritualities or have begun to construct their own communities. It was, in fact, in the study of women in alternative religions that I first began to think many years ago about whether certain religious ideas were more conducive to the religious participation and leadership of women than were others.[11]

The second principle of selection is that the writings are in some sense feminist. By this I mean that the authors consider the fact that they are women significant for the work they are doing, and their work is directed not exclusively but wholeheartedly to transformation of religious traditions in order to make possible the full participation of women. These women are not satisfied with things as they are now. Thus "women," as I use it in this book, is shorthand for religious thinkers who fit my criteria.

This principle of selection means that there is an obvious bias that can be construed as "liberal" in many of the writings I cite, and I have therefore given serious consideration to whether what I am calling "women's religious thought" is simply another form of liberal religious thought, and if that is the case, what difference it makes. It is certainly true that most of the women I refer to manifest in their writings some of the major characteristics of liberal rather than conservative religion in America: an emphasis on the immanence of the sacred; a reliance on the authority of lived experience as a counter to traditionally authoritative religious claims; a willingness to engage insights from secular culture in the construction of religious ideas; and an understanding of theology as, finally, more expressive than prescriptive or even descriptive.[12] But, just as I am unwilling to label the ideas I am considering as any one kind of piety or as an over-arching women's spirituality, I consider the multiple worldviews in this study too various and complex to be confined solely, simply, and profitably to the realm of liberal religious thought. I do not, for example, see various feminist manifestations of New Age thought as reflective of liberal theology as it has been understood in American religious history. It is also the case that the American liberal vision of "inclusion of all" has taken a beating in recent years for its failure of vision in regard to "difference" in American culture.[13] In addition, I have intentionally included some references to the strategies and theological interpretations that women in more conservative communities make use of to foster their greater participation.[14]

In sum, in regard to matters of selection, it is my hope that the variety of women's theological work I cite, while not all-inclusive and while obviously shaped by my own interests, experience, and inclinations, will serve as an invitation for further exploration. It is not so much that some communities count more than others but that I have had to make choices, determined in part by the fact that this is a textual study and I have therefore paid attention to communities that have produced what I consider powerful and significant texts. The fact that I am still worried about this issue after quite a few years of working on the project illustrates that the choices, finally, are not always easy to make. It is also possible, I think, to see my difficulty as a hopeful sign that there is now so much to choose from.[15]

Rationale for Focus

The time period on which I have chosen to concentrate is in some sense arbitrary, but the years between 1985 and approximately 1997 signal a time of growing maturity in American women's religious thought.[16] The early years of contemporary feminism in the area of religion were mostly taken up with the effort to discover, understand, and critique the reasons for male dominance in most religions. This included research aimed at recovering women's theological work from the past and the beginnings of new visions for religion and society based on the insights and experiences of women.[17] There is no doubt that all five themes I explore in this study were in evidence in that earlier work. More recent religious thought builds on the foundation of that scholarship as women now have the opportunity to elaborate on the implications of earlier insights and to develop new ones.

Mary Daly's early call for the "transvaluation of values" offers a good illustration of what I mean. In a well-known chapter in her 1973 book *Beyond God the Father*, entitled "Transvaluation of Values: The End of Phallic Morality," Daly calls for honoring in religion those qualities of women's experience that traditionally have been ignored and denigrated—and honoring them to the extent that a whole new world is created. One of the three epigraphs preceding the chapter comes from Sojourner Truth: "If the first woman God ever made was strong enough to turn the world upside down, all alone—these together ought to be able to turn it back and get it rightside up again: and they is asking to do it. The men better let 'em."[18] To turn the world upside down is one thing; but to figure out the details of what the world will be like once it is turned upside down is quite another task, one whose fruits do not become immediately apparent but rather emerge over time.

The early and pivotal insights of any religious or cultural movement need to be worked out, however powerful their appeal at first glance, in contrast with what has gone before. It is the results of this working out over time that I am interested in and that are becoming more apparent in women's religious thought as women see the implications—positive and negative—of earlier feminist thought and as they become more aware of emerging challenges. There are at present three generations of women engaged with matters of religion, theology, and gender: women in their 60s and 70s, for whom the women's movement emerged mid-life and mid-career; women in their 40s and 50s, whose lives, work, and education were marked by the early years of the movement; and younger women, who have lived most of their lives in a culture that is aware of gender issues. And there is by now—nearly forty years after the beginnings of the contemporary feminist movement—the opportunity to see what broad patterns are emerging.

We are now accumulating sufficient writings by women from many traditions to support the kinds of speculations and generalizations I want to make about how gender consciousness is shaping religious thought and what it has to contribute to understandings of particular traditions and theology and religion in general. We can as yet only guess about how and whether women's participation in the formulation of the religious thought of various traditions over time may permanently affect the direction of overall themes in American religious thought or the theologies of particular traditions. We are just beginning to learn about how women's contributions to American religious thought will change prevailing assumptions about its major themes.

The Place of Gender in American Religious Thought and Where to "Place" Women's Religious Thought

Typically, American religious thought has been articulated in chronological surveys confined mostly to mainstream groups or in studies devoted to individual thinkers, to separate denominations, or to the analysis of theological movements such as Protestant or Catholic modernism or evangelicalism.[19] As students of American religious history, we are still struggling to figure out how to shake up the dominant narrative of American Protestantism even as we are more and more aware of how many strands need to be incorporated into it, in authentic rather than contrived ways.[20] Perhaps we are now at a time in the history of American religion when it is possible to see what will emerge when religious studies scholars can make use of common issues like gender to tie together or compare and contrast the religious thought of many different communities. The effects of circumscribed gender roles in religion and elsewhere—an experience common to both women and men—do not yield their mysteries very easily in terms of accurate or long-lasting generalizations. In a recent essay on gender and religion in American culture, David G. Hackett suggests that "[s]ince the early 1980's, advances in the study of gender in American history have come primarily through an unmasking of the assumptions of earlier studies."[21]

Thus, there is another subject that is of concern in this book, and that is how to better integrate American women's religious thought into the mainstream of American religious thought, even if one must also continue to ask where that mainstream lies. Standard works on American religious thought have not acknowledged the influences of gender consciousness; and until recently there has not been much publicly available to acknowledge. We do not yet know very much about how consciousness of gender issues and differences is shaping and will continue to shape American religious thought. And we do not yet know much about where to place women's religious thought within the larger framework of American religious thought. We have little experience as theologians, religious studies scholars, and historians at interpreting women's religious thought in contexts broader than concerns about gender.

Historically, women's religious thought has been tied to dissent, primarily because the women whose names have survived the filtering process of history typically have been those who have departed in some way from established traditions. In an early book on women in American history Gerda Lerner directs readers who consult "religion" in the index to see "Dissenters; Ministry." The text on dissent mentions in passing Anne Hutchinson and the Quaker Mary Dyer, who was hanged in Boston in 1660; Mother Ann Lee, founder of the Shakers; and Jemimah Wilkinson, founder of a very small eighteenth-century communal group.[22] Mary Baker Eddy, who might well have been included as a religious dissenter, is included in a section of the book called "women emancipators."[23] There is only one paragraph on ministry in the book, and it includes a reference to women in "Law" as well. In it Lerner mentions Antoinette Brown, the first woman ordained in the Congregational Church (in 1853) and Anna Howard Shaw, the first Methodist clergywoman (ordained in 1880). Lerner adds the fact that most Protestant denominations excluded women from ordained ministry.[24] In fact, both Brown and Shaw struggled for ordination against cultural and theological expectations for them, and neither stayed long in ordained ministry.

It is not startling that Lerner would have included so little about women and religion in a book published in 1971, but it is interesting to note that with not much information at her disposal she intuited the connection between women and dissent, a pattern that has existed for four centuries in American religious history. As colonial historian Laurel Thatcher Ulrich points out in an article on ministerial literature about women in the seventeenth and eighteenth centuries, "Well-behaved women seldom make history."[25]

It is not necessary to look to previous centuries to find evidence of this phenomenon. A compelling example is Re-Imagining, an international, ecumenical theology conference "by women for women and men" held in Minneapolis in 1993. The first Re-Imagining conference drew over 2,200 people, more than 2,100 of them women. Most of the thirty main speakers were established feminist theologians from North America and other parts of the world. On the day of its conclusion, the conference planners, 140 women and a few men, Minnesota laity and clergy from many denominations, considered the event an immense success as a celebration of women's theological creativity deeply rooted in the Christian tradition.[26]

Within days of Re-Imagining's end, it was denounced by conservative factions, particularly among the United Methodists and Presbyterians (U.S.A.). Member congregations of these denominations were urged to send cards to national offices announcing that they would withhold annual apportionments and contributions in protest against Re-Imagining. Many of them did, thereby threatening the Presbyterians with losses exceeding $4 million over several years. Among many charges, critics accused participants of goddess worship because of references to "Sophia," or Wisdom, as a feminine name for the divine, ridicule of traditional doctrines of the church such as the atonement, "tasteless rituals" that inappropriately emphasized women's sensuality, and the celebration of "lesbian lifestyles."

In the nationwide publicity that followed in both the religious and secular media, interpretations of the conference became increasingly polarized, nearly obliterating Re-Imagining's origins as very much a grassroots effort of Minnesota church women. It had been planned over a four-year period by women who had long served the churches—as clergy, professional staff, members of religious orders, seminary professors, organizational administrators, and volunteers.

There was fear that the controversy would split the Presbyterian Church (U.S.A.), whose Women's Division had contributed a significant amount of money to the conference. At its 1994 General Assembly, delegates finally voted 98 percent in favor of a resolution calling on all sides to "cease and desist and to allow healing to happen and trust to be rebuilt."[27] In the case of the Presbyterian Church (U.S.A.), the controversy needs to be seen within the broad context of this denomination's many-year struggle over issues of sexuality. But the readiness with which large numbers of Presbyterians and members of other denominations expressed intense fear and anger about women's theological work is indicative of the larger and persisting pattern of seeing women's religious thought as primarily dissenting in nature and as dangerous to religious orthodoxy.[28] There have been several smaller Re-Imagining gatherings since 1993, most recently one of approximately 1,000 in April 1998, and these, also, have elicited publicly expressed concerns about women's orthodoxy.

Why does this view of women's religious thought as primarily dissenting persist? For one thing, there is the reality that women, whether inside or outside the established traditions, have been drawn to ideas that present an alternative vision of the world and of religious communities—visions that necessarily serve as critiques because they almost always insist on the full participation of women in protest of the status quo. In this respect, if one is looking at it from a mainstream perspective that wishes to keep things as they are, women indeed have been dissenters and no doubt will continue to be. Further, women themselves take on the identity of dissenters. It is a way of saying that they do not wish to feel too at ease in an institution that keeps them on the margins, no matter how intimate a knowledge they have of its workings and however intense their loyalty to its best insights.[29]

For these reasons, I would argue, we have not been so readily able to see the conserving aspects of women's religious thought. It is my strong belief that "conserving" has much more to do with preserving the vitality of a religious tradition and its symbols than it does with attempting to protect what is perceived as the stability and certainty of the past or to guard the boundaries of a tradition. Sometimes conservation takes the form of pushing at boundaries in order to foster radical new perspectives about the wisdom and the depth of ancient truths. Dissent that is thorough and authentic is its own kind of participation and does not necessarily exclude conservation. It requires extensive knowledge of a tradition, a desire to take it seriously, and a willingness to endure conflict with the hope that it will ultimately be more productive than destructive for religious communities.

Concern about gender equity has often been the entry point, the motivating factor, for women's beginning participation in theological work, and it remains a central aspect of women's religious thought. But to see only that aspect is to overlook the extent to which women are participating in far-reaching conversations about religion and religious ideas. It is to miss out on much of the creativity and complexity of what women are contributing to many different religious communities and to the understanding of religion in general at the end of the twentieth century.

Where I Stand

This is a book that rides the boundaries of the several different—mostly interdisciplinary—areas of study that for many years have shaped my perceptions of women's religious thought and many other subjects: American studies, American religious history, religious studies, women's studies, and theology. Because I do some methodological and disciplinary roaming, I would like to conclude this introduction with a few clarifications about my own stance toward the ideas in this book and the writings I cite. While I don't think it is possible or necessary to adopt a tone of neutrality in this study—I am obviously an advocate of women's full participation in their traditions—I have not wanted to sound either defensive or triumphalist in my analyses. I have not wanted to expend energy defending the stand that women's religious thought needs to be taken seriously and that it is sufficiently rigorous and systematic. Nor do I have any intention of claiming that women's religious thought is the ultimate revelation. In fact, if there is any theological assumption that undergirds this study, it is that women are human—with all the gifts and flaws that are part of being fully human. I have been interested, rather, in looking at both the distinctiveness of women's religious thought, its originality and creativity, and its connections with ongoing theological themes and issues in American religious history.

Methodologically, I am a thoroughgoing pluralist, long since persuaded by William James that we learn more about religion by paying attention to a variety of manifestations than by trying to reduce this variety to any one thing. Theologically, I am something of a hybrid. I have been formed by the sacramental worldview of Roman Catholicism, the community to which I have belonged all my life. For better and for worse, these are my people, and I suspect that, in ways that are both obvious to me and partially obscured, even my choice of subject matter issues in some way from this reality. I have also been on the faculty of a liberal Protestant seminary for more than twenty years, and I have learned to take the Protestant principle seriously: that there are no institutions, symbols, rituals, or teachings that do not stand in need of ongoing critique and reform. This inclination toward critical distance had early encouragement in my childhood visits to the many households of my mother's large extended family, where I spent hours reading publications of the Missouri Synod Lutheran Church. There I came upon some rather startling critiques of Roman Catholicism that countered my inclinations to think that my own community was perfect. I have no doubt that this experience fostered in me a lifelong interest in thinking about what realities must be acknowledged about a religious tradition before any authentic commitment can be made.

In spite of these declared methodological and theological inclinations, I do not function in this study as a theologian. It is not my intent to speak to or on behalf of a particular religious community. I am a student of American religion and culture who is attempting to find themes and patterns in American women's religious thought and experience. In that regard, the concept that best defines what I am consistently drawn to is one for which it has taken me longer than it probably should have to find a name: "theological creativity." That is, the desire, the commitment, the capacity to construct religious worldviews that are intellectually and emotionally motivating, not necessarily to me but to their communities, at a given moment in history. I am intrigued by this phenomenon wherever I find it: inside or outside established traditions; in obviously religious sources or in aspects of culture regarded as secular. At this moment in the history of American religion and culture, it is my strong conviction that women's religious thought offers us not just insights into possible relationships between gender and religion but powerful examples of theological creativity. It is this dimension that I am particularly drawn to and that I wish to illustrate in the following pages.

2

Ambivalence as a
New Religious Virtue

*The Creativity of Women's Contradictory
Experiences of Their Traditions*

However controversial it has become—theologically, philosophically, psychologically, sociologically—one of the most powerful catalysts for fostering
American women's religious thought is the concept of "women's experience."
Credit for its discovery as an intellectual entity is almost always given to religious studies scholar Valerie Saiving. In 1960, the year she began teaching at
Hobart College, she published what has become a famous article: "The Human Situation: A Feminine View."[1] Nearly forty years after its publication this
somewhat tentative, not-yet-angry article continues to be cited over and over
again. I have not conducted a quantitative study, but I am not hesitant to esti-
mate that three-fourths of all the books of women's religious thought I've read
mention this article, if not in the text then in footnotes.

Persisting references to Saiving's essay give evidence of how powerful an
act it was to discover and give name to what has now become the obvious: that
(1) for a variety of reasons and to varying extents women experience religion
differently from men; (2) to ask what has seldom been asked in the past—"what
is it like to be a woman in a particular religion"—opens up an immense territory of inquiry with implications for history, theology, ritual, and polity;
(3) women's narratives and interpretations of their experiences have almost
never been publicly incorporated into the theologies and institutional structures of religious communities; and (4) when they are, major symbols, rituals,
stories, teachings, and manifestations of authority begin to take different shape.

Saiving begins her article with this simple statement in which masculine language is obviously still the norm: "I am a student of theology. I am also a woman. Perhaps it strikes you as curious that I put these two assertions beside each other, as if to imply that one's sexual identity has some bearing on his theological views."[2] She had originally written the essay as a paper for a graduate course at Union Theological Seminary. Her professor, Daniel Day Williams, suggested that she publish it, an idea that Saiving says "never would have occurred to me, never."[3] Saiving was greatly surprised by the immediate success of the article. After it was published, a *Time* magazine editor wrote an article about it, and Saiving received positive responses from all over the world. Speculating about the reasons for the article's success, she said, "Maybe the reason it struck a note that made people notice it was because, although other people had written about injustices to women, nobody in our century had addressed the question of a male-dominated religion. Maybe that's why it seemed so original."[4]

If the immediate appeal of Saiving's idea lay in its originality, the long-term effect has been to open up an area of inquiry that had never before been acknowledged or systematically articulated. In a recent analysis of the effects of feminism on theological education, theologian Rebecca S. Chopp speaks of "the space cleared by [Saiving's] criticism," because she "probed the nature of woman's experience as different from man's and the need for theology to reflect upon the experience of women."[5]

Ambivalence: A New Religious Virtue

This chapter looks not at women's experience in general but at a particular experience with their communities that women relate over and over again: that of being simultaneously outsiders and insiders. I am particularly concerned with how feelings of contradiction and ambivalence shape women's religious thought and promote the telling of certain kinds of stories. To a great extent, the purpose of this chapter is to set the mood for those that follow, chapters that will have more specific theological content. It becomes clear from stories about women's experiences of their insider/outsider status that there are many different places in relation to the center from which to offer contributions to their communities in the realm of religious thought. To pay as much attention to the ways women express creative attachment to their traditions as to how they express critique offers opportunities to see the intensely participatory nature of women's religious thought. And to stress the intensely participatory tone and content of women's religious thought does not require the downplaying of the negative critique they offer. In women's religious thought both go on simultaneously.

The women in this chapter are mostly those who are explicit one way or another about their relationships to particular communities. Some of the women have remained active and visible in their communities. Others have said good-by without leaving. And still others no longer have any kind of formal association with former religious communities but continue to acknowledge their influences. For these women both protest and participation, as they define it, require absence but not silence or total repudiation. As will become apparent, there are many different ways to stay in a community and many different ways to leave.

I did not expect to find a phrase that sums up the general mood of this chapter in an article about smoking in the *New Yorker*. I came upon it just when I was searching for a way to articulate what I was discovering as I read narrative after narrative about women's dual responses to their traditions—whether they had remained within them or had left to form or join others. The author, a former smoker, describes a woman who is lighting a cigarette in a distant window as "inhaling contradiction and breathing out ambivalence."[6]

In the narratives I have gathered, many of which come from feminist reinterpretations of religious traditions, women often begin the story of their relationships to their traditions as an exercise in inhaling contradictions. They describe themselves as breathing in the contradictory messages their communities convey to them about who they are by their very natures as women and what that means about their place in the community. Historically, communities have excluded women from publicly acknowledged arenas for leadership—preaching, teaching, administering—because they are not men. Over and over again women across many traditions relate stories about coming to see themselves as outsiders in communities with which they have been intimately involved for a lifetime.

At the same time women tell of hearing repeatedly from their traditions that they are ultimately if differently equal to men and valuable, in fact indispensable, to their communities in their assigned roles. They acknowledge as well that, in spite of excluding them from positions of public authority, their traditions have shaped and sustained them, given them communities and religious histories, and offered them language, symbols, teachings, and rituals by which to articulate their own religious ideas. Women write of the many ways their traditions have been more imprisoning than liberating, more stultifying than transforming, more death-dealing than life-giving. Yet they write as well of their love for their traditions, their almost visceral connections with them, and their hopes for the transformed futures of these same communities.

To illustrate: Lutheran liturgical theologian Gail Ramshaw describes herself as "paradoxically richly nurtured by a church that constrained me."[7] She recounts the story of one of her professors, who, "after four years of teaching me the theology of Christian worship, advised me that I had no future in the field because I am female. Clearly," says Ramshaw, "I heeded his teachings but not his advice."[8] Asian-American theologian Rita Nakashima Brock, a member of the Disciples of Christ, speaks of herself as both nurtured and wounded by her tradition.[9] In a newspaper article, "Faithful Iconoclast" (aptly titled for this study), about Brock's departure from the faculty of Hamline University in St. Paul, Minnesota, to run the Mary Ingraham Bunting Institute at Radcliffe College, she is quoted as saying, "Some days I'm fed up with Christians. And then some days I love Christians."[10]

Having inhaled the contradictory nature of their experiences, women breathe out in their religious thought an ambivalence toward their traditions. Their ambivalence is grounded in a deep sense of belonging, familiarity, and commitment and an equally strong sense of alienation and distrust. This distrust is not so much of their traditions' most central insights, but of the traditions' failings particularly in regard to women. They have come to acknowledge the capacity of their religious communities to distort their deepest wisdom and thereby inflict great harm in the name of that same wisdom. They point to the failure of their traditions to be transformed by—or even respond to—what has become obvious: that the community has never been aware of or incorporated the experiences and insights of half its members. Judith Plaskow gives voice to this experience from the perspective of a Jewish feminist: "Thus Torah—'Jewish' sources, 'Jewish' teaching—puts itself forward as *Jewish* teaching but speaks in the voice of only half the Jewish people. This scandal is compounded by another: The omission is neither mourned nor regretted; it is not even noticed."[11]

But this is not all Plaskow has to say. She does not choose to give up her Jewish identity; she affirms Judaism and its value for her, "as a central part of my identity," along with other particular identities, including feminism. For Plaskow, "being part of a community with its own history, convictions, customs, and values can add richness and meaning to life; I believe these things are worth preserving—not as frozen forms, but as elements in dialogue with changing social and historical reality."[12] Like Ramshaw, Brock, and most of the other women included in this study, Plaskow does not, finally, base her identity as a Jew on either/or prescriptions: either Judaism is without flaw or I can't be a part of it; either I am afforded full participation as a Jewish woman or I won't participate at all. Given women's acute awareness of religious communities' capacity both to harm and to transform their members, any woman—or man—who wants to remain a member of one cannot abide by absolutist standards. This does not mean, however, that there is resignation on the part of women to the way things are. It is this volatile and creative combination of women's feelings toward their communities—ambivalence, I choose to call it—and how it works to shape the religious thought of women that I want to explore further.

Ambivalence about one's religious tradition—about where one stands in relation to it—has seldom been promoted as a virtue. In popular usage the term indicates a state of confusion or indecisiveness, of simultaneous love and hate, or even of paralysis. It connotes the lukewarm attitude, the wishy-washiness, the holding back from full commitment that religious communities preach against. On the surface, ambivalence appears to vitiate the kind of dedication that religious communities demand of their members. It is, one would think, not a good state to be in—a state, in fact, that requires resolution one way or the other.

I contend, to the contrary, that as women describe their contradictory experiences with their traditions, ambivalence emerges much more as a virtue to be cultivated in creative and dynamic ways than a vice to be avoided—that there is a vitalizing quality to its manifestations.[13] It is a willed ambivalence, a sustained and cultivated ambivalence, an aware ambivalence. This is an ambivalence that requires women always to be vigilant, always to be critical of their communities' inclinations toward exclusion and distortion and at the same time to be open to new possibilities to hold up and reform or transform or dig up, from wherever they have been hiding, their traditions' most liberating and healing insights. It is an ambivalence that demands wariness that does not lapse into cynicism, loyalty that does not succumb to docility or resignation, creativity that flourishes on the margins without losing sight of the center. It is an ambivalence that expands the circumference of the center and points out that it is a dynamic rather than a static configuration.

A cultivated ambivalence fosters a triple task in women's religious thought. It requires constant critical distance from one's community; conservation of its deepest insights; and innovation, which I see as imagining and constructing new visions by combining a tradition's insights with revelations that come from many places in the culture. The virtue of ambivalence stirs up love and hate, attraction and repulsion, devotion and impatience, and an affection that is sometimes tender and often critical. There is a ruefulness and a wryness detectable in women's religious thought that is generally absent in what has tended to be a more earnest genre of religious writing.

I might have chosen to interpret the narratives that follow in terms of ambiguity or paradox (first cousins of ambivalence), or even old-fashioned doubt. It does not take much reading between the lines to detect evidence of all three. But these responses have a more cognitive focus than I want to project at this point. I choose to emphasize ambivalence, because I particularly want to pay attention in this chapter to the emotional quality of what women have to say about their traditions.

I begin with stories of alienation. This is often where women themselves begin: with their discovery of how they are perceived as "other" in their traditions and why, in spite of the mostly negative connotations of this discovery and the pain it brings, "otherness" is a category that has been extremely useful to women in terms of encouraging creative religious thought. I move next to a compendium of some phrases women of different communities use to express the quality of their insider/outsider status and then on to a consideration of how women describe their attachments to their communities. I conclude with some observations about what insights women's experiences of ambivalence contribute to conversations about American religion in general at this time in history and to an understanding of what it means to be committed to a religious community.

Women's Discovery of Themselves as "Other": Identifying the Quality of Their Feeling of Exclusion

The late 1960s through the 1970s saw the widespread emergence of women's realization that their names and their contributions to their religious communities had not been recognized, much less acknowledged; therefore they are not recorded in the histories of their communities or religious histories in general. One can chronicle the evolution of feelings in reaction to this discovery, from gradual awareness to astonishment to bewilderment to rage to theological creativity. Women have been motivated by the discovery of their absence in history and theology to look to the past in order to recover what they could of their histories and to the future as well to make sure that their stories will not be obscured again, and to work for full participation in their traditions. In doing so, they have made several other discoveries related to both past and future.

One was that the end of the twentieth century was not the first time women recognized that they had been excluded from full participation in their traditions. But consciousness of gender inequity by women in previous centuries had not persisted, nor had it brought about significant or lasting change. Another discovery was that the obvious evidence that their traditions had excluded half their members from full participation did not lead to the traditions' taking quick action on women's behalf. In fact, they were resisting.[14] In other words, it became clear to women that remedying the exclusion and oppression they had suffered was not a matter of pointing out the obvious and having it rectified as a matter of justice. There was something less rational and straightforward going on. Women began to suspect that there must be another set of rules that applied to them.[15] This was indeed the case, because the established norm was male, and women were different: they were "other."

The recognition of their own otherness has helped women to define the nonrational and often irrational quality of women's experience of exclusion from full participation in their traditions. Change does not come "naturally." It is not even a matter of offering evidence of women's capability in teaching or preaching or administration, since such evidence has not so far resulted in widespread changes.[16] Thus there is the discovery that common sense and rational argument will not be sufficiently powerful approaches in women's religious thought to bring about systemic change. That will require a theological creativity that goes far beyond the re-working of old symbols. It will involve a much more probing critique and a more assiduous search for resources in particular traditions.

Claiming and analyzing "otherness" as the particular quality of their sense of exclusion has been very much an intellectual stimulant for women's theological work. But I want to emphasize in this section the more affective elements of the experience—how, according to women, it feels to be "other." The chapters that follow will elaborate on a different question: When the Other begins to speak, what does she have to say?

Women of different traditions have distinctive ways of describing this feeling. They relate it to the particular stories and theologies of their own communities. Jewish theologian Judith Plaskow draws from Simone de Beauvoir's writings on women as Other to illustrate her contention that historically Jewish women inhabit a "terrain of silence." As Plaskow puts it, "Where women are Other, they can be present and silent simultaneously; for the language and thought-forms of culture do not express their meanings."[17] Women are not absent in Jewish teaching, she says. Stories are told about them, but these stories are told by men. Even the stories centered on strong women—Sarah or Rebekah—speak of God's covenant not with these women but with Abraham and Isaac. The experience of otherness in their own tradition is intensified for American Jewish women, according to Plaskow, because they already belong to a group that exists on the margins of the dominant Christian culture. Thus, Plaskow points out, Jewish women experience a sense of otherness not only in their own communities but in a broader sense: "As the 'other's Other,' we take in both the images of Jews and specifically Jewish women in the wider society, and also the projections of Jewish men."[18]

Roman Catholic theologian Anne Carr sees women in Catholicism, a tradition that does not yet ordain women, as constituting an official "oddity" that must be accounted for by means of a special theology for women.[19] Controversy over the failure to ordain women is an ongoing and pivotal issue in Roman Catholicism, and it is a focus, although not the only one, for women's expressions of discontent. The various and continuing pronouncements by the Catholic hierarchy that women cannot be ordained and the recent pronouncement by the Vatican that the matter should not even be discussed reinforce the experience Catholic women describe of being other-than-the-norm. Their women-bodies cannot, according to the hierarchy, represent Christ at the altar during the celebration of Mass. There is something in their very nature as women that makes impossible their sacramental efficacy, according to church tradition, even though they are considered to have other essential gifts to contribute that are complementary. Catholic feminists insist that the church's traditional teaching of the complementarity of male and female—both necessary but requiring different roles—really works not to include women but to emphasize their otherness. Their point is intensified by a Mormon woman, a member of another tradition that does not ordain women.

In pointing to the roles of priesthood and motherhood in Mormonism that are described by Mormon authorities as "complementary," Carolyn M. Wallace says, "The LDS priesthood and motherhood may be complementary, but . . . they are not symmetrical."[20]

Another Roman Catholic, Catherine LaCugna, author of a well-received book on the Trinity,[21] perceives the issue of ordination as one that is grounded in theological anthropology—what it means to be fully human. Issues of gender, she says, are tied to the most central symbols of the tradition, including the nature of the divine. If gender is theologically significant, as LaCugna sees it, both in terms of biology and in its "social-psychological-political" interpretations, "then gender must have something to do with who God is."[22] LaCugna follows this contention with a series of questions designed to point to the very basic issues that are at stake in Catholicism when women are excluded from ordained ministry: "Are women persons in the same way that men are persons? Is the personhood of women a full image of the triune God? Do the obvious biological differences between men and women amount to a qualitative difference in personhood? Is woman's personhood derived from man's personhood? Has God eternally decreed that in the orders of creation and redemption woman be subordinate to man? If so, then who is God?"[23] Thus matters of gender address not merely social roles but the questions of whether a tradition teaches that women are human in the same way that men are human and whether its models of God are sufficient to demonstrate the full humanity of women.

In *Buddhism after Patriarchy*, Rita M. Gross, a feminist Buddhist, makes the claim that traditional Buddhism is thoroughly androcentric; that is, its teachings and traditions have come down to the present day through male interpreters. Therefore, it should not be a surprise that when the subject of women arises in Buddhism, it is from the male perspective: woman as object rather than subject. "The question, the issue," says Gross, "is always what to do about women, what special rules they would have to observe, whether or not they can become enlightened, whether they could progress as far as men on the Buddhist path." Women in Buddhism, according to Gross, "are experienced and discussed as the other, as objects, as 'they' rather than 'we,' as exceptions to the norm that need to be regulated, explained, and placed in the world."[24]

"What *am* I doing in a religion whose formal expression is a highly defended, medieval, male, sexist hierarchy?" asks Kate Wheeler, a Buddhist practitioner who is also a contributing editor to *Tricycle*, a well-known Buddhist quarterly. In an essay called "Bowing, Not Scraping," Wheeler says that there are not many people with whom she can discuss thoughts like these: "My secular-humanist friends pity me; the Buddhists tell me to go and meditate until I feel better." And there is the recurring theme of her female otherness. "Buddhist logic says that if I'm mad and sad because I'm a woman, I'm also a woman because I'm mad and sad. It's karma. If I keep indulging negative thoughts, I'll be reborn a woman again—or worse, since the lowest hell is reserved for those who criticize Buddhist teachings."[25]

Evangelical Protestant women also describe their experience of otherness—their sense that their tradition sees them as by nature different from men—in terms of their particular theological worldview. They tell of their dismay that, according to the excluding rhetoric of their tradition, the redemption of the world and of humankind does not appear to apply to them in the same way it applies to men since in many evangelical communities there are prohibitions against women's participation in public ministries.

Evangelical scholar Patricia Gundry reports receiving a letter from a church woman who recounted her growing despair at church-generated materials about the inferiority of women. "I was so devastated," she says, "that I was beginning to almost believe the Holy Spirit in me was not the same Holy Spirit that indwelled 'the brethren,' or if otherwise, why am I to keep quiet in the church and not let the Holy Spirit speak through me, simply because I have a woman's body?" The woman went on to offer her own beginning theological analysis: "God surely makes more sense than that."[26] But she considered herself ready to sink under the burden of hearing male authorities point to the Scriptures for proof of her inferior status. "Bring your pies, ladies," she felt them saying to her, "but leave your ideas at home."[27]

Gundry herself has felt "other" in her own tradition. At a Sunday morning class convened to discuss women's equal partnership in the church, she noticed that only men were speaking: "The women's faces were drawn tight, their bodies held totally still. The atmosphere was electric with tension, yet they said nothing." Gundry felt herself as "immediately seized with a terrible fear. On some level I knew that I was alien and unwelcome—not because I was a visitor, but because I was female."[28]

Evangelical women who are also feminist scholars of religion feel in particularly acute ways the pressures of living in two different worlds and having to explain themselves to both evangelicals and feminists. Diana Hochstedt Butler, a religious studies professor and author of a prize-winning biography of an evangelical Episcopal bishop, explains that "[o]n one side I am challenged by fellow evangelicals who question whether a woman should have any career outside the home, much less one teaching church history and theology; on the other, my academic colleagues doubt that the words 'evangelical,' 'female' and 'academic' can be used in the same sentence—unless the sentence reads, 'Evangelicals hate female academics.'"[29] Butler herself does not experience the two worlds she inhabits as mutually exclusive. She describes herself as "evangelical, thoroughly trinitarian and orthodox, committed to biblical authority, convinced of the need for a personal inward relationship with Jesus Christ." But she is just as firmly "a feminist desirous of making women's voices heard from the history of Christianity and in the theology, speaking against the ways that the orthodox Christian tradition (which I deeply love) has oppressed my own gender." Butler does not despair because of the pressures she experiences.

She sees the entry of more evangelical women into the church's intellectual life as a reality that will have a significant, reshaping effect on evangelical theology. "Finding oneself in the middle of conflict can have its benefits," she says.[30]

One could multiply these stories endlessly. The very frequency with which they appear in women's religious thought and the variety of ways they can be articulated in many different traditions offer evidence of how congruent this insight is with the way women experience their places in their traditions. When women of many different traditions speak—as women—about how they experience themselves in their traditions, one dominant set of stories they choose to tell is about the sense of existing in essential ways on the margins—as a species, or a kind of sub-species, set apart. And they feel themselves set apart because of what they have no power—or desire—to change: the fact that they are women. But this is a chapter on ambivalence, and these stories are not the only ones that women have to tell about their experiences of otherness in their traditions.

Positive and Ambivalent Uses of Otherness

Otherness is not presented only as a totally negative category of experience in women's religious thought. The discovery of their own "otherness" as a category of experience also has positive meanings. The stories above convey women's experience of being "dangerously other" or "irrelevantly other." But "otherness" has a long and polyvalent history in religious thought, and it is a term with both positive and negative connotations. It is used in the monotheistic religions to designate the greatness, the transcendence, of God—a strategy to ensure that the divine—the Totally Other— is never confused with the created world.[31] The term is used, also, to point to "some one or something. . . . truly from outside—outside our skin, our thinking, our believing, our world."[32] This use of the term, in a way that is meant to be provocative rather than indicting, offers perspectives that are useful for women.

In *Pure Lust: Elemental Feminist Philosophy*, post-Christian feminist Mary Daly turns "otherness" upside down. This is a strategy she uses often in her writings in order to transvalue qualities that typically have been associated with women and therefore denigrated. Daly urges women to claim their Otherness as a creative means to the shaping of an independent self. She ties Otherness to "leaps of transformation." Daly claims that the starting point for a woman to bring about the kind of radical change needed in society is "an ontological intuition of her Otherness in relation to all of the shapes imposed upon her by patriarchy." As Daly sees it, faithfulness to their intuitions of Otherness gives women a kind of double vision: "A woman knows her Otherness not only in relation to the androcentric atrocities, however. She knows it most certainly through Realizing her Elemental powers—through evolutionary leaping itself."[33] Thus, early on in the contemporary women's movement there was the sense that being Other is a status that can be claimed as well as imposed. And when it is claimed, rather than imposed, it brings with it certain kinds of freedom and power.

Protestant theologian Paula M. Cooey presents another approach to the transvaluation of otherness, one that emerges from feminist analysis and inter-religious dialogue, particularly with Buddhism. Cooey acknowledges that at the present time it is difficult to find feminist discussions of otherness that are positive. And, for good reason, she says, as she sums up many of the negative meanings of otherness as they have been imposed upon women: "Defined as essentially other, *woman* comes to represent all that androcentric consciousness fears and denies within itself but at the same time cannot live without. This includes the qualities of finitude, physical suffering, and sexuality associated with embodiment, and by extrapolation the qualities of necessity, causality, inevitability, repetitiveness, and continuity associated with the natural order."[34]

Looked at more positively, according to Cooey, as it is possible to do once "otherness" is demythologized and demystified, otherness has a dynamism about it that is necessary for differentiation of self and community in relation to other selves and communities. "Transvalued," says Cooey, "otherness, as it is associated with both central religious symbols and philosophical concepts, challenges static, complacent views of person and community."[35] But, when "good other" is associated with God and by extension with maleness and "bad other" with women, then, as Cooey puts it, "The dualism of male-identified self and female-identified other that should have been a dialectic of self and other ongoing within each human identity and available to all human beings contaminates every theory of identity and every claim to universality including the claim to universal love."[36]

Because it is not the case, then, that otherness is always interpreted negatively, here again is another kind of ambivalence that is born of women's efforts to say to their traditions, "I am not other" and at the same time to say, "My otherness has its own purposes, its own wisdom to contribute to the tradition." If one's theological or artistic creativity does, in fact, come to some extent, or even to a great extent, from one's identity as "other," then how much of it is it possible to give up or repudiate in one's present life without losing something essential to the development of the creative self? In an interpretation of both the rage and the hope she finds in American Indian women's poetry, American Indian writer Janice Gould uses poet Wendy Rose's experience of ambivalence toward her otherness as an epigraph: "I hate it when other people write about my alienation and anger. Even if it's true, I'm not proud of it. It has crippled me, made me sick, made me out of balance. It has also been the source of my poetry."[37] But, again, it is one thing to be labeled "other," and it is something else to claim that status for oneself.

Laurel Thatcher Ulrich's interpretation of herself as a Mormon feminist makes it clear that it is possible to have both these experiences simultaneously and to use them in creative ways to interpret one's status in a religious tradition. Her self-interpretation runs parallel to that offered by evangelical feminist scholar Diana Hochstedt Butler. Ulrich is a Pulitzer Prize–winning American colonial historian, a Mormon wife and mother of five children, and a religious education teacher who has been active in the church all her life. She describes herself as "an active, believing Mormon" who is also a feminist. That she can be both is a surprise to many who are not familiar with the extent of contemporary Mormon feminism. That she is sometimes considered "other" by both Mormons and feminists offers insights into the complexity of women's experiences of otherness.

Often called upon by both Mormons and non-Mormons to explain herself, Ulrich makes connections between feminism and the theology of her religious tradition. As a feminist she identifies "with women across the centuries who have had the courage to claim their own gifts," and "as a Mormon," she says, "I embrace ideals of equality and a critique of power that also shaped early feminism."[38] She has "tasted equal worship in the Church of Jesus Christ of Latter-day Saints. Unfortunately, I have also observed the smug condescension of men who have been called as lord and tutor. Against such behavior I assert both my Mormonism and my feminism."[39]

Ulrich credits her Mormon religious education for making it possible to see the tradition's true values in spite of injustices. She is "grateful for a religious education that taught me how to be different, though I had no idea it would sometimes make me feel like a stranger among saints."[40] Historian of Mormonism Jan Shipps recounts an incident when Ulrich was indeed treated like a stranger. When the planning committee for the 1993 Brigham Young University—LDS Relief Society Annual Women's Conference suggested Ulrich as the keynote speaker, BYU vetoed the proposal. Shipps ties the veto to church administrators' concern that women's history is raising questions about the church's conservative stance toward women by pointing to earlier eras when women participated more fully and that women's history is also motivating the development of a Mormon feminist theology grounded in the concept of Heavenly Mother.[41]

Shipps reports Ulrich as being more bewildered than angered or hurt by the rejection. She asked, "If I'm not safe to speak at BYU, then who is?"[42] For her part, Ulrich confesses that although she has sometimes felt like a woman without a country, "perhaps the experience of 'otherness' can be a source of strength." As she understands it, being "other" in her own tradition, and often among feminists as well, gives her the distance to better perceive "a net of assumptions and prejudices we cannot see." She continues to cherish her identity as an "OxyMormon," a Mormon and a feminist.[43]

There are women in other traditions who find, like Ulrich, that their feminist sense of injustice as well as the means to overcome it have their theological origins in the tradition itself. In a conversation between two women members of the Church of the Brethren, L., a seminary student, and K., a former campus minister and now a mental health worker, the subject arose of the connections between their tradition and feminism. L. said, "It does feel like Brethrenism in every way leads into feminism. There's almost a way that—for women growing up in the Church of the Brethren—it's very difficult *not* to become feminist, if you take the theology seriously. But one tripping point seems to be that we still have somewhat of the sectarian Anabaptist understanding of the church."[44]

K. responds with her own experiences of conflict: "We're taught all these things and nurtured to be a certain way, and then, if you are that way, as a woman, then you kind of get knocked down, because you have to fit into this mold. But if you listen to what you've been taught from day one in Sunday School, you *can't* fit into that. I think that's where the dilemma comes for me in terms of loving the Church of the Brethren—a deep-felt, family-like love—yet at the same time, feeling stifled by it, too, like I don't fit."[45]

Both these women were part of a group of Brethren women who decided together at the Re-Imagining conference in 1993 to make a public announcement that they were from then on going to call their denomination "The Church of Reconciliation." This was a change that had been discussed for some time in Brethren circles as in keeping with the theology of the church and a membership that includes both women and men. It was the women's recollection that "[w]hen we were talking about that beforehand (we were out in the hallway, reaffirming that this was the right thing to do and that everyone was comfortable with it), the comments being made were, 'This is what I've been taught to believe in,' and 'This is everything about who I am as a person and what I believe.' "[46]

In the details of Ulrich's Mormon and feminist experiences and in the conversation between two feminist Brethren women (one can see why they desire a change in name), we have the opportunity to see more specifically what Daly and Cooey describe in the abstract. They, and women of many traditions, embrace "otherness" as a strategy for the transvaluation of values, a means of developing and defining a self, as a catalyst to individual and communal transformation, as a gift of multiple interpretations and critical distance to a tradition. We hear again the echoes of Ramshaw and Brock as they speak about traditions that both "nurtured and constrained," "nurtured and wounded" them. Whatever its creative benefits, this is not to say that the role of officially designated Other is an easy one. It gives women a place to stand—on the margins looking to the center and back again—and the kind of freedom that comes with being on the margins. It is also a stance that requires a constant questioning of one's identity and a prodigious expenditure of creative theological energy to maintain.

Insider/Outsiders, Defectors
in Place, Resident Aliens

In the years since 1985 women of different traditions have developed a variety of ways to describe their sense of being both insider and outsider in their communities, both other and intimate. Sometimes these phrases appear in book titles, other times in the texts of women's religious writings. All of them speak to the doubleness of women's roles as they experience them in their communities. Over and over again they express the feeling of being in two or three contradictory places at once, constantly in a state of ambivalence, and at the same time aware of the creative potential of such unsettledness.

The contradictory and ambivalent nature of women's experiences in various traditions is reinforced by the title of a book of autobiographical essays published in 1985: A *Time to Weep and a Time to Sing.*[47] These are essays by women who are academics, narratives of the mixture of pain and joy that marks the lives of academic women in particular. They have experienced the realities of gender bias in their religious traditions and academic settings, the liberating power of scholarship, and the ongoing search for a religious life that is both committed and critical.

For some women the ambivalence seems to have been lifelong. Mary Jo Meadow, one of the editors and a professor of religion and psychology, says, "For as long as I can remember, God and I have not been able to leave each other alone. And on that bitter cold winter day in St. Louis when my parents baptized me into the Catholic church, an enduring love-hate relationship with institutional religion was born."[48]

Another contributor, Sheila Graeve Davaney, a former Roman Catholic, now a professor of theology at a United Methodist seminary, refers by name to the ambivalence she experiences in her own profession, an ambivalence that is derived in part from the traditional assumption that a theologian is a man: "A feminist theologian sounds to many women, including quite often myself, like a contradiction in terms. It is a personal and professional identity that is filled with tension and ambivalence." Yet, Davaney says, "despite its ambivalent character, I believe it is not only an appropriate but also an essential one for myself as a woman committed to the transformation of the social order."[49] Davaney's reference to the tasks of feminist theology as related to social transformation foreshadows the description Rebecca S. Chopp offers ten years later of feminist theology as "saving work"—that is, work that must have practical outcomes in its uniting of critique and construction, ethics and epistemology. Chopp contrasts feminist theology as saving work with the more abstract concerns of a theologian like Paul Tillich, who begins his systematic theology with a definition of religion as ultimate concern.[50]

Some women describe the conflicting experiences within their religious traditions as "walking in two worlds," the title chosen for a book of essays based on presentations given at an ongoing series of lectures, "Theological Insights," delivered each year at the College of St. Catherine, a women's college, in St. Paul, Minnesota. For more than ten years, hundreds of women have gathered on Friday mornings to hear two presenters—presenters who are chosen specifically to unite the theological creativity of academic and non-academic women. The first presenter shares her life story, with all the ambiguities of her experiences in her religious tradition. These are women who, as the editors say, "never dreamed they would stand before a large audience and share the intimate details of their life stories, let alone see those details in print." The second presenter is always a scholar, a woman more experienced in public speaking, who presents her research, which is usually not yet common knowledge, and its implications for interpreting lives in their religious traditions and in broader arenas.[51]

The phrase "walking in two worlds" sums up the common theme of the weekly presentations, a theme, the editors say, that "was an experience before it was a book"—that of inhabiting the often conflicting worlds of patriarchal church and culture and the world they know as women. Episcopal theologian Elizabeth Dodson Gray, who began the program at Harvard Divinity School on which the St. Catherine program is modeled, describes the ambivalence of inhabiting more than one world: "To walk in these two worlds—of patriarchal power and women's body/life experiences—is to know confusion and silence, invisibility and worthlessness, pain and betrayal, yet amazing hope and renewal."[52]

Another phrase that points both to women's dual experience of their traditions and to the stance many presently choose to claim is "defecting in place." The authors of a recent study of black and white Catholic, Protestant, and Protestant-related women and their relationships to their communities describe "defecting in place" as an apt metaphor "to capture the paradox of the Christian feminist position in relationship to the church."[53] Many women, as the authors discovered in a study funded by the Lilly Endowment, choose to stay within their religious traditions on their own terms and to take responsibility for their own spiritual lives.[54] Nonetheless there is a sense of alienation that comes with this decision. As the authors interpreted their findings, they concluded that "[t]he movement may be seen by outsiders as rooted in dissent, but proponents believe just the opposite. Their stance is positive, not negative, for their dissent flows from a prior assent to the initiatives of the Spirit. Their 'yes' to the Spirit is the basis for their staying within congregations or denominations to work to bring about change."[55]

Womanist theologian Delores Williams uses the term "two-edged sword" to describe the particular experience of women in black denominations. In *Sisters in the Wilderness: The Challenge of Womanist God-Talk*, she recounts the struggle to create black women's theology that will speak to the church and to the academy and to those beyond the community of black women "without compromising black women's faith."[56]

Williams acknowledges that African-American churches have served as refuges for black women, where they have come not only to vent their pain but for "decidedly theological reasons." But she claims as well that "the African-American denominational churches function like two-edged swords. They sustain black women emotionally and provide 'theological space' for black women's faith expressions. But they suppress and help make invisible black women's thought and culture."[57] Williams goes on to say that through uncritical use of the Bible and patriarchal theology the African-American denominational churches keep women from asking critical questions about their own oppression and how the male-dominated Christian churches contribute to it. Out of this dual experience has emerged womanist theology as a corrective—a perspective born of ambivalence and contradiction, "a prophetic voice reminding the African-American denominational churches of their missions to seek justice and voice for all their people, of which black women are the overwhelming majority of their congregations."[58]

Another womanist theologian, ethicist Katie Geneva Cannon, describes her dual identity as emerging from a dilemma that Zora Neale Hurston called "trying to hit a straight lick with a crooked stick." Cannon says that, in essence, she sees her role as speaking as "one of the canonical boys" and as at the same time embodying "the noncanonical other." On one hand, her task as a Christian ethicist is "to transcend my blackness and femaleness and draft a blueprint of liberation ethics that somehow speaks to, or responds to, the universality of the human condition. On the other hand, my task as a *womanist liberation ethicist* is to debunk, unmask, and disentangle the historically conditioned value judgments and power relations that undergird the particularities of race, sex, and class oppression." She sees the inclusion of black women's moral reasoning within the structures of traditional ethics as a pioneering endeavor. And Cannon experiences herself as both participant and other.[59]

Yet another way women describe their contradictory experiences is by referring to themselves as "resident aliens" in their communities. Roman Catholic theologian Elisabeth Schüssler Fiorenza uses this term to describe one who is both insider and outsider: "insider by virtue of residence or patriarchal affiliation to a male citizen or institution; outsider in terms of language, experience, culture, and history."[60] In fact, she goes further and suggests the image of the feminist theologian as "a troublemaker, a resident alien, who constantly seeks to destabilize the centers, both the value-free, ostensibly neutral research ethos of the academy and the dogmatic authoritarian stance of patriarchal religion." Nonetheless, she says, women should not do their work from the boundaries "but should move it into the center of academy and religion."[61] Rebecca Chopp picks up on this theme in *Saving Work* and describes the difficulty of being a resident alien: "One is never really at home, except where one can create even partial visions of a home with a table to which all are readily and eagerly invited." But she sees this status as the best of presently available op-portunities for women in their religious communities, particularly in contrast with either "doing it like a man" or fleeing, if that were even possible, to all-women enclaves.[62]

Not all descriptions of insider/outsider status are negative or in some cases even ambivalent. As a feminist Buddhist, Rita Gross understands her insider/outsider perspective to be part of a two-stranded methodology. She describes herself as deeply committed to a comparative approach in the study of religion, which includes making use of insights from the social sciences, especially an-thropology. Gross is also clear about herself as a practicing Buddhist, so Bud-dhism is not, for her, at least in one sense, a religion like all others. Being a comparativist does not make her a relativist. "Thus," she says, "I work simulta-neously as a comparativist and as a Buddhist theologian, both as an insider and as an outsider. I see no conflict in this method; rather, it is a complete and well-rounded approach."[63]

When it comes, however, to her experiences as a woman in Buddhism, Gross is very articulate about how a traditionally male-dominated Buddhism needs to be "revalorized," as she calls it, according to feminist insights, because Buddhism, like many other traditions, has until very recently seen women as "other." Thus Gross is both insider and outsider in Buddhism in ways that are similar to those described above. And other Buddhist women find yet another phrase, "women on the edge," to describe their sense of place within the tra-dition. In a book of essays similarly titled, editor Marianne Dresser offers a set of perspectives from what she describes as "the fertile margins of the dominant discourse." She sees the "view from the edge" as "panoramic, clear, less ob-structed by received knowledge or codified notions of 'correct' views." But her conviction is that this view from the edge has as its goal "the reclaiming of our rightful place at the very *heart* of Buddhism."[64]

The fact that so many women from so many different communities choose to describe themselves as inhabiting more than one world, seeing from multi-ple perspectives, embodying ongoing contradiction in relation to their com-munities imparts an obviously ambivalent tone to women's religious thought. It is a functional ambivalence that offers a contrast to the certainties of tone that are typical of much religious thought. It is also an ambivalence that re-quires the telling of detailed stories about their wary and rueful, deeply loving and knowledgeable, experiences of their traditions.

Beloved Communities

What experiences do women choose to emphasize when they tell stories about what motivates them to remain within their traditions—or at least to continue to take them seriously? How do they talk about their relationship to their com-munities, their love, their loyalty? Most often, in surprisingly noncognitive terms. One does not get a sense that women are rationalizing their commitments or that they are making the best of a bad deal. For the most part what follows are not conversion stories, and they are certainly not attempts to convince anyone that they remain in their traditions because those traditions are superior to all others. That subject never seems to come up. There is no point-by-point exposition of the truth claims of the tradition, although women offer moving testimonies to the shaping power of their religious heritage.

I am not claiming that women's religious thought is devoid of compelling point-by-point intellectual discourse. Quite the contrary, as will become apparent in the following chapters. But I am choosing here to convey stories women tell about their affective attachments to their traditions—again, an emphasis on tone. There is a clear-headedness in these accounts about the intensity of emotional ties that keep women in their communities. It is not an inability to see injustice or distortion, nor a willingness to overlook them. These are also not exercises in nostalgia. They are stories that combine affection and loyalty with an obvious realism. In 1990 Judith Plaskow said of her tradition, "If Judaism is patriarchal, I do not believe there is any nonpatriarchal space to which I can go to create a new religion."[65] In 1997, Laura Levitt, also a Jewish feminist, wrote more specifically about the nature of her embrace of an imperfect Judaism (and an imperfect feminism, liberalism, and granddaughter-of-immigrants' American dream), "I no longer feel bound by a desire for guarantees or permanence."[66]

What I find particularly interesting is the fact that many women no longer look on the shaping power of religion as primarily insidious and therefore to be resisted, as was more typically the case earlier—as a product of the tools of the master, whose house can never be dismantled by those same tools. In the following stories, the formative powers of religion are regarded as constituting a more dynamic reality with the capacity for both good and ill. By acknowledging their willingness to shape this formative power in ways that are transformative, women make it clear they do not experience themselves at the mercy of their traditions but instead are responsible for them along with other members of their communities. Buddhist Kate Wheeler cites a German biographer of the Buddha who suggests that the historical Buddha didn't respect women very much (the extent to which the Buddha did or didn't intentionally include and respect women is a subject of debate among Buddhist feminists). Rather than denying this possibility, Wheeler responds, "This attitude can be considered secondary, if we feel entitled to form our own judgments about what's valuable in Buddhist teachings and what isn't."[67] In fact, she goes even further: "In the case of women, the Buddha was wrong—and we have to have the courage to say so."[68]

For some women the connections they maintain with their traditions are tenuous or nonexistent in terms of formal affiliation. Here is a graphic description by Emily Culpepper of how her southern Protestant Christian past figures in her present life: she sees her early years as "compost." Asked by a woman who knew that Culpepper no longer considered herself a Christian whether she nonetheless considered Christianity her "roots," she realized that she could not claim that metaphor: "The ecology of my spiritual life is more complex than that, with moments of radical discontinuity." Thus, thinking of her Christian background as compost seemed to make more sense: "It [her Christianity] has decayed and died, becoming a mix of animate and inanimate, stinking rot and released nutrients. Humus. Fertilizer. The part of organic life cycles with which everyone gets uncomfortable and skips over in the rush to rhapsodize growth and progress and blossoms and fruition and rebirth." Culpepper finds that she can extend this metaphor very elaborately, and she concludes by declaring, "If our traditions and symbols are truly part of living, then they are organic and will have rhythms of living and dying."[69]

Lutheran theologian Elizabeth Bettenhausen describes Lutheran women she knows who "stay because one central belief is what holds their life together, even while other teachings or rituals threaten to tear it apart." For others, "the local congregation is home, community, and the most tangible form of a distinctive culture left." Bettenhausen says that she has "talked with many women for whom Lutheran theology is largely irrelevant but for whom the Lutheran congregations to which they belong are precisely where they feel they belong."[70]

In a similar manner, *mujerista* theologians Ada María Isasi-Díaz and Yolanda Tarango speak of the Roman Catholic church as providing not only a religious framework but a culture for Latina women, "the main paradigms of our 'moods and motivations' in life."[71] Isasi-Díaz and Tarango are often asked why they even bother with religion, why they put energy into battling with church officials and doing theology. They offer several reasons, all of them related to the multiple themes of constraint and nurture, harm and healing, frustration and transformation, ambivalence and commitment. They describe religion, particularly Roman Catholicism, as a major part of Latin American culture, one that cannot be eradicated from Latinas' lives if they are to retain their central identities: "As Hispanic women," they say, "we have been very hurt by the Catholic church in a number of ways—and this does not refer only to hurt feelings. Many of us have even walked away from the Catholic church and other Christian churches. Yet, as a group of us told a U.S. Bishops' Committee, 'We cannot leave the Church. It is part of our culture, of who we are.' "[72]

Many Roman Catholic women reinforce this sense of their religious community as an essential part of their identity, however flawed they experience its teachings in regard to women. The tradition as not just the institution but that which belongs to the inner self is described by Kathryn Terry, one of the subjects of a doctor of ministry thesis about Roman Catholic feminists who choose to stay in the church. When asked why she remained Catholic, Terry responded not with theological justifications but this way: "Because it's in my bones. Where would I go? Because I'm Catholic. It's who I am. Because I love the saints. Because I love ritual. Because all my formation was in this tradition.

It's like asking, why do I remain Irish? Even if I didn't go to church, it's not what it's about. It's in my thinking; it's in my vocabulary. It's who I am."[73]

The theme of "not being able to leave" is common and powerful among women of many different communities. But it doesn't always mean not being able to leave the institution. The artist Meinrad Craighead no longer holds formal membership in Roman Catholicism, but nonetheless claims its formational power for her art. Craighead, for many years a member of a contemplative religious order, does not see herself as part of the institution, but neither does she consider herself as having left the Catholic church. She describes herself as having internalized the structure of Catholicism. "I haven't left the church," she says. "It would be like leaving my family. You might have all sorts of arguments. You might not fit in, you might outgrow them, but your family's still your family. My original soil, going back countless generations, is the Catholic Church, and I honor it."[74]

As one example of what she means, Craighead describes the profound effect that childhood participation in the communal recitation of litanies had upon the art that is now her work. In *The Litany of the Great River*, a book of paintings and texts, she writes that "the rhythmical flow and the precise syllable of the sacred language got inside our bodies; the step-pause-recite-pause-response movements were as regular and drumlike as our heartbeats. All the spirits and holy ancestors we were invoking seemed to walk with us, our re-membering made them present."[75] Years later Craighead learned about "the principle of indefinite extension" in an art history class. She made the connection with the litanies of her childhood, the body-memories that now inspire her painting, with the "indefinite extension" of all that had formed her across the boundaries of the institution and into a new way of being religious.[76]

Using the language of another tradition to express her commitment to Buddhism, Rita M. Gross says, "Karmically, I am a Buddhist. That is the simplest explanation for my strong sense of affinity and familiarity with Buddhism. I needed only to determine for myself that my gender would not be made into a major obstacle."[77] This does not mean that she experiences Buddhism as free from negative views of women. It is, she maintains, "flawed, sometimes seriously," in terms of gender issues. But she considers this reality an institutional failure rather than lack of depth in core Buddhist teachings. For Gross the experience of Buddhism's potential for liberation conveys sufficient authority to keep her in the tradition.[78] And Buddhism's capacity for liberation, as Gross sees it, emerges in great part from what it holds in common with feminism: an emphasis on experience over doctrine that Gross considers contrary to most of Western philosophical and theological thought. According to Gross's perception, "both began with experience, stress experiential understanding enormously, and move from experience to theory, which becomes the expression of experience. Both share the approach that conventional views and dogmas are worthless if experience does not actually bear out theory."[79] A whole variety of Buddhist women not only affirm with Gross the coherence of Buddhism with feminism but agree that what finally keeps them within the tradition is "the practice."[80]

For some women the attachment to their tradition emerges from the reclaiming of a past that had been rejected. In the introduction to *My Soul Is a Witness: African-American Women's Spirituality*, Gloria Wade-Gayles tells of rejecting religion beginning in her twenties and into her forties. "Yes, that late," she says, because "I thought people who believed in the working of something as invisible and undefinable as 'the Spirit' were flirting with an illogic that, if they were not careful, could have dangerous consequences. They could become disconnected from the real world which, in my thinking then, meant the world we see and hear and move in as corporeal beings."[81] Now Wade-Gayles ties that rejection to her desire to demonstrate that she had become an intellectual in male-dominated rational Western society and had stepped back from all the religious practices of "the folk." "This," she admits, "was no easy task, given the resonance of the Spirit in my upbringing."[82]

The collection Wade-Gayles edited brings together writings from African-American women in many different religious traditions. In it she refuses to operate out of contemporary culture's prevailing distinction between "religion" and "spirituality," which by "denying them the right to breathe in the same space and doubting their ability to achieve the same goal — is tantamount to playing god, goddess, or the Spirit, and thereby, assuming a power that we as finite beings simply do not possess: to see within a person's soul."[83] What holds these essays together, according to Wade-Gayles, is their rejection of "male-controlled pulpits" and their affirmation of the "threads" of faith that have come to them from their mothers and from other African-American women of the past. In spite of the differences of the contributors, they have in common not a monolithic "mother's faith" but "their belief that only when we are spiritually connected can we realize our highest selves, become one with all of humanity (as the Spirit says we must), and transform the world in which we live."[84]

Rita Nakashima Brock, who remains a member of the Christian Church (Disciples of Christ), writes of the irony that it is in many ways anger at Christianity that has kept her in it. She sees her exploration of feminist spirituality, with its quest for the Goddess and its search for a way to be wholly religious outside sexist institutions, as having affected her profoundly: "They have nurtured spiritual parts of myself not accessible to me through the church." But her explorations repeatedly brought her back to Christianity "and to the examination of my anger at the subtlety and extent of androcentrism in theological doctrines. Connections that provoke such anger are not easy to leave behind."[85]

Anger is not the only experience that holds Brock to her tradition. In 1995 she and two co-editors, all of them members of the Disciples of Christ, published a collaborative introduction to feminist theology. The editors and the other contributors wanted this collection to be "[m]arked in some discernible, yet not exclusivistic, way by the values and concerns of the Disciples tradition."[86] During the years of collaboration that included summer seminars spent in each other's company, these women were struck by how much they shared, in spite of many differences, based on their grounding in the Disciples tradition. They noted similarities that were sometimes "softly present" and other times more obvious.

As they worked together, they articulated what they thought had shaped them as Disciples and influenced their theologies. They experienced themselves as "uniquely positioned to speak theologically to traditions ranging from Baptist to Episcopal to Roman Catholic" due to their membership in a tradition that is low church in polity yet highly liturgical because of its weekly practice of communion. They shared as well a "sense of being called to a Christian fellowship that is deeply ecumenical in spirit, our collective 'looseness' on issues of doctrinal/credal correctness, our firm rootedness in the scriptural story, our discomfort with rigid ecclesial and social hierarchies, and our abiding love for the local church."[87]

What is noteworthy is that this obviously loving and highly knowledgeable description of the most particular qualities of the Disciples tradition serves as the introduction to a set of essays that is meant to foster a feminist critique of the tradition as well as to construct new visions for it. The capacity to do both, as these women demonstrate, comes from the heritage and the ongoing vitality of their community—to which they see themselves contributing. There is also testimony in this example that goes beyond gender issues, indicating that attachment to the specificity of denominational identity is not necessarily a thing of the past.

Some women experience and express their devotion to their traditions in terms of love for sacred texts and faith in the deep and abiding truth and wisdom of these texts—however they may have been used to exclude women from full participation in their communities. Constance Parvey, a pastor and theologian in the Evangelical Lutheran Church in America, describes herself as "unwilling to let go of a faith that is based on the Bible as authority. As Jacob wrestled with the angel and would not let go until he was blessed, so I too have wrestled with the Bible as the authoritative text for my life, and I have been unwilling to let go until I received a blessing."[88] Parvey recounts her forty years' struggle with biblical authority as beginning in her seminary days in the 1950s. In those years she ignored the negative references to women in the epistles of St. Paul, considering them outdated and irrelevant to contemporary women— "context-bound," she called them. She emphasized, instead, the text as a whole and ignored those passages "that did not resonate with my faith experience of God's love and justice and God's gift of integrity to every human person."[89]

In the late 1960s, when she and others in her denomination were debating whether women could be ordained, Parvey discovered that the passages she had ignored were being used to argue against women's ordination. Parvey realized that she could no longer consider them irrelevant: "I had to deal with them head on," she said, "and at many levels." She developed a three-fold method that required her to examine the passages in detail in their own biblical context, to look at them not as isolated passages but in terms of the whole message of Paul and the Christian Scriptures, and to ask what these texts meant in their own time and what they mean now. In other words, Parvey became a biblical scholar. By confronting the texts she had once ignored, she concluded that they simply did not have sufficient authority, given the overall message of equality in the Bible, to stand in the way of women's full partnership either in the early church or in contemporary times.[90]

Riffat Hassan began her career as a feminist theologian "almost by accident and rather reluctantly." As the only Muslim faculty member at Oklahoma State University in the 1970s and thus adviser to the Muslim Students' Association, she was asked to present a paper at a seminar of the group. Although there was no tradition of assigning faculty members topics, Hassan was given her subject: Women in Islam. She knew the topic was assigned to her "because in the opinion of most of the chapter members it would have been totally inappropriate to expect a Muslim woman, even one who taught them Islamic Studies, to be competent to speak on any other subject pertaining to Islam." Hassan resented being assigned a topic and describes herself as not even very interested in the subject of women and Islam—at least not at that time.[91]

Hassan agreed to give the paper because she knew it was a breakthrough to address an all-male, mostly Muslim group and because she was tired of hearing men "pontificate" about the status of women in Islam in the ever-increasing number of publications on the issue. She began her research reluctantly, more out of a sense of duty than from any awareness that she was setting out on "perhaps the most important journey of my life." She does not know exactly when her academic study became "a passionate quest for justice on behalf of Muslim women," but she does know with certainty that "what began as a scholarly exercise became simultaneously an Odyssean venture in self-understanding."[92]

In Hassan's story, as in Parvey's, we find all the elements of discovery of "otherness" that are a part of so many women's stories of their relationships with their traditions: growing awareness of exclusion, loss of innocence, and anger—to be followed by a turn to scholarship and a desire to search out the tradition's texts and traditions, symbols and rituals, in order to see whether anything lay deep within that affirmed the full equality of women. At the heart of Hassan's scholarship was the increasing and disillusioning awareness of the discrepancy between the ideals of Islam as she had always understood and experienced them and Muslim practice as it pertained to women. It became her goal to illuminate the essential equality of women and men as it was set forth in the Qur'an in contrast with the view of women that had become commonplace in Islamic culture through the *ahadith*, the oral and written commentaries on the Qur'an: that men are superior to women; that a man's share in inheritance is twice that of a woman; that the witness of one man is equal to that of two women; and that women are deficient in prayer and in intellect.[93]

In order to accomplish this goal Hassan expanded her field of study in two areas: *hadith* literature that pertained to women and the writings of Jewish and Christian feminists who were attempting to trace the theological origins of antifeminist ideas and attitudes found in their own traditions.[94] Hassan's continuing efforts go beyond critique toward formulating Islamic theology based on women's experience of the tradition and her own knowledge of "the justice and compassion of God reflected in the Qur'anic teachings regarding women."[95] For Hassan the Qur'an remains the primary source of hope for equality between men and women, a hope that she has not lost "despite everything that has gone wrong with the lives of countless Muslim women down the ages due to patriarchal Islam."[96]

I will conclude this chapter with some speculations about how ambivalence serves women and shapes their religious thought and about what the new virtue of ambivalence has to contribute to our understanding of religion. Before doing so I would like to offer an extended example of how one woman's mind has changed in regard to a particular aspect of her tradition and how that change has led to a reinterpretation of her relationship to her community—what it demands of her and what it offers her.

In 1993 Rachel Adler, a Reform Jewish feminist theologian who had previously been Orthodox, published an article in *Tikkun*, a Jewish journal of religion and culture: "In Your Blood, Live: Re-Visions of a Theology of Purity."[97] In this article Adler refutes what she had written twenty years earlier in a much acclaimed article about Jewish menstrual impurity laws. This is an essay for which women continue to express gratitude that Adler no longer feels she can accept: "What I owe to those who read and were persuaded by my theology of purity is not merely to outline abstractly my revised conclusions but to tell a richly detailed story about a particular process of rupture and transformation in a specific time and place."[98]

In the earlier article she had "attempted to reframe the meaning of women's menstrual impurity laws (*niddah*) by reintegrating it with other, broader purity regulations stipulated in the book of Leviticus rather than focusing on it as a unique phenomenon."[99] Adler's interpretation offered newly feminist Jewish women the opportunity to understand the purity laws related to menstruation in a more positive light. Adler now sees herself as having denied the negative effect the purity regulations have had on Jewish women's self-understanding. Eventually, she asked herself, "What did it mean to formulate a theology of purity that was blind to gender differences and silent about gender stigma [as she was attempting to do], when the only kind of impurity with behavioral consequences in Orthodox communities is gender specific—menstrual impurity."[100]

As she understands it now, her mistake lay in denying the reality of her own experience and setting aside her doubts that "God's Torah could be in error: Whatever I was or saw that did not fit had to be cut off, had to be blocked out. The eye—or the I—was alone at fault. I tried to make a theology to uphold this truth, and as hard as I tried to make it truthful, it unfolded itself to me as a theology of lies."[101] Eventually Adler placed her lived experience as a Jewish woman in dialogue with the teachings of Torah, and she found Torah wanting. Adler did not then repudiate Judaism and Torah, but she changed her mind about its authority in relation to her own life and that of other Jewish women. She found that she needed a new interpretation of Torah and what the life of the community should look like in relation to it.

What Adler conveys in this story is a lengthy process that in her distinctive way parallels much of what has occurred among women in other traditions. As they describe it, it involves coming to trust that the experience of feeling alienated and de-humanized—"other"—has theological significance that must be pursued and elaborated. As Adler saw it, her identity as a member of the community conferred on her the authority to speak. And the authority she claimed carried with it the obligation to speak.

Adler found herself changing her mind not just about the impurity laws. She needed also to claim the authority of Torah in a new way, not as a repository of immutable truth but as a living, changing compendium of what it means to be a human person who is Jewish and a woman. "When I was Orthodox," she remembered, "I thought God's Torah was as complete as God: inerrant, invulnerable, invariable truth. I thought that I, erring, bleeding, mutable creature, had to bend myself to this truth." Now, she says, she asks Torah "to speak to us in human. . . . Human is not whole. Human is full of holes. Human bleeds. Human births its worlds in agonies of blood and bellyaches. Human owns not perfect, timeless texts because human inhabits no perfect, timeless contexts. Human knows what it weds need not be perfect to be infinitely dear."[102] Adler concludes with a claim about Judaism that might have been made by most of the women in this study: "Sacred need not mean inerrant; it is enough for the sacred to be inexhaustible."

In this narrative Adler brings together the several themes of this chapter as they emerge from the stories of women who are both insiders and outsiders. She is a lifelong Jew and a scholar of the Jewish tradition. She is a woman and a feminist who is acutely aware that her tradition has put forth as irrefutable and as essential to the maintenance of the tradition laws that have set her apart as impure. For many years of her life she attempted to deny the negative identity of otherness that emerged from her adherence to these laws and to interpret them in a way that mitigated her experience that these laws, unlike others in Judaism, set women apart as impure during the time they were menstruating. Her gradual acceptance of the reality of her negative experiences and the legitimacy of her claiming them led not to a repudiation of Judaism but to a reinterpretation of what it requires of her. By implication, she demands that the tradition must acknowledge both its capacity for error and distortion and its willingness to change.

In Adler's case, like that of many other women, ambivalence leads not to final resolution of issues affecting the equality of women but to an ongoing commitment to a tradition that, she believes, will continue to offer both limitation and transformation. What I want to emphasize particularly is not that Adler decided that the menstrual impurity laws were not good for women or for the Jewish community, since that is a subject about which there is much debate among Jewish women in all branches of the tradition. Rather it is the fact that Adler asks of her tradition what anyone might ask—that it be inexhaustible in its capacity to respond to the lived experience of its members.

Conclusion

As much as anything else, in this chapter I am interested in the tone of what women have to say: not only the sense of ambivalence they convey toward their traditions but their bemusement and affection, their anger and contempt, their willingness to leave some things behind and to take others along in the midst of trying to fashion something new. To emphasize varieties of tone and thus emotional content moves one to consider what happens to religious thought when there is more "story" in evidence, more sense of the origin and history of convictions. A greater variety of emotional content tends to confound typologies, to blur the lines among categories, to shake up assumptions not only about what is proper content for religious thought but what are proper feelings in regard to one's religious community. We have traditionally heard from insiders and, more recently, quite a lot from outsiders as well. Those who experience themselves as both insiders and outsiders—in this case women—can add another set of complexities to American religious thought.

The first set of stories in this chapter illustrates women's need to express the worst about their traditions. Sheila Redmond, a psychologist and religious studies scholar who counsels HIV/AIDS patients in Ottawa, Canada, quotes a statement attributed to Thomas Hardy that she has written in the middle of the blackboard in her office: "If a way to the better there be,/It exacts a full look at the worst." That quote and her experience with Christianity have inspired Redmond to make this claim: "Whenever we fail to take a full look at the worst, whenever we deny the imperfections of our belief system, whenever we deny the evils our theologies have created and perpetuated, whenever we deny the abuse we ourselves have caused and suffered in the name of our Christian beliefs, we risk, at the least, perpetuating the present violence and at the worst, causing more harm even inadvertently."[103]

The second set of stories offers testimony to another reality that women experience: that a tradition does not need to be perfect in order to be compelling. However grave its distortions, it may well have within itself the wisdom to effect its own (partial) transformation, even though this wisdom never comes in a form that is undiluted by self-interest. These stories are from women who,

41

by virtue of the time in history in which they live, have experienced two major shake-ups of the foundations: the revelation of their own exclusion in their religious communities and the de-stabilizing of truth claims that is part of post-modern thought. Wherever one stands in regard to the questions of meaning raised by postmodernism, those questions cannot be ignored. Thus women who choose to expend their energies in the arena of religious community and religious thought do so with a certain kind of realism. "I am not naive," says Jewish scripture scholar Tikva Frymer-Kensky. As a late-twentieth-century person adept at various kinds of critical theory, she describes herself as well aware that her conscious participation shapes her Jewish identity.[104]

The stories women tell about their relationships to their traditions vibrate with the tensions that are incorporated and held together in their religious thought. Women tell about their anger and disillusionment at being excluded and marginalized. They also convey that there is freedom and perspective that derives from marginalization. Women express regret that the deepest wisdom of their traditions is diluted, compromised, deadened, and distorted in captivity to patriarchal domination. They also continue to probe their traditions and find their symbols and rituals endlessly extendible, often, in fact, far beyond institutional boundaries. Women acknowledge the truth claims of other religious traditions, but they choose to speak in the language of their own, however foreign it sometimes seems. Women decry the blindness and rigidity of religious institutions. They also give testimony to the value of community. Women insist on the need for the transformation of symbols and rituals in ways that are coherent with the ways they experience their lives. In so doing they conserve and revitalize these same symbols and rituals. Women push at the boundaries of their traditions and in so doing discover their depths.

Altogether these contradictory feelings and experiences compose a stance of ambivalence. The contradictions that women once resisted or for which they sought resolution or that they "read as a kind of internal prohibition against the discipline of theology itself" have now become, as Protestant theologian Catherine Keller describes it, the stuff of theological methodology.[105] If the volatility of ambivalence continues to be put to good use, it may have numerous theological and organizational functions. Maintaining a creative ambivalence might guard against women's expecting either too much or too little from their religious communities. It might push women beyond solutions that demand either resolution or departure, but either way close down theological engagement and inquiry. It might help to foster new forms of community that will promote and sustain women's full participation.[106]

Whether a piety of ambivalence is one that can or should be sustained in the long run by both women and men is a compelling question. It may force living in a tension that is as difficult to hold together as the Calvinist insistence that one's actions in the world had no effect on one's ultimate salvation.[107] Or it may promote strategies like "defecting in place," which provide a major and permanent means to enable women to remain within their religious communities and which result in a new kind of gender-based "separate spheres"—different in form from that which prevailed in the nineteenth century, but just as divisive.

On the other hand, one could argue that cultivating the virtue of ambivalence is just what all religious communities need to do to prevent reification of symbols, rigidity of teachings and rituals, and the failure to be aware of the needs of all their members, no matter how various. It may be the case that sustaining an ambivalence that is intensely aware of the simultaneous need for critique, conservation, and innovation will be an ongoing major contribution of women's religious thought to their communities and to other forms of institutional life in American culture as well.

3

The Immanence of the Sacred

*Women's Religious Thought
Comes Down to Earth*

American women's religious thought fosters a strong allegiance to the party of immanence without requiring a farewell to the party of transcendence. Witness the following excerpts taken from the religious writings of women from nine different religious communities: Jewish, Roman Catholic, Mormon, African-American Protestant, American Indian, Goddess-oriented feminist spirituality, liberal Protestant, Buddhist, and Muslim. It would be easy to add many similar excerpts. I have chosen these particular passages to provide examples of the frequency of women's affirmations of divine immanence and to point to some of the distinctive ways women express this concept.

"My *berakhot* [blessings] do not bless a 'lordGodKing of the Universe' or, indeed, any 'sovereign' at all. Instead, they point toward a divinity that is immanent, that inheres in all creation and nurtures all creativity" (Marsha Falk).[1]

"Nor does the Spirit's dynamic power arrive as an intervention from 'outside,' but is immanent in the world that is becoming" (Elizabeth A. Johnson).[2]

"One evening while I was praying to know Heavenly Mother, my mind was filled with this thought, 'you already know her, for you know yourself'" (Suzanne Werner).[3]

"My womanist voice comes from deep within myself. It rests in my innate God consciousness present in the breath of my ancestors from the Motherland" (Anonymous interviewee in womanist theology questionnaire).[4]

"A community of spirits,
kopisty'a, some in flesh,

some embodied words. A presence
don't you know. All in mind" (Paula Gunn Allen).[5]

"A psychology that can lead us to encounter the mysteries must be rooted
in an earth-based spirituality that knows the sacred as immanent. What is sacred—whether we name it Goddess, God, spirit, or something else—is not
outside the world, but manifests in nature, in human beings in the community
and culture we create" (Starhawk).[6]

"God's immanence, then, being universal, undergirds a sensibility that is
open to the world, both to other people and to other forms of life, as the way
one meets God. In this picture we do not meet God vis-a-vis, but we meet God
only and always as mediated, as embodied" (Sallie McFague).[7]

"My self is intentional, having a unique connection with the Creator and
the Creation. I belong to Allah, whose domination extends over the heavens
and the earth. Looking toward the light within, I see a reflection of the divine
light without" (Amina Wadud-Muhsin).[8]

"The great Completeness tradition speaks of an innate awareness (*vidya*,
rig pa) considered the mind's natural condition (*sems gyi chos nyid*). Innate
awareness is in this sense the ultimate collateral energy of mind and body"
(Anne C. Klein).[9]

"Immanence" does not mean exactly the same thing in all these different
worldviews. Nonetheless there is a consistent emphasis on sacred presence in
the world and, by implication, accessibility to the ultimate that is not surprising given women's history of lack of institutional access to the divine.[10] A fuller
exploration of the contexts from which these quotes come would illustrate
that interpretations of immanence are shaped by particular histories and cos-
mologies, multiple understandings of ultimate reality, and different theological issues and tensions. But for the moment I want merely to illustrate that in
women's religious thought there is persistent testimony to the conviction of
sacred presence permeating the world and accessible to humankind. In what
follows I will explore some of the directions an emphasis on immanence takes
in the religious thought of women in different traditions and where this emphasis fits in broader patterns of American religious thought.

In the opinion of many women, an emphasis on immanence does not
signal a chromosomatic predisposition to theologies of immanence. It does not
mean that women in every tradition manifest their loyalty to the same extent
or for the same social or theological reasons. It does not mean that women
have no use for "transcendence" in their religious thought; in fact, they expend
much energy in redefining it. If there was a tendency early in the second wave
of religious feminism to toss out bad transcendence in favor of good immanence, the more recent perspective is that various meanings of transcendence
need to be transformed, not obliterated. "Transcendence" is simply too useful
a theological concept to lose.

In *Our Passion for Justice*, Episcopal theologian Carter Heyward acknowledges "the complaint voiced frequently against feminist theology . . . that we have no place in our theology for 'the transcendent.'" She counters by saying that as a feminist she rejects not "transcendence" itself but traditional definitions of it that depict a static deity "stuck" and "sealed fast" in limited cultural movements. For Heyward "transcendence" really means—"to cross over" or "to bridge." Heyward sees herself and other feminists claiming transcendence as "a wonderfully mysterious power truly crossing over into and through and from our lives into the lives of all created beings—and that this power is indeed God, transcendent precisely in the fullness and radicality of her immanence among us."[11] From a very different part of the theological spectrum feminist and Orthodox Jew Tamar Frankiel also uses the image of divine transcendence as a bridge "across supposedly male and female views." She claims that "[t]he point of view represented in Torah, prophets, and classical rabbinic interpretations holds that it is God's mercy—not his thought, mind, intellect, spirit, logos, or other Greek philosophical characteristics—that exemplifies his transcendence, because it comes from a place beyond the natural order of things."[12] At the same time she holds that Judaism teaches a God who is "related in and to the world."[13]

An emphasis on the immanence of the sacred—within nature, within human souls and psyches, within relationships, within culture— means primarily that this traditional theological concept has emerged as a fruitful and versatile theme with a catalyzing effect on women's theological constructions. It fosters worldviews and theological interpretations that women consider conducive to full participation in their religious traditions and in society and that make more sense in terms of what we know about how the universe operates at this time in history.

"Immanence" is, in fact, a sub-theme in all the chapters that follow. The sacredness of the ordinary depends upon the assumption of sacred presence throughout the universe. Relational theologies and ethics, based on claims about the inter-connectedness of all things and the integrity of women as moral agents, likewise take for granted the indwelling of the divine. And women's theologies of healing are predicated on assumptions about an inward capacity to bring about healing of sin and sickness, individual and social.

But the focus of this chapter is concerned primarily with women's uses of immanence to do two things: to bring the religious enterprise out of the heavens and down to earth and to reinterpret "God" or ultimate reality from the perspectives of women.[14] I am interested in exploring why "immanence," a broad and even ordinary religious concept, is so useful in women's religious thought. And, further, to look at why grounding religious thought in earthly rather than other-worldly concerns makes such good theological sense to multiple communities of women: both for reasons of critique of traditional teachings and as a basis for construction of new interpretations. "This-worldly," in the sense I use it here, does not imply a materialist or mechanistic worldview, one devoid of spiritual presence. Rather women define "spiritual" and "religious" and "transcendent" in ways that draw their significance almost totally from the life we live on earth. Of particular interest from my perspective as a student of American religious thought is the extent to which in the following examples women maintain continuity with the symbols of their traditions. They do so even as they take for granted that the sacred is immanent in the world and that any form of transcendence must be grounded in this assumption. Further, women maintain this continuity in the midst of vigorous critique of their traditions.

The chapter takes shape as follows: (1) a brief discussion of traditional meanings for immanence and transcendence; (2) a few examples of sources of immanentist thought in American religious history; (3) a survey of the efforts of women from several different religious traditions to use immanence as a theological concept to bring religion down to earth; (4) an extended discussion of how women of several different communities take on the task of reinterpreting symbols for God or ultimate reality and what they think is at stake in this enterprise for women and for their particular traditions. The theme of ambivalence is muted in this chapter, although it bubbles along beneath the surface as women have some things to say about losses and gains in new interpretations of the holy.

Immanence and Transcendence in the Abstract

"Immanence" and its correlative, "transcendence," are ancient ideas in Western and Eastern religious thought. Broadly defined, immanence refers to the presence of the sacred or of ultimate reality within the world and its inhabitants. "Transcendence," by contrast, is a concept traditionally used to designate the uniqueness and the apartness of the divine from creation, and ultimate reality from the penultimate or the transitory. In the biblical religions, particularly, much theological energy is expended to maintain a creative tension between immanence and transcendence. If there is too much emphasis on transcendence in a tradition, the sacred, whether manifest theistically or non-theistically, becomes too removed. And remoteness often promotes either fear or indifference. Too much emphasis on immanence, at least in the biblical religions, is seen to invite the dual dangers of idolatry and pantheism: the temptation to worship that which is not God and to confuse the boundaries between the creator and the created. There is also the concern that a highly immanentist theological system will be inadequate in its capacity to cry out against evil—or even to detect it with sufficient radicality. If the sacred is infused throughout the universe, then where does evil come from, what does it look like, why does it persist, and how do we work against it?[15]

As with most polarities, immanence and transcendence carry with them a history of evaluative connotations. Even a secular source like a dictionary suggests that "transcendence" refers to that which goes "beyond ordinary limits," that which is "superior" or "supreme," in contrast with "immanence," which is assumed to be concerned with common matters.[16]

What is at stake in the weight given to either the immanence or the transcendence of the holy in a religious system are generally three issues: how to describe the divine or ultimate reality; how the sacred is known and expressed in the world and thus the number and kinds of possibilities for access to it; and the relative worthiness or sacredness of the world and its human and non-human inhabitants. Typically, the greater the emphasis on transcendence, the more limited and regulated the possibilities of access to the divine. It is also more likely that the world and its inhabitants will be considered fallen or illusory, in need of salvation, enlightenment, or liberation—most often available in ultimate form from a source outside normal human capacities.

Generally, the more immanent the divine in a religious system, the more available it is to human experience and use; the more sacred the world and its inhabitants, the more the arena for religious thought and action becomes this world and the greater is the assumption of the human capacity, by whatever means, to effect our own salvation or enlightenment or liberation. Immanental theologies are also more likely to find meaning, even revelatory meaning, in aspects of culture rather than to see cultural forms as mostly adversarial to religion.

On the other hand, the more immanent and available the divine, the more difficult it is to discern, define, regulate, and control. Too-much-immanence, from the perspective of those who guard the boundaries of institutions, stirs up access to the sacred as a volatile commodity in a religious system, a potentially dangerous substance or capacity in need of control. It is not only perceived as a temptation to idolatry and pantheism (especially in the biblical religions); it is also looked upon—for good historical reasons, actually—as an invitation to claim "private revelation"—individual access to divine intentions that, acted upon, threaten religious orthodoxy and social stability. Further, too-much-immanence fosters fears of secularization, whereby the distinctiveness of religion as a contribution to culture is collapsed into other aspects of culture such as psychology or politics.

It is not my intent here to offer a cynical rendering of these concerns or to make light of them, even though I would maintain that in the exaggerated forms they sometimes take they are certainly bars to theological creativity. They are all related to religious communities' efforts to insure the distinctiveness and authenticity of their worldviews, an enterprise in which women are deeply engaged. My primary interest is, rather, in demonstrating why and how contemporary women are expending so much effort to expand the importance and multiple meanings of immanence.

Immanence in American Religious Thought

In American religious thought, an emphasis on immanence in the work of a particular thinker or tradition or school of thought has frequently emerged in conjunction with new ways of thinking theologically. It more often signals innovation than conservatism. Immanence tends to be associated with rejection of dogma judged to be rigid and unaccommodating to new information about how the world works. It is an emphasis that frequently coincides with a renewal of interest in pondering the spiritual significance of the natural world or in finding new ways to relate science and religion.

One can point to any era in American religious history and find evidence of immanental theologies. Immanentist thought is consistently evident in the worldview of the Quakers, who have placed their confidence in access to inner light since the seventeenth century. And however much it was concerned about what it considered Quaker excesses in this matter, Puritan theology was by no means devoid of references to the immanence of God. In his study of American religious thought, William Clebsch points to various ways divine immanence is manifested in the religious thought of Jonathan Edwards (1703–1758), whose popular reputation persists as the great defender of God's sovereignty and transcendence.[17] The New England transcendentalists, who might just as well have been called immanentalists,[18] offer another school of thought that insisted on the reliability of inner wisdom grounded in access to the divine through nature. The metaphysical religions—Christian Science, New Thought, Theosophy—that emerged during the last half of the nineteenth century insisted to greater and lesser degrees that knowledge of the divine and the spiritual meaning of reality are accessible to human knowing. And it is a truism of American religious history that women have been attracted to these movements in disproportionate numbers.[19]

Varieties of immanentist thought in the nineteenth century found their way to America through European religious and philosophical idealism as well as from the introduction of Eastern religious thought into the culture. The growing interest in occult ideas that appeared in religious movements such as Spiritualism and Theosophy offered another source. Immanentist thought also took significant shape particularly in liberal Protestant theology, but in evangelical theology as well during the last quarter of the century and into the twentieth.[20] And regardless of how they have emphasized this theme at any given historical moment and with what qualifications, Roman Catholic and Jewish theologies have always looked upon the world as filled with the presence of the divine.

Aspects of late twentieth-century religious thought have additional contributions to make to immanental theologies. Among them are speculations about the theological implications of subatomic physics; ecological worldviews that insist on the inter-relatedness of all things; and the human potential movement that has elaborated into multiple self-help and twelve-step programs that depend for success on the assumption of an inner power—usually connected to a higher power—for transformation. And one can make the generalization that postmodern thought, with its insistence on the socially constructed nature of religious ideas, looks to the authority of theological creativity and the capacity for world construction that dwells within humankind.

Women and Immanence

What does all of this have to do with gender? It is a frequent claim in women's religious thought that the shape the immanence/transcendence tension takes in a tradition makes a significant difference in the status of women. Because Christianity and Judaism have tended to place greater emphasis on the transcendence of the divine, they are perceived by many women as reinforcing a concept of a God who is (1) remote from the world; (2) static rather than dynamic; (3) distortedly anthropomorphic—more precisely, male; (4) impossible to reconcile with what we now know about how the universe came into being and continues to operate; and (5) accessible only by regulated means—official persons, rituals, and ecclesiastical structures—that historically have excluded women.

The result, according to the critique, has been a doctrine of God that promotes alienation and separation as the primary relationship between God and the world—including humankind and particularly women—and drains from the world a sense of sacred presence. Further, an over-emphasis on transcendence is seen to obscure and even to deny the variety of ways to imagine the divine available in the sacred texts and traditions of many different religions. The reluctance to give God many names, including feminine names, is interpreted as yet another by-product of too-much-transcendence that has negative implications for women.

The feminist critique of too-much-transcendence coincides to a great extent with the dissatisfaction expressed more and more widely since the nineteenth century with the model of God known as classical theism: an omnipotent, omniscient, unchanging monarch who rules his creation from a distance.[21] But women's critique of classical theism goes in another direction as well. Women of many different traditions tie their most negative experiences of being considered "other"—those experiences documented in the previous chapter—quite directly to the inadequacies of classical theism as a model of the sacred that promotes the full humanity of women. The elaboration of this claim has had sufficient public exposure in the last thirty years that there is no need to go on at length here.[22] Let it be enough to repeat women's rejection of the traditional assumption that women, as more "earthly" beings than men, are that much more carnal and therefore more alienated from God; that much weaker morally and intellectually and therefore in need of greater regulation than men (the special rules, categories and circumscriptions noted in Chapter 2); and that much more "bodily" and finite than men and therefore in need of more purification rituals. Such assumptions, according to the critique, foster negative interpretations of women's bodies, women's psyches, and women's capacity to be moral agents. These interpretations range from assuming that women are morally weaker than men to seeing women as evil or at least as "ambiguously evil."[23]

At the same time, as many historians have pointed out, women have experienced highly unrealistic adulation of themselves as more sentimentally spiritual, pure, and moral than men and thus more in need of protection from the demands of public life and exclusion from its responsibilities. This is a purity and a morality, women contend, that is not grounded in the realities of a full life. The result is the Eve or Mary constellation of characteristics that feminists like Mary Daly denounced early on in the contemporary feminist movement. Numberless women have pointed to this construct as totally incongruent with the ways they experience themselves—neither as pure as stereotypes of Mary, the mother of Jesus, nor as tempting as Eve was supposed to have been.[24] Women describe a grotesque lack of fit between how they experience their lives and the religious roles available to them that is even more pronounced among women of color and working-class white women. What emerges, then, in women's developing theologies of immanence is at one level an attempt to stir up more complexity and more possibilities in how women and men experience themselves in relation to the sacred, to other people, and to the world.

American women have a history of using the immanence of the divine to overturn limits on participation in their religious communities, although marginalization in various forms has often been the price. In 1637 Anne Hutchinson declared at her civil trial in Massachusetts that she spoke the truth of her conscience as she knew it, a truth that had been revealed to her by "an immediate revelation," which she described as "the voice of his own spirit to my soul."[25] That declaration along with other circumstances accounts for the exile of her and her family from Massachusetts Bay and their excommunication from the church. Even a brief reference to this incident renews our memory that historically women have assumed public authority in American religious history by claiming an inner revelation that allows them to subvert institutional barriers to their public speaking or teaching. Thus, claims of the indwelling of the divine have often served as strategic means to claim both authority and autonomy.

It is necessary to consider also the nineteenth-century African-American women preachers whose journals recount the means by which they claimed their ministries: an individual call from God in spite of the objections of their communities.[26] Or the female Spiritualist mediums whose insistence that the spirits spoke through them relieved them of their responsibility for breaching the proscription against women's preaching.[27] Or the Pentecostal women ministers whose narratives of their call from God to preach overcame the objections of their conservative communities.[28] Nor does one have to go beyond the mainstream to find examples. American theological seminaries, both liberal and conservative, are filled with women who tell their stories of being called to ordained ministry, even when family or church either failed to acknowledge their claims or actively discouraged them.

The "call" for all these women and many others emerges from a conviction that an interior voice can be revelatory of divine intent—irrespective of the limitations placed on women by religious institutions. Thus, the evoking of authority by means of declaring access to the divine within has always been available as a strategy for women to attain fuller participation in their traditions, however reluctantly or circuitously granted. This is a strategy that has not necessarily required new definitions of immanence and transcendence or elaborations of a theology of immanence, because to a limited and well-controlled extent, the possibility of direct knowledge of the divine will or mind is part of most religious traditions.[29]

Against this backdrop of critique and history, women of different traditions are constructing theologies that seek to explore what takes shape when the implications of divine immanence are probed more assiduously. This work is a manifestation not just of protest against distorted concepts of transcendence but more prominently of the creative uses of the concept of immanence. As women have developed a greater historical awareness of those few circumstances under which women have claimed religious authority, it has become clear that a merely strategic invoking of divine immanence is not sufficient to bring about major institutional change, in terms of either structure or theology. What is needed, as women see it, is the development of theologies of immanence that will reshape and thus transform all aspects of their traditions: symbols, rituals, teachings, and institutional structures. The dual goals of this reshaping are to fashion systems of religious thought that promote gender equality and that are coherent with contemporary knowledge about the nature of reality. Women not only want full participation in their traditions; they also want to construct and embrace theologies that are intellectually and emotionally compelling at the end of the twentieth century. For many women these goals cannot help but overlap.

Transcendence Downward: The Earth as Home

Pope John Paul II reiterated in 1995 that Roman Catholic theology and tradition could not permit the ordination of women, having said a year or so earlier that the matter should not even be discussed. In response *Commonweal*, a Catholic journal devoted to religion, politics, and the arts, featured a question about whether Rome's ban on the ordination of women was infallible. Among the several respondents was Michael Novak, a conservative Catholic thinker. Novak argued on the side of infallibility and in doing so distinguished between denominations that ordained "priests" and those that ordained "ministers." "A priest is not a minister," he said, although he granted that "in ministerial roles, women do as well as, if not better than, men. The priestly role is cultic and representational. Religions in which there are not priests, only ministers, will of course ordain women."[30] In this article Novak uses the term "priestess" to refer to women who are ordained in sacramental communities like the Episcopal Church.

One might want to argue with Novak on many grounds, including his exploiting of the negative connotations of the term "priestess" in Western culture and religion. But more interesting to look at for my purposes are his fears about what will happen to Christian theology if women are ordained in sacramental traditions such as Catholicism. Novak claims that the role of churches, like the Episcopal Church, that are now ordaining women is uncertain, but he predicts that their doing so will bring about radical theological changes: "A quite different theology of the body; a quite different doctrine of Incarnation and the resurrection of the body; a quite different symbolic approach to the Trinity; a depreciation of the role of Mary, the Mother of God; a different theology of the sacraments; and a radical devaluation of the tacit wisdom embodied in tradition." In other words, Novak predicts change in the most central elements of the tradition; and, without reading too much between the lines, one can assume that change for Novak means "loss."[31]

Novak invokes fears of ancient heresies when he speculates that the ordination of women will move Christian theology in the direction of gnosticism, a belief system that originated in the first and second centuries of the Common Era. Gnosticism rejected the goodness of creation and the ultimate reality of matter. "A church of priestesses," Novak claims, "might be tempted to become a church of the 'spirit,' rather than the far more humble, limited, despised, and rejected Incarnation. The figure of Jesus Christ, a male, will become 'problematic' to it—as it already was to the Women's Ordination Conference during its 1995 meeting. In short, we should anticipate a different and quite modern gnosticism, appealing to many, spreading rapidly, and ordaining its own priestesses and establishing its own counter-church (probably *within* the true church because that's cheaper)."[32]

Novak is concerned only with Christianity, but I read him as wrong on all counts about women in Christianity and other traditions as well. The overall theme of women's religious thought across many Christian traditions is not anti-body, not anti-world, but highly immanental. One of the major features of women's religious thought is that it brings the entire religious enterprise down to earth.

Women readily acknowledge the complex realities of life in this world in their religious thought and acknowledge the world as the arena of their suffering. But there is no hint in the theological writings I've encountered of a desire to escape to other realms or to devalue earthly life either as less spiritually authentic or as merely a prelude to something better elsewhere.[33] I have not found intimations, except in the writings of very conservative women (whose writings are not generally included in this book), that women are inclined to wait upon the rescuing efforts of a God who is external to the world to remedy injustice. Rather there is the sense that God is present in the struggle for equality. Nor is there a pattern among women of non-theistic traditions like Buddhism to look upon spiritual disciplines and practices as avenues of escape from this world. Because of its persistent concern with the status of women, women's religious thought is intensely taken up with efforts to promote justice and what Buddhist Rita M. Gross calls "sanity" in this world. If the world is the scene of women's suffering, it is, also, decidedly the arena of their joy and liberation. Women claim the earth as their home. They contend that whatever is necessary for the living of a full religious life can be found on earth; they are not strangers here. "Conversion to the Circle of Earth," is what Roman Catholic theologian Elizabeth A. Johnson calls this perspective.[34]

Women's theological creativity in this arena points to the capacity of major religious symbols to be transformed in new historical contexts without losing their power or their deepest meanings—their "dearness" or their continuity with their traditions. As women make use of them to further the full participation of women in their communities, it becomes apparent that traditional religious language and symbols, even "beliefs," are not so dependent for their vitality or credibility as once was thought on positing a reality that exists outside the known universe. Nor must they ground their most ultimate expression in "spirit" defined as metaphysically contradistinct from and superior to nature. In the following section I have selected examples of the work of Roman Catholic, liberal Protestant, and Buddhist women to support this claim.

BRINGING MARY BACK TO EARTH

In *Mary: Mother of God, Mother of the Poor*, Brazilian liberation theologians and Roman Catholic sisters Ivone Gebara and Maria Clara Bingemer put forth a new Marianist theology for the poor of Central and South America, one that refutes traditional teachings about Mary, the mother of Jesus, that emphasize her passivity and other-worldliness.[35] I begin with this example, because it is among poor and uneducated women that one might be likely to find, if anywhere, expressions of the anti-world tendencies Novak anticipates in women's religious thought. Gebara's and Bingemer's starting point is the experience of Latin American women. They offer a theological anthropology that they see as moving from male-centered, dualistic, idealist, one-dimensional assumptions to those that are human-centered, unifying, realist, and pluri-dimensional. The center of this theology is Mary, and they look at her from the perspective of scripture, Marian dogmas, and traditional devotions to Mary. There is an obvious awareness on the part of these theologians of the intellectual and emotional demands that their new interpretations must bear.

Will their approach knock the foundations out from under traditional Roman Catholic theology, making its symbols useless to contemporary believers? Not as these authors see it, because the persistence of meaning in these symbols, in particular that of Mary, does not depend upon an understanding of the eternal as unchanging. They hold that "'the eternal,' whether in values, persons, or deities, is always historical; that is it always retains the imprint of time—it begins, grows, changes, ages, dies, is renewed. Such a perspective permits an ever-new understanding of the figure of Mary."[36]

What will happen to divine transcendence in this new theology? Can it be maintained? To demonstrate that it can, the authors collapse immanence and transcendence in speaking of the "presence of transcendence" in human persons, male and female. They are concerned with valuing what is "autonomous and original" in each one. "Transcendence," Gebara and Bingemer say, "is not synonymous with higher experience or other-worldly experience, or experience beyond history, or to put it another way, transcendence is not a break in the forward course of history. God's transcendence is manifest in God's creatures."[37]

This study, grounded in the life and contemporary meanings of Mary, the Mother of God, for the women of Central and South America, is a lengthy exercise in theological creativity that takes its life from an emphasis on divine immanence. "The divine takes place in the human," say the authors, "in its entire flesh, in its precarious wholeness."[38]

One can open the book almost anywhere and find Gebara's and Bingemer's new interpretations of traditional theological concepts. The authors insist that it is the understanding of the divine as immanent that frees traditional theology from the rigidities that have depended for their persistence on an understanding of God as mostly transcendent and "other." As they describe it, the whole focus of religious energy and activity shifts from "up there" to "down here." Judgment, for example, is still a valid expectation in their theological worldview, but judgment takes place not "up there" by God after we die. Instead, "Our brothers and sisters on earth are our only judges!" In this shift of focus—and locus—Gebara and Bingemer acknowledge the Bible as a human product. It is not the word of God in a literal sense but the word of humans about God. This does not mean, say the authors, that the Bible tells us nothing reliable about divine mystery: "Some texts in the Old Testament and in the New Testament recount experiences so profound, so essential to us that we say, 'this is the word of God.'" But, as Gebara and Bingemer see it, these are texts that have to do with our relationships to each other, thus keeping "revelation" grounded in earthly experience. They consider the parts of the Bible that are particularly inspired to be "those texts that speak to us of sharing, forgiving, mercy, and compassion."[39]

The authors also take on the task of re-interpreting the meaning of "dogma" as they look at traditional teachings about Mary in order to see what makes sense in light of the realities of contemporary Latin American women's lives. "What is permanent in dogma," they say, "is its deepest foundation, the original mystery out of which it emerges."[40] They do not reject Marian dogmas: the Immaculate Conception, the Virgin Birth, the Assumption. But neither do they accept them in their traditional, literal interpretations, all of which require divine interruption of natural and historical processes. They examine the scriptural warrants—or lack of them—for these teachings about Mary; they investigate the history of traditional church teachings about them. And then they find ways to relate them to the lives of the poor women they serve.

The poor have their own "dogmatics," they say: "What is important for the people is saving life—their own individual, collective, and cultural life."[41] Thus, the teaching about Mary's bodily assumption into heaven can become a way to restore and reintegrate "woman's bodiliness into the very mystery of God"[42] rather than to emphasize, as the tradition has often done, that Mary has moved up and away from women to a heaven far removed from their sufferings on earth. One hears echoes here of Rachel Adler's claim that a tradition need not be inerrant in its interpretations of its central symbols to retain its dearness to the community, only inexhaustible.

No doubt these more metaphorical and non-literal interpretations of Marian tradition are easier to accept intellectually than the traditional ones. But why do the authors see them as good for women? Or for men, for that matter, or for the world? Why is a Mary who gives rise to innumerable stories and interpretations better for women than a pure and removed, immaculately conceived Mary who is Queen of the Universe and intercedes with God for the good of the poor? For one thing, the intention of these authors is to demonstrate that "the human word about God in Mary" and "God's revelation in women" can only emerge from the lives of the women who are devoted to Mary. And what emerges from the stories of their lives is testimony to both the sufferings they experience and the hope they work for and embody. It is the lives of these women that, in fact, give the authors their inspiration for new interpretations, and it is the reciprocal energy between these women's lives and the tradition's claims about Mary that keep this central symbol alive for poor Roman Catholic women in Latin America.

According to Gebara and Bingemer, a feminist theology of Mary that starts with the lives of poor women serves notice not just to society but to the church, particularly, to examine whether it has been a sufficiently strong advocate for women. "If the church earnestly compares itself with the person and figure of Mary," the authors say, "such reflection will entail examining and discerning whether it has truly said 'yes' and whether it has had the courage to say 'no' at the right time."[43] It is an earthly Mary, then, a Mary who is "with us" that these liberation theologians continue to claim as essential to their faith, a Mary they interpret in ways they see as faithful both to the tradition and to the lives of living women.

THE NATURALIZING OF THEOLOGY

I have chosen as another example of the catalytic power of ideas of immanence to women's religious thought three influential, liberal Protestant theologians whose work is widely known: Sallie McFague, Marjorie Suchocki, and Sharon Welch. They do their theological work in very different cultural contexts from Gebara and Bingemer, but they are moved by the same immanental, earthward impulse. McFague works extensively with ideas about theological language, particularly its metaphorical nature, and she has identified numerous theological issues connected with "bodies" as a common thread that runs throughout her own theological journey.[44] Suchocki has taken on the Christian doctrine of original sin and redefined it as "rebellion against creation" in contrast with the more traditional "rebellion against God." And, using as a focus the nuclear arms race, Sharon D. Welch offers an "ethic of risk" in opposition to an "ethic of control." For all three women an emphasis on divine immanence and new definitions of transcendence are pivotal in their construction of religious worldviews they consider more compelling to this moment in history and more reflective of women's experiences of their religious traditions.

Sallie McFague, who identifies herself as a Christian, a feminist, and, more recently, an ecological theologian, has published four volumes of theology since 1982. *Metaphorical Theology*,[45] what she calls the deconstructive phase of her work on religious language and on models of God, was followed in 1987 by *Models of God: Theology for an Ecological, Nuclear Age*, the constructive phase of her efforts. In this book she offers chapter-long extensions of three relational metaphors for God: mother, lover, and friend. She put them forth tentatively, as "thought experiments" that would "try their chance at demonstrating the creative, saving, and sustaining activities of God in relation to the world."[46] McFague describes the three models as a trinitarian construction and says they reflect, also, her predilection for personal models of God. They work, in her estimation, to counter the heavy emphasis on God's transcendence that for too long has been a part of the Christian tradition and, in McFague's opinion, has been detrimental—dangerous, actually—to the needs of a nuclear, ecological age.

In 1993 McFague published *The Body of God: An Ecological Theology*, based on the metaphor of the world as God's body, about which I will say more in a moment. In 1997, she published *Super, Natural Christians: How We Should Love Nature*,[47] which argues for a change in how Christians view nature. She says its thesis can be stated simply: "Christian practice, loving God and neighbor *as subjects*, as worthy of our love in and for themselves, should be extended to nature."[48] McFague argues in this book for what she calls "horizontal Christian sacramentalism." By elaborating on this concept, she hopes to contribute to a change in Christianity's history of using nature in too functional a way to point beyond itself to God. "Natural forms," she says, "are not transparent to the divine; they are first of all themselves, and as such, in the intricacy and uniqueness of who, what, they are, they speak elliptically of God."[49]

Particularly in her later work, McFague calls more and more specifically for a theology that is earthly. This is especially evident in *The Body of God* and her contention that "the world as the body of God" offers "a way of thinking about transcendence in an immanental way," that "the world is our meeting place with God."[50] For her an earthly theology is less abstract, general, and "spiritual." It is more humble, less pretentious, and less inclined to suggest that it issues from direct communication with the divine mind. An earthly theology holds that concepts like sin and salvation are "fleshly, concrete, particular matters having to do with disproportion and well being *in relation to* the forms of God's presence we encounter in our daily, ordinary lives: other bodies."[51]

McFague also becomes more self-disclosing in her later works, a rhetorical strategy that is common in feminist writings and one that typically is used to indicate the contextual, and therefore partial, perceptions of any given theologian. At the conclusion of *The Body of God*, she includes a story about her own conversion to what she has come to see as "nature" spirituality, "a spirituality that finds renewal and hope coming from what the eye sees and not just what the ear hears."[52] McFague confesses that "as a Protestant" she was once a person for whom "only 'the Word' that reached my ears conveyed the presence of God, never the sight before my eyes"—that is, nature as "divine habitation."[53] Her most recent book, *Super, Natural Christians*, it seems to me, is part memoir. It is engaging for being so and illustrative, also, of McFague's insistence on the partial nature of all theological efforts.

What happens to traditional definitions of "immanence" and "transcendence" when "immanence" assumes the lead, as it does in the hands of contemporary Protestant theologians like McFague? As I see it, they take on much broader meanings than they have had previously, but they remain grounded in the Christian worldview nonetheless. McFague herself uses the term "radical" to characterize her new interpretations, because she sees them based not just on human history but on the history of earth and the universe. As she sees it, the model of the universe as God's body "radicalizes transcendence of *all* of the fifteen-billion-year history and the billions of galaxies in the creation, the outward being, of the One who is the source and breath of all existence." And she holds that the same radical possibilities exist for new understandings of immanence: "The world (universe) as God's body is also, then, a radicalization of divine immanence, for God is not present to us in just one place (Jesus of Nazareth, although also and especially, paradigmatically there), but in and through all bodies, the bodies of the sun and moon, trees and rivers, animals and people."[54]

McFague is a liberal Protestant feminist. She is committed to her tradition and acutely aware of its shortcomings, but she does not want to abandon "God." She chooses, in fact, to elaborate on personal models of God that are already part of her tradition—very familiar models, in fact. The creative possibilities of emphasizing immanence as the grounding ethos of her models of God and the world do not push her to the point of leaving behind the Christian tradition's teachings about the transcendence of God or even of the uniqueness of Jesus.[55] Instead, they remain the foundation of her creativity.

In *The Fall to Violence: Original Sin in Relational Theology*,[56] Marjorie Suchocki, a process theologian (that is, one whose theological worldview emerges from the philosophy of Alfred North Whitehead), moves "sin" in its entirety—causes and consequences, repentance and forgiveness—down from infinite celestial regions and within the boundaries of nature. The book had its origins in Suchocki's serving as Juror No. 1 in a "mundane drug case" that ended in a unanimous verdict of guilty. Although she went home relieved that the trial was over, the questions that had been raised subliminally began to emerge more insistently, mostly in Suchocki's wondering about the extent to which her world as an academic dean in a theological seminary overlapped with what seemed to be the alien world of the drug pusher—a world that was both very far from and very close to her own. " 'My' world was geographically close," Suchocki says, "but had I ever intentionally done anything at all to touch the lives in the 'other' world? Was I only involved to judge its inhabitants? Or was there not a sense in which I was a participant in that world as well as mine, even if that participation were as an absentee neighbor?"[57]

Motivated by these experiences[58] Suchocki began work on a theological study that is grounded in ancient questions about evil and violence: "Why is it that we humans are so capable of such great harm to all of creation, including ourselves? How is the horror possible that humans can and do delight in causing pain?"[59] Her response is to point to new ways to understand both sin and transcendence within a worldview that assumes the presence of the divine and does not need to look outside the creation for explanations of evil. Suchocki defines sin as "the violence of rebellion against creation," because, as she argues, the traditional understanding of sin as rebellion against God and a desire to be god-like does not do justice to the way most people think about what they are doing when they "sin." "One must do mental gymnastics," she says, "with the concept of rebellion against God to apply it to most of the deeds of ill-doing in the world today, where rebelling against God or being god-like is often irrelevant to the consciousness or intentions of most perpetrators of evil."[60] Her working definition of sin is "participation through intent or act in unnecessary violence that contributes to the ill-being of any aspect of earth or its inhabitants."[61]

Suchocki's interpretation of sin depends for its cogency, as do McFague's models of God and the world, on a worldview that emphasizes divine immanence and redefines transcendence—a transcendence, as Suchocki says, that is immanent in the world, that does not go outside the natural world to find "limits, norms, judgment, and meaning." For her, traditional terms like "transcendence" and even "infinity" no longer require an ultimate referent that is out-of-this-world. She is talking about an understanding of transcendence that is "extraordinarily ordinary," one that does not require "the vantage point of a lofty perspective surveying the universe from above. . . . It may indeed survey the universe from within." This mode of transcendence "is gained not through isolation from all others, but through relation to all others."[62]

Suchocki's effort to bring sin down to an earth in which the divine is immanent fits in several different ways with broader themes in women's religious thought. Her efforts are consonant with contemporary feminist insistence that sin is not only individual, it is "systemic," "relational": so intertwined with the workings of the world that no one is innocent. Her work also contributes to a move beyond definitions of sin that have often been gender-differentiated: sin interpreted as pride or the desire to be god-like (recall Saiving's essay), an interpretation that feminists say speaks primarily to privileged males; or sin as sensuousness, an absorption into nature, that is more often attributed to women. She is looking in her new definition for ways to subvert the traditional dichotomy that associates women with earth and nature and men with spirit— to the detriment of possibilities of wholeness for both.

Interestingly, and in keeping with the inclination of many forms of women's religious thought to be ultimately more hopeful (not cheerful) than gloomy about the human condition, Suchocki concludes her book about sin with the claim that both sin and guilt are "salvific words," "words of grace." For Suchocki, "The naming of sin bespeaks a vision where violence is not the norm; it bespeaks transcendence through imagination of a new and different future."[63] Like McFague, she does not leave the terms of the Christian tradition behind but redefines them in keeping with her conviction that the sacred dwells within creation.

Sharon D. Welch is a third Protestant theologian who finds the source of the divine within the world rather than outside it. Based on that assumption, she proposes what she calls a feminist ethic of risk for members of the Euro-American middle class. [64] She defines an ethic of risk as less absolutist, perfectionist, utopian, intolerant of conflict, and liable to cynicism and despair than its opposite, an ethic of control. As Welch sees it, an ethic of control has predominated in the white middle-class response to issues such as the nuclear crisis; and, because total control is never possible, there ensues a sense of helplessness that makes all action seem futile.

One of Welch's primary sources is the literature of African-American women like Toni Cade Bambara, Paule Marshall, and Toni Morrison. For her, their writings "express an ethic of risk, a definition of responsible action when control is impossible." In Welch's interpretation these authors "name the resources that evoke persistent defiance and resistance in the face of repeated defeats."[65] An ethic of risk, as Welch defines it, carries no guarantees of "quick solutions or total solutions or obvious success." She says, instead, "that the creation of fairness is the work of generations."[66]

The theological correlate of an ethic of risk, Welch says, is a theology of immanence, one that provides "the benefits of a theology of transcendence without the social costs." Here again we find not only the construction of new perspectives but the implicit, and often explicit, re-interpretation of traditional definitions of immanence and transcendence. In Welch's theology, "transcendence" has to do not so much with "God." It is "produced," one might say, by loving acceptance of an ethical imperative to work for justice that involves seeing the complexity of life; celebrating the wonder and beauty of life; transcending conditions of oppression that devalue life, self, and others; and working for social change.[67] In Welch's theology of immanence, there is no need to look beyond the finite for sources of grace. "Divinity," as she understands it, points to a quality of relationship and being, not to a deity that is exterior to the world: "Grace is not that which comes from outside to transform the conditions of finitude. Divinity, or grace, is the resilient, fragile, healing power of finitude itself."[68] Welch does not deny the comfort that belief in God or the Goddess can bring, but for her these constructs are no longer adequate for the social and theological circumstances in which we find ourselves at the end of the twentieth century. She claims, instead, a multi-imaged, adjectival or adverbial understanding of divinity.[69]

THE EARTHLY GOALS OF BUDDHIST SPIRITUAL PRACTICE

Discussions of sacred indwelling are prominent among American Buddhist women, but they take their own particular shape. As many women point out, Buddhism already has significant strong points from a feminist perspective. Its founder, though a male, was a human person, not a deity, and Rita Gross considers Buddhism's non-theism one of its major advantages for women. "Count your negative blessings," she says in *Buddhism after Patriarchy*, and she includes non-theism (in contrast with the predominantly male-imaged God of the biblical religions) under the category of "battles we don't have to fight."[70] Buddhism also takes for granted that Buddha nature, the potential for enlightenment, is inherent in every person. Further, in America, anyway, since the 1960s, it has developed as very much a this-worldly religion. One might assume, then, that Buddhism is already so thoroughly immanentist, so down-to-earth, that the feminist inclination toward immanental theologies would not be much in evidence. To the contrary, I see the immanentist religious thought of Buddhist women particularly in two areas: the issue of women teachers and leaders and the distinction between immanence and transcendence as it affects understandings of what Buddhist practice is for.

Increasing in intensity from the 1960s through the present has been the expressed longing of Buddhist women for women teachers of the Dharma, the path to enlightenment taught by the Buddha. In the male-dominated Asian leadership that found its way to America, women teachers were for many years very rare. At the very least the issue of women's leadership is related to the obvious feminist principle of "modeling": women who see other women in leadership positions can likewise imagine themselves in that capacity. But women's leadership in Buddhism is related as well to the ancient question about women's capacity for enlightenment and whether they achieve it to the same extent and in the same way as men. If that issue is to be resolved in an American feminist Buddhism that considers women and men equal in their capacity for enlightenment, then, say Buddhist women, women teachers are required. Sandy Boucher, for example, makes the strong claim "that an egalitarian Buddhism is possible only if the very top leader and teacher [in a Buddhist *sangha*, or community] is a woman, and one with socially enlightened views," although she says at the same time that she has no wish to denigrate the spiritual development of women who study in centers with male leaders.[71]

Many of the reasons Boucher gives for her claim are related to her experience that women bring distinctive qualities to the teaching of Buddhism, qualities that I see as related to a more immanental, daily-life-oriented, and particularized practice. Women, she says, are more likely to acknowledge the emotional aspects of life and Buddhist practice and to adapt "their message to the twentieth century, psychologically-oriented consciousness of their students." Boucher also experiences women teachers as more likely to experiment with innovative forms of practice, to bring in elements from other traditions, and to insist on less hierarchical arrangements in Buddhist centers.[72] Women teachers and innovative practices, in the opinion of many Buddhist women, make "the path" visible within a variety of people and life circumstances and thus more widely accessible. And accessibility to the divine, as the history of American religious thought demonstrates, is one of the functions of an immanental theology.

Accessibility, in turn, will make Buddhism more versatile and therefore more available to communities other than the white, educated, middle- and upper-middle-class people to whom it has typically appealed. Jan Willis, an African-American teacher of Tibetan Buddhism, has a great deal to say about accessibility from this perspective and relates it to issues of race and even more to class: "It seems clear," she says, "that the question of accessibility is one of *class*, not — at least not *necessarily* — one of race. In order to study and to practice Buddhism in America, two requisites are absolutely essential: money and leisure time."[73] Thus, in putting forth her several meanings of "accessibility," Willis is at the same time pointing to multiple ways that Buddhism needs to come down to earth.

Accessibility to the divine also fosters the kind of innovations in practice that are particularly associated with women teachers in America. Because of the strong perception that there is something new emerging among American Buddhist women, innovations in practice are viewed as not only a privilege, a freedom, but also an obligation. According to Karen Gray, one of the women Sandy Boucher interviewed for her book about American women who are creating the new Buddhism, "The big issue is, what is going to be born here in America in terms of Buddhism? I think what's going to be born that's really new will be born among women." She uses the language of immanence when she goes on to suggest that what American Buddhism needs is not women teachers who are successful because they mimic men: "What we really need is to do this very hard thing of looking inside of ourselves and saying, What *is* being born here. What is it that is developing within us? And I deliberately use women's symbolism. I do think of it as a kind of fetus developing, that we are giving birth to something that will outlive us."[74]

Buddhist women are articulate about the connections between women's innovative leadership and practice and devotion to traditional goddess figures like Tara and Kuan Yin—myth models, Rita Gross calls them—and particularly how such devotion fosters women's confidence. Here again is immanental language. Female deities, says Buddhist teacher Miranda Shaw, "represent the divine potentiality of all women," and in the Buddhist worldview, where the dividing line between human and divine is not strictly delineated, "the goddess represents the innate divinity of all women." She, like Boucher, insists on the need for women to receive initiation and instruction from women: "It makes the extraordinarily empowering statement that women can tap directly into the ultimate source of power, energy, and truth in female form. It powerfully communicates the sufficiency of female embodiment as a vehicle of total freedom."[75] Shaw is also convinced about the self-esteem and "divine Pride" that Buddhism—in Shaw's case, Tantric practice—fosters in women. This is a confidence that she sees as diminishing the need to seek outward sources of approval and the chance that discouragement will bring practice to a halt. In Shaw's estimation, then, it is both the ancient goddess figures of Buddhism and women teachers, that is, "women who have realized their divinity and attained enlightenment"—goddesses come down to earth, one might call them—who promote this divine pride in women.[76]

In a different kind of approach to immanence and transcendence in Buddhist women's thought, Rita Gross points to how these concepts are illuminating about different and even contradictory understandings of Buddhist practice. Buddhism, according to Gross, teaches both that we are basically good and enlightened beings and that "we are not fully in touch with that goodness and enlightenment." She relates the former stance to immanence and the latter to transcendence and sees the challenge of Buddhism as requiring that we hold on to both: "Without both, one will fall into either trivial superficial spiritual materialism of the 'love and light' variety, or one will fall into rigid and depressing dualistic otherworldliness."[77] She interprets them, also, as indicative of the conflict between what have been typed as masculine and feminine spiritualities: "patriarchal world-denying spiritualities of longing, dissatisfaction, quest, and transcendence" and "feminist spiritualities of acceptance, joy, community, and cycles." Imbalance and one-sidedness in the long run, says Gross, are the consequence of settling for either extreme.[78]

Masculine spirituality is the predominant mode in classical Buddhism, the kind of Buddhism, according to Gross, in which most Westerners have been instructed, and it needs the balance of feminist Buddhism. It was, in fact, this masculine kind of spirituality that compelled her as "a poverty-stricken farm girl . . . to leave home, to seek to understand and be transformed, to reject as inadequate the conventions laid out for me because of gender and class." People are drawn to this kind of spirituality, as Gross sees it, by what she describes as a "volatile combination" of both vision and unwisdom based on pain. It leads them to seek a means to live apart from the dictates of conventionality but also "to seek a heaven-oriented transcendence" and "to glorify renunciation, aloneness, and self-sufficiency, to become alienated from much that is deeply sane about earth-oriented immanence."[79]

Gross looks to feminism to provide a "countervailing weight" to this renunciatory inclination, but by itself, she says, it is inadequate because it does not foster sufficient vision and discontent to keep us from being satisfied with things as they are. Gross claims sorting out the excesses of either kind of discipline as a difficult but necessary task for a balanced spiritual life—one of the major tasks of Buddhism after patriarchy. This balanced practice, she contends, must lead to productive life on earth.

According to Gross, serious, ongoing, disciplined practice is a necessary part of a whole Buddhist life, and there are things in one's life that will need to be put aside for it. Yet the goals of Buddhist practice, in her opinion, are earth-oriented. Gross does not think it is necessary to sense the presence of realms other than the earthly or to enter "exalted, euphoric states of consciousness" or gain esoteric knowledge, although if one achieves these things it is a bonus. "But when they are pursued," she says, "instead of one's immediate concern with earth and one's fellow human beings, they are counterproductive."[80]

Charlotte Joko Beck, who teaches at the San Diego Zen Center, tells a story about one of her students that illustrates and confirms Gross's point. The student called her at 1:30 A.M. to tell her about a good book he had read on enlightenment and to complain that he didn't think his own practice was sufficiently enlightened. When Beck suggested to him that it wasn't a good idea to call people in the middle of the night, he said, "Oh, is it the middle of the night?" Beck responded, "Enlightenment is about awakening; and if you're going to be awake, you need to know what time it is." The student confessed that he had never thought of that.[81]

Immanence, Down-to-Earth Theology, and Talk about the Ultimate

It is apparent just from the few examples above that bringing religious worldviews down to earth requires new ways of talking about God or ultimate reality, particularly in those traditions whose God-language was once dependent upon supernatural understandings of the divine. The rest of this chapter is devoted to explorations of some of the insights women in different traditions are contributing to ideas about the holy.

Women approach the subject of ultimate reality with an interwoven set of concerns. They do so as members of particular religious traditions with histories of creating religious symbols, and as members who are women. They want the symbols for the sacred their communities embrace to reflect the experiences of women and to foster the full humanity and participation of women. They bring to the conversation as well all the other social particularities of their lives and communities.

Further, women participate in the creation of God-language as inhabitants of American culture at the end of the twentieth century, whose exposure to questions about how religious language functions necessarily influences their theological work. They ask not only, "What are the most fruitful ways for us to talk about the sacred in our communities and still maintain continuity with the tradition?" They also acknowledge the reality that God-language is no longer assumed to be made up of "stable" words that point to a discernible reality—however imperfectly revealed—that lies behind them. There is an acute awareness that God-language, like the language of any other discipline, is constructed within all the entanglements and disparities of power and knowledge and social arrangement that make up human communities.

Acknowledging both the communal and the created nature of "the symbol" gives rise to a self-consciousness about God-language. What is a symbol for God or ultimate reality supposed to be doing? What is it for? How does it function? If a particular understanding of God is acknowledged to be a human construction, can it inspire commitment? Is there anything of the transcendent about it at all? While this awareness of the nature and function of religious language is faith-shaking in some respects, in others it is highly conducive to theological creativity exercised on behalf of the community. "The symbol gives rise to justice," is the way Roman Catholic theologian Mary Catherine Hilkert puts it in an essay on "rethinking the image of God."[82]

There are several questions I consider foremost in an exploration of women's ideas about God and ultimate reality in addition to the theme of immanence that underlies the entire chapter. How do women talk about what is at stake for them and their communities in the creation and transformation of language about the ultimate? What do they hold dearest in their traditions— or, put another way, what do they choose to renew and enhance rather than leave behind? What contributions are women's religious ideas making to a broader understanding of how symbols of ultimate reality are revitalized and continue to function at various times in history?

What I am particularly interested in demonstrating in this section is what women "do" with the concept of immanence in re-interpreting the major symbols of their traditions—in this case, "God" or ultimate reality. What new meanings emerge? What, finally, do women say is at stake for their traditions in these new constructions—in terms of both critique of the old and possibilities for re-vitalization?[83]

USING MANY IMAGES TO ENHANCE JEWISH MONOTHEISM

One of the most prominent and prolific Jewish feminists is Judith Plaskow, author of *Standing Again at Sinai: Judaism from a Feminist Perspective.*[84] In a variety of her writings, one of the most central claims of her feminist reformulation of Judaism is that women are fully members of the Jewish community. Their experiences must be included in any understanding of it or in any formulation of the meaning of Torah and God, or it is not truly Judaism. This principle of inclusion sounds straightforward and fairly simple on the surface, but in Plaskow's estimation it requires far-reaching changes: rewriting Jewish history; altering and expanding the boundaries of Jewish memory; re-arguing and reconstructing Jewish law; creating liturgies that include the experiences and spiritualities of women; and creating new symbols for God.[85] Up to now, Plaskow argues, women have been part of the covenant community, "but precisely in a submerged and non-normative way."[86]

It is one of Plaskow's theological assumptions that God is present—immanent—in community and is experienced in community. Therefore the arena in which new understandings of God and new names for God emerge must also be the whole community of Jews, men and women. Like many other women in this study, Plaskow rejects "the notion of a supernatural God who singles out a particular people," but she has no desire to deny the loyalty to God that is the center of Jewish identity or "to reject the God who is met in community and wrestled with in history."[87] The immanence of God within the Jewish community is signaled in new ways by women's liturgies, women's leadership, and women's new names for God, whether these are anthropomorphic or not (Plaskow suggests that McFague's models of God might be explored to good end by Jewish feminists). "It may be," she says, "that truly satisfying communal images of God await the creation of new communities, for communal structures and communal metaphors are mutually related."[88]

As Plaskow sees it, women draw on Jewish understandings of God that are already part of the tradition when they seek new metaphors for God. They are concepts that "emerge out of the Godwrestling of our ancestors and represent their efforts to name and comprehend the God they knew as with them on a long and various journey."[89] These symbols, she says, are privileged because they are a formative part of Jewish memory, not because they say all there is to be said about God. She understands the traditional ways of talking about God not as binding on the community but as offering examples for how the community constructs viable models of God: the "listening, struggling, and constructing meaning in historical context that we go through in trying to make sense of our religious experiences."[90]

Plaskow does not propose female imagery for the divine as the only answer to Jewish feminists' prayers for new God-language. Female imagery can motivate an examination of the tradition, but it doesn't necessarily address the nature of God as "dominating other."[91] On the other hand, Plaskow does not by any means see female imagery for God as "sullying" Jewish monotheism and pushing it toward paganism and polytheism—typical accusations directed at Jewish feminists. In fact she sees feminine language as a test of whether Jewish monotheism is sustainable: "Is our God sufficiently God that we are able to incorporate the feminine and women's experience into our understanding of the divine?"[92] One assumes that her answer to this question is "Yes, of course."

She does not, though, find it theologically adequate that images for God be primarily nurturing in nature, because that mutes the issue of God's moral ambiguity, an issue that Jews in a post-Holocaust world cannot ignore in their attempts to understand and image God. Plaskow herself does not always experience the holy in her own life as aligned with the moral, an insight prompted by seeing a huge waterfall on the border between Brazil and Argentina and being moved to speculate that "Such sources of the power of nature are one source of a theology of immanence, embodiment and ambiguity."[93] God's ambiguity, in fact, is one of the theological issues that particularly intrigues Plaskow. She distinguishes "ambiguity" from the classical theological problem of theodicy, which requires a reconciliation between the evil that happens in the world and a model of a deity who is perfectly good. Ambiguity is a different issue, in Plaskow's opinion, one that moves us to ask, "How do we name the power in the world that makes us know our vulnerability, that terrifies and overwhelms us?" For Plaskow, a feminist revision of God-language that does not confront the ambiguous ways we experience God's power omits reference to a "profoundly important dimension of human existence. Unless the God who speaks to the feminist experiences of empowerment and connection can also speak to the frightening, destructive, and divisive aspects of our lives, a whole side of existence will be severed from the feminist account of the divine."[94]

On whose authority and with what safeguards will new images for God in Judaism emerge in a worldview that looks so decidedly to the immanence of the divine? The authority of the community, says Plaskow, which will make its own gradual decisions about which new images of God to retain and which to reject. And the issue of authority is one on which feminism has particular insights to offer, "Not because it has solved the problem of authority, but because it has had to confront it head on." [95] Plaskow credits feminism with pointing to the authority of the community in the interpretation of texts and of the tradition itself. Speaking for herself, she says, "I did not get my feminist perspective from God, but neither did I or any other individual woman invent it in a vacuum." Her point is that "religious authority rests in a community of interpreters that—whether to enhance its own power or give voice to the experience of a larger community—seeks to understand texts and/or experience in ways that give meaning and structure to human life."[96] The community, then, no longer understands itself as invoking the outside authority of divine approval; it confers authority on its own members.

In order for this to be the case and so the process will work with integrity, there must be the assumption that immanent within the community there is a wisdom about ultimate matters, an authority that is available to its members: "Authority is, or ought to be, responsive—to the meanings in Jewish sources, to the changing demands of Jewish and human community, to the Eternal You that sustains and enlivens all our efforts to give our lives purposes." In fact, Plaskow says, reaching for an absolute foundation for authority in the mind of the Eternal may well be an evasion of responsibility on the part of the community. "' It [authority] is not in heaven,' the rabbis remind us."[97] In order to be authentic to the needs of the community, as Plaskow sees it, interpretive authority must come down to earth. And this God, who can be called by many names, "is experienced not only in relation to nature, but also in the coming together of human beings who see their communal purpose as transparent to a larger purpose in which it is grounded."[98]

This is the immanent God that undergirds the Jewish theology of *The Book of Blessings* Marcia Falk published in 1996. In a publication preceding the book, Falk describes the understanding of divinity on which these blessings stand: not a "'LordGodKing of the Universe' or, indeed, any 'sovereign' at all. Instead, they point toward a divinity that is immanent, that inheres in all creation and nurtures all creativity."[99] However much she rejects traditional kingly images of God, Falk has no intention of abandoning Jewish monotheism. Like Plaskow, she sees the multiple images in her blessings reinforcing monotheism, but this is a monotheism that assumes diversity: "Because I believe in a monotheism that does not deny diversity but instead celebrates differences, I use a multiplicity of images to point toward an underlying unity—the unity that embraces all creation."[100]

Falk's blessings hold up for celebration the ordinary moments of this life, in faithfulness to Jewish understanding: "We are embodied selves, and Judaism acknowledges our embodiment. *This* life, *this* world, *this* moment in time: we acknowledge, we embrace, we claim."[101] She describes her blessings as having "their roots in classical Jewish sources: Bible, *midrash*, piyyut—although, of course, most are turned to reflect my own poetic sensibility."[102] In Falk's understanding, to confine the divine to only a few traditional images is not being true to the Jewish understanding of reality. If people ask "where is the divine" in all her blessings, she responds this way: "Nowhere in particular—yet potentially everywhere that attention is brought to bear. If everything is capable of being made holy, as rabbinic Judaism teaches with its scrupulous attention to the details of everyday life, then surely we need not—we *ought* not—localize divinity in a single apt word or phrase. We may find it wherever our hearts and minds, our blood and souls are stirred."[103]

Sometimes Jewish feminists call God "Shekhinah" (the word has various spellings in Jewish and Christian writings). Plaskow refers to the Shekhinah, "as opposed to the totally unknowable *Kadosh Barukh Hu* (holy one, blessed be he)," and she describes this understanding of the divine in light of her own emphasis on community as "precisely that aspect of God with which we can be in relation . . . experienced in joint study, community gatherings, lovemaking, and other moments of common and intimate human connection."[104]

In *She Who Dwells Within: A Feminist Vision of a Renewed Judaism*,[105] Lynne Gottlieb, a Reform Jewish rabbi, translates the Hebrew word *Shekhinah* as denoting "the female presence of God." In this book Gottlieb chronicles her early searching for sources of feminist images for God in Judaism and her worries that "Jewish monotheism . . . seemed to preclude incarnate images of the divine, particularly the Goddess."[106]

She recounts her experience of attending a gathering of Christian and post-Christian feminist scholars at Union Theological Seminary in New York in the winter of 1975. She had various responses, mostly negative and apprehensive, to the meeting and to the women's speculations about how the Goddess might fit into their particular traditions. Finally, she asked a question of Ann Barstow, who had told the group the story of being affirmed as a woman upon seeing an immense figure of the Goddess giving birth.

Why, she asked Barstow, does an oversized statue with breasts affirm your womanhood? Because, said Barstow, the experience enabled her to feel pride rather than shame in her womanhood and in "the numinous nature of her physical and spiritual being." "Did she whisper to me then?" asks Gottlieb. "What if I permitted other words, other images, of God? What if I imagined YHVH as a woman giving birth? The rabbinic sages record a folk legend that describes the God witnessed by the Israelites at the shores of the Red Sea as a man of war, and the God of Sinai as a learned sage. What if I replaced the Man of War with a Woman giving Birth?" On her way home on the subway that evening, Gottlieb whispered to herself, "Yes, I need the Goddess. I need her to midwife the spirit that sings with a woman's voice inside me."[107]

Gottlieb began to look for ways to claim the indwelling feminine aspects of God that are inherent in the Jewish tradition, searching for Jewish texts that might tell her about Shekhinah. She discovered traces of Shekhinah in Jewish mystical and midrashic texts from the first millennium C.E. onwards. "I felt like an orphan," Gottlieb says, "who uncovered documents that proved that her mother was not dead." She sought further sources about Shekhinah that had been written by women but discovered only those written by men, a situation that in her opinion needed to be remedied: "Without women's voices interpreting and composing Shekinah texts for themselves . . . we can never fully grasp women's experience of the divine."[108]

Within what framework of understanding Judaism does Gottlieb place her work? Like Plaskow, she is looking for a transformed and renewed Judaism that takes women into account—that responds to their experiences and benefits from their particular kinds of wisdom. She is not looking for a new religion, even though that is one of the frequent criticisms directed at Jewish feminists who talk about the Goddess: that they have crossed over into something that is no longer Judaism. Rather, the search is for a new theological language, as Gottlieb sees it, that will permit the tradition to say better what has always been a part of it. She sees the development of "Shekinah" language, based as it is on an understanding of the divine within, as one way to do this: "The many images associated with the Shekinah can become a source for women's encounter with the divine today as well as a bridge to our past. Women yearn for this possibility. When women speak of God She, we can finally picture ourselves created in God's image."[109]

An interest in God as Shekhinah is not restricted to Reform Jewish women. Orthodox Jewish feminist Tamar Frankiel claims that "Shabbat represents the feminine in powerful form, the Shekhinah manifest in her unity." Very important in Jewish mysticism, "the whole concept of the Shekhinah, the divine Presence in the world, . . . suggests that insofar as we know God's presence in the world—in the forces of nature, in the ordinary course of our own lives—we know it as feminine."[110]

Frankiel does some creative work with the concepts of immanence and transcendence based on her dual claim about how male and female are related to Jewish understandings of God and the universe. "The universe," she says, "rests on the delicate balance of male and female, one that we must work out in our families, our communities, and the public world."[111] And in Judaism, as Frankiel interprets it, "God's oneness, the divine unity, is the marriage of female and male, the transcendent union that is neither mind nor body, spirit nor matter, nor anything else we can comprehend."[112]

What makes Frankiel's interpretations of transcendence and immanence intriguing from the perspective of my interest in theological creativity is how as an Orthodox woman she confounds popular definitions of liberal and conservative, feminist and traditionalist. She announces in the preface to *The Voice of Sarah: Feminine Spirituality & Traditional Judaism* that it is her intention "to stand firmly within the bounds of generally accepted halacha."[113] (The word "halakha" has various spellings in Jewish and Christian writings.) In other words, even though she is sympathetic to—and knowledgeable about— feminism and women's experiences of injustice within Judaism and other traditions, she cannot advocate changes in Jewish practice. She bases what might be called a conservative refusal to do so on what are typically considered "liberal" claims: a well-developed theology of the immanence of the divine and confidence that as a member of the Jewish community whose "inner voice," is shaped by Jewish practice, her interpretations carry authority within that community.

For Frankiel, it is the *doing* of Jewish practice that has been powerful for her rather than some of the justifications for it she has been offered. "As a feminist," she says, "if I had only been listening to the words, I wouldn't have stayed around for more than a few weeks."[114] But it is the case for her that deepening her commitment to Jewish practice has also intensified her feminist consciousness. It is Frankiel's concern that changing Jewish practice in matters related to the masculine-feminine structure of Jewish life might undermine the power of the whole system. She is seriously doubtful that having women rabbis and scripture scholars—a male-egalitarian paradigm for Jewish women—is the best way for women to become full participants in their tradition. She has, instead, worked to develop her own understanding of the role of women in Judaism, because she did not find satisfactory explanations to "why this ancient practice was so powerful to me" either in feminist literature or in explanations by Orthodox rabbis or other observant writers—only "bits and pieces" here and there.

And yet Frankiel is as highly immanentist in her theology as many Jewish feminists who call, unlike herself, for significant changes in practice. She sees women's theologically immanentist contributions to Judaism as inherent in and already being fostered in Jewish women's practice as it presently exists. She is convinced that as women recover and take back the power of private and public speech, as they write midrash and prayers, as they contribute the immanentist emphasis of their own spirituality, halakha will be affected positively "from the place of immanence, from our connection to the divine hiddenness, from our knowledge of Shekhinah, of Rachel weeping with us." In the process, women will also "ask men to call back to their consciousness the knowledge of immanence."[115] All of this is possible, says Frankiel, without changing Jewish practice as it now exists.

Plaskow, Frankiel, Falk, and Gottlieb very self-consciously identify themselves as participants in the Jewish community who draw the inspiration for their new theological formulations from traditional Jewish sources. They see themselves as conservators of Jewish monotheism, particularly in their insistence that monotheism cannot be obliterated or compromised by multiple images for the divine. Their more radical move is to insist that not only is monotheism safe in light of multiple images of the divine, including those emphasizing immanence, but it can be enhanced by them—feminine images, nature images, that in their multiplicity are nonetheless unified by the foundational Jewish assumption that God is One.[116]

MORMONISM'S HEAVENLY MOTHER

Judaism and traditional Christianity in its Protestant and Catholic forms are monotheistic but have within their scriptures and traditions female images for the divine. Mormonism, which I see as a form of Christian polytheism and, like Christian Science, neither Catholic nor Protestant, has within its religious system not only female images for the divine, but a female deity: Heavenly Mother, the consort of Heavenly Father and the mother of the spirit bodies of Mormons. Devotion to Heavenly Mother is permitted on an individual basis (although some women report that even this is discouraged), but she is not revered institutionally by the Church of Jesus Christ of Latter-day Saints.

Even in a religious tradition like Mormonism, which is highly earth-centered in a number of ways and whose view of heaven is very much an earthly paradise, women make the connection between a theology brought down to earth and greater possibilities for female images of God. In her memoir, *Refuge*, which unites the story of her women relatives' deaths from cancer—particularly her mother's—and her concerns for the bird life and ecology of the Great Salt Lake region, Terry Tempest Williams speculates about the Holy Ghost in the Mormon Godhead as a female presence. The voice of conscience, the "still, small voice" that she connected with the Holy Ghost as a child, she chooses today to recognize as "holy intuition, the gift of the Mother." It is her conviction, also, that "[i]f we could introduce the Motherbody as a spiritual counterpoint to the Godhead, perhaps our inspiration and devotion would no longer be directed to the stars, but our worship could return to earth."[117]

There are numerous Mormon feminists working on recovering, renewing, and creating images of Heavenly Mother, and often that creativity depends upon an understanding of Heavenly Mother already present—immanent—in the Mormon community, if only the community had eyes to see. It is also common to see theological speculations about Heavenly Mother tied to efforts to gain the priesthood for Mormon women, who, like women of many other traditions, are denied ordination[118]

One of these feminists, Margaret Merrill Toscano, sees a female priesthood and a heavenly mother as "doctrinal attestations of the equality of women." She does not understand these concepts as having been invented by feminists and imposed on Mormonism from the outside, but as revelations given to Joseph Smith by God. As Toscano sees it, they are part of the "restoration of all things," a restoration that cannot be complete until women have the priesthood restored to them. "And," says Toscano, "until God the Mother is accepted as the equal of God the Father, we as a church will remain bereft of the fullness of the Spirit of God. Zion, our Mother, cannot return until we are ready to receive her."[119] Like feminists of other traditions, Toscano maintains that the tradition cannot be whole until the Mother of Mormonism is fully acknowledged.

Janice Allred is another Mormon woman who is working toward a compelling theology of God the Mother. In her work she sounds the familiar feminist theme of the nearness of the divine, and she asks women to speculate from their own experience: "[W]hich of you mothers does not know that your children need you to be with them? If you, then, being selfish, will sacrifice to be with your children, how much more is our Mother, not in heaven, but here with us?"[120] And here is the testimony of another Mormon woman: "When I let myself be quiet and listen—listen to the feeling in my gut, I experience spirituality. When I respond to my voice within, confusion disappears. I feel strength and wholeness. I have clarity. I feel the truth of my life. Perhaps this experience is God. And so, for me, if God has gender, God is female."[121]

Mormon theology has always fostered the possibility of private revelation and thus direct access to the divine will, although it has carefully regulated the extent to which such revelation—and whose revelation—has implications for the entire community. Traditionally, the revelations of women have had significance only for themselves and their children. However, some Mormon women are obviously claiming the power of revelation as significant for the larger community and, in an effort to expand the theological understanding of who Heavenly Mother is and can and should be in Mormonism, are pooling their insights and experiences of Heavenly Mother.

EVANGELICAL FEMINISM AND CONCERNS
ABOUT THE IMMANENCE OF THE DIVINE

A move to the evangelical part of the Protestant feminist spectrum reveals another theological conversation with a different sense of what is at stake in feminist constructions of God-language. Christians for Biblical Equality was founded in St. Paul, Minnesota, in the mid-1980s. Its membership includes women and men from numerous evangelical and pentecostal denominations and some mainline churches as well. This organization is committed to the full participation of women in public, ordained ministries among evangelical Christians. It is dedicated to exploring biblical warrants for women's full inclusion as well as investigating social problems like domestic violence in light of scripture. CBE publishes a quarterly journal, *Priscilla Papers*, which offers feminist articles by women and men.[122] It is a good resource in which to look for evidence of how evangelical women approach the issues of constructing images for God and where they draw the line, not only because it contains compelling work but because it offers a good reminder of the variety of women's theological voices, often within the same tradition—in this case Protestantism.

Anyone familiar with contemporary American women's religious thought is likely to have come across references to "Sophia," often defined as "wisdom" or "inner wisdom" to evoke feminine images of the divine. It is, though, a controversial term, one that provides a focus for evangelical women's concerns about how much is too much in terms of innovative language for God. Tina J. Ostrander, an evangelical Christian feminist, asks whether "Sophia" is the long-awaited "bridge between traditional Christianity and feminist concerns. . . . Who is Sophia, and where did she come from?"[123] Ostrander analyzes the uses of "Sophia" at the 1993 Re-Imagining conference (and the smaller conferences that followed) as a point of departure for her own theological analysis of Sophia from an evangelical perspective.[124]

Ostrander rejects interpretations of "Sophia" as a reference to the God of Israel in the imagery of the Goddess, which she attributes to Roman Catholic theologian Elisabeth Schüssler Fiorenza. She rejects as well Sophia as either a divine person or an abstract concept, interpretations she saw in evidence at Re-Imagining. "The biblical understanding of Sophia which is most true to the biblical context is that sophia is none of these things," says Ostrander. "Sophia is nothing more than a Greek noun describing an important attribute of God. Wisdom is personified not because it has an existence of its own, apart from God, but as a literary tool used to stress its importance. . . . .The introduction of a goddess, however, merely obscures the fact that God is neither male nor female"[125] According to Ostrander, the very real needs of women in Christianity must be met apart from references to the Goddess.

Evangelical scholar Aida Besançon Spencer is willing to grant the good faith of the women at the Re-Imagining conference who claimed in response to widespread criticism of references to Sophia that their prayers were directed nowhere other than to the Christian God. But it is her interpretation that the rituals and prayers at Re-Imagining, with their references to God within as "the Presence within you," moved from immanence to universalism to pantheism, and perhaps even to blasphemy. "Our naming of ourselves *is* less sacred than the naming of God," says Spencer. "To equate our name with God's name is blasphemy."[126]

In spite of Spencer's concerns that the invoking of "Sophia" at Re-Imagining took immanence too far, she does not advocate "highlighting the very opposite of what these speakers and writers say" because "any of these reactions will lead us to heresies as serious as those espoused in these words"[127] (which I interpret to mean an excessive insistence on the transcendence and otherness of God and the unworthiness of humankind). Further, she is an advocate of gender-inclusive language. In a recent article in the *Christian Century*, Spencer is adamant in her disapproval of the International Bible Society, which developed the new International Version of the Bible. In response to protests by conservative Christians the Society decided not only to abandon plans for a gender-inclusive Bible but to excise gender-inclusive revisions already made in the New International Readers Version, whose audience is adults and children for whom English is a second language. Spencer says that "[i]nstead of dollars being spent to spread 'light' and truth around the world, they will be used so that females may hear that 'all men,' but not 'all people,' might believe."[128]

For Ostrander and Spencer there are boundaries that must be preserved in terms of what the symbol "God" can encompass, no matter how fervently they favor women's inclusion in all aspects of their traditions. In the midst of such concerns there is also experimentation with language for God among evangelicals. Here is a meditation on Shekhinah by Kristin Johnson Ingram published in *Daughters of Sarah*, a journal attuned, particularly in its earlier years, to more evangelical kinds of Christian feminism and to the expression of "varying viewpoints." Ingram pulls out all the theological stops when she describes Shekhinah as "God's fiery female face": "She is the Life-Giver, the Paraclete, the wildest force known to God. She is God and she is God's breath; she is the Spirit of God, she is the wind that blows suns and Magellanic clouds and gravity and particles from Kingdom Come and back again. And she is God."[129] Ingram describes, as well, the ambivalence of her beginning understandings of Shekhinah. "Scarey," she calls them: "I love Jesus, and I didn't want to leave him; yet after years of adventure with a very masculine savior I was beguiled by the Spirit I glimpsed as not only a feminine *name* but as a female presence."[130]

God and Nature: Panentheism or Pantheism?

The creative uses to which women put the concept of immanence and the underlying question that undergirds this effort—how much immanence is too much immanence?—show up in interesting ways in conversations about the extent to which the divine or the ultimate should be distinguished from nature. In this conversation one of the terms that emerges most frequently is "panentheism," usually interpreted to mean "God in everything and everything in God." This is in contrast with pantheism, which generally holds that everything *is* God. "Panentheism" functions as a kind of theological *via media*, a way of talking about how the divine presence is infused throughout the world but is also more than the world—a way to say that God is in everything without saying that everything is God. My interest is in seeing what women do with this term theologically—what kinds of ideas about God it generates—in the effort to connect an emphasis on immanence and the construction of new God-language with the full participation of women in their traditions and to shape vigorous definitions of transcendence as well.

One well-known interpreter of panentheism is Roman Catholic theologian Elizabeth A. Johnson, whose book *She Who Is: The Mystery of God in Feminist Theology* has been widely acclaimed. In this volume and other publications, Johnson draws on the classical tradition of Catholic theology and contemporary experience to make the case for the theological necessity of addressing divine mystery as "she." Johnson is concerned in this project not only to make the case for "God-she," but also to offset the tendency of classical theology to insist on God's transcendence to the point where "divine immanence tends to slip from view."[131] When transcendence is too greatly emphasized, she says, "The equation is thus set up: male is to female as transcendence is to immanence, with the feminine Spirit restricted to the role of bearing the presence of God to our interiority."[132] Johnson uses "immanence" to expand the traditional understanding of "Spirit" to include women's experiences and to address large public issues such as the inequality of women and the ecological crisis.

Positing a strong doctrine of immanence gives Johnson a way to sacralize the world as hospitable to divine presence: "If we ask more precisely which moments or events mediate God's Spirit, the answer can only be potentially *all* experience, the whole world. There is no exclusive zone, no special realm which alone may be called religious. . . . The historical world becomes a sacrament of divine presence and activity, even if only as a fragile possibility."[133]

Johnson makes a strong case for claiming that the way a community talks about God has tremendous implications for the status of women, because symbols for God don't just point to a meaning beyond themselves; they function in ways that shape social relationships. The symbol for God is the lodestar of a religious community, she says; it "expresses a community's bedrock convictions."[134]

Johnson's worldview emerges from the sacramental vision of Roman Catholicism. She very carefully—and in strong language because of what she considers to be at stake—distinguishes this worldview from pantheism, which she defines as a "suffocating deception." A pantheistic worldview, in her opinion, tempts women to submerge themselves in the "all," whether that be "the 'all' of a man or family or institution."[135] What is at stake for the Christian tradition, as Johnson sees it, is an understanding of God that preserves the divine mystery and incomprehensibility and thus the capacity for this symbol to give rise to a vast number of images, including female images. What is at stake for women, in addition to the possibility of female images for the divine, is personal autonomy in relation to a God who is not totally identical with nature. A God who is collapsed into nature offers no ultimate point of reference with which or whom to have a relationship.

It is certainly possible to look at Christian women like Johnson, or Sallie McFague (who likewise wants to preserve a personal, trinitarian God with whom relationships are possible), primarily as guarding the boundaries of Christian identity. I'm not inclined to insist otherwise. But I want to put the emphasis elsewhere and suggest that it is also enlightening—in terms of understanding more about theological creativity—to see their efforts as issuing from a desire to preserve the creative potential of their tradition's insights by maintaining a sense of what constitutes an authentic interpretation of its best insights. And we are then back in the territory of inexhaustibility and the "dearness" of one's tradition about which Rachel Adler speaks.

For some communities of women, the conservation of their traditions that is at stake for Johnson, McFague, and other women who espouse biblical religions is simply not at issue. Among them are the spiritual feminists described by Cynthia Eller, who see no need to maintain the Goddess as in any way separate from nature—even in order to have a relationship with her. "Certain trends emerge," says Eller, "when women discuss the goddess and other divine players. She is nature, she affirms life and sexuality, she is in each woman." As Eller interprets it, immanence and pantheism are at the core of feminist spirituality. Its participants acknowledge no theological restrictions against pantheism and are happy to claim the term.[136]

Yet there are some Goddess feminists like Carol Christ who are not willing to go so far. Christ finds the Goddess in nature and in herself, but she also experiences the Goddess as a personal presence. "While I find the philosophical notions of immanence and pantheism attractive," she says, "in the end they fail to do justice to my experience of the Goddess."[137] Christ, an academically trained theologian who is now among the best known Goddess thealogians (the spelling many of them favor), uses the concept "panentheism" as it is expressed in process theology to make the case that the Goddess is transcendent as well as immanent, but She does not exist apart from the world, omniscient and omnipotent, like the God of classical theism: "The power of the Goddess is a limited power that operates within a finite and changeable world."[138]

The most thoroughgoing pantheistic stance I've come across other than in Goddess materials is articulated by American empiricist philosopher Nancy Frankenberry. She suggests that pantheism has fewer flaws than either classical theism or panentheism in its potential as a source for feminist God-construction. Frankenberry, who describes her work as philosophical rather than theological, acknowledges the existence of a wide variety of God images, but, according to her, classical theism, panentheism, and pantheism are the "only three broad conceptual models . . . in the Western discussion for rendering religious language of devotion into philosophy's language of reflection. . . . Logically, these three forms exhaust the possibilities of relating the terms *God* and *nature*, by locating the reference range or ontological target of God-language either 'outside,' 'inside,' or coincidental with, the whole of reality."[139] And for Frankenberry, it is "logic" that is at stake rather than the insights or symbols of a religious community or the preservation of "God."

Like many women across a wide theological spectrum, Frankenberry quickly dismisses classical theism as devoid of any possibility of feminist rehabilitation and goes so far as to suggest that anyone who can continue to espouse classical theism at this time in history probably needs psychological help. But neither does she find compelling the efforts to construct a Mother Goddess. "My own view," says Frankenberry, "is that these efforts do not get to the root of the anthropomorphic problem." It is not just that the emperor has no clothes, in her opinion, but that there is no emperor. Thus she finds any anthropomorphic model of ultimate reality, even one that emerges from women's experience, flawed, because, she argues, such a project "may not sufficiently take into account the prior construction of these experiences by an androcentric culture and language in which, as French feminists remind us, 'woman is only effect of man.'"[140]

Frankenberry also finds panentheism inadequate for several reasons. First, because as a model it maintains a distinction between God and the world, and this is the very distinction that Frankenberry suspects of perpetuating "the image of male 'mind' exerting control over the 'unruly' feminist body." In addition, she says, if the feminist project is to tear apart "pervasive webs of dominance and exploitation then panentheism with its insistence on holism and unity does not provide much 'elbow room' for women who traditionally have suffered not from fragmentation but from repressive unity."[141] Thus, ironically, for the same reason that Elizabeth Johnson espouses panentheism—liberation from cosmic and social unities that oppress women—Frankenberry finds it inadequate to sustain a feminist construction of ultimate reality.

Frankenberry holds that a pantheistic worldview can furnish adequate resources for ethical systems. A pantheistic worldview, she says, is most coherent with the organic and paradoxical way women tend to generate religious symbols. The whole conversation in which there is the likelihood of "assimilating *God* to *nature* in order to avoid assimilating a God-of-the-gaps, may raise the suspicion that one of the two terms is semantically superfluous."[142]

In Frankenberry's estimation, functionalist arguments for the necessity of retaining the symbol "God" fail to take into account that "God" can be used in negative ways. She is also skeptical of the extent to which one can believe in a symbol that one knows has been constructed: "Both productions, the theological construction of God-concepts and the social construction of gendered subjectivity, converge on the interrogation of the extent to which something that is socially and historically constructed and known to be so can also be personally appropriated and lived out with a measure of authenticity."[143]

Frankenberry has two other objections to panentheism. One is the insistence of those who espouse it that in order to be of value something—in this case God-language—has to endure forever. Why, she asks, "[i]s it not sufficient that our fragile, novel, risk-filled acts of radical contingency can strut and fret their hour across the stage, even if they are heard no more?" The other is a dismissal of the process theology version of the ontological argument, because it fails to prove the reality of God—the divine necessity, as she calls it. Her conclusion is this: "If all the places panentheism proves problematic turn out to be instances in which it departs from pantheism, the suspicion grows that pantheism might be the more straightforward option. Indeed, perhaps panentheism is just pantheism for Ph.D's."[144]

What Frankenberry proposes—feminist constructions of ultimate reality and a religious (one assumes) worldview within which "God" is not necessarily a useful symbol—will require a religious creativity that is not attached to the symbols of a particular religious tradition. It will emerge, instead, from the worldview of American empiricism and from the language of American pragmatism's search for ways to find words for the sacred: like William James's "more," words that suggest not one but a variety of religious experiences. It will be intriguing to see what symbols of ultimate reality feminist empiricists like Frankenberry will fashion that work to promote the full participation of women in society as an essential component of the common good.

God-Language and Survival

For some communities of women, what is described as at stake in constructing models of God and language for God is, starkly, survival. This is the case for the Latina women from different Spanish-speaking cultures who are the subject of Ada María Isasi-Díaz's theological work. Isasi-Díaz describes the triple oppressions experienced by Latina women in ways that are analogous to but not identical with those articulated by African-American, Asian-American, and Native American women. It has to do, says Isasi-Díaz, "with the fact that we are women, that we are Hispanics, and that the majority of us are at the bottom of the economic ladder in the U.S.A. We understand that our gender, our ethnicity, and our economic status have been made into social categories that play a very important role in the domination, subjugation, exploitation, and repression that we suffer."[145]

Among Latina women, the emphasis on divine immanence emerges in terms of the intimacy of their relationship with God. Isasi-Díaz sees a radically immanent God, one with whom an intimate relationship is possible, as essential in the development of self-worth and a sense of moral agency and autonomy among Latina women: "It is not only a matter of believing that God is with us in our daily struggle, but that we can and do relate to God the same way we relate to all our loved ones. We argue with God, barter with God, get upset with God, are grateful and recompense God, use endearing terms for God."[146]

We might speculate as to why Isasi-Díaz has not discovered an omnipotent, rescuing God as the one most desired by Latinas. Perhaps it is not appealing or necessary that God be all-powerful, since, given their histories, Latina women can offer only meager testimony that the omnipotent but remote God of classical theism has exerted His power on their behalf. What is required instead is a God with whom one can have an intimate relationship: a God who is present in the daily struggle for survival, which for Latina women does not mean, according to Isasi-Díaz, just "barely living" but is concerned "with the struggle to *be* fully."[147]

As Isasi-Díaz sees it, it is an immanent God, a God with a capacity for intimacy, who is essential for Latina women to develop as moral agents, to learn to trust the inner wisdom that comes from their own experience as women in their communities. This requires, for one thing, a transformation of the traditional term "conscience." Latinas, she says, need to move beyond an awareness of "conscience" as an admonishing inner voice—*Mi conciencia me dice*—to a more fully developed moral confidence that helps them ascertain values, make choices, and discern the difference between suffering that is inevitable because it is part of life and nature and suffering that is caused by the dominance of oppressive systems. Then they must act on their own behalf.[148]

As Isasi-Díaz has experienced the lives of Latina women, including her own, she has come to see that their sense of self-worth has its foundation in a very strong sense of the presence of God, a God who fosters not self-recrimination but self-love. As she describes it, "authentic self-love becomes a basis for a relationship with the divine, with God transformed from one who is radically beyond the person to one who is radically immanent to the agent, the God who is the *'algo me lo dice de mi'*: the voice inside and the daily guidance in their lives."[149]

Like Isasi-Díaz, womanist theologian Delores Williams has searched for ways to talk about God that illuminate the experiences of the community that is hers: African-American Christian women. Williams puts forth her thesis about black women's theological insights in *Sisters in the Wilderness*, a book she subtitles *The Challenge of Womanist God-Talk*.[150] The objects of her challenge are black liberation theologians, African-American denominational churches, and feminist theologians of other races and cultures. All of them offer possibilities of fruitful dialogue, according to Williams. None of them, in her estimation, adequately reflects the particular experiences of black women, because they do not get at either the reasons for or the extent of the exploitation of black women's bodies. Williams uses the concept of "surrogacy," both coerced (during slavery) and voluntary (primarily as domestics in white families), to point to the reality of black women's lives.[151]

Williams's womanist God-talk is grounded in the biblical story of Hagar, the slave-woman of Abraham and Sarah who, pregnant with Abraham's child, is banished into the wilderness without resources. Eventually, God tells Hagar through an angel to return to Abraham and Sarah with her son Ishmael. This will ensure their survival but not their freedom. The story of Hagar is traditionally used by African-Americans as a story of liberation from oppression. Williams refutes that interpretation on the basis of African-American women's experience. For Williams this is a story, black women's paradigmatic story, in fact, of "survival and a positive quality of life for black women and their families in the care and presence of God."[152]

This alternative reading of the Hagar story requires black women to reject widely accepted biblical interpretations in the black community and in liberation theologies, both African-American and South American, that "God acts on behalf of *all* the oppressed." Williams says there is no clear indication in either the Old or the New Testament that God is against slavery—or at least against the slavery of Hagar or the surrogate role she played in the household of Abraham and Sarah.[153] This reading requires as well, according to Williams, that the Christian doctrine of atonement be revised to insist that the significance of Jesus was his life, his "ministerial vision of righting relations," rather than his death. The traditional doctrine that sees Jesus' surrogate suffering for humankind has not been a good thing for black women, Williams says: "There is nothing divine in the blood of the cross. God does not intend black women's surrogacy experience. Neither can Christian faith affirm such an idea."[154]

One might conclude that rejection of historical Christian interpretations of God's liberating power and Jesus' atonement would require Williams to construct a radically nontraditional model of God for African-American women. This is not the case, although she suggests the need to look beyond as well as within Christian and Jewish sources for God-language—West African, for example, and Egyptian (Hagar was Egyptian). Williams's concept of God is of a deity very much present with African-American women in their suffering and accessible to them. She, like women of many different races and traditions, refers to Celie, Alice Walker's main character in her novel *The Color*

Purple, and her declaration of faith in a God who is not confined either to institutional religion or by male or female images: "She [Walker] shows that the black mother's religion must move beyond male-female imagery in order to accommodate the black mother's realization of self-esteem, autonomy and liberation. The idea of the divine spirit working within humans is more efficacious for women's development of self-worth than notions of God in male or female form." [155]

Like Isasi-Díaz, Williams connects black women's capacity to survive and even to prosper to a sense of self-worth derived from awareness of a history of "making a way out of no way" and of relying on God. Here again in the religious thought of Williams we encounter an elaboration on the immanence of the divine from the perspective of yet another community of women and the combination of "orthodox substance and daring expression." [156] Williams concludes *Sisters in the Wilderness* with a testimony to black women and a reference to God that could hardly be more traditional or more orthodox: "The greatest truth of black women's survival and quality-of-life struggle is that they have worked without hesitation and with all the energy they could muster. . . . They depended upon their strength and upon each other. But in the final analysis the message is clear: they trusted the end to God. Every important event in the stories of Hagar and black women turns on this trust." [157] However immanent the divine in Williams's religious thought or however many critiques of male black liberation or denominational theologies she offers, bedrock for her is "God," and she depends upon both traditional and innovative meanings of God to undergird her theological claims and to sacralize the experiences of African-American Christian women.

Women and Immanence in Metaphysical Traditions

Before concluding, I want to explore a long-standing arena of women's theological creativity and emphasis on immanence that first emerged from the "metaphysical" religious movements during the last quarter of the nineteenth century: for example, Christian Science and New Thought and some of their direct and indirect descendants like the Unity School of Christianity and Divine Science.[158] I include as part of this lineage many religious movements presently characterized as "New Age": metaphysically oriented, eclectic in the sources of their teachings, and historically, if not exactly—and not always admittedly—related to the nineteenth-century metaphysical movements.[159]

These movements have always drawn disproportionate numbers of women members and leaders, and from their beginnings they have been repositories of immanental worldviews. They offer doctrines of God that depersonalize deity, often referring to God as Spirit or Mind or Principle.[160] Their theologies of human nature are optimistic; they run counter to doctrines of humankind that insist on pervasive, inner sinfulness, a doctrinal excess that women of many traditions describe as particularly harmful to them. They are also, typically, healing movements, concerned with physical, emotional, and spiritual well-being, and they have been associated, particularly, with "women's healing." Reference to some of them will recur in Chapter Six. Often criticized and sometimes caricatured for their inadequate doctrines of evil, the metaphysical traditions hold in various ways that sin and suffering are due to false perceptions of reality. Thus, the site of struggle and change is "mind," an arena open to all regardless of circumstances.

In terms of the over-all theme of this chapter—how women use doctrines of immanence to bring religion down to earth and construct new models of ultimate reality—the theologies of the metaphysical religions strike me as suspended somewhere between heaven—or at least spiritual realms—and earth. They are focused on health, well-being, and prosperity (not always defined as "wealth"), but in their worldviews what is ultimately real is spirit, not matter, and "mind," not body.[161] Thus they do not fit at all neatly with many of my generalizations in this chapter, but they are much too important in the history of American women's religious thought to ignore. They have in common with the immanentist emphasis in other forms of women's thought the insistence on the indwelling of the sacred as a way to claim human worth, often women's worth in particular, and participation in the divine. A major departure from most of the other women referred to in this chapter lies in the lack of ultimate reality they ascribe to body, earth, and nature.

One of the most popular contemporary heirs of the broad metaphysical tradition is Marianne Williamson, author of the best-seller *A Return to Love: Reflections on the Principles of A Course in Miracles*.[162] I see this volume as a kind of metaphysical systematic theology that begins with a chapter on "hell," defined as "a network of fearful perceptions." It concludes with a chapter on "heaven," defined as the "transformation of . . . events within . . . mind,"[163] a transformation that is followed by changes in the physical world. Williamson's interpretations of God as "love" and of humankind as "perfect creation," based on *A Course in Miracles*,[164] coincide with the teachings of the metaphysical religions. Williamson's eschatological claim—her perception of the "end times"—is both a study in immanentist thought and a clue as to how her metaphysical worldview departs from the more earth-oriented theologies of women like McFague or Plaskow or Suchocki or Johnson, for whom "spirit" is infused in matter but does not claim metaphysical superiority or reality. Here is what she says about the end of the world: "The end of the world as we know it wouldn't be such a horrible thing, if you think of all the ways in which the world is full of pain and suffering. In the 'end days,' we will not escape the horrors of the world through vehicles that soar into outer space, but through vehicles that soar into inner space. Those vehicles are our healed minds, guided by the Holy Spirit."[165]

Williamson is not overtly concerned with issues of gender in this first volume, but in conjunction with A Woman's Worth, published in 1994, "for women who have been to hell and back," there is the opportunity to see how she applies metaphysical teachings about divine immanence to matters of gender. She describes A Woman's Worth as a book about "women's inner life" where "we are our real selves, while in the outer world we are imposters."[166] Williamson argues that for many reasons, including popular perceptions of what women should be and do, "womanhood is a mass pain of unspoken depth."[167] According to Williamson, the pain that women experience comes from lack of self-knowledge, from not knowing the perfection of their true selves. This ignorance and the pain it causes keep women from awareness of their cosmic destination. And here again is the immanentist claim with a metaphysical twist: "This destination is far, far away, a place so deep inside us that we have barely glimpsed its outer walls."[168] It coincides with much New Thought and New Age literature about trusting the self as the repository of divine wisdom that has its source in ultimate reality. For Williamson the "inborn escape hatch" is "deep inside us": "It's a love that doesn't end or waver or make money off us or play games with us or stomp on our hearts. It's our spiritual core. Within it, we exist as cosmic royals: mothers, sisters, daughters of the sun and moon and stars."[169]

This kind of writing is easy to caricature, but I think we do better to take it seriously as an effort to create a theology of human nature that includes women's experiences of their lives as perceived and described by Williamson.[170] The sources of Williamson's religious worldview and practice are eclectic and not what scholars would call systematic.[171] But she is obviously a religious thinker who is grappling with a significant theological question: What does it mean to be a human being who is a woman and how do our understandings of God and reality shape our responses to this question? Suspended as they seem to me to be between earth and other realms, her writings and that of other New Thought and New Age thinkers illustrate the versatility and also the conflicts of various concepts of immanence in women's religious thought and the variety of worldviews they serve. And they maintain a historic and theological connection with some of the nineteenth-century religious movements that offer insights into how women's experience has shaped certain manifestations of American religious thought.

Conclusion

From its earliest years, the second wave of American religious feminism has demonstrated a critique of what it has identified as dualistic thinking based on the tendency particularly in Western thought to construe reality in terms of polarities. In dualistic thinking, one of the poles is looked upon not only as the "opposite" of the other but as its superior: spirit/matter; mind/body; reason/

emotion; heaven/earth. It is also the case, says the feminist critique, that the lesser of the poles—matter, body, emotion, earth—has traditionally been identified with women. What would happen, women began to ask, if these polarized entities were turned upside down—transvalued— and those previously considered lesser took on not only increased prominence in theological worldviews but more positive value? How would our theologies and our institutions be changed? This chapter reflects my effort to respond to some extent to that question.

Immanence and transcendence are among the more abstract and less dramatic of the historical tensions in religious thought, but their transvaluation and transformation in American women's theological writings have been far-reaching in their implications and in the kinds of creativity they have fostered. Both historically and at present, women have claimed immanence as a religious idea with significant potential for increasing women's access to the divine, promoting the full humanity and self-worth of women, and developing women's trust in the authority of their own experiences. All of these are related to women's desire for full participation in their religious communities. In the process of pursuing these goals, women have also become participants in the ongoing task of every generation's efforts to keep the symbols, rituals, texts, and teachings of religious communities intellectually and emotionally compelling, even if for some this has required the founding or joining of new religions. Thus, in addition to its focus on how immanental theologies promote the full participation of women, this chapter has been particularly concerned with how women have used the concept of immanence and new meanings for transcendence not only to bring theology down to earth but to construct models of God and ultimate reality that are, in the words of theologian Gordon Kaufman, both "humanizing" and "relativizing." That is, they function to make us more profoundly what we are supposed to be as full human beings and they offer a point of ultimate reference that draws us beyond ourselves and serves as a foundation of critique of all that is not ultimate.[172] In order to be fully humanizing, women insist, constructions of God and ultimate reality must incorporate the experiences and insights of women. And in order to be relativizing, all theological constructions must have a built-in acknowledgment of their ultimate inadequacy.

Unlike participants in some earlier immanentist movements in American religious history, women at the end of the twentieth century are not making claims about a religious universalism that undergirds the pluralism of religious forms. In fact, the opposite is the case. One of the notable aspects of women's use of immanence is the extent to which it is not dependent on any one religious worldview. As mentioned earlier, the prominence of immanence has had a particularizing, not a universalizing, effect on women's religious thought. Commitment to the wider goal of gender equality has not prompted women to abandon the symbols and issues of their traditions for the hope of a universal religion. Women are often highly cognizant of what women in other communities are saying about gender issues, but they are immersed, however ambivalently, in their own. The symbols of their communities are the stuff of women's creativity. What women demonstrate in their reconstructions of God-symbols and interpretations of ultimate reality is that an emphasis on imma-nence does not seem to lure its adherents into the kind of relativism—a con-viction that any religion is as good or as bad as any other—that those fearful of the effects of religious pluralism anticipate. Neither does it diminish women's desire to expend theological creativity in search of new meanings for transcen-dence, the relativizing aspect of doctrines of the sacred. Nor, in the process of bringing theology down to earth, have women's immanentist inclinations moved in the direction of extolling human progress; they are more likely to offer a critique of assumptions of human progress than to uphold them.[173] Rather, there is more a sense of divine presence in the struggle for full equality. "Empowerment" is a term frequently used to denote this theme. Finally, as another characteristic of women's immanentist thought, there is the extent to which an emphasis on the immanence of the sacred requires a creative con-servation of the power and depth of meaning in traditional religious language and concepts, even for those women who go far beyond the boundaries of in-stitutional religion. In relation to a concept usually associated with theological innovation, this conserving quality of women's religious thought has been an intriguing one for me to discover.

Immanental theologies have implications for aspects of religion other than their understandings of the sacred. In the next chapter, about how women claim the revelatory power of ordinary life, there is an assumption, often un-stated, that this is the case because the sacred dwells within all aspects of life. In turning to what women of many communities have to say about the theo-logical significance of their daily lives, we find the opportunity to see from another angle how an emphasis on immanence can influence religious world-views and judgments about what is considered appropriate subject matter for religious thought.

4

The Revelatory Power of the Ordinary and the Ordinariness of the Sacred

Mixed Blessings

In 1591 Sor Juana Inés de la Cruz, a Mexican nun, published a spiritual and intellectual autobiography that was to become famous as *La Respuesta a Sor Filotea*.[1] "Sor Filotea" was the pseudonym for the bishop of Puebla, Mexico, who had sent Sor Juana a letter admonishing her for writing and making public her critique of a forty-year-old sermon by a Jesuit priest. Sor Juana's reply to the bishop is the work of a learned woman who bases her defense of women's intellectual life on references to Scripture, church history, classical learning, theology, and her own experiences. She describes her struggle to lead a life of study and still meet the demands of living in a religious community and to do both in a world and a religious institution that are disapproving of her efforts.

In her reply Sor Juana recounts an incident in which "a very saintly and ingenuous Abbess" commanded her not to study. Sor Juana relates that, in accordance with her vow of obedience, she did not pick up a book during the three months the abbess had power over her: "But that I study not at all is not within my power to achieve, and this I could not obey, for though I did not study in books, I studied all the things that God has wrought, reading in them, as in writing and in books, all the workings of the universe. I looked on nothing without reflexion; I heard nothing without meditation, even in the most minute and imperfect things."[2]

Sor Juana elaborates for the bishop. She watched children play spillikins. The triangular shape into which the sticks fell reminded her of Solomon and his building of the temple, and she saw in the same shape a foreshadowing of the Christian doctrine of the Trinity. She made further observations in the kitchen. The frying of eggs in butter and oil had its own truths to reveal about "natural secrets," as did other domestic activities, and Sor Juana suggests to the bishop (addressed throughout as "my lady") that "had Aristotle prepared victuals, he would have written more."[3] She confides that her superiors finally permitted her to read again when it became apparent to physicians that "a grave upset of the stomach" occurred "because so vigorous and vehement were my cogitations that my spirit was consumed more greatly in a quarter of an hour than in four days' studying books."[4]

Sor Juana's reply to the bishop is a poignant study in mixed emotions—ambivalence. There is an expression of subservience that the reader knows can only be ironic. She acknowledges the power of a superior in a hierarchical system but does not bow to it in spirit. There is the manifestation of the brilliance, erudition, and wit of a woman who was considered "the most learned woman in Mexico." There is the demonstrated capacity to make do with what one has. And there is the pathos of a woman struggling to find institutional outlets and support for what is natural to her: studying, writing, and teaching. When the "most learned woman in Mexico" says to the bishop, "But, lady, as women, what wisdom may be ours if not the philosophies of the kitchen?" there are insights into much of the creative ambivalence, the contradictory responses many contemporary women express when they so frequently proclaim the sacredness of the ordinary and the domestic. There is the desire to move beyond the identification of women as custodians of the ordinary in ways that are trivialized, sentimentalized, and circumscribing. And there is the simultaneous effort to broaden the meaning of "ordinary," to claim its wisdom as well as the compelling questions, insights, and transformations that emerge from theological reflection on the ordinary.

To reinforce this sense of ambivalence, here is another description of the religious implications of attention to the ordinary: a description of what anthropologist Barbara Myerhoff calls "the domestic religion" in *Number Our Days*, an ethnographic study of elderly eastern European Jews who belonged to a community center during the 1970s in Venice, California. Rachel, one of the women who frequents the center, enters a conversation about differences in the ways women and men experience Judaism: "What the girls had is different from the boys. Now what ideas Moshe and Nate got, they came to through schooling. We girls had another kind of religion. We couldn't doubt it too much because we didn't know enough. You could say, from this we were always in a positive way."

In Rachel's opinion the boys' intellectual study of Judaism led to arguing and doubt, in contrast with the inculcation into Judaism she received through domestic rituals: "The boys in cheder could learn the words and forget them, but in this domestic religion, you could never get rid of it. . . . You could not just put it aside when you don't agree anymore. When it goes this way, Jewish comes up in you from the roots and it stays with you all your life."[5] As I interpret Rachel's words, I understand them not as a defense or sentimentalizing of a piety without intellectual grounding or lack of religious education as a guard against loss of faith, but a description of the nonverbal knowledge of religion that is powerfully felt and conveyed in all these stories by educated women as well.[6]

In the stories of Sor Juana and Rachel there is implied a whole history of women's connections to the ordinary tasks of daily life, most often considered "domestic" in nature. Even though "ordinary" and "domestic" are not synonymous, there is an overlapping that women describe as characteristic of their lives. Buddhist Rita Gross categorizes this whole area of concern as that of the "householder style, involved in domestic and livelihood issues" that is often seen as an obstacle to spiritual development and religious practice.[7] These are stories of a particular kind of opportunity and also of a lack of choice—the circumscription of possibilities for engaging wider arenas. There is acknowledgment of what can be learned of a religious nature by participation in the life of the home, in a life exclusive of the study of texts. These two women, Sor Juana and Rachel, are very different from each other in terms of historical moment, privilege, background, religious community, and education. That makes it even more compelling that women so far apart in most ways tell similar stories about what is gained and what is lost in the lives of women whose pursuits of religious experience and understanding are bounded by their communities' assumptions about what is permitted for women.

Contemporary women's religious thought demonstrates a strong desire to contribute their reflections, ambivalence and all, on the religious depths and intricacies of ordinary life. There continues to be ongoing and creative reference to the domestic arena. What Ada María Isasi-Díaz describes as true of Latina women receives similar testimony among women of other communities: "Instead of devaluing and rejecting our traditional roles in our families, what Latinas want is the opposite: we want the value of those roles to be recognized and their status to be enhanced."[8] But, without wanting to set aside the satisfactions or the lessons imparted by domestic concerns, women manifest, also, a greater and greater awareness that "ordinary life" encompasses more than the domestic. Women find themselves in possession of experiences and insights from the domestic arena, broadly defined, that they wish to contribute to their religious communities. Many women, in fact, do as their foremothers did—in the temperance movement, for example—and expand the concept of "home" to include both the political arena and the ecology of the planet—the earth as home. At the same time women express an impatience with needing to justify all their activities, intellectual, religious, economic, political, in terms of "home."

Jewish ethicist Laurie Zoloth-Dorfman describes women as feeling caught between two ideological claims. "The slogan," she says, "that the personal is political is a way of saying that every aspect of one's life counts in the political arena, that every choice is a public, moral choice." Or, for the purposes of this book, has significance for religious thought. But she goes on: "Yet, (and simultaneously) the imperative of feminism demands an attention to the liberation of the female self from the constraints of the female role and demands of us a radical rethinking of the nature of obligation and dependency."[9] The ambivalence women feel about the ordinary life, its responsibilities and rewards, its limitations and frustrations, like the ambivalence women feel toward their traditions, I would argue, is a particular impetus to the creativity of their religious thought. The ordinary life is sacred, women say, but it is also a mixed blessing. "Sacred" doesn't mean perfect.

In this chapter "ambivalence" takes a different shape from its manifestations in Chapter 2. In their theological reflections on the ordinary, women demand and create theological responses to the details of the ordinary life that neither gloss over nor wallow in the mixed blessings that human life is made up of and that are so marked in the chronicling of ordinary days. My interest in this chapter goes beyond the claims from women of many communities that the ordinary is sacred, that it has religious significance. I am particularly concerned with how this claim generates religious thought. What do women do with this conviction theologically? What issues do they take on in conjunction with it? What insights do they offer as a result of their reflections on the sacredness of the ordinary or the ordinariness of the sacred? The details of the ordinary life are until recently more likely to have been recounted in devotional literature, fiction, and poetry, rather than in theological writings. But in this book I am looking specifically at more obviously theological writings to see what women are saying as the ordinary becomes a category for theological reflection in new ways.

There are three sub-themes I particularly want to explore. The first involves women's efforts not just to sacralize the ordinary, to make it significant rather than trivial, holy rather than profane or corrupt, but to expand its meanings and the theological meanings of the ambivalence it generates. The second is the use of the ordinary as a category to demystify that which has been rendered as "overly sacred" by religious institutions and therefore inaccessible to women for reasons of gender. This theme often takes the form of the ordinariness of the sacred and moves one into the realm described by Marjorie Suchocki as the "extraordinarily ordinary." Rituals offer a good arena in which to investigate this work. The third is a brief look at some of the moral and ethical implications of an emphasis on the ordinary in women's religious thought. What can we learn about good and bad, right and wrong, better and worse, if the ordinary is the focus of theological reflection?

The Revelatory Power of the Ordinary and the Ordinary Expanded

What were often-invoked truisms of the early years of second-wave feminism—bodies are sacred, daily tasks are sacred, and the like—have become more complicated in their implications, particularly with the insights generated by women with disabilities, women of color, and aging women. The connotations of ordinary are not always bland, harmless, or routine. Violence and privation make up the ordinary in many communities of women. Sickness and death can hardly be defined as other than ordinary, even if not routine, in most people's lives. In women's religious thought the daily, the ordinary, and the domestic are intertwined. They encompass those tasks that must be done routinely to sustain life and tradition and order—at home and beyond home. The daily in women's religious thought is more than the domestic, although the daily encompasses the domestic. One aspect of women's critiques in regard to the ordinary addresses the assumption that any ordinary day requires tasks that must be carried out and endured so that more important things can be accomplished—often by more important people. Further, goes this line of thought, women have always had more than their share of responsibility for these tasks, and their religious significance has never been adequately articulated: their connections to the sacred have been lost. The most powerful symbols of a tradition, women of many traditions claim, are grounded in ordinary life. Creative religious thought needs to restore and embellish these connections. It must restore them in such a way that the ordinary and the sacred become reintegrated and reciprocally illuminating.

Affirmation of the ordinariness of the sacred and the sacredness of the ordinary takes for granted the immanence of the holy within the world. In that sense, this chapter is a continuation of some of the theological implications and themes of the previous chapter, although it generally refers only implicitly to issues connected with ultimate reality.

Until recently there prevailed in women's religious thought a general sense of "ordinary" as that in women's lives which needed valuing and sacralizing because it was unremarkable and unremarked upon and yet essential to the sustaining of family and institutional lives. That still useful perception prevails to some extent. It has also given way to a more complex opening up of the term to encompass the significance of what constitutes an ordinary day or an ordinary task in the lives of many communities of women. In other words, recent women's religious thought has fostered an expansion of thinkable thoughts about what "ordinary" means as well as what it means to call something "sacred." Simply deciding what is "ordinary" has political, social, religious, economic, and aesthetic implications.

I begin this section with the stories of women who analyze the theological significance of what "ordinary" means in the lives of those who are suffering physical or psychic pain or disability—those who cannot take the details of their daily lives for granted. Reflection on their lives expands the meaning of "ordinary" and its religious meanings and at the same time demonstrates the ordinary as an arena of theological creativity for women. It also illustrates one of the major contentions of women's religious thought: that theology needs narrative and detail in order for us to know to what extent and for whom it is compelling.

DISABILITY AND ORDINARY LIFE AND MEANING

In the beginning of her book entitled *The Disabled God: Toward a Liberatory Theology of Disability*, Nancy L. Eiesland, a woman with physical disabilities, acknowledges her high school creative writing teacher, Barbara Johnson, for encouraging her to write about her ordinary life. This was after Eiesland responded with disgust that she had nothing to write about after having spent months in the hospital.[10] What she writes about in this book is what she calls the hard-won accomplishment of learning how to live a life that is not disabled. As she has experienced it, "The difficulty for people with disabilities has two parts, really—living our ordinary but difficult lives, and changing structures, beliefs, and attitudes that prevent us from living ordinarily."[11]

In her work Eiesland incorporates her own experiences and theological insights, but she also makes use of the writings of two other women with physical disabilities, Diana DeVries and Nancy Mairs. In Eiesland's interpretation, they "reveal a type of ordinary life that has heretofore been too often categorized as extraordinary. These two individuals recount their experience of painstakingly inhabiting their bodies and of disputing with society about their proper social place. In the process, they de-mythologize disability and refuse to acquiesce to society's stigmatization."[12] Eiesland insists that there can be no liberating theology of disability without the specific stories of people with disabilities. At the same time she is adamant that these stories must not be contrived into tales about heroic personal efforts to overcome physical limitations and social barriers: "The real-life stories of people with disabilities interfere with these portrayals."[13] If there is anything that Eiesland stresses, it is the ambivalent nature of the ordinary life she leads as a disabled woman. "I try to chart a middle ground," she says, "recognizing in the experience of disability grace and dignity, but not avoiding the disgust and disillusionment of this nonconventional life."[14]

But the ambivalence engendered by her ordinary life has a revelatory quality to it. Because she cannot take her body for granted, because it is "nonconforming," she and other disabled people for whom the "corporeal" is the most real dimension of life pay attention to what she calls the "kinesis of knowledge," a kind of body knowledge that "disclose[s] new categories of thinking and being." One such category has to do with what it means even to be embodied, to have a "natural" body. She points out that Mairs and DeVries use wheelchairs and braces and include them as integral parts of their bodies, thus revealing an alternative understanding of embodiment that suggests to Eiesland that embodiment itself "is a social accomplishment, achieved through attentiveness to the needs, limits, and bounty of the body in relation to others."[15] Their narratives illuminate disability as part of an ordinary life, but Eiesland does not mean by this that there are no differences between the disabled and the able-bodied or that claiming "ordinariness" does away with the need to combat "false and oppressive explanations" of the nature of those differences. She uses the insights she gains from her ordinary life to refute traditional assumptions that "disability denotes an unusual relationship with God and that the person with disabilities is either divinely blessed or damned: the defiled evildoer or the spiritual superhero,"[16] both common themes that women with disabilities point to as pervasive in biblical and religious literature.

THE ORDINARY EXPERIENCES OF SICKNESS, LIMITATION, AGING, AND DEATH

In her contention that corporeality gives rise to new ideas and categories of thought, Eiesland is joined by Protestant theologian Melanie May, who, in the midst of experiencing breast cancer, depression, the death of her mother, and the pressures of institutional and academic work, wrote a book (completed two days before her mother's death) called A Body Knows: A Theopoetics of Death and Resurrection.[17] May points to a "revelatory insight" at a meeting of the National Council of Churches of Christ when she asked herself how she knew what she knew theologically: "My most formative ideas on what it means to be the church today, on the worldwide ecumenical movement, on the practice of ministry, on preaching and on the task of theology have taken shape in me not according to the formalities of my rationally trained theological mind, but as I think in my body."[18]

Thinking in her body, she says, is a way of theological knowing that she ties to feminism's insistence on the authority of experience as the basis for making religious truth claims. But she connects bodily knowing, as well, to everyday life. Her guard against making false universals about all women's experiences based only on her own is to stress the singularity of the source of her knowledge: "My most formative theological insights have come from my body as knower."[19] She is not only "guarding against" in this statement or protesting that "complexity is most often forbidden to the oppressed," one of Eiesland's points as well. She is also offering "a proclamation: particularity need not be divisive but may be the sign and substance of the promised abundance of life together."[20] May uses Christian imagery of death and resurrection to say, with Eiesland, Mairs, and DeVries, that life in the body is a mixed blessing and so is making public what one knows about it. "Daring to descend into hell," she claims, "we practice resurrection; resurrection encompasses the tragedy as well as the glory of our particular physicality,"[21] and particular physicality can only come from the details of ordinary life.

Like May, Adele B. McCollum, a woman who has lupus, makes use of the body knowledge that comes to her through ordinary life to open up new meanings for religious concepts, in this case the familiar themes of immanence and transcendence. "Let me examine briefly," she says, "what the paradox of transcendence and immanence might mean when generated from body, change, and deterioration."[22] Women with disabilities are "ambushed," according to McCollum, by "three thought impediments: disdain for body, scorn of different realities, and insistence on fixed realities."[23] McCollum is adamant that there is no salvation nor any knowledge outside the body, that the body is "the origin of constructed reality": "Any idea that salvation, transcendence, rapture or anything else will occur without the body is an absurdity without ground." At the same time, because of the nature of her illness, she also thinks of her body as "the great betrayer. Today it jogs or at least walks briefly. Tomorrow it may gasp for air. Today I pace before the class; tomorrow I teach from a wheelchair. Today my fingers type flawlessly. Tomorrow they are red, swollen, painful and can't even open the medicine that brings relief."[24] The unpredictability of McCollum's experience of daily life and health has theological significance for her not only in terms of content but also of method. It has motivated her to reject "notions of fixed reality, permanent ideas or identities, unchanging gods, predictable archetypes or patterns."[25]

These experiences have also led McCollum to reject traditional understandings of transcendence that depend too much on soul or mind and leave body behind. McCollum has a different interpretation: "Overcoming barriers and locating freedom in physical restrictions constitute my idea of transcendence."[26] She now espouses an understanding of immanence and transcendence "generated from body, change, and deterioration," which are, of course, ordinary experiences not just for the physically disabled but for every human person.

In a satirical critique of traditional theologies' assumptions that women are more carnal than men and therefore less able to participate in transcendence, McCollum suggests that if women are considered disabled males because of their female bodies, then "perhaps . . . women with physical disabilities are less disabled. Perhaps the disability renders her asexual and consequently less female and carnal than her sisters. If so, perhaps she can be engaged as a model of transcendence since her 'natural' disability of womanhood is somehow canceled or overcome. Shouldn't this then give women with disabilities both a spiritual and epistemic advantage?"[27] Beneath the bantering tone, there is the implied reality that women with disabilities do not perceive that they are afforded either spiritual or epistemological advantages, that they are often perceived as "overcomers," or as embodiments of evil, as we have already heard from Eiesland, or in the words of another disabled woman, as "the one whose job it is to represent or overcome sadness"[28] for others. None of these is an adequate description of the way women with disabilities describe their ordinary lives; nor do the theologies that underlie such categorizations prove useful to them.

As women with disabilities point out, it is not only traditional religions that have shaped their worldviews without contributions from those whose ordinary lives would refute some of their most deeply held assumptions. Feminist theologies have their own sins to confess, one of them a tendency especially in the earlier years to offer uncritical adulation of "the body" in opposition to what has been experienced as anti-female body patterns in patriarchal religions.

In response to this excessive tendency, Valerie Saiving calls feminist theologies to account by stating, "As an older woman, I sometimes wonder whether the women's movement is made up exclusively of women between the ages of sixteen and forty-five, for so little is ever said about what it means to be human after the later age. Moreover, the women's movement woman typically seems to be a healthy person, not chronically ill, severely and permanently disabled, or facing death."[29] The women's movement, says Saiving, has not seemed to pay much attention to issues of illness and death from a feminist perspective: "In our search for a new understanding of the relation between our bodies and ourselves, we must somehow take account of the fact that bodies, by their very nature (because they are alive), not only are born and grow to maturity, but also grow old, sicken, and die."[30]

Saiving wrote this paper for publication in the midst of experiencing arthritis, depression, and heart disease (she died in 1991). She recounts the feeling of her younger years that "she" was not somehow divorced from her body in any essential sense and could not "imagine that I had once been or would later become a disembodied spirit." "The problem," she says, "was not so much the inadequacy of traditional arguments for immortality of the soul; it was rather a matter of my not being able to conceive of myself as disembodied, so essential did my bodily feelings seem to my sense of who *I* was."[31] She also remembers being glad that this was the case. When she asked herself as an older woman how that youthful conviction had held up, she answered candidly, "not very well." But, as it turns out, this was not because she had lost her conviction that being alive in a human body is "the greatest gift imaginable," but because "my younger self had an inadequate and superficial view of what constitutes a full human life."[32]

What does Saiving do theologically with what for most people is an ordinary experience of aging, illness, limitation, and impending death? What are the religious thoughts these experiences generate—that she thinks are good, as well, for women and that will maintain the joyful affirmation of embodiedness that she continues to hold as bedrock truth? She does not consider bitterness or stoicism adequate responses, nor is she interested in the kind of rage against death that denies it as a part of life. "Is there no way," she asks, "in which we can affirm our bodily life in its *totality*, including the realities of sickness, aging, and death?"[33]

Saiving offers suggestions to her question, even though she characterizes none of them as an answer: "To propose an answer, even a tentative one would contravene my own experience, and in fact I am still struggling toward an answer."[34] The limitations she describes in the article are the very ones she has experienced while writing it: "In particular, the limits of what I can promise to others have become clearer in the course of its writing."[35]

The religious ideas Saiving develops are all in relation to her counsel that we need to accept our finitude, our limitations. To do this, according to Saiving, requires not the passive acceptance of particular suffering individuals, but three changes of heart and action: "the elimination of some of the most painful forms of illness and death by the creation of a new, life-affirming social order [Saiving suspects that many of our death-denying strategies in fact hasten death]; the transformation of the quality of pain by the full presence of other human beings in our sickness and dying; and the internalizing of a new view of the relationship between self and environment."[36] This last suggestion issues from Saiving's questions about how to view the "self," if there is such an entity—as immanent or transcendent in relation to the body.

Saiving acknowledges her debt to Alfred North Whitehead and to process theology. Her way of articulating and organizing her responses is shaped by these influences, but it is the specificity of the ordinary experiences she describes that give life to abstract issues about "finitude" and the nature of the self and its relationships. In the immanental worldview Saiving describes, one in which life in the body is the greatest gift imaginable, wisdom about the religious significance of this claim can be gained only by acknowledging, as she asks feminists to do, the complexities and bitter-sweet realities that a human body experiences over a lifetime.

Nancy Eiesland writes about both the grace and the disgust of her experiences of embodiment; May about the heaven and hell, the death and resurrection, of what it means to live an ordinary woman's life; McCollum about the roller-coaster ride of inhabiting—being—a body whose onslaughts of illness are unpredictable; and Saiving about the search for an embraceable embodiment that is realistic about the ordinary things that happen to everyone sooner or later—we get sick or injured and we die. The emphasis on these ordinary experiences of life, these ordinary and painful experiences, opens up for the women who tell about them new ways to think about some of the central insights of their traditions: grace, death and resurrection, immanence and transcendence, and finitude.

THE DAILY PAIN, ANGER, HOPE, AND ENDURANCE OF NATIVE AMERICAN WOMEN

Living with grief, sickness, aging, and dying are part of the ordinary lives of most women and men. Having to negotiate all of these and in addition the demands of conflicting religious and cultural worldviews is the constant reality of the everyday lives of American Indian women. Women like Iris Heavy Runner of Minneapolis, a member of the Blackfeet tribe and originally from Montana, live simultaneously in two cultures. Heavy Runner is coordinator of native cultural services at a large medical center and is an interpreter of Indian values for both Indians and whites who don't know about them. She moves as well within the institutions of the dominant culture.

Part of her first job in Minneapolis involved training professionals outside her community about the effects on Indian identity of the Indian Child Welfare Act. She is particularly eloquent about the cultural tensions experienced by Indian children placed in non-Indian foster homes: "You say, 'I'm *never* going to be able to go back home. I'm here to *stay*. Do I fit in or do I fight? If I fight hard enough, I'll probably end up in prison. If I assimilate, then even my own people won't accept me, even though I might look like them.'"[37] She also interprets the dominant culture for Indians, serving very much as a bridge between the two cultures. In her work with Indian alcoholism, she is aware, for example, of how many cultural differences make 12-step programs, the major approach to addictions in Minnesota, difficult for Indians, from the insistent emphasis on "talking" in 12-step groups to assumptions about a "higher power." Heavy Runner reports that Indian people ask, "Iris, can you help me understand 'higher power'? Because the way I've been taught, my power is inside of me. How can it be higher than me?"[38]

Heavy Runner describes herself as always feeling the pull from the mountains of Montana "where the spirits reside." Paula Gunn Allen claims as one of the themes that pertain to American Indians that "Indians and spirits are always found together."[39] Heavy Runner confirms this contention and says that she is helped in her work by the knowledge that the spirit of her grandmother and other spirits are always near: "They're here in our dreams. They're here during hard times. They're here when we're laughing."[40] A reporter who interviewed Heavy Runner related that when she mentioned her grandmother, there was a "sudden, sweet, and very pleasant" fragrance detectable in the room. "Only later," says the reporter, "does Heavy Runner explain that when the scent came, she knew a spirit had entered the room."[41]

One is more likely to find evidence of the religious fruits as well as the costs of the life experiences of women like Iris Heavy Runner in the literature, especially the poetry, of American Indian women than in works of academic theology. In the fiction and the poetry there emerges the kind of everyday detail and interpretations of those experiences that have for so long been missing from outsider descriptions and interpretations. And it is in these writings, as well, that one encounters what it means to live not only between cultures but between literary styles: the oral and the written, the Indian in its many varieties and the Euro-American. Cherokee poet Diane Glancy, who teaches creative writing and Native American literature at Macalester College in St. Paul,

describes cross-cultural dynamics as highly significant in her own writing in terms of both style and religious content. "I often write," she says, "about being in the middle ground between two cultures, not fully a part of either. I write with a split voice, often experimenting with language until the parts equal some sort of whole. . . . I write from everyday circumstances, old ordinary life, and the stampede of the past."[42] She is also very eloquent about both the overlap and the disparities between native religions and Christianity in a poem like "A Confession or Apology for Christian Faith," which begins, "How could I believe this stuff?/ A white child in a manger." She goes on to chronicle some of the similarities she sees between Indian teachings and rituals and those of Christianity, between Jesus and Indian men: "Christ wears body paint? He goes for tattoos? When I read/of the writings on his thigh, I see war-paint." "Maybe," she concludes the poem, "it's easier if the Indian traditions/are seen as a type of the Old Testament. & Christianity is a fulfillment of the old ways. But who can be fulfilled with-/out the star quilts on the church walls, the burning of cedar/at the altar, & the drum hymns."[43]

In an essay about American Indian women's poetry, Janice Gould, an Indian poet herself, offers another perspective on the "split voice" of Indian women's poetry: that in its strategies it embodies both rage and hope. Much of what Gould points to in her survey and analysis of American Indian women's poetry makes central the role of rage among women whose recent ancestors have experienced genocide and who themselves carry not only this memory but its continuing after-effects. "The roots of Indian anger are long and deep," says Gould, "and I sometimes imagine that grief and rage have been encoded in the genes."[44]

But Gould is also highly cognizant of the themes of hope and healing in Indian women's poetry. "Ultimately," she says, "the rage that is found in American Indian women's poetry is always tempered by sorrow, and balanced by humor and hope." Those poets whose work she cites ground their hope as much as their rage in the everyday, in the ordinary. She cites poems like Joy Harjo's "Deer Dancer," in which a woman who is "related to deer" walks into a bar on a freezing cold night and dances naked in front of the "Indian ruins" who are drinking there. One man is so enchanted by her that he returns home and pays back a debt he owes the narrator. And like "Workday" by Linda Hogan, who looks back at the people she has just left on the bus and thinks of how they will look walking home, "the beautiful feet,/ the perfect legs/ even with their spider veins,/ the broken knees/ with pins in them."[45]

Gould sees poems like these as testimony to the convictions evident in American Indian women's poetry that the miraculous emerges from the mundane, that "the sacred and the profane balance each other in the Indian world."[46] If one follows her lead and surveys further some of the poets she mentions and others as well, it is obvious that her interpretations are compelling, that they are grounded in "the old ordinary life" of which Diane Glancy speaks. Others of Linda Hogan's poems, for example, like "Gate" in *The Book of Medicines,* point to the nearness of the sacred and the possibilities for hope in the everyday world. In this poem, Hogan says of the people in a "town, nearby" that "They think heaven is so far away,/ beyond the farthest towns,/ not beneath the mortal sky,/ not the radiant fields of potatoes/ brown with dust."[47] Or Joy Harjo's poem, "Perhaps the World Ends Here," about the centrality of the kitchen table in the drama of the world's creation and eventual going out of existence. "The world begins at a kitchen table," writes Harjo in the first line of the poem. "No matter what, we must eat to live." And it will end there as well, she concludes, "while we are laughing and crying, eating of the last sweet bite."[48]

American Indian women write often about how attention to the conscious experiences of everyday life serves the purposes of those who write from the borders of both oral and written cultures. Wisconsin Oneida poet Roberta J. Hill puts it this way: "Each morning I take time to appreciate the place where I stand on earth. Intuiting the relationship between a language and the earth involves a struggle, for in dreaming and speaking I must believe in the power of language to capture my experience, yet I know that my vision will always push against the limitations of that language. . . . When we take time to feel alive on this earth, these forms of thought aid our survival by strengthening us."[49] Janice Gould, too, emphasizes the efficacy of "words" and of poetry for American Indian women's transformation of both world and worldview. For Gould, poetry integrates both oral and written cultures. Poems are not just literary texts in her understanding but also "the vehicle for prayer, song, and oration." When American Indian women write poetry out of the experiences of their everyday lives of both anger and hope and from the borders of both oral and written cultures, Gould says, they are also writing on the assumption that words are magic, potent, and efficacious in bringing about change. "That is where hope must be located," she says, "in our self-assurance that we can affect the world through language, a language that permeates boundaries, that we can perceive from beyond ourselves."[50] In the capacity to bring about change through the efficacious use of language, Hill and Gould are suggesting, lies also the strength to interpret, to transcend when necessary, and to persist and endure—not with resignation, as the case of Iris Heavy Runner demonstrates—but with personal and communal creativity.

TEXT, ORAL CULTURE, AND ORDINARY REALITY
IN AFRICAN-AMERICAN WOMEN'S LIVES

American Indian women are not alone in asking about the religious and personal significance of moving from oral to written culture. What are the benefits, the risks, the trade-offs, in moving the oral tradition and its stories of African-American women's daily lives to the pages of a literary text? There are African-American theologians like ethicist Katie Geneva Cannon who have

entered the world of the academy, the world of the "canonical boys," as she calls them. But the literary and theological origins of women like Cannon are in an oral culture, origins that "seem to arise from the flowing waters of the 'live river' within me. . . . The voices of women, black women, that I have known and read about, call to me from the river."[51]

For womanist theologians, the issue of moving from an oral to a textual culture is not just a matter of the conventions of different rhetorical styles. It has theological and epistemological implications as well. It is not only about remembering and interpreting the wisdom of the everyday realities related by the oral culture. It also involves, according to Cannon, the recognition that what most students took for granted as true and ordinary in the seminary classrooms of the 1970s and 1980s was not part of the pasts or the cultures of most African-American women. Nor did they encounter much that was familiar in terms of the lives they were living at the time: "We entered every discussion with a developing awareness that the indisputable norms of established truth would not be the norms of our daily existence."[52] Cannon writes of occasionally encountering other African-American women seminarians and becoming aware together that they felt themselves in every situation to be "sister outsiders," to use Audre Lord's famous phrase. The details of the daily lives these women lived in their communities and carried in their histories revealed dissonance and strangeness in the taken-for-granted theological and epistemological claims they were encountering in seminary.

The new question Cannon sees emerging from the clash of the ordinary expectations of two different cultures is this one: "How do we remain both beholden to our inherited religious culture materials as well as responsible in favoring the extension of oral texts for posterity?"[53] When two literary cultures, the oral and the written, come together—and when they originate in different racial cultures as well, Cannon asks implicitly—what new things might emerge?

One response to Cannon's question lies in Cheryl A. Kirk-Duggan's womanist theological work on Spirituals. In *Exorcizing Evil: A Womanist Perspective on the Spirituals*, Kirk-Duggan brings together all the experiences and knowledge of her own particular life in an analysis of African-American Spirituals as they were used by antebellum slaves in nineteenth-century America and during the civil rights movement of the 1960s. Kirk-Duggan is an academically trained womanist theologian and an ordained minister in the Christian Methodist Episcopal Church, one of the historic black denominations in the United States. She is also an academically trained professional musician who sang her first Spiritual solo at four. She grew up in a family that "loved and depended on God through the mornings of new life, the evenings of death, and the mountains and valleys of daily existence."[54]

The major theological theme of *Exorcising Evil* is theodicy, the category of a theological system that addresses the relationship between suffering and evil and the nature of ultimate reality, in the case of Christianity, God. One of Kirk-Duggan's mentors suggested to her that Spirituals are actually applied theodicies. They became a natural focus of inquiry for her, because she identifies music as "the arena where I wrestle with good and evil, suffering and pain."[55] As oral texts, musical texts, the Spirituals not only address in encoded language the realities of daily life and suffering among antebellum slaves; they also, according to Kirk-Duggan, "know literary independence as they stand on their own as a particular cultural form, especially as they exude Black distinctiveness."[56] They are, it would seem, natural vehicles for exploring Katie Cannon's commitment to remaining faithful to inherited religious culture materials and at the same time saving and extending oral texts of African Americans' lived experience for posterity.

One of the particular aspects of Kirk-Duggan's approach is that she includes not only textual analysis but musical analysis of taped live musical performances. She speaks of the solo and communal singing of Spirituals as "musicking," a term she uses to indicate the kind of participation in creating music and musical performance that exists in African-American culture, in contrast to what she sees as the Western assumption that music, especially performance, is the province of trained and talented professionals. The Spirituals, "stories in song," she calls them, come out of a more ordinary reality. They "celebrate the communal and the interrelationships between music and life via the religious and the theological."[57]

Kirk-Duggan places her interpretation of Spirituals and their theodicy of both resistance and hope within her own womanist goals for social transformation. "Womanist theory," as she claims it, "challenges us to shift from pure individualism, apathy, blaming others, being victims, and bemoaning all our present social ills toward a place of having an outrageous joie de vivre for life, wholeness, and proactive possibility." In her opinion, singing the Spirituals can serve as a catalyst for this kind of transformation.[58] She is also very clear that she has not superimposed an academic, theoretical theodicy on the Spirituals; it is already there in the lives of the people who have sung them historically and who sing them now. She sees her work as typical of liberation theologies in that she moves from praxis to theory, "from the bottom up." "In the African-American setting," she says, "the sacred and the secular, together with politics and piety, are integral to daily life. That intimacy arises from a strong communal sense and a sense of being intimate with the divine."[59]

As academic womanist theologians, Katie Cannon and Cheryl Kirk-Duggan demonstrate a facility with traditional European and American male theology. They are familiar with Augustine and Aquinas, Calvin and Schleiermacher and Karl Barth. They know white feminist theology and *mujerista* theology as well and do not count anyone out of the conversation. But the catalysts for their own theologies and the creativity of their work emerge from their distinctive interpretations of African-American daily life, particularly the lives of women, historic and contemporary. "Womanism," says Katie

Cannon, "requires that we stress the urgency of the African American women's movement from death to life."[60]

PRESERVING TRADITION THROUGH EVERYDAY LIFE

Jewish theologian Carol Ochs uses the metaphor of individual life itself as a text to point to how the holy is revealed in the ordinary work of a community and how such work sustains the community in the best and worst of times. She makes the case that the Jewish people have received two revelations: the Five Books of Moses and Miriam's Way. In a new midrash (an elaborated interpretation of an event in Jewish scripture and history) that she calls "Miriam's Way," Ochs claims that "[e]ach life . . . is a revealed text through which we may encounter the nothing—and everything—of the holy in daily life."[61] In this midrash that focuses on the five references to Miriam—the sister of Moses and Aaron—that Jewish scripture has preserved, Ochs points to the Jewish tradition's claim that the child receives its Jewish identity from the mother. "One has to wonder how this came about," she says, "given the central role in ancient Judaism of Temple worship, which lay entirely in the province of male priests, and the subsequent turn to Torah study, which was denied to women. Just what, we may ask, were the women passing on when they passed on their faith?"[62]

Ochs argues that when the Israelites wandered in the desert after their escape from Egypt and before their entrance into the Promised Land, Moses "recognizes, too late, what Miriam had contributed to the shaping of the Judaic religious consciousness." In Ochs's new midrash, Moses thought about Miriam as he lay dying and pondering the nature of future leadership, "but, not recognizing what she had contributed to preserving the faith, he had made no effort to have someone else assume her role." What began to dawn on him was that he had made no provisions for passing on the faith to future generations. Thus, says Ochs, Moses withdrew from the people in order to think and pray about the identity of Miriam's successor.

In Ochs's midrash, it is Miriam who reminds the women that revelation does not always come in dramatic moments through those who remove themselves from the community in order to receive it. In Moses' absence, "Miriam visited the women one at a time, as they cooked and stirred, rocked their children and comforted them, and she pointed out, 'Revelation is taking place right now as you cook and comfort, tend the fires, and nurse the young.'"[63] Neither does revelation always fill in the gaps with answers; sometimes it enables a people to confront nothingness and uncertainty about the future without resorting to false worship (the golden calf) in order to fill the emptiness with false gods.

Biblical scholar Tikva Frymer-Kensky uses not a new midrash but an exploration of halakha,[64] Jewish law, from the perspective of daily life to speak to issues of continuity and community among Jews, particularly among liberal Jews, for whom "obligation" in terms of Jewish law must be redefined. For liberal Jews, "the performance of a *mitzvah* (commandment) is its own re-ward," since "the flouting of abrogation of Halakha carries no sanctions. . . . And in the post-Holocaust era, few believe in supernatural sanctions."[65]

In Jewish communities where adherence to halakha is not what consti-tutes the boundaries of the community, Frymer-Kensky argues, non-ritualized daily life becomes extensively secularized and seems to lie outside "the realm of the holy." As she sees it, liberal Jews have paid a high price by "forfeiting the attempt to live constantly surrounded by God and holiness."[66] It is this high price that Frymer-Kensky has in mind when she talks about the need to find a new rationale for living out halakhic law in daily life. For her the rationale be-hind halakha is not obedience to rules: "The ultimate purpose of the Halakha is to infuse our daily biological and social activity with a sense of divinity, pur-pose, and community, so that we can truly live in the path of God."[67] This is what it means to be a holy people, to continue the identity of the community.

For Frymer-Kensky, being a holy people requires a constant revisioning of the past, because "Ancient Israel could not foresee everything. The Bible never transformed its own social structure."[68] Jews must therefore continue to ask questions about halakhic requirements in order to interpret them in terms of contemporary lives and with reference to specific cases. And this means bringing discussions of halakha down to earth and out of the realm of "theo-retical, mythical, and at times even mystical language."[69] Frymer-Kensky tries out some of these questions, which range from issues specific to the Jewish community to culture questions about such things as the death penalty: "*Does the Halakha accord everyone his/her full humanity? . . . Should milk be kept separate from meat? . . . Should we observe* shaatnez, *the avoidance of fabric composed of both wool and linen? . . . Should Halakha permit the death pen-alty? What about homosexuality?*"[70]

To these questions Frymer-Kensky gives different responses and reasons for her response—all in terms of issues concerned with contemporary daily life. If the rationale for observing halakha has to do with the holiness of daily life at this time in history, she says, then "Judaism should always be open to the idea that a particular guideline in the received Halakha should no longer be Halakha." As to how such decisions will be made, that authority, says Frymer-Kensky, must be left to the whole community rather than only to ex-perts, however daunting the creation of new ways of making halakhic decisions might be.[71]

TRAVELING WITH CHILDREN:
THEOLOGICAL INSIGHTS FROM HOME

In concluding this section on some of the ways women of various communities are opening up the meaning of "ordinary" and its implications for theology and religious thought, I look at the work of two women, one a Protestant theologian in pastoral care and counseling and the other a Jewish ethicist. Both women elaborate on the ordinary tasks and the ordinary tensions experienced by women who are the mothers of children they delight in and who are also academic women with the desire to contribute creatively to their professions by teaching and writing. Likewise, both women point to the workplace, including the feminist academy, as theologically unresponsive to these same tensions. From different disciplines and out of the grounding of two different religious traditions, Bonnie J. Miller-McLemore and Laurie Zoloth-Dorfman speculate about what new theological visions of mothering, family, and work will diminish the ordinary pain of women who find themselves constantly torn between the requirements of the two roles.

Zoloth-Dorfman sets for herself the challenge of constructing "an ethics of ordinariness without sentimentality about the daily moral choices that are made by women and to reflect on the theology that is partner to such an ethics."[72] She makes explicit as background for this constructive work a critique of theologies and sacred texts that depict the spiritual quest as a solitary male pursuit away from the ordinary and toward the holy, which is considered separate from it—with no clues as to who is supporting this quest by making it possible. Texts like that about Moses at Sinai or Jacob's wrestling with the angel, says Dorfman, "always leave me muttering about who is watching the four-year-olds near the water, who is bouncing the babies to sleep at the edges of the gathering, who is washing the plates after dinner, who is dyeing the cloth for the sacred raiment."[73]

In reflecting on the theological fruits produced by the tensions in her life as a mother, Zoloth-Dorfman describes what she has come to see as a theology of interruption. She goes so far as to say that "the ontological status of my life is constructed around the interruption, which is to say that the interruption creates a foundational pattern for the radical recognition that the needs of the other compel immediate moral attention."[74] In attempting to make theological sense of this reality, Zoloth-Dorfman asks, "Is such a claim Jewish?"

She answers that it is not only Jewish but feminist: "Much of the religious honor given to the daily reflects a choice that we can claim as feminist. The attention to the details of the work of a human life, the concern with the work of childbearing, of reproduction remind us of a rabbinic regard that is a deliberate theological decision about power and importance."[75] Nonetheless, she claims, it is not very easy to discern the value of a life whose structure is continually interrupted, and it is not a life that is supported by "the structure of the workplace, the academy, even the feminist academy."[76] In spite of what she experiences as a lack of institutional support and few written models for the kind of journey she is on, Zoloth-Dorfman finds grounding for her theological interpretation in the Book of Ruth, in the Jewish regard for the sacredness of everyday life, and in "Talmudic discourse and text that allows the creation of a community of shared meaning, interrupted by the case and the casuistic reflection that both offers and comments on a model of the interrupted discourse for ethical reflection."[77]

Zoloth-Dorfman says that it is out of the ordinariness of the interruption in her life as the mother of five children that she has come to insights about "the power of the daily in ethical choice," insights that she claims are only rarely pointed out in the sacred scripture of most traditions.[78] What does the spiritual quest look like, she asks, when one travels at the slow pace of children whose needs necessarily interrupt any efforts to achieve sustained time for reflection and writing?

Embracing that question, Bonnie J. Miller-McLemore speaks particularly of proceeding "according to the pace of children" and of what that ordinary reality means for a more realistic understanding of "generativity." This is a concept that she adapts from psychologist Kai Erickson and that speaks to the human need to live a life of "productivity, creativity, and procreativity."[79] Her critique of established religion is that "in speculating on the meaning of creation and human fulfillment, theology seldom pulls the life experiences of mothering into its arena for anything but limited, and even oppressive commentary. And it certainly never has entertained seriously what mothers think, feel, desire, and know about creation and revelation."[80]

Miller-McLemore and Zoloth-Dorfman are not looking for advice. They are seeking, instead, companions on the journey and ways to discern and articulate theologically what their ordinary lives reveal about the inadequacies of conventional understandings of home, family, and work. Their issues are pragmatic but not only pragmatic; they look to the heart of what their religious traditions have to say about their lives and ask, in Miller-McLemore's words, "What is the promised life for which God created us and for which we should strive?"[81] And they ask as well—and tell—what do mothers know about it? No adequate responses can be constructed, these two women from different traditions insist, without a detailed knowledge of what the everyday life is like.

In telling their stories, Zoloth-Dorfman and Miller-McLemore offer the kinds of details with which their lives are filled: nursing babies, picking up children after school, writing during naptime, and suppressing the terrors that if one wishes too hard for the kind of time required to lead a scholarly life, it might be granted in catastrophic ways. "One day," says Miller-McLemore, "while trying to revise a manuscript during the naptime of one of my sons, I recall feeling torn between a desire for total uninterrupted silence and horror at my fantasy that a capricious god might grant my impulsive wish and I would lose my children forever."[82] Appearing as it does in a theology about the revelatory nature of the tensions in ordinary mothers' ordinary obligations, Miller-McLemore's self-disclosure also makes clear the power of traditional expectations for mothers and the fear of cosmic proportion that questioning them brings. This, again, is the stuff of ambivalence, never far from even the most optimistic and creative of women's theological endeavors. Like Proteus, "ambivalence" seems to change shape to suit the occasion.

In *Dakota: A Spiritual Geography* Kathleen Norris has a very brief chapter entitled "God Is in the Details," based, I assume, on information offered by a neighbor in the tiny South Dakota town where this poet and writer lives: "He

said: 'You want to hay your brome and crested wheatgrass. They're the taller, more lush grasses, not native, and they'll lose their nutritive value quickly. Any moisture and they'll frost-kill, But the native shortgrass—that's your grama and buffalo grass, sedges and switch grass—makes for good winter pasture. You let it stand, and it cures on the stem.' "[83]

Without the title as a clue, this description of instructions for growing shortgrass does not appear to offer much in the way of insight about God or anything else generally considered religious. It is the title that compels one to think about what Norris has in mind, what she thinks this description reveals about God, and, further, what understandings of God and the details themselves are being revealed. The women whose writings I've cited claim that the sacred is in the details, and that therefore the details must be conveyed. But the details cannot stand alone. If they are to reveal the sacred, they must do so within an interpretive framework of the kind we see emerging in women's religious thought, a framework that comes from the depths of their particular traditions. "Check your guidebook," says Zoloth-Doorman, by which she means "the particularity of the religious tradition."[84] To know that a woman who suffers from lupus has swollen hands one day and dexterous hands the next is not enough. But the implicitly theological statement "life is mixed" is not enough, either; it needs the details to back it up. That is why we get so many details about the ordinary in American women's religious thought; the details offer a path to understanding the sacred. And, in fact, the details lend themselves to women's discovery of the sacred's very origins and grounding in the ordinary.

The Ordinariness of the Sacred

If the ordinary reveals the sacred, then, according to many women, manifestations and invocations of the sacred often partake of the stuff of ordinary life. Lying behind this claim is the familiar critique that historically women have had little access to sacred offices and rituals and have seldom participated, publicly at least, in the shaping of religious symbols, rituals, teachings, and disciplines. It is not surprising to discover that one means women use to gain access to the sacred is to create interpretations that render it more accessible and comprehensible. One way to do this is to point out the connections of the holy to the ordinary rather than to the remote and mysterious, the regulated and the set apart. We have seen this in reference to understandings of ultimate reality and the resulting emphasis on theologies of divine immanence. Another fruitful area in which to encounter this strategy is in the area of ritual.

There is a widely articulated perception that ritual among women tends to be more horizontal than vertical, de-emphasizing traditional forms of leadership that set one person apart as more in touch with the divine and thus less ordinary than the rest of those gathered. Further, says Lesley A. Northrup, "when women ritualize, they use the stuff of everyday life, rooted in earthliness and women's domestication of space; homely crafts like quilting; meal preparation; experiences of childbirth and raising; plants and flowers, innate rhythms of months, seasons, light and dark; bowls and dishes; stones; *a capella* singing; robing; and so on."[85] A prominent Goddess feminist, Hallie Iglehart Austen, remarks as well on the element of de-mystification in rituals among spiritual feminists, a perspective that takes for granted the immanence of the divine: "Women's spirituality is a process of de-mystifying spirituality. It is about making spiritual practice accessible to each one of us in our everyday lives. We can write our own scriptures, create our own rituals, since each of us has access to the inner wisdom from which all the great practices come. . . . We always need to come back to our own inner selves where the heart of wisdom resides."[86] Here it all is: de-mystifying, re-sacralizing, using the ordinary to render the sacred accessible; relying on inner wisdom as well as the wisdom of the community as a source of inspiration and validation.

In keeping with my emphasis on women's religious thought, I am interested not only in what women do and use in rituals but particularly in how they reflect on what they are doing. As women of many traditions frequently point out, their rituals—even those of Goddess feminists—do not come out of a vacuum. Women want not just to create new rituals but to connect them to the histories of their traditions. In the process of thinking about the nature of these connections women cannot help but enter the realm of religious thought, where they are compelled to ponder where their traditions are lacking and where they have life. One theme that becomes apparent quickly is women's conviction that demonstrating the rootedness of ritual—and the sacred—in the ordinary has the effect of revitalizing religious traditions—pointing to their inexhaustibility—rather than rendering them lifelessly mundane. "When women trust their instincts and each other," says Penina V. Adelman, in reference to *Kos Miriam*, a new Jewish women's ritual of drinking from the cup of Miriam that has emerged since 1989, "they can find ways of invoking the ancestors. This brings them the strength that is needed spiritually, emotionally, intellectually, and physically to contribute to the survival of the Jewish people."[87]

At one level, it is the simple inclusion of women in rituals from which they have been barred that has a de-mystifying and re-vivifying effect on a tradition. Often there is the additional benefit of countering the sense of essential unworthiness that many women describe in the stories they tell about their communities and rituals. Rabbi Lynn Gottlieb, who creates Jewish rituals for women, gives as much opportunity as she can for women to ascend the *bimah* (the platform in the temple or synagogue on which the Torah scrolls are kept and from which the rabbi and the cantor hold forth) and read from the Torah. "We women," she says, "are still seeking our place on the bimah." Her purpose is to "invite them to hold the Torah, to read from the Torah, to dance, laugh, and cry with the Torah to overcome their intimidation, sense of shame, fear, and hesitancy about possessing this inheritance as their own." When women stand on the *bimah* and hold the scrolls, "What was forbidden is now permitted."[88] The space that was once too extraordinary in its sacredness to permit the presence of women is rendered accessible and therefore de-mystified. De-mystified in one way; it is also re-sacralized by including the presence of the other half of the Jewish community.

As straightforward as this sounds in theory—using ritual to promote the ordinariness of women's presence on the *bimah*—Gottlieb acknowledges that traditional understandings of what is sacred are not so easily subverted; they are too deeply internalized. Here again we encounter some of the ambivalence that women experience when they step over boundaries that have been so influential in shaping their understandings of what is right and proper for salvation and inclusion in the community. This is the case, according to Gottlieb's experience, "even when everyone present is a declared feminist." Presenting new ritual visions of what the community should look like is risky business, because it requires improvisation—a clear sign of departure from the solid foundations of the past. "Some grow afraid," says Gottlieb. "They think crossing over the line means falling into an endless abyss. Everything is challenged, everything is possible. How will we know what works, what doesn't, what saves us and what damns our souls?"[89]

The ordinariness of women's inclusion in ritual takes another form among grass-roots Latinas who belong to an organization called LAS HERMANAS. This group of women has struggled for many years with the issue of celebrating Mass at its conferences and meetings, which requires the presence of a male priest, "something many of us find disempowering." The issue, says Ada María Isasi-Díaz, "is not lack of belief in the Eucharist but the exclusion of women from ordained ministry in the Catholic church."[90] Over the years the group has moved from having a traditional Mass to developing their own liturgies, in which only women have leadership roles.

Many considerations shape the creation of these liturgies, all of which involve both de-mystification and re-sacralization as these two simultaneous processes are aided by grounding in the ordinary elements of Latina women's lives. First is the desire to claim the place where they meet and the fact that they meet as sacred, "an important way of asserting our share in the holiness of God." Another is the need to make sure that the liturgies "remind us of the sacred spaces that many of us carve out even in the humblest of houses." Most Latina women, says Isasi-Díaz, no matter what their economic, educational, or social status, have altars in their homes or pictures of Mary, Jesus, and the saints hanging on the walls. This was an effort to make grass-roots Latina women feel at home: "For some of them this was the first time they stayed in a hotel, the first time they were in a conference with only women, the first time they heard a woman preach, the first time it was one of them who broke the bread."[91] The intent of the liturgies was not only to celebrate the gifts and presence of Latinas but also to subvert the mystification of the sacred that Isasi-Díaz sees as a "control mechanism" used by "religious professionals."

In their particular ways, Gottlieb and Isasi-Díaz are talking about what Miriam Therese Winter calls "the politics of ritual" and how women's rituals—and all religious rituals—need not just "rehearse the past," as she says, but point to visions of "the way it could and should be."[92] This is the prophetic dimension of ritual, its capacity to render visible the ways the status quo is inadequate. Winter is a Roman Catholic sister and author of many books of women's prayers and rituals. Her critique of most of the traditional rituals of religious communities is that they are designed to "celebrate victories." They sustain and intensify the status quo "that theology supports and embellishes, structures maintain and perpetuate, and canons guarantee."[93] Ritual loses its power to point beyond the status quo when, as Winter puts it, it "disdains the common touch," its grounding in the ordinary experiences of women's lives as they have been and continue to be a part of the community.

In her understanding of what is needed for women to participate in "the universe of power," Paula Gunn Allen, a woman of Laguna Pueblo, Sioux, and Anglo heritage who is a well-known interpreter of American Indian women's spirituality, refers to "the common touch" in terms of women's need to be grounded in ordinary tasks. When an interviewer asked her, "How can those of us who feel separated from the universe of power use ritual to re-member our relationship to that universe?" Allen responded that this was a difficult task for those not raised in a ritual tradition.[94] But her advice was this: "The most important thing you need is the ordinary life. If you read a story and you want to think about it, then go do the dishes. Sweep the floor. Tend the garden. Talk to the kids. Be with that story, and let it work itself out through your hands. Through your feet. In your mind. It will show up in your house. It will show up in your job. That is the entrance. That is how you get into this other level where the universe of power is."[95]

The everyday kinds of discipline required of a person on the medicine path—keeping your house clean, keeping yourself clean, learning to live with chronic illness—offer a startling contrast to the drama of Allen's description of entering the universe of power by getting on the medicine path: "It will probably kill you in very unpleasant ways." In *Grandmothers of the Light*, Allen's book about Native American goddesses and supernatural beings, she outlines the seven-fold path that women on the medicine path must follow: "As a woman, you gain discipline through being a good daughter, a good householder, a good hunter/gatherer, a good cook, a good parent, a good grandmother, whatever it is you're doing. That discipline is the thing that keeps you in some kind of balance."[96] At the same time, she says, "You have to learn how to focus mentally. You have to be ruthless. You have to be able to tell everybody whom you care about, 'Look, I don't have time for you.' "[97] The implication seems to be that the ordinary tasks performed by women can be understood as serving a purpose other than taking care of others.

Allen sees the power of the universe emerging through the busyness of what is required of women in their ordinary lives, but at the same time she describes the essential nature of the cosmos as "female intelligence," God as "spider grandmother," the one who, like the mountains, has the ability to endure. This is in contrast with "the men who do the implementing. What you don't see is who started the process."[98] Taken altogether, Allen's advice and her perceptions of female and male discipline and power do not always sound consistent (one of the minor virtues of creative religious thought as far as I'm concerned). I attribute this to another manifestation of the ambivalence that shows up when women are working to find their way between both the power and the entrapment of traditional women's tasks.

One of those traditional and ordinary tasks is feeding the hungry. This is a point that Roman Catholic feminist sacramental theologians make, both when they offer a critique of the exclusion of women in their tradition from celebrating the Eucharist—getting a meal on the table, one might call it—and when they construct new theologies of the Eucharist. In her feminist interpretation of sacramental theology and its relationship to embodiment, Susan A. Ross takes as a starting point the perception of another theologian, Christine Gudorf, that women will benefit if the sacraments are reconnected to ordinary life. Ross finds compelling Gudorf's assessment that "sacraments are, at their heart, celebrations of what women do naturally—give birth, feed, and comfort—physical experiences that have been taken up by men and sacralized. Men can now do what women do, but on a higher, more spiritual plane; women's bodily experience is now seen as less holy than men's."[99] Ross and Gudorf agree that the sacraments (there are seven in the Roman Catholic tradition, as opposed to two in most Protestant denominations) have been divorced from their grounding in ordinary activities and that, as a result, the ordinary activities from which they spring appear to be less holy than their sacramental counterparts.

What would be the theological consequences, the changes in understanding of, for example, the Eucharist, if it were to be more closely understood from a feminist perspective as an ordinary rather than an extraordinary meal? For including women is not just a shift in personnel but a catalyst for new interpretations of the Eucharist and of ordination (one of the common themes of the women-church movement in Roman Catholicism is a lack of desire to be ordained to the priesthood as it now exists). For one thing, says Ross, the focus of the ritual will change from the presider—the male priest—to the community that is gathered: "When the focus is on the assembly, the Eucharist is a lavish gift to be shared, not scarce gold to be parceled piecemeal only to those who qualify. Like the multiplication of the loaves and fishes, the eucharistic feast ought to be a living symbol of the openness and generosity of the Christian community. That it so often fails to live up to this generosity is a scandal."[100] Further, this change in focus from presider to assembly might well change the understanding of what "priesthood" means in the Roman Catholic tradition. Ross says by this she does not mean to suggest that there is the possibility of a "complementary notion of women's common priesthood" that might exist alongside the ordained male priesthood, but "that the experiences and gifts women would bring to the priesthood would inevitably change the office." [101] These changes, according to Ross, would emerge from women's experience with the sacramental ministry of the church that has been practiced for centuries but never acknowledged.

A group of Disciples women, whose tradition has a less sacramentalized but nonetheless central tradition of communion, likewise grounds this ritual in ordinary life. Disciples have communion weekly, unlike many Protestant traditions that celebrate monthly or quarterly. Kris Culp, one of the participants in a lengthy discussion about the memories and meaning of communion for Disciples women, associates communion and the passing of communion trays with images of potluck suppers from her childhood: "Women often prepare both sets of meals, whether as deaconesses or as CWF [Christian Women's Fellowship]." [102] Nancy Claire Pittman, another participant, says that her "earliest memories of communion do not have as much to do with the worship service as they do with the cleanup afterward." [103] Pittman and her sister helped their mother, who was a deaconess, and her friends wash the communion trays and little cups after the service.

The Disciples women talked together about numerous concerns related to communion in their tradition: the role of women in presiding at the communion table, changes in ritual that test traditional meanings of communion, issues around who is invited to participate, changes in theology and the role of ritual, and the power of communion as a symbol and ways its meanings can be expanded. The conversation, as these women agreed at the end of it, was its own kind of communion. It "happened in a cramped hotel room. . . . Most of the floor space was taken by a room-service cart on which sat half-eaten pizzas, soft drink cans, and pieces of chocolate dessert. Nine women, one nursing a baby, sat munching and sipping together as we talked about the holy meal that lies at the center of our communities of worship and faith." It was this conversation and meal, also, that convinced one of the participants that what they had experienced together was communion. Bonnie Miller-McLemore confessed that she had wondered before the conversation why they were planning to talk about communion in the first place, but came to realize "that I have a feminist Disciples theology and I share it with you." [104] For these women the more ordinary setting for a traditional ritual prompted changes in its form and a broadening of its meaning.

Rita Gross envisions similar changes in the rituals of Buddhist practice if more ordinary goals are set for its use and more ordinary interpretations offered for its benefits. These changes involve the dual processes of re-sacralization and de-mystification. For too long, she says, Buddhist practice and "the householder lifestyle" have been seen as antithetical to each other. If the duties of the household can be see as another arena in which mindfulness and detachment can be practiced, then "ordinary domestic life will be seen much more directly as a *Buddhist* rather than merely a secular or a lay problem." [105] Such changes in perception are not minor in Buddhism, particularly in North America, because they are related to large questions about the value of monastic practice versus lay practice.

These changes in understanding motivate Buddhists to examine other major assumptions as well. In keeping with her emphasis on an earth-oriented post-patriarchal Buddhism, Gross asks a pivotal question regarding Buddhist spiritual discipline: "For what purpose? What do we hope will result from the practice of spiritual discipline? What changes will it effect?"[106] Gross does not think that the traditional idea of engaging in Buddhist spiritual practice as a preparation for death will survive post-patriarchal changes. Instead, there will be increasing emphasis on what the practice of such disciplines can contribute to the sanity and deep peace of the individual, to the possibility of communicating with and comforting each other, and to the well-being of the community and the earth. These she sees as more ordinary goals than experiencing the presence of other realms, becoming deities, or envisioning the palaces of the deities. "When we look out our windows," says Gross, "we will see the palaces of the deities. When we comfort each other, we will converse with the deities."[107]

In agreement with Gottlieb and Allen, Gross does not equate "ordinary" goals with what is easy to accomplish. She sees no way around the need to engage in spiritual disciplines that go "against the grain" of conventional life lived without reflection. She is convinced that "without such disciplines, few people transcend trivial, conventional repetitive styles of immanence for those grounded in deep peace." [108] But a move to the more earth-oriented, the more ordinary, goals of this against-the-grain discipline, Gross thinks, will change the nature of Buddhist discipline itself.

"Prayer," another of the spiritual disciplines of many traditions, likewise partakes of the ordinary life of the person who participates in it and also offers an interpretive framework within which to interpret ordinary life. Disciples of Christ clergywoman Kay Bessler Northcutt looks to Christian prayer as something that is not set apart from daily matters. "A prayerful life," she says, "is not the custody of an elite class, ordained or otherwise set-apart 'holy' people nor is a prayerful life set-apart 'holy' experience."[109]

Northcutt uses as an example of prayer her own mother's attention to the folding of Northcutt's diapers, which the mother had hung out on the line in January, contrary to the advice of Northcutt's grandmother, who thought her daughter would catch cold. Northcutt's mother said to her, "Those frozen-dry diapers were as soft as you could imagine after the wind had whipped the ice out of them. You see—it was all in the fold; I spent many hours debating your Aunt Shirley about how to fold a diaper the best way. You just couldn't get diapers to fold right after they dried over the furnace. They were stiff. And hard."[110]

"*That*," says Northcutt "is prayer. It is the devotion of absolute attention." The way to achieve this intensity of attention is to cultivate "the gift of seeing the holy in the ordinary."[111] As Northcutt understands prayer, it is not withdrawing from the world, but paying attention to it. It is also not a solitary pursuit, even if it is sometimes enacted in solitude, but a discipline that requires "the solidarity of spiritual friends" and what Northcutt calls "a living response to one another." In this sense the ordinary goal of a life of prayer is similar to the effects Rita Gross calls for from the practice of Buddhist spiritual practice—an enhanced capacity to communicate with and comfort others. There is an affinity here, also, with the Buddhist concept of "mindfulness" as Gross describes it. Focusing on prayer as absolute attention to the ordinary moves the function of prayer away from petition and closer to what an immanental worldview would seem to call for: awareness of divine presence in the world and in others. "With wisdom's quickening," says Northcutt, "we number our days as we bring our absolute attention to the work of ice-diapers and babies' bottoms to the translucent skin of aged ones whose work is death. In absolute attention we pray . . . admiring in silent anguished wonder the passing moment that each life is."[112]

CLOTHES AND THE ORDINARINESS OF THE SACRED

One of the issues that brings some women face to face with the interweaving of the sacred and the ordinary is the matter of clothes in those religious communities where there are decisions to be made about the extent to which one wants to give an outward sign of affiliation or feels obligated to do so. Choosing whether to wear distinctive clothing can force an examination of where one wants to stand in relation to the world outside the religious community. In Marcia K. Hermansen's study of several different communities of American Muslim women—immigrant and native-born, white and black—she concentrates on issues of acculturation and relates individual choice to issues of situation: liminality and communitas. Because Hermansen's study incorporates a variety of circumstances in which Muslim women find themselves, generalizations need to be qualified in terms of context. The situation of Muslim women born into Arab culture is different from that of American women who marry foreign-born Muslim men is different from African-American women who become Muslims, and so on. But the issue of how or whether to signal one's identity by means of dress is a daily matter and one that exists, as Hermansen puts it, "everyday, perhaps every hour."[113] Decisions must be interpreted within a religious worldview that co-exists with secular American culture—what to wear to work, for example. And, to complicate matters further, "the choice, once rationalized at the personal level, is still raised overtly or subconsciously when associating with other Muslims."[114]

What this clothing dilemma raises, it becomes clear, is a need for a theology of everyday dress, one that acknowledges in some way how Muslim women in different contexts see the overlapping or the separation of their religious and secular lives—how much and why they want to make clear or conceal their identity as Muslim women. Hermansen looks at this issue in terms of the an-thropological terms "liminality" and "communitas," but these, of course, are terms that have theological implications as well. The everyday questions that emerge for women from being Muslim in America—what to wear being only one of many—call for "an ijtihad (interpretation of Islamic law and values)," which, interestingly, as Hermansen points out, "in its radical nature reasserts the initial impetus of the Islamic revelation to break down tribal/ethnic iden-tifications."[115] One might guess from this that the move will be toward greater assimilation, but whether or not that is the case is a question that Hermansen thinks will be answered only by the next generation of American Muslim women. Hermansen's study, then, points to a need for an interpretive world-view, one that includes attention to dress that is other than prescriptive— more like "how do we think about these things?" than "this is what you must do."

Hermansen's article offers an entry into a discussion of how distinctive re-ligious clothing is related to issues of ordinary life. Helen Beach Cannon's meditation on the significance of Mormon sacred clothing offers more detail about how one woman from a particular religious community integrates the issue into an interpretation of her own spiritual journey and how she under-stands the role of sacred symbols in her life: in other words, how she thinks about these things. Her reflection on sacred garments and her ambivalent feel-ings toward them takes the form of spiritual autobiography. Cannon's article began as a response to a presentation by Colleen McDannell at the University of Utah on her research—as an outsider—into Mormon sacred garments.[116] Cannon had not worn the garments for more than twenty years when she wrote the article, although her husband had continued to do so, as had one of her married daughters.

At one level Cannon talks about decisions concerning the care and wear-ing of sacred garments in terms of highly practical, even funny, everyday deci-sions. She tells the story of a friend who doesn't know whether to wash her visiting daughter's and son-in-law's garments with other clothing, because "It doesn't seem kosher to put these sacred garments with secular undies."[117] But, like the Muslim women Hermansen has studied, Cannon needs to see the everyday decisions in terms of a broader context of religious identity. She tells of contemplating whether to wear blouses that would reveal that she doesn't wear garments when she helps to teach Gospel Doctrine classes in her ward and what is at stake, as she sees it, in making that decision: "So not only am I a woman, an academic, and not conventionally active in the Church, but I wear no garments. In my ward these four descriptions constitute four near-heresies when it comes to Gospel Doctrine teachers. My lessons therefore are not above suspicion."[118]

Cannon's meditation is a study in ambivalence toward the garments. She may sometime choose to wear them again, and she honors their significance even if at the moment she does not wear them. It is an ambivalence that is carefully reflected upon and that has many sources. One is her desire not to symbolize, by wearing them, a separation from her parents, who had not done so. Yet this wish is complicated by the fact that her husband and at least one child do. There is also what Cannon experiences as the pull between Mormonism's de-sacralized worldview and its insistence on the rational (whereby every miracle can ultimately be explained in terms of natural law) and its historical connections with folk magic.[119] As a result, when it came time to put on the garments after her marriage in the temple, she felt torn: "How could I put on sacred garb when all I had known prior to the temple experience had been my own wrongful disdain for clothing as symbol? In my unwillingness to acknowledge that every human experience is capable of being lived on a different plane, it logically followed that the garments could signify no more than is visible. It could be no more than an item of underclothing, uncomfortable, not only in its spiritual fit but in its physical feel as well."[120]

It has been Cannon's encounter with Jewish friends and Judaism that has given her new ways to think about the meaning of the sacred garments in her life: what they have meant, what they don't mean, what they could mean. Judaism's insights on sacred objects have been valuable to Cannon because of this tradition's lengthy history of pondering the complexities of religious observance. These insights have prompted Cannon to become more "receptive to symbol and sanctification in new ways," particularly regarding her own faith.[121] She began to see the religious significance of her ambivalent and contradictory feelings. "To me, wearing the garment seemed to separate me from my family, my roots, my people, my own identity. I believe that a deep spiritual impetus and faith prompted me to make the decision and prevents me now from wearing the garment and entering the temple. I believe in the power and symbolism of the garment. I do not at this time consider myself worthy to wear it. If and when I decide to put the garment back on, I will not take that act lightly. It will have utter significance. I've thought sometimes that perhaps I should just 'do it' with less commitment, less honesty."[122] For the moment, she says, she needs to be content with another insight from Judaism, a saying that says, "When the heart is truly open, there is room for yes and no."[123]

The Ethics of the Ordinary Life

Is the arena of the ordinary sufficiently large to encompass issues of social transformation? That question is generally close to the surface in women's religious thought, fostered by the ethical complexities apparent in the most ordinary tasks.

As she was concluding a dissertation on ethics and agriculture, Protestant ethicist Judith N. Scoville found herself in the supermarket looking for something easy to grill for dinner, like pork chops or chicken. "But as I surveyed the packages of chops," she says, "I was seized with misgivings."[124] These misgivings led her to think about the fact that pork is more and more being produced by the same kind of factory farming that produces most of America's broiler chickens. She thought further about low wages and injuries in packing plants, the suffering of sows in gestation crates, the pollution caused by hog factories, the chemicals used to grow the grains for pig food, the forcing of small farmers out of business. She concluded, "Buying pork chops would involve me in many things I don't want to be involved in." Even contemplating becoming a vegetarian was not much comfort: "I stand in the produce department surveying the broccoli, carrots, and grapes and I wonder: What do I know about this produce?"[125]

Scoville's trip to the supermarket prompted a move from attention to the details of an ordinary task to reflection on what this same task elicits in terms of ethical questions. She found herself compelled to dwell on the endless meanings of who we are and how we are connected to the land and to the natural world in the midst of the deceptively simple job of figuring out what to have for dinner. Scoville's reflection emerged from her conviction that in the act of eating "we experience our own most intimate connection with the world."[126] She has integrated this conviction with her efforts to develop a theological ethics that is appropriate to agriculture and that differs from some well-known wilderness ethics. My interest in what she has to say revolves particularly around the extent to which she finds the catalyst for her theological work in the questions raised by the specifics of daily existence. Once attention is focused on the details of ordinary life and is aroused to the ethical implications of it, what next?

Sometimes there is no obvious "what next?" Careful attention to the details of the world and our ordinary life within it does not always lead to moral analysis or claims. Pamela A. Smith makes this point in an analysis of the works of writer Annie Dillard, famous for her observation and description of both small details and larger patterns in the natural world, including its human inhabitants. "She watches like mad," Smith says. "She records what she observes; she refrains from recommending that anyone do anything about what she sees."[127] What Smith is asking of Dillard, or at least points to as missing in her work, is that she move beyond the ordinary as only a descriptive category and begin to make some ethical judgments about the way the world works, in view of what Dillard has observed. Or perhaps Smith is asking for just a few clues as to how Dillard thinks human persons should be involved in the world other than to observe and endure. Whether or not this is a fair request depends of course on the theological perspective from which one makes it. Many of her interpreters would claim that what Dillard is advocating is mindfulness, attentiveness, to the world she describes, which is its own kind of religious stance and one that is sufficient. Wherever one stands on this matter, it is at the very least provocative of worthwhile discussion.

Ethics and the Ordinary as a
Category of Religious Thought

All the stories in this chapter yield implications for involvement and change — theological, ritual, social, and economic. All of them suggest that one reason to draw attention to the ordinary is to make its contours known in the lives of women of particular communities, but also to make judgments about what is valuable and what needs to be changed. I want to use the work of one particular woman thinker, Ada Maria Isasi-Díaz, to elaborate on "the ordinary" not only as a descriptive category but as a more complicated theological category, one that is acquiring depth of meaning as women use it to elicit the details of their lives.

From Isasi-Díaz's earliest works, she has insisted that her theology and that of the Latina women with whom she works must have as its source the lived experience of their daily lives. *Lo cotidiano*, she calls it. *Lo cotidiano* refers to all the multiple elements that make up the daily lives of Latina women: from speech patterns to class and gender, power and family relationships, the experience of authority and various expressions of faith. It is what provides the "stuff" of Latina women's reality.[128] In her analysis one finds all the mixed blessings, all the ambivalence and disgust and outrage, all the celebration and hope that characterize women's descriptions of their ordinary lives and their theological reflections upon their lives.

When Isasi-Díaz points to *lo cotidiano* as "more than a descriptive category," she is insisting on it as a source of theological reflection. *Lo cotidiano* has hermeneutical importance and epistemological implications. She is particularly interested in conveying that *lo cotidiano* is not an effort to present Latinas' experiences as an undifferentiated way of knowing. Neither is it meant to refer to a fixed and universal category: "*lo cotidiano* points precisely to the opposite of that: it points to transitoriness and incompleteness."[129] It is not, either, an objective reality that Latinas observe and relate to; instead, it "is a matter of life and death," which includes the need to feed, clothe, and shelter children as well as to survive physical abuse.

Isasi-Díaz is particularly concerned not to romanticize *lo cotidiano* or to make it "a criterion for judging right and wrong, good and bad." *Lo cotidiano*, the quality of everyday life, is too mixed for that: "Yes, there is much that is good and life-giving in *lo cotidiano* but there is also much that obstructs understanding and tenderness, allowing to appear an abundance of postures of self-defense that are full of falsehoods, of lies, that turn *lo cotidiano* into a behavior that is not open to life."[130] As Isasi-Díaz sees it, "liberation" is the criterion by which Latinas judge what is right or wrong and is "the essential element of Hispanic women's morality and of all morality."[131]

Lo cotidiano and the specificity of what it evokes about the lives of Latina women is, as Isasi-Díaz uses it, a denunciation both of false universals and of the oppression of Latina women's lives. Just as important, *lo cotidiano* has intellectual content; it is "a way of understanding the divine, what we know about the divine." Isasi-Díaz sees it as a contrast to institutional religions' inclination "to see theology as being about God instead of what we humans know about God. *Lo cotidiano* makes it possible for us to see our theological knowledge as well as all our knowledge as fragmentary, partisan, conjectural, and provisional."[132] She does not reject the past, only "regurgitation of the past." But it is clear to her that "our communities have their own living religious traditions. The religious beliefs and practices of grassroots Latinas are not *ex nihilo*, but rather are rooted in traditions passed on from our ancestors and certainly rooted in Catholic and more recently, in Protestant religious teachings."[133]

Isasi-Díaz presents Latina women as "organic intellectuals" who must be seen as moral agents, capable of reflection on their own lives, on what makes them oppressive, and also on what liberates them from that oppression—not just in society but in the church as well. This is a kind of reflection that is related to action—"praxis" in the contemporary language of theology and theological education: "the insistence that grassroots Latinas do *mujerista* theology and that so doing is a liberative practice indicates that they too are intellectuals."[134] In her work with Latina women, Isasi-Díaz feels the obligation to present the details of their lives as well as the character of their piety and their struggle.

Conclusion

Isasi-Díaz's description of the Latina women she works with as organic intellectuals, whose lives have an epistemological cast and theological content, returns us to Sor Juana Inés de la Cruz and to Barbara Myerhoff's Rachel. Their stories offer testimony about two kinds of religious knowledge that emerge from the obligations, the restrictions, and the opportunities of daily routines and domestic rituals. One kind of knowledge demonstrates the reflections of an educated woman. The other is the knowledge of a tradition that comes from immersion in ritual and other kinds of participation. Each of these women speaks of restrictions in her life. Sor Juana has no public outlet for her learning; Rachel is aware of but has never experienced the study of Torah and rabbinical writings available to Jewish men that might deepen her appreciation of a religious devotion that she describes as immune to doubt; it is a kind of body wisdom about her tradition that does not depend for its integrity upon verbal interpretation. In the religious thought of contemporary American women one encounters over and again efforts to integrate these different kinds of knowledge, to see them as reciprocally illuminating rather than opposed to each other.

The influence of this effort at integration by focusing on the ordinary is visible in American women's religious thought from several different angles. Methodologically, a focus on the ordinary requires attention to the details of specific lives; it requires that religious thought incorporate not only narrative but the kind of detailed narrative one finds in discussions about wheelchairs, arthritis, and whether or not to throw sacred garments in the wash with regular underwear. If God is in the details, so are the clues to the realities of people's lives and what kinds of theology are adequate not just to interpret them but to get at underlying patterns: those that are life-giving and those that need to be discarded or transformed. Response to the details of ordinary life gives theology life and integrity, say women of many different traditions.

Theologically, say women, a focus on the ordinary decreases the tendency of religious traditions to universalize about the meaning of life—or, perhaps better said, to universalize too soon—in ways that obliterate significant differences among members of any one community and across communities as well. In addition, such a focus offers new insights about what sustains a religious community across time or what it is about rituals that keeps them alive rather than "pathological," to use Ronald Grimes's term, or merely boring. Details about ordinary life also open up the category of religious virtues to include those that have been heretofore unacknowledged, like ambivalence or survival.

Epistemologically, an emphasis on the ordinary expands on multiple meanings of religious knowledge. It questions in creative ways whether legitimate knowing must always be expressed in the language of a particular tradition or whether it must be expressed verbally at all. Many scholars claim that the wisdom, knowledge, and commitment of women, and no doubt men as well, can be lost to a tradition, because it is not expressed in specifically theological language. Explorations of this issue, a matter of "discourse," appear in the work of women in several different traditions. In a study of several generations of Episcopalian women and how they expressed their devotion to their traditions, Joanna B. Gillespie discovered that going over the transcripts of interviews with these women revealed almost nothing phrased in traditional theological language: "At first glance, the interview transcripts appear totally mundane because they have no 'church words' such as *salvation* or *discipleship*. On paper, unaccompanied by facial expression and the language of the eyes, the spirituality they express appears to be wordless." Gillespie's challenge and that of her colleagues was "to discern what language—or nonlanguage—they did employ about concerns of the spirit and their inner lives."[135] The point of Gillespie's study and others like it is not to *make* women use the language of the tradition, but to move scholars and religious traditions to do more creative work in learning and acknowledging multiple ordinary ways to talk about or otherwise express religious knowledge. Like Isasi-Díaz, Gillespie and other scholars with similar projects are looking for the extraordinarily ordinary in what women have to say about their daily lives.

In terms of ethical issues, the telling and interpreting of the details of women's lives raises questions about what suffering is to be resisted because it comes from systemically inequitable social arrangements and what is to be accepted as part of life. It raises questions, as well, about what kinds of happiness or success or gain are to be celebrated as part of what one should hope for and work for and what kinds of happiness come too much at the expense of others. Reflecting on a task as ordinary as buying—or not buying—pork chops can move one into the realm of ethical reflection.

Now, by the conclusion of this chapter, it is becoming more apparent how the themes treated in this book work together to shape an interpretive world-view broad enough to elicit women's narratives from many different traditions. There is much overlapping and cross-pollination of themes—more, in fact, than I had expected or intended in the beginning. That will be even more the case in the following chapter, on relationships and their complexities in American women's religious thought. A theology of immanence rests to one extent or another on a view of the inter-connectedness of all aspects of reality. What that claim means for women of particular traditions and how it functions as a catalyst for theological creativity expressed in the language and issues of those traditions is the subject of the next chapter.

5

"Relationship" and Its Complexities

Inhabiting the Cosmic Web

During her 1980 inaugural lecture as professor of Christian ethics at Union Theological Seminary, Beverly Harrison stated that "the most important base-point for a feminist moral theology is the centrality of relationship." Harrison acknowledged that, like anything else, "relationship" can be bought and sold in a capitalist economy, but she was talking about what she calls "the deep sociality of all things. All things cohere in each other. Nothing living is self-contained, if there were such a thing as an unrelated individual, none of us would know it." In this address, Harrison refers to her vision of reality with a term that turns up over and over again in women's religious thought—that of reality as a "vast cosmic web." Her conviction is that "no moral theology that fails to envisage reality in this way will be able to make sense of our lives or our actions today."[1]

Harrison was voicing a theme—"relationship"—that was already a prominent part of American women's religious thought. Five years previously Roman Catholic ethicist Margaret A. Farley had published an essay about relationships and ethics that is still widely quoted.[2] Protestant theologian Letty M. Russell's books on a theology of partnership emerged both before and after Harrison's address.[3] Two years later psychologist Carol Gilligan published *In a Different Voice*, a study that in my experience vies with Valerie Saiving's 1960 essay and Alice Walker's novel *The Color Purple* as among the most frequently cited sources in women's writings about religion. In her book Gilligan established what has become a famous and controversial thesis: that women reflect on ethical issues from within a network of relationships and an ethic of care

120

rather than by reference to abstract principles of justice.[4] In the same year Episcopal theologian Carter Heyward, who is widely known for her theological emphasis on relationships, published *The Redemption of God: A Theology of Mutual Relations*, a work that also offers new interpretations of immanence and transcendence.[5]

"Relationality" is not a specifically theological concept. Nonetheless, its meanings have expanded and made their way into women's religious thought with sufficient frequency to occasion Nancy Frankenberry's comment that "relations" is an idea that should be paid overtime. My interest in this chapter is to demonstrate why and how relationality, with its vision of reality that Harrison and others present as "a vast cosmic web," has been fruitful in women's religious thought. In a broader context, this chapter is concerned with women's ideas about who we are to each other as individuals and communities. The various responses to this question have insights to impart, as well, about American religious pluralism at the end of the twentieth century, a subject I will save until the conclusion of this book.

This is also a chapter in which ambivalence makes another appearance, especially toward the end of the chapter. If emphasizing "relationship" rather than abstract principles of justice in making moral decisions and ethical assessments seems "truer" to women's experiences of the world, it does not necessarily make decisions easier. Usually, in fact, the opposite is the case: decisions become more complex. In fact, this is a chapter about moral complexity as much as it is about relationality. It is an interesting irony, I think, that women's efforts to expand the meanings and implications of relationality have sometimes resulted in near impasses about how much women of different communities can claim in common.

The following quotations give a small sampling of how women from different traditions and scholarly disciplines refer to relationships and relationality. These are the words of women who come from Buddhist, Jewish, Catholic, American Indian (Muscogee), Protestant, eco-feminist, and Goddess communities. Their subject matters vary, and they use the concept of relationality for a variety of reasons, but it is evident that the emphasis on the relational nature of reality in women's religious thought is widespread.

"The politics of Buddhism is the interconnection of all beings" (Kate O'Neill).[6]

"Any understanding of Israel must begin with the recognition that Israel is a community, a people, not a collection of individual selves. The conviction that personhood is shaped, nourished, and sustained in community is a central assumption that Judaism and feminism share" (Judith Plaskow).[7]

"By acknowledging our common ground we are given 'new eyes' with which to see each other: the eyes of love and compassion. Because people otherwise alienated can together praise God, there is in Christianity an authentic basis for the hope that differences or divisions can be overcome in the Spirit of God, giving way to new bonds, new relationships, new joint commitments, new affections, a new future in the reign of God" (Catherine Mowry LaCugna).[8]

"We gather at the shore of all knowledge as peoples who were put
here by a god who wanted relatives.

This god was lonely for touch, and imagined herself as a woman,
with children to suckle, to sing with—to continue the web of the
terrifyingly beautiful cosmos of her womb" (Joy Harjo).[9]

"My contention here is that liberative power is exercised within the context of a relationship, of a give-and-take between dominant and subordinate agent in which not all the giving is done by the dominant and not all the taking by the subordinate but in which both agents give and take" (Ada Maria Isasi-Díaz).[10]

"The ancient church developed a notion of 'original sin,' clothed in mythic structures, that spoke to conditions set in force long before our individual births that nonetheless orient each of us toward sin. The notion carried conviction for more than a millennium of Christian history, but lost ground in the age of Enlightenment. We now live in a world deeply attuned to the extensiveness and intensiveness of relationality" (Marjorie Hewitt Suchocki).[11]

"What is the relation between an imagining subject and the body in the context of religious life and practices?" (Paula M. Cooey).[12]

"Dare I suggest that, with the paradigm of interrelatedness, we approach a degree of ultimacy, and that the reason it eludes articulation and conceptualization is that relational truth—like all truth—is forced to express itself through the inadequate, distorted vehicle of language?" (Mary Grey).[13]

"Ecofeminism stresses relationship, not solely because it has been women's domain, but because it is a more viable ethical framework than autonomy for transforming structures that are environmentally destructive" (Carol J. Adams).[14]

"The moral challenge of our time is whether human beings can find ways to live in greater harmony with each other and all beings in the web of life" (Carol P. Christ).[15]

At its most basic, the concept of relationality holds that we inhabit a universe made up of a network of relationships, an assumption that appears explicitly and implicitly in the quotations above. The vision of the universe as a cosmic web, a network of relationships that assumes the inter-connectedness of all things, is a predictable corollary of theologies of immanence. And, like immanence, this vision has many sources in American religious thought and culture from which women draw. They include traditional religious sources like process (relational) philosophy and theology, the relational theology of H. Richard Niebuhr, the sacramental worldviews of Catholicism and Judaism, American Indian worldviews, and Eastern religions. But there are other sources as well: nineteenth-century metaphysical religions, nuclear physics and ecology, magic, the occult and New Age worldviews. There is no scarcity of sources. We could go back to Plato and Aristotle to seek them out, if we so chose. But all of them must be adapted and interpreted in light of women's particular interests in their traditions and beyond.

The concept of relationality suggests that there are no autonomous entities in the universe—neither individuals nor communities, neither living nor nonliving parts of the universe. What bears on one bears in some way on all. In general, women's critique of traditional religious thought is that most thinkers and systems of thought have proceeded on the basis of another assumption. They have offered tribute to a deity who is remote from a universe that is perceived as more parts than whole, more fragmented than integrated, and more profane than sacred. Like ambivalence, immanence, and the sacredness of the ordinary, relationality provides an ethos as well as a shaping of content to women's religious thought. And like these other concepts, its implications must be worked out, not just proclaimed, if they are to have any substance.

Without further investigation, it would be easy to assume that women's widespread praise of relationality with its connotations of harmony and inter-connectedness fosters agreement among women that requires only minor qualifications for use within particular communities and raises few questions. But that is not the case. The fact of inter-connectedness, no matter how fervently claimed, does not guarantee adequate responses to the questions of what "woman" means in any universal way, who women are to each other, and what women owe each other, not even when they are members of the same community. To say something too general about all women is perceived by many as promoting an essentialist view about women's nature that obscures the distinctive histories, experiences, and insights of women of many different traditions. To refrain from making any claims that go beyond the issues in one's own sometimes very small community does not, it is feared, go very far toward promoting the solidarity of women to bring about widespread cultural changes. In addition, to refrain from making such claims seems to belie the very insistence on relationality that is so much a part of American women's religious thought.

Many earlier generalizations about "women's experience" that were intended to hold together assertions of commonality have since been categorized as falsely universalizing. As more and more women relate the particular experiences of their daily lives, the complexities and difficulties of offering broad-based interpretations about "women" have became only too obvious. Given the various circumstances of women's lives, it appears that it is never—well, hardly ever—possible to speak in terms of all women's experience with authenticity and moral force. "What does the universality of our intentions (should we still share them) have to do with the particularity of our circumstances?" asks religious studies scholar Paula M. Cooey in her study of the body and the religious imagination.[16] Or, as Roman Catholic ethicist Mary E. Hunt puts it, the issue is "how to keep from absolutizing oneself, one's community,

123

and/or one's perspective while at the same time claiming that one has some-thing to say."[17]

The result is that the highly contextual nature of women's religious thought, that is, the emphasis on the distinctive aspects of particular communities, has made it difficult to make universal moral claims on behalf of all women. How, then, to combine women's insistence that the commitment to justice for all is non-negotiable with the equally intense demand that ethical reflection and action must acknowledge all the realities of particular lives and communities, realities that often demand very different forms of justice?[18]

As it turns out, this multi-pronged intellectual dilemma, so widespread in modern and postmodern culture, not just in women's religious thought, has been much more creatively provocative than paralyzing in women's religious thought. But it has fostered a strong sense of the complexities and limitations of most theological and ethical claims by women and about women, and a methodological self-consciousness that sometimes is creative and sometimes gets in the way of forceful, content-filled theological statements. Thus, both the centrality and the complexity of a relational worldview have been stirring the theological imaginations of women in recent years.

Structure of the Chapter

I have divided this chapter into two major sections that illustrate both the crea-tivity and the complexity of women's widespread use of references to relation-ality. The first section offers illustrations of how women of different traditions use an emphasis on relationality to construct new interpretations of major sym-bols of their traditions. These are interpretations that women consider more conducive to the full participation of women and that they see as more crea-tive and compelling understandings of what these symbols mean at the end of the twentieth century. The second section address women's relationships with each other across various boundaries of particularity. In it I explore some of the reasons for women's loss of innocence about the extent to which universal claims can be made about women. I also look at several of the strategies and perspectives women are constructing to make possible more authentically far-reaching claims that do not obscure distinctiveness or eradicate historical re-alities. Complexities notwithstanding, this chapter is about the pervasiveness and versatility of the concept of relationality in American women's religious thought.

What subjects, what issues, do women take up in their own traditions in response to an emphasis on relationality? To illustrate, I have chosen the works of women from several different communities, all of whom have made particu-larly prominent use of relationality in their work but for different reasons. In-terwoven with these examples are many of the issues that religious thinkers, women or men, must contend with at the end of the twentieth century and particularly as they apply to women. I have chosen them, also, for their variety and creativity and because they deal with broad issues in religion and theology that are not exclusive to single communities. Interwoven in them are references to debates over relationships between self and community and the ways different communities are related to each other. There are disagreements about whether there is any "thing" or "presence" in the universe that is not socially and historically constructed, and if not, on what we base our ethical and theological claims. There is conflict over whether women are more oriented toward relationships than men; if so, why, and if not, why does it appear that way? And there is controversy over whether utter certainty about moral issues can ever be attained within a religious community. All of these issues in one way or another have to do with the prominence of relationality as a theme in women's religious thought. I have chosen the following examples for their creativity and for the variety of their sources and approaches.

Relationality and Theological Creativity

THE COMPASSIONATE SELF AND WORLD LOVING IN BUDDHISM

Two Buddhist women, Anne C. Klein and Joanna Macy, use the concept of relationality to interpret two different, major aspects of Buddhism. Klein turns her attention to the compassionate self and what Buddhism and feminism have to say to each other about its development. She places her interpretation within the broader issue of essentialism and cultural determinism. Macy looks at how emphasizing the relational aspects of Buddhism provides perspectives and strategies for responding to ecological and nuclear disaster.[19]

In *Meeting the Great Bliss Queen: Buddhists, Feminists, and the Art of the Self*, Anne C. Klein has set herself a two-fold task. The first is to bring the "profoundly different" worldviews of Tibetan Buddhism and Western feminism into conversation.[20] The conversation itself is designed to pool the wisdom of two partially incommensurate worldviews that have much to teach each other, in Klein's opinion, about the nature of human dignity and the development of the self. The second task is to dissipate what Klein considers the ultimately useless tensions between essentialists, those who espouse the theory that women possess an essentially female nature, and postmodernists, who hold that the self, including gender, is totally the product of social construction.

Here, then, is a rendering, within a Western Buddhist context, of questions that trouble and intrigue us at the end of the twentieth century and that affect women and men across traditions: does there exist anything that can be called a "self," that construct on whose basis much of Western theology and philosophy has been formulated? If there is, how does that self develop morally and how is it related to others? In her work Klein addresses issues that are of major importance in women's religious thought, because they have far-reaching implications for how broadly the very term "woman" can be used.

Klein offers an interpretation of a Western Buddhist feminism that can mediate "the powerful pulls between the experiences of relatedness and autonomy, connection and separateness, that 'essentialism' and 'postmodernism' entail."[21] Whatever their differences, Klein sees both Tibetan Buddhism and Western feminism, which have appeared in the West at approximately the same time, as concerned with fruitful relationships between theory and experience that make a practical difference in the lives of real people. They both, likewise, concentrate on issues of self and identity. And, says Klein, "They also share a radically critical view of the status quo in which they find themselves. For feminists, everyday assumptions about gender and identity are marred by age-old male-based models and agendas. For Buddhists, ordinary (mis)understanding causes us to believe ourselves and others to be enduring in ways that Buddhist analyses find absurd."[22]

"Is it possible to have a compassionate connection to others and still retain a powerful sense of self"?[23] This is the question Klein asks in order to open up a discussion of what kind of reciprocal wisdom might emerge from a comparison of compassion in Buddhism (usually considered male and self-empowering) with relatedness in the West (more often considered female and undermining of the development of an autonomous self).

Klein finds in Tibetan Buddhism's interpretation of compassion a way of integrating the two different kinds of responsibility Carol Gilligan identified in A *Different Voice*, her study of women as moral agents: reciprocity and response. The former is based on an assumption of equality and sameness between oneself and another. The latter is grounded in a sense of obligation to give to another what that particular person seems to need. Gilligan found the latter to be more typically the approach of women. According to Klein, the Buddhist seven-fold and four-fold methods of cultivating compassion can be seen as fostering both categories of relationship, but Buddhist compassion does not require choosing between them: "Rather, it lies with the artful understanding of which criteria facilitate compassionate behavior in specific situations, and with knowing how to embody compassion effectively."[24]

On the other hand, Klein makes it clear that a discussion of relationship in Buddhism is not necessarily the same thing as a discussion of compassion, which in a Buddhist worldview "results less from interpersonal dynamics than from intentional cultivation."[25] She is not simply suggesting that Western feminists trade relatedness for compassion. The Western feminist concept of relatedness has things to teach Buddhism as well. For a Buddhist worldview and practice to be compelling to Western women—and, one assumes, men—it must also cultivate the personal inter-connectedness and telling of stories and sharing of pain that are part of Western ways, particularly women's ways, of developing both selfhood and compassion. Klein says that "[i]n a synthesis of Buddhist and Western feminist sensitivities, and given Western investment in the uniqueness of every individual, the 'getting to know' that is not traditionally emphasized in Buddhist or philosophical literature has an important place."[26]

It is Klein's conviction that adversarial gender polarization related to the question of whether an autonomous self can be compassionate—a polarization that serves neither men nor women well—can be mitigated and understood more dynamically in a Buddhist/feminist synthesis. And this synthesis can contribute, also, to emerging understandings of self in both Buddhism and feminism that need be captive neither to essentialism nor to theories that insist on the totally constructed nature of reality. Buddhism provides the conversation with more nuanced ways of understanding relationships. Feminism provides Buddhism with correctives to traditional Buddhism's inclination to be disengaged from the kind of personal narrative that makes relationship an important feature of self-construction for women in Western religion and society.

The importance of relatedness in Western women's views of the development of self stimulates Klein to articulate both traditional and new meanings for compassion in a Western feminist Buddhism. In so doing she points to what she calls "lacunae" in both. At the same time she makes use of central insights in each to expand the meanings of both relationship and compassion and add depth to their meanings. Thus she is developing "relationship" at two levels: within her tradition and across worldviews that have some common and some very different assumptions. She is using relationality as it is found in both Buddhism and feminism to soften the dichotomy that has developed between essentialists and constructionists in late twentieth-century religion and culture. She contends thereby that the kind of adversarial approach to the issue that has so often brought women's conversations with each other to a standstill need not persist.

Joanna Macy is a social activist with her own particular interests in Buddhist understandings of "self." She is best known for her work in the ecology and peace movements and for "despair work and empowerment"—the intentional bringing forth of repressed feelings of despair about the fate of the earth in order to prevent numbness and paralysis and to motivate action. Macy's despair work came out of an insight from Tantric Buddhism that emerged in response to her own despair about nuclear weapons. She "conceptualized the notion of, rather than countering our despair with hope, to move *through* it. . . . It's what I call 'the Tantric flip.' That if you can move with where the energy is, then you can flip it over."[27]

For many years Macy has worked to integrate the Buddhist notion that there is no abiding individual self with her conviction that we are indeed accountable for taking action in response to the various crises facing the world. "The basic question," she says, "is the connection between what we do and what we are."[28] Or, put another way, does it matter what we do? Macy has found the intellectual and emotional grounding for her work in the early Buddhist teaching of "dependent co-arising," what might be called the Buddhist version of the cosmic web. Macy says that this concept "fills me with a strong sense of connection and mutual responsibility with all beings."[29] She has combined this insight with contemporary systems theory, which, according to Macy, has much in common with the Buddhist claim that we are not helpless victims of either the past or the present—that we live in a world in which all our actions are inter-related and efficacious. Taken together, says Macy, dependent co-arising and systems theory form the basis for a socially activist Buddhism, one that interprets "karma" not in fatalistic and deterministic ways but as "a dynamic process of interdependent factors."[30]

The various ways Macy has lived out her convictions about the interconnectedness of all things are particularly evident in the workshops she offers all over the world. In addition to the despair work and to the creation of "spiritual exercises for social activists," Macy is involved with workshops that summon The Council of All Beings; participants engage in a three-part ritual of mourning, remembering, and speaking for other life-forms. "We meet in Council," says the ritual leader, "because our planet is in trouble. It is fitting now, and it is important, that each of us be heard."[31] There are other workshops that ask participants to speak for past, present and future generations. Being "[i]n league with the beings of the future," Macy calls this exercise, one that asks us "through our moral imagination, to break out of our temporal prison and let longer expanses of time become real to us."[32] The idea came to her in part from her participation in a citizens' lawsuit to stop the Virginia Electric Power Company from unsafe storage of high-level nuclear waste. "Our citizens group lost its suit," says Macy, "but it taught me a lot. It taught me that all the children for centuries to come are my children."[33]

Macy sees herself participating in what she calls the Third Turning of the Wheel, this moment in history that calls for the contributions of Buddhist social activism. In a claim of the kind now very familiar in this book—the thisworldly nature of authentic religious commitment—she says, "Our mission is not to escape from our world, or to fix things by remote control, looking at charts and pushing buttons, but to fall in love with our world. We are made for that, because we co-arise with her—in a dance where we discover ourselves and lose ourselves over and over."[34]

Several years ago Macy was asked by Sandy Boucher, who interviewed her and many other Buddhist women for a book on contemporary feminist Buddhism, whether her identity as a woman had contributed to her ideas about "the great net of being connecting us all." "There's no question," she answered, and went on to cite the importance of Carol Gilligan's work for the way she understands herself and her work.[35] For Macy the pain we feel for the suffering of the world is "natural and healthy," because it demonstrates our inter-connectedness with all that is and our obligation to act on behalf of the whole planet.

COMMUNITY INSIDE AND OUTSIDE JUDAISM

Jewish theologian Judith Plaskow uses the concept of relatedness and community to open up new ways of understanding Judaism. Like Klein, she addresses issues of selfhood and argues that selfhood is not diminished but developed and enhanced by communal relationships: "To develop as a person is to acquire a sense of self in relation to others and to critically appropriate a series of communal heritages."[36] Plaskow emphasizes community as a potential source of liberation rather than constriction. This is wisdom that comes out of women's experiences of the world, as Plaskow sees it, and it is also traditional Jewish wisdom: "Jewish memory is communal memory and centers on community even as it forms and is formed by community."[37]

Plaskow's feminist critique of Judaism is that it has submerged and silenced half of its community: its women members. Plaskow points to several kinds of suffering that women experience as a result: not only exclusion from public participation but also spiritual deprivation. "There is no Jewish way," she says, "to go off into the desert and have an independent relationship to God. Relationship to God is experienced and mediated precisely through the community that maintains women's marginality."[38] If feminist Buddhists look to women's emphasis on the necessity of relatedness in Buddhism to insist upon the importance of community, Plaskow turns in another direction— toward the redefining of her community: "Israel" itself. Plaskow says that the challenge to Judaism comes "not when women as individual Jews demand equal participation in the male tradition, but when women demand equality *as Jewish women*" and do so in a community "that will allow itself to be changed by our difference."[39]

Plaskow's redefinition of Jewish community is multi-layered, because it involves not only Jewish women and men but relationships, also, to the societies in which Jews live. Plaskow makes the case not against difference—men and women, Jews and non-Jews—but against institutionalizing differences in hierarchical relationships, which she sees as a negative part of Jewish history from its beginnings. She finds parallels between the ways women are excluded from full participation within the Jewish community and the various ways Jews have been set apart in the societies they live in.

Particularly interesting is Plaskow's taking on the issue of "chosenness" as a vehicle for finding new ways to think about Jews' relationships to each other, to other traditions, and to the societies in which they live. Plaskow understands "chosenness [as] a complex and evolving idea in Judaism that is by no means always associated with claims to superiority"[40] except by a few, but she is convinced that it would be better to think of Jewish self-identity in terms of "distinctiveness." "Distinctiveness," according to Plaskow, has not so many temptations for the Jewish community to think in terms of hierarchy either within the community, particularly between women and men, or in relationship to other communities. Instead it promotes thinking of relationships in terms of parts and whole, an arrangement that has three advantages: the possibility of retaining the uniqueness of a group that is also part of a larger community; an awareness that "there is no whole without all the pieces;" and a way to avoid defining normative humanity without including groups that appear to be valued less, such as women or non-European Jews.[41]

If Jews give up their identity as the chosen people of God, will they thereby be giving up their identity entirely or losing their relationship with God as it has been defined historically? Plaskow is convinced that this is not the case. "Jewishness," she says, "is a rich and distinctive way of being human, of linking oneself with God and with other people, of finding a pattern within which to live that gives life depth and meaning. That is enough reason to be a Jew," and one that "needs no supernatural vocation."[42] Plaskow extends her concern about Jewish identity and equality of relationships to the state of Israel and elaborates on those relationships, with women and with Palestinians in particular. She expresses the fear that from a feminist perspective "the enduring inequalities of the Jewish community have found new and complex embodiment in the laws and structures of a nation state struggling to secure its existence and survival."[43] Plaskow makes connections between women as Other in the Jewish community and Jews as Other in the broader society. She is convinced that when the relationships between women and men are no longer arranged hierarchically in Judaism there will be new understandings also of how Jews are related to the societies they live in.

ROMAN CATHOLIC WOMEN LIBERATING
CONSCIENCE AND RECLAIMING THE TRINITY

Anne E. Patrick and Catherine Mowry LaCugna are Roman Catholic theologians who likewise choose to open up new meanings of "community." They do so in different ways by bringing the concept of relationality to bear on two major symbols of the tradition—the conscience and the Trinity. Patrick's reinterpretation of conscience is part of her effort to bring an entire new ethos to Roman Catholic moral theology. LaCugna's project is to give renewed life to an ancient Christian doctrine that in her opinion has diminished in vitality and significance over the last several centuries.

In *Liberating Conscience: Feminist Explorations in Catholic Moral Theology*, ethicist and theologian Anne E. Patrick, like Plaskow, takes on the issue of hierarchy and relationships within community. She does so from the angle of Catholic tradition, with its emphasis on the primacy of conscience in matters of morality. Patrick identifies the longing for certainty in moral matters that is so much a part of traditional Catholicism and its hierarchy with the institution's unwillingness to grant women full participation.[44] Because women's moral experience has not been incorporated into discussions of conscience,

women are considered "moral minors." In addition, says Patrick, the magis-
terium (the teaching office) of the church has always exhibited excessive certainty on issues of sexuality and reproduction that have a great impact on
women, even though it has a high tolerance for ambiguity in matters like eco-
nomics and war.[45]

Patrick is making a case for the liberation of conscience from the perspective of a feminist-egalitarian paradigm, one that de-emphasizes control and instead "operates with a sense of power as the energy of proper relatedness. Discipline is still valued, but it is less rigidly understood."[46] In this way of
looking at the moral life, variety of perspective is not only tolerated but valued
as essential. Dissent is perceived as a vitalizing contribution to the community.
Patrick's own position is that debate about moral issues is necessary and healthy
and that "thinkers who responsibly dissent from Vatican positions are supporting the hierarchical teaching authority rather than subverting it. Indeed, such
theologians are helping to prepare the Catholic community for a day when
central church leaders will be more trusting of the Spirit of God present in the
faithful than current Vatican officials appear to be."[47]

Patrick rejects definitions of conscience such as a little voice inside an
individual or "moral radar equipment" and looks at it instead as an aspect of
self that is more akin to "intelligence." "We all have some of it," she says, "but
degrees vary greatly, and even a lot of it is no guarantee we'll always be right."
Patrick's own definition of conscience is a dense one, worked out over time.
She claims it as a "personal moral awareness, experienced in the course of
anticipating future situations and making moral decisions, as well as in the
process of reflecting on one's past decisions and quality of one's character, that
is, the sort of person one is becoming."[48]

Conscience, insists Patrick, is not just a matter of individual responsibility
but "a social phenomenon" developed within a community. It is, in fact, a
matter of relationships, because "the individual is always a self in relation to
others."[49] Communities need to work out together the parameters of the moral
life, and "only time will finally sort out authentic virtue from its counterfeit."[50]

Patrick is not wildly optimistic about how quickly change can be accomplished in the Roman Catholic tradition, particularly because she thinks that
adopting this new, less certain, tolerant-of-diverse-opinions way of approaching
the moral life will require a radical conversion on the part of the institutional
church. For example, in the area of sexuality, the Vatican teaches that there
are "intrinsically evil" actions, which Patrick interprets as partly a strategy pro-
tecting traditional authority. But, she grants, "it also stems from a conviction
that human welfare requires a very clear and very restrictive sexual code."[51]
This, in her opinion, is a claim that requires "honest, extensive research." She
appends to her opinion a list of questions about sexuality that must be answered, such as, "What are the human needs where guidelines for sexual behavior are concerned? Is it possible that these vary over the course of a lifetime?
Could they be different for females and for males? For those whose attraction

is primarily for the same sex and for those attracted primarily to the opposite sex?" Patrick says that to open up questions like these in a tradition that has always claimed full knowledge of God's will in the area of sexuality "requires a profound conversion."[52]

Patrick grounds her hopes for such a conversion and an end to the present impasse between conscience and authority in a theology of immanence, a confidence in the indwelling of the Spirit that not only offsets the legalism and absolutism of traditional Catholicism at its most dogged but also prevents a tumbling of the tradition into either relativism or isolating subjectivism: "The belief that God's Spirit dwells in us grounds our hope that openness to new data and the cautious revision of sexual ethics it requires will not lead to disaster, but simply to a new stage on our pilgrimage through history."[53] For this to be the case there must be new understandings of the relationships between conscience and community, authority and dissent, and women and men.

Catherine Mowry LaCugna uses "relationship" in a very different way to construct new interpretations of the traditional Christian doctrine of the Trinity—the belief that God is made up of three persons, Father, Son, and Holy Spirit, but is nonetheless one God.[54] The Trinity is one of the central doctrines of Christianity, but it has been "defeated," as LaCugna puts it, over the last several centuries, because it has become so entangled in abstruse and esoteric speculations about the inner relationship of the three persons that have little connection with the life of the community. In fact, says LaCugna, "Christianity and Christian theology seem to have functioned quite well, for several centuries, with a doctrine of the Trinity relegated to the margins,"[55] and it is only recently that interest in it has been renewed.

LaCugna's dual goal is to have people think about the Trinity again and to think about it in new ways, because she sees it as "an eminently practical doctrine with far-reaching consequences for Christian life."[56] One of her major tasks is to move trinitarian theology away from concentration on "the Trinity as Father, Son, and Spirit in relation to each other, but intrinsically unrelated to anything or anyone else."[57] LaCugna uses very traditional Christian language to make the case that at its heart the Trinity is about relationships and that God is by nature relational and not remote. "Indeed," she says, "trinitarian theology is par excellence a theology of relationship: God to us, we to God, we to each other."[58]

What does LaCugna's interpretation of the Trinity have to do with women and with feminism? She acknowledges that in the early stages of the contemporary feminist movement many women either rejected the Trinity or ignored it. But, "now some feminist theologians appeal explicitly to trinitarian theology in support of a relational view of human personhood and the values of mutuality, equality, and community."[59] I see it as an interesting irony, in fact, that centuries' worth of discussion concerning the various ways the three male persons of the Trinity are related to each other might now contribute to some rather sophisticated ways of thinking about relationship in general from a feminist perspective.

LaCugna's book has only one section of one chapter that refers directly to feminism and feminist interpretations of the Trinity. On the other hand her entire inquiry is shaped by an effort to overturn theological assumptions about God and the world and the human community that women have seen as detrimental to the equal dignity of women as human beings. It is this claim—that women are fully human—that LaCugna defines as the basic belief of feminism. Part of establishing the equal dignity of women and men requires new definitions of "God" and "person" and an elaboration of what these new definitions have to do with the way we live our lives together. "Persons in communion," a phrase that LaCugna uses over and over again and to which she devotes a lengthy chapter, refers both to God and to the human community. She draws from ancient and contemporary sources to make her case that we are radically relational beings sustained by a radically relational God.[60]

A PROTESTANT RELATIONAL THEOLOGY OF ORIGINAL SIN

Protestant process theologian Marjorie Hewitt Suchocki also assumes the relational nature of reality in order to embark on new understandings for another traditional Christian doctrine, that of original sin—the belief that we are sinful by our very natures, by virtue of being born. Her aim, as with LaCugna's interpretation of the Trinity, is to offer an understanding of original sin that is practical—that is, a teaching that makes more sense in light of contemporary experience and that, in turn, makes sense of contemporary experience. I have already referred to Suchocki's interpretation of original sin in the chapters on immanence and the sacredness of the ordinary.

For the purposes of this chapter, I want to stress Suchocki's insistence that sin is only secondarily directed against God (sin as an offense against God is the traditional Christian definition) and is primarily a "violation of any aspect of creation" and thus a rebellion against creation. In this context, her work provides an apt illustration of yet another way a woman religious thinker makes use of the assumption that reality is by nature relational, dynamic, in constant process. In Suchocki's understanding, "sin" involves not so much the act of one person against another; it is a communal act because of the inter-relatedness of all things. She does not hesitate to say that sin is rebellion against God as well, but that is not the angle she wants to explore in this work.[61]

Much of women's religious thought in the nineteenth and the twentieth centuries has refuted the doctrine of original sin as particularly detrimental to the full humanity of women.[62] Thus it is interesting to investigate how and why Suchocki reinterprets it and, one might say, rehabilitates it, at the end of the twentieth century. For Suchocki, emphasizing the relational nature of sin as violence to any aspect of creation opens up some new ways to understand why we continue to harm one another and the creation. As Suchocki sees it, "the doctrine of original sin must be reappropriated in such a way that it speaks to our condition, and allows us to name our condition."[63]

Suchocki looks at the "structure of sin" from three different angles. One is our tendency to violence as a human race, which she sees as "the ground of sin." Another is the result of "our solidarity with the human race. We are individuals, but we are also participants in an organic whole much greater than ourselves, the human species."[64] The third is our participation in sin through "social inheritance," or in other words, the relationship between social institutions and sin.[65] All these taken together in Suchocki's interpretation "conspire to create conditions for each human individual that are analogous to the ancient concept of original sin."[66]

This sounds like a rather hopeless situation, one that might suggest that we are "undone," as Suchocki puts it. But Suchocki's hopeful response to what she has depicted comes out of the same assumption of an ultimately relational reality as does her understanding of sin. She concludes the book with a discussion of forgiveness as an alternative response to violence that can break the cycle she has described, although she acknowledges forgiveness as "the most difficult of virtues." Here is how Suchocki defines forgiveness: "an action of the will toward the well-being of victim and violator in the fullest possible knowledge of the nature of the violation."[67]

Forgiveness, as Suchocki interprets it, doesn't require the emotions of either love or "accepting violators into one's physical space." Nor does it require forgetting. Sometimes, she acknowledges, these feelings are possible or develop over time, "but forgiveness must not be enmeshed in any essential way to these qualities, as if forgiveness could not be forgiveness without them."[68] What is most important to Suchocki is that forgiveness breaks the cycle of violence. What makes that possible? One reason Suchocki gives is that it redeems the distortion of time whereby past, present, and future are robbed of possibility, because without forgiveness "the horror remains fresh and perennially present." Forgiveness makes possible a new future. Social forgiveness for our guilty participation in institutional sin comes from examining social structures and attempting to transform them. Sin, according to Suchocki, is so pervasive because "in a relational world we are individuals-in-community." And forgiveness is possible for the same reason.

RELATIONSHIP, MORALITY, AND GODDESS RELIGION

Up to this point in my examples of women's use of relationality, I have concentrated primarily on the reinterpretation of religious symbols in communities that have been long established. In Carol P. Christ's *Rebirth of the Goddess: Finding Meaning in Feminist Spirituality*, referred to by some as the first systematic Goddess thealogy, it is possible to see how a thealogian uses relationality in the construction of a new (or ancient, depending on one's perspective on this issue) worldview, since Goddess thealogy is a religious movement in the process of being created.[69]

Although I suggested earlier that "relationality" is not a specifically theological term, that statement requirements some qualification in regard to Goddess religion, which has placed a very pronounced emphasis on the relational nature of reality since its beginnings in the late 1960s. Here, for example, is part of Christ's definition of the vision that undergirds her book's worldview: "The Goddess is the power of intelligent embodied love that is the ground of all being. The earth is the body of the Goddess. All beings are interdependent in the web of life. Nature is intelligent, alive, and aware. As part of nature, human beings are relational, embodied, and interdependent. The basis of ethics is the feeling of deep connection to all people and all beings in the web of life."[70]

The task for those who are creating Goddess religion is not so much to bring a highly transcendent religious worldview down to earth, because "earth" has been its location from the beginning. It is rather to find new understandings with which to respond to those issues of an ultimate nature that are the province of religion and theology. In other words, what will be the building materials for the construction of a new religion? What will constitute the foundational values for the moral life of the community?

Christ sets up a contrast between traditional, particularly monotheistic, religions and Goddess religions in terms of where they seek out grounding for a system of morality. "In Goddess religion," says Christ, "the source of morality is the deep feeling of connection to all people and to all beings in the web of life. We act morally when we live in conscious and responsible awareness of the intrinsic value of each being with whom we share life on earth. When we do so, we embody the love that is the ground of all being."[71] Christ denies that in order to develop an ethical framework, one that relies on "duty" in order to motivate people to form responsible relationships with each other, a religious system needs laws revealed by a deity who exists outside nature and history.

In an earth-based religion like Goddess spirituality, moral behavior must issue from a love of life for its own sake, according to Christ. Moral codes must emerge from nature, but this is possible only if one assumes, as does Christ, that nature is intelligent and loving rather than "brutal and blind." Christ's optimistic view of nature, however, does not tempt her to hope that total justice is possible. If morality is grounded in natural values, which, finally, are finite, then, "This means that our ethical decision making will always occur within the context of the ambiguities of finite life."[72] Admitting that both our intelligence and our morality are limited, Christ acknowledges, is "deeply sobering," but "liberating" as well, because the moral life in a nature-based system demands not perfection but persistence: "If we value our feelings of deep connection, if we love life on its own account and through others, and if we find the courage to act together on what we know, then maybe, just maybe, we can build a better future for ourselves, our children, and all the other children of earth."[73]

Throughout *Rebirth of the Goddess* Christ makes extensive use of two terms that she borrows from anthropology, particularly the work of Clifford Geertz: "mythos," meaning a religion's shared collection of symbols and rituals that indicate what is to be valued, and "ethos," the religion's way of life expressed through activities, customs, and institutions. In Goddess religion both mythos and ethos value relationality as an ultimate good and the assumption on which the entire worldview rests.

WOMEN CLERGY SUPPORTING EACH
OTHER IN ONGOING RELATIONSHIP

A group of clergywomen and their ongoing relationship with one another provide the final example of how relationality motivates new perspectives in women's religious thought. In *Holy Women, Wholly Women* anthropologist Elaine Lawless interprets the lives of ten women from different denominations who participate in a women's ministerial association in a Midwestern state.[74] It was during her previous work with Pentecostal women preachers that Lawless encountered an occasional clergywoman from a mainline denomination and knew that some day she wanted to compare the lives and ministries of these two different groups of women.

Lawless's entire study can be described as an exercise in the analysis of relationships, but there are three aspects of her work that I particularly want to emphasize. First, there is Lawless's own relationship to the women she studied and the method she refers to as "reciprocal ethnography." Second, there is the clergywomen's initial omission of references to personal, particularly family, relationships from their life stories. Third, there is the sameness with which women with very different life stories interpreted their "call" to ministry as coming through relationships with other people.

Reciprocity and collaboration made up the dynamics of what Lawless sought by way of method and process as she worked with the ten clergywomen. She met with them, listened to their individual stories, and attended regular lunch meetings where these women talked about their lives, their ministries, and their preaching. In a sense she wrote her book "with them," because they responded to drafts of her book as she was writing it. As Lawless did her anthropological work, she was looking for a kind of give and take, "a sharing and building knowledge based on dialogue and shared/examined/re-examined knowledge."[75] She saw this method as not only reciprocal but feminist in its focus on how women come to know what they know. Lawless expected to be changed by her relationship with these women and what she calls their never-ending story, and she was. This is the concluding sentence of her book: "Women like these are changing the world, they are changing the perimeters and expectations of ministry; they are changing their denominations; they changed me."[76]

On the other hand, Lawless's book is not simply a chorus of praise for "relationship," since one of her discoveries was the difficulty professional women experience when they attempt to tell their life stories and discover that "their lives and their ministries segment, and fragment, their narrated experiences."[77] Upon first reading transcripts of the stories they had told Lawless, the ten women hated them: "They felt uncomfortable about their stories because they recognized the stories as only skeletal representations of their actual lives. They regretted that they had deleted important figures in their lives from their stories; they were frustrated that they did not communicate what they believed to be the meaning of what they did relate; they were dismayed by the 'professional image' that prevailed, one that, in the end, they felt did not capture them as people at all."[78] Lawless interpreted their omission of personal relationships as a sign of their own ambivalence and worries about their personal identities and their status in their various denominations. In conversations about their life stories, the clergywomen "revealed that being 'relational' was, in fact, a terribly important part of the way they perceived themselves; they were also explaining that to be 'relational' was obviously perceived by others as being 'female,' and carried, then, a less than serious value."[79] The women confessed to each other that in their desire to be valued as professional women they had learned to tell their stories in ways that de-emphasized the relationships that were central in their lives—and to feel ambivalent about those parts of their lives as well.

Yet, however much these clergywomen felt they had truncated the relational emphasis in their life stories in some respects, in another way their very choice of career had depended upon them. As they talked about their "call" to ministry, defined as the conviction that this was what God wanted them to do, they did not report "voices in the night" or dramatic revelations. For most the choice to enter ordained ministry developed over a long period of time and was often influenced by someone they had known when they were young. "What is important in these stories," says Lawless, "is that they reveal that "the 'call from God' came through their connection with and support from *other people*."[80] This is in contrast to most traditional call-to-ministry stories as based on individual and often lonely decisions. Lawless says that she hears echoes in the women's stories of Gilligan's thesis about the relational orientation of women and that the subjects of her study were telling stories that stemmed from their experiences *as women*.

A final reference to Lawless's study provides a transition to the next section of the chapter about women's relationships with each other across religious and social boundaries. Lawless described the clergywomen she studied as finding ways to talk with each other across denominational boundaries. Their conversation gave rise to a group song without abandoning their individual voices. From Lawless's perspective, they spoke from their experience, not from within the authorities of their traditions: "They had not relied in these discussions of their religious beliefs on the codified treatises of the United Methodist, Disciples of Christ, or Episcopal churches. They have spoken from the heart; they have spoken from their own personal experiences with themselves, with their families, with each other, and with God. They know what they know based on what they have experienced."[81] Based on my own reading of Lawless's subjects, I would say that they did indeed speak as women whose hearts, experiences, and responses had been formed by their own traditions. But they chose to speak collaboratively, pooling their insights, rather than competing. My point is not to emphasize a disagreement with Lawless, even though we see this matter somewhat differently. It is, rather, to emphasize again one of the ongoing subtexts of this study: that women are not religious in general, but religious in particular. How to be religious in particular and still create and maintain relationships with women of other traditions is the subject of the next section.

The Challenges of Relationality

RELATIONSHIPS AND WOMEN'S LOSS
OF INNOCENCE: A BRIEF HISTORY

There have been enough acrimonious exchanges among women of different communities in the last twenty years to shake the confidence of those who wish to cite commonalities in women's experiences of their lives. There is no longer a sense that any one group can speak for all communities of women, or even that women in the same community with different perceptions about issues of gender will be able to understand each other, much less stand together. There is no assurance that the anger women often express will not be directed at each other as much as it is at male dominance and systemic oppression. The inter-connectedness of all things does not necessarily mean the harmony of all things.

There is now in women's religious thought a compendium of stories about women calling upon each other to recognize and repent of serious limitations in their visions of commonality. Among the most famous are Audre Lord's criticism of Mary Daly for ignoring the particular oppression of black women, Delores Williams's admonishing of Rosemary Radford Ruether for failing to take into account issues of class and race in some of her work, and Judith Plaskow's and Annette Daum's criticism of Christian feminists for denigrating Judaism in order to emphasize the liberating power of Christianity.[82] Nor is it only recent history that has raised problems for how much black and white women or Jewish and Christian women can say or do together. Another disillusionment about the possibility of women's solidarity across racial lines came from Barbara Andolsen's research about how nineteenth-century white suffragists exploited white male fears of black male enfranchisement in order to make a better case for white male support, particularly southern, of women's suffrage.[83]

It is typical to find in the religious writings of women acknowledgments that they are acutely aware that their work is both undertaken and received within a network of multiple relationships. As one example, here is Delores

Williams asking in the introduction to her womanist theology how to take into account the need to maintain relationships within and without the black community and address issues of race, class, and gender: "How do I shape a theology that is at once committed to black women's issues and life-struggles and simultaneously addresses the black community's historic struggle to survive and develop a positive productive quality of life in the face of death? How do I design theological language and devise theological methods that not only speak in the academy but also speak to African-American women and the African-American community in a language they can understand? How does my black female theological voice join the chorus of nonblack women's voices and male voices in theology without compromising black women's faith? How do we black female theologians speak with *all* our strength when some white female and some black male scholars work together to crowd out our voices or take control of our words?"[84]

Race is not the only issue that requires thoughtful consideration of a community's internal and external relationships. In *Like Bread on the Seder Plate: Jewish Lesbians and the Transformation of Tradition*, Reconstructionist rabbi Rebecca Alpert looks at how lesbians are making their presence known and felt in the Jewish community. She offers suggestions for "reinterpreting and transforming Jewish texts from a uniquely lesbian Jewish perspective."[85] In the concluding chapter Alpert mentions thirteen other groups of Jews to whom she sees the concerns of lesbian Jews related in terms of coalition building. They are heterosexual feminists, gay Jewish men, heterosexual intermarried couples, bisexual Jews, transgendered Jews, those who can't or don't wish to raise children, single heterosexual Jews, other Jews "who have been uncomfortable with traditional prayer and observance," Jews "who find the Torah both fascinating and alienating," other liberal Jews who are looking for "a way to create a Jewish life that is not based on halakhic (legal) precedent but is driven by a Jewish ethics that relies on values," progressive Jewish educators, "scholars of women's history, mysticism, and Mizrachi Jewish communities," and "Jews who are discouraged by the values of some in the Jewish community who care only if something is 'good for the Jews.' "[86] Like Williams, she is aware of the multiple relationships she must take into account if her work is to be effective. If Alpert had chosen to do so, she might well have added many other categories of people both in and beyond the Jewish community for whom her work has implications, even if they might not all be seen by her as coalition builders.

Crossing traditions and communities brings another set of complexities. In *Anti-Judaism in Feminist Religious Writings*, Katharina von Kellenbach describes her journeying "in and between communities which are torn apart by mistrust, agony, fear, guilt and suspicion. The Jewish and German Jewish and Christian, feminist theological and Jewish-Christian dialogue communities each speak in their own specific languages." Von Kellenbach inhabits them all, tries to assimilate all their languages and create dialogue among them. Further, she says, "I am also involved in a passionate struggle against antisemitic sentiments lurking behind each of these identities."[87]

Sometimes the sacred text that is meant to bind women of one tradition together is seen so variously by different members of a community that it keeps them apart instead. In her work on women's issues for the World Council of Churches, Lutheran theologian Constance F. Parvey participated in an "explosive study group" on the New Testament story of Martha and Mary in which women used the same text to affirm new roles as biblical interpreters but also older traditional, domestic roles. At another international consultation on women's experience and the authority of the Scriptures, women from Latin America, Africa, and Asia reminded North American women that "although the Bible creates problems for them as women, they would not let go of the authority of scripture because scripture also serves them as a significant transcultural critique of sexism."[88]

At other times it is the absence of a common culture that keeps women apart. In *Encountering God: A Spiritual Journey from Bozeman to Banaras*, a book she calls "a theology with people in it," world religions scholar Diana Eck tells the story of a conference on women, religion, and social change held at Harvard in 1983. As women from several continents spoke of their concerns for justice, two women from Japan who were obviously becoming more and more frustrated, finally asked, "What do you really mean by 'justice'? Why does everything come back again to 'justice'?"[89] Eck says she was "dumbfounded" by their questions and finally asked the Japanese women their word for "justice." When that question was not helpful, she continued to press and ended up asking, "What would right relations be called?" After conferring, the women decided that it would be something like what the other women thought of as "harmony." Eck says that was the beginning of a revealing discussion, one that needed to acknowledge significant differences in values among the assembled women: "Is justice harmony? Is harmony justice? What do we mean by these words? What might the Japanese mean? What if justice produces no harmony? And what if harmony produces no justice? Our very criteria of value are at stake here."[90]

Add to these few examples all the theological, social, cultural, and methodological complexities, all the demographic variables of age, ability, region, economic status, and education that shape the daily lives of women, and it begins to look as though women cannot say much about anything that matters beyond their own communities. The list of binary oppositions women have discovered in their efforts to make claims about women in general seems endless: women of color and white women, Jew and Christian, lesbian and heterosexual, evangelical and liberal, young and old, disabled and able-bodied, Goddess feminists and members of established religious communities; essentialists and constructionists.

At one level the articulation of these oppositions has elicited multiple stories from many different communities; at another it has shaped impasse-oriented scripts of denial, accusation, and confession that have made it difficult for women to make strong claims about their relationships to each other.[91] And yet women recount experiences that keep the vision of interrelatedness alive, some of them grounded in ecumenical work and inter-faith dialogue.[92] Both the negative experiences and the positive efforts are part of women's coming to terms with what it means to live in a religiously plural culture, wherein the efforts of one community of women are necessarily noticed by, used, or criticized by the women of other communities. Like their ambivalence toward their traditions, women's acute awareness that they do their theological work in a plural culture has been a catalyst to creativity.

Women are involved in creating ideas and strategies that make possible claims of commonality among women of many different communities that at the same time take differences into account. There are two strategies that I want particularly to look at in this section of the chapter. The first deals with "bodies" and how women from three different traditions with varying issues at stake find ways to situate the human body as an anchor for establishing relationships among multiple communities—and how one woman says that it is "bodies," perceived as separate entities, that keep us apart. The second is concerned with "discourse," the distinctive languages that shape and are shaped by interpretive communities, and several ways that granting the legitimacy of different discourses expands the possibilities for unlikely relationships. I have chosen them, because, with one exception, they demonstrate efforts to establish bonds of commonality that do not require the fostering of universalizing beliefs; rather, in both cases they require a willingness to respond with compassion to the other.

BODIES: UNIVERSAL AND PARTICULAR

Contemporary women's religious thought about bodies and embodiment has become more complex since the early days of this feminist movement, when it seemed a sufficient transvaluation of cultural norms simply to declare women's bodies and all their functions and fluids, shapes and colors, "good." In the intervening years gendered bodies have been problematized, deconstructed, reconstructed, and even "disappeared" in some of the more esoteric forms of postmodern discourse. Now some theological approaches to human bodies are emerging that interpret them as the site and sign of our common humanity. Bodies, as it turns out, are the perfect vehicles to fill two supposedly opposing categories: the universal—everybody has one—and the particular—there are no two alike.

In her book *Religious Imagination and the Body*, religious studies scholar and Protestant theologian Paula M. Cooey explores the question of what constitutes legitimate knowledge in a culture. In her study of feminist theologian Nelle Morton, Brazilian political activist Alicia Partnoy, and Mexican painter Frida Kahlo, Cooey looks upon the female body and its capacity for pleasure and pain as a metaphor for alternative knowledge. Her broader task, as she

141

describes it, is to raise "over and over again the question of the relation between religious imagination and the body."[93] By making this question so central, Cooey places her work in the contemporary discussion about gender, bodies, and knowledge and how all three are related to religious imagining and constructing. She explicitly rejects two different kinds of theories related to them: "those that reduce gender differences to the body and [those] that tend to claim that the body is so socially construed that it is irrelevant to theories of knowledge."[94] The broadest framework of all to which she applies her work is that of relationships, particularly the relationships between particularity and universality in the matter of religious symbols and "the relations of the many communities, religious and academic, which each thinker represents to one another."[95]

Cooey's is a dense, often abstract, and closely argued project that is certainly intellectually compelling. She is talking about a difficult subject: what kind of epistemological authority does "the body" have—and, further, what is "the status of the female body as an alternative to culturally accepted modes of knowing"?[96] But her work is also emotionally moving due to her descriptions of the pain experienced by all three of her subjects and her speculations about what pain—or pleasure—has to do with the religious imagination—what it has to do with how we know and what we know. Here, for example, is what she has to say about Alicia Partnoy's torture: "Through a macabre mimicry of educational processes, she is being taught at the time of her incarceration that there is no order outside the arbitrary exercise of her captors to break her down. The primary pedagogical resource is her body, turned as weapon upon her."[97]

What interests me most about Cooey's work is her contention that its most basic goal is justice. Her study of "body," gender, and the religious imagination is not directed only toward more precise formulations. Rather, she says, "the ultimate epistemological issue is justice itself."[98] She sees her emphasis on the body as furthering the goal of justice because human bodies are the site of both particularity and common humanity. Our bodies and their sentient knowledge relate us to each other, Cooey says: "Although it provides no single all-purpose solution, the body, in all its particularity and in its ambiguity as artifact in relation to sentience, serves nevertheless as one common condition that relates us to all other sentience, a condition that further stands as an ethical criterion by which to assess the significance of our work, one from which we should not detour."[99]

Roman Catholic ethicist Lisa Sowle Cahill uses the reality that we are related as bodies for a different project from Cooey's, one that requires, she says "a modest defense of moral objectivity."[100] Cahill finds grounding in Roman Catholic tradition for "the ideal unity of sexual expression, sexual pleasure, commitment of partners, and shared parenthood [that] can contribute to a more complete Christian ethic of sex as an embodied and social reality."[101] But she acknowledges as well that, however much the tradition offers, "[i]ts lack of demonstrated commitment to the equality and well-being of women worldwide remains the greatest liability of official Roman Catholicism's message on sex."[102] One of Cahill's major criticisms of institutional Catholicism's teachings on sexuality is, in fact, that they ignore personal, family, and social relationships and concentrate too much on "the morality of individual acts."[103]

Cahill is often talking about much the same epistemological and ethical issues that concern Cooey, even though her specific task is very different—that of articulating a feminist ethic of sexuality. Like Cooey, Cahill is unwilling to say that everything in human experience, including bodies, is socially constructed. As Cahill sees it, "no consistent feminist critique can maintain that practical good and evil in matters of sex and gender are culturally constructed to their very roots and in value utterly relative to social approbation."[104] But she is more than willing to acknowledge that sexual identity, mores, and gender roles are always historically and culturally shaped and therefore revisable. If Cooey is looking for epistemological grounding in bodily sentience that can promote common efforts across communities for the sake of justice, Cahill is seeking on feminist grounds moral norms that are consistent and persistent across cultures. Otherwise, she says, social change can be based only on "the acquisition of enough power to shove aside those who formerly monopolized it."[105] She is also looking for ways to articulate the bases on which human flourishing is possible in terms of sexuality.

What do bodies have to do with the search for moral norms that might relate cross-cultural communities? Human bodies have certain common physical and social requirements for flourishing, however various these may be and however ambiguous embodied life may be. For Cahill, "the body" functions as a base point for moral reflection and social action: "If socialization is always culturally various, human existence in the body provides at least a base point for communication, empathy, and critical assessment of the relationships and institutions which mediate experiences of maleness, femaleness, and sexuality."[106] However much women have suffered, according to Cahill, because of objectification and commodification of women's bodies, women will suffer more if we give up all efforts to formulate moral foundations that sound familiar and appealing across cultural and moral traditions. Cahill chooses to do that work within the Roman Catholic tradition with its history of reflection on "natural law," which holds that however many particularities of culture and history there are, human experience and reason can come up with at least some modest consensus about human beings' moral obligations to each other.[107]

Cahill is concerned in her study with broad categories. Frida Kerner Furman takes on a more specific project and looks at the relationships between aging bodies, psyche, and self-worth among a group of elderly, mostly Jewish, women who frequent a fictionally named Julie's International Salon in Chicago. This is a study Furman has conducted in order "to explore the experience of aging and the meaning of old age through its literal embodiment; that is, my aim is to understand women's experience of old age in relationship to their bodies."[108] Furman wants as well to "deconstruct the ways in which the female aging body encodes cultural values, social relations, and patterns of domination and subordination." But she also wishes to identify ethical elements of aging, and she joins Cooey and Cahill in the territory of universal and particular bodies when she sees these two categories "both as internal, individual processes and as socio-cultural constructs."[109]

Furman describes physically many of the women she meets during the time of her participant observation and informal interviewing. She lets us hear their conversations as well. We hear these women talk about physical decline, the diminishing of joy, the loss of beauty, and the fact they have not by any means lost the desire to be attractive. That is why they frequent Julie's. Some of the women are accepting; others are angry, resentful, and fearful. Furman writes of the body as a means of self-presentation and the fact that "just about everyone I ever talk to at Julie's International Salon takes it as a given that looking old is bad, looking young is good."[110] Many of the women report to Furman that they feel younger inside or that they do not see their real selves in the image the mirror offers them.

Furman tells an especially poignant story about seventy-seven-year-old Evelyn looking at a Polaroid photo Furman has just taken of her: "Her response is dramatic and astonishing. . . . I am ill-prepared for it. 'Oh, God, I could cry!' she whimpers. 'I look like a birth defect. Oh, God! I don't want to see it. . . . Oh, God, I'm never going out of the house again. How could I look so . . . I got to look like an animal, like a beast. . . . I can't stand to look at myself I look so ugly! You cannot imagine what it feels like to look so ugly, so grotesque. How could that be me?'" Even more poignant is the question Furman asks about Evelyn's reaction: "There is clearly some distortion going on here. I do not see what she sees. But what kind of moral order does Evelyn inhabit that causes her this kind of suffering?"[111]

In the process of studying these elderly women, Furman finds that she has changed her mind about how to interpret their struggles with the bodily manifestations of aging: "When I first began hearing women's claims that they felt young inside, I thought these claims revealed personal defensiveness, denial, or coyness."[112] Now she sees their interpretations more positively, as both resistance and an effort to maintain a continuity in self-identity. In Furman's change of mind and heart, it is possible to hear echoes of exactly what Cooey and Cahill are talking about when they speak of "the body" and its vulnerabilities and strengths as a source of alternative knowledge about women's lives. Differing approaches to the body in women's religious thought are serving to suggest knowledge that can be acted upon of a common humanity, an interconnectedness of all bodies and thus an empathy and compassion that can be elicited across cultural and religious differences. It is a knowledge based on sentience, women say, that has implications for learning better who we are to each other and increasing the possibility that people across communities can act together to make social changes.

I do not want to leave the subject of bodies and relationality without acknowledging that there are also religious worldviews espoused by women that see too much emphasis on "embodiedness" as a bar to the fullness of human community. This is particularly true among the metaphysical religions, whose stance on spirit as more ultimately real than matter, as indicated in Chapter 3, is also a departure from what the majority of women in this study hold to be true. In *A Return to Love*, Marianne Williamson has many positive things to say about the body: that it offers a means of communication, that it is an instrument, a "holy expression" of loving purpose, "an important classroom."[113] But, in keeping with the metaphysical traditions' worldview, she says, also, that "[o]ur real identity lies not in our body, but in our mind. . . . Neither is another person's body who they are, either. The body is an illusionary wall that appears to separate us, the ego's chief device in trying to convince us that we are separate from each other and separate from God."[114]

The broader question Williamson is addressing is that of self-in-relation, which, in one form or another, is one of the major issues of this chapter. Finally, says Williamson, we are not separate bodyselves; we are one: "If you go deeply enough into your mind, and deeply enough into mine, we have the *same mind* . . . at our core, we are not just identical, but actually the same being. There's only one of us here."[115] It would be difficult to get farther away than Williamson from some of the anti-essentialist, anti-universalizing claims about bodies that are prominent across traditions in much of contemporary women's thought. But it is important, I am convinced, to give some idea of the wide range of religious worldviews that support women's claims of who we are to each other and the importance of relationality.

DIFFERENT DISCOURSES AND THE POSSIBILITY OF COMMON BONDS

Another strategy women are exploring for fostering relationship is the investigation of different communities of discourse and the attempt by scholars to understand the women of these communities on their own terms. At its simplest, "discourse" refers to modes of speaking or writing that characterize the linguistic forms and interpretations of particular communities. In its more complex forms, "discourse," serves as a code word for post-structuralist theories of language and interpretation that make certain claims about the relationship between language and reality: namely, that discourse constructs reality rather than represents or somehow unveils it. Whether in its simpler or more complex forms, women use discourse analysis to build relationships intended to contribute to the wider well-being of women. Sometimes these relationships take the form of actual coalitions; in other cases the goal is a better understanding of another community at a more theoretical level.

In *Changing the Subject: Women's Discourses and Feminist Theology*, Mary McClintock Fulkerson uses the highly theoretical tools of discourse theory to conduct an inter-textual analysis of "three resisting regimes found in the practices of women whose faith performances are as diverse as they are graciously productive."[116] The three regimes are a small group of Pentecostal mountain women; Presbyterian Women, an organization of the Presbyterian Church (U.S.A.) made up of mostly white middle-class homemakers; and several Christian feminist theologians, particularly Mary Daly and Rosemary Radford Ruether.

Fulkerson wants to construct a feminist liberation epistemology and a feminist theology of difference that will be more authentically inclusive than appeals to "women's experience." Fulkerson is a Protestant feminist theologian who says that the theological commitments she invokes in her interpretation of theories and practices are her own: "My commitments come from a Christian reading of creation, its God-dependence, violations of that dependence in socially displayed forms of domination, and a view of redemption appropriate to the structures of fallibility."[117]

Discourse analysis, according to Fulkerson, helps to reveal how women whose religious practices are not feminist as defined by feminist theology manifest various kinds of resistance to gender-based oppression. She asks in the case of Presbyterian Women, "What does resistance look like in a community of women on record more than once as denying that it wants independence from the male half of the church? What possible feminist registers can be found in a group that has to be implored by male leaders to make its opinions known when women's ordination is up for consideration by the ecclesiastical body?"[118] What she concludes by analyzing their discourse is that Presbyterian Women's "transgressions" of the constraints upon them are very real and available to those who know how to see them. Of Pentecostal women, who are not feminists if that designation requires espousing feminist ideas, Fulkerson says, "The practices of Pentecostal women are manifested in a real contradictory discourse: the refusal to claim a will, an expertise, a forwardness, precisely along with the gaining of a place, a presence, an authority."[119]

Fulkerson is not trying to turn Presbyterian Women and Pentecostal women into feminists. Her contention is that feminist theology's blindness to signs of resistance to gender oppression that are not expressed in the "right discourse" has limited its capacity to make connections with multiple communities of women. For Fulkerson, this failure has obstructed the possibility of building relationships among communities of women that appear at first to be disconnected from each other. She does not intend to base the possibility of new connections, new relationships, on collapsing the identities of various "others." She calls, instead, for feminist theologies of "affinity" rather than "identity." "Affinity," she says, "acknowledges love's inability to know the other." Fulkerson says that this presently is "the best we can hope for in developing feminist theology toward the respect for all subjects now defined as women and support of the end of dominations that texture their lives."[120]

In *Mama Lola: A Vodou Priestess in Brooklyn*, anthropologist Karen

McCarthy Brown presents an intricate study of multiple voices and relationships, not the least of which is the friendship between herself and Alourdes, the Haitian woman who is the subject of her study. She confesses that "[i]t was neither an easy nor a direct path that brought me to such familiarity."[121] Unlike Fulkerson, who is not very optimistic about the extent to which different communities of women can finally come to know each other, at least at the level of discourse, Brown says, "I have thought many times that academics have overemphasized those things that separate individuals and cultures from one another."[122]

In her study of Alourdes, her family and community and the Vodou she practices, Brown uses the strategy of differing discourses to "develop a style of narrative analysis in which the flow of the text is determined by story lines that from time to time evoke an analytic voice," a voice that speaks in asides.[123] The multiple voices Brown chooses to interrelate and use are those of Alourdes and the stories she tells; Brown's own scholarly voice; another voice that is also Brown's but one that "risks a more intimate and whole self-revelation"; and "perhaps the voice of Gede."[124] Gede, or St. Gerard, is the Vodou saint of the dead, a trickster, master of the cemetery, guardian of sexuality, protector of small children, and one of the spirits who frequently possesses Alourdes.

Brown does more than study and write in plural discourses. She spends time with Alourdes and her family, travels with her to Jamaica and Haiti, and eventually chooses to be initiated into Vodou: "I am now," she says, "one of the 'little leaves' (ti-fey) on Alourdes's Vodou family tree, and she introduces me as her 'daughter.'"[125] The process of friendship and initiation prompted a change in the way Brown viewed her professional work, as she found herself unable to maintain her detached observer status. She describes herself as knowing that there were both gains and risks at stake in this transition. As a scholar she stood to gain a greater depth of understanding about Vodou, and that turned out to be the case. She also knew that she risked "losing the important distinction between Vodou interacting with the life of a Haitian and Vodou interacting with my own very different blend of experience, memory, dream, and fantasy. My experiences with Vodou are and are not like those of Haitians."[126]

Finally, there was no "pure" discourse available to Brown to convey accounts of Alourdes and Vodou: neither that of the objective scholar nor that of a practitioner of Vodou unaware of the theoretical underpinnings of the anthropological work she was doing. Her choice was to write in the multiple voices described above and thus to create something new that came from the mixing of cultures: "The stories I tell about these experiences," she said, "have authority only in the territory between cultures."[127] Brown suggests at the very conclusion of Mama Lola that Alourdes, too, is creating something new in her relationship with the spirits who possess her. At a birthday party for Papa Gede, whom she describes as "unrelievedly male," Brown witnessed the brief appearance of "Gedelia," a feminine manifestation of Gede. Brown has not experienced her presence since, but she saw Gedelia's name written on a bus in Haiti and suspects "that Alourdes is not alone in recognizing the need for her."[128]

From the perspectives of their different disciplines, theology and anthropology, Fulkerson and Brown look for ways to create bonds across cultures by taking seriously the discourses and practices of communities to which they do not belong. Cognizant of multiple barriers to that enterprise and the complexity of the relationships they are undertaking, they proceed nonetheless.

In their emphasis on relationality we find women of different traditions taking positions that reflect an acute self-consciousness of all that stands in the way of proceeding together on behalf of women, men, and the world. But their conviction is that making claims for the common good and acting on them must go ahead. Lisa Cahill suggests, for example, about her own discipline, Christian social ethics, that "at the level of experientially recognized and practically important needs, social ethics proceeds on the assumption of a shared humanity and at least a fundamentally shared moral vision, whether or not the philosophical warrants for that assumption are clearly in place."[129] It is meeting practical needs, Cahill is convinced, responding to suffering bodies and communities, that will go a long way toward helping people of different traditions to recall what they hold in common about the meaning of a just society.

Rebecca Alpert, who speaks from the particular perspective of a Jewish lesbian, insists that "we cannot make a choice between accepting ourselves, caring for our circle of loved ones, and doing justice in the world. These efforts must be woven into one framework." What picture of a just society do "human beings who are Jewish lesbians" paint? A very general one, as it turns out, that does not refer to sexual orientation. A just society, according to Alpert, is one in which all people have enough to eat and a place to live, "health care, safety, education, and work," moral autonomy, and the opportunity to live on a planet without war.[130] This is a vision based on very general goals that are not attached to a particular religious worldview. But Alpert's contribution to its attainment will come, she says, from her willingness as a Jewish lesbian to be visible in her own community: "This is the beginning of justice. For only if we speak about who we are can we create the opportunity for justice for ourselves."[131] The just society for all, as Alpert sees it, is related to and comes from the particular contributions of the many.

Conclusion

If relationality is a concept that works overtime in women's religious thought, it is because it is moving women's religious thought in so many different directions. Explorations into ways women are opening up various meanings of "relationality" reveals quickly that its fruitfulness goes far beyond claims and speculations about whether women are more relational than men.[132] In fact, that is a subject I have mostly avoided in this chapter. Asking "who are we to each other and how do we talk about these things and act on what we discover" has motivated women to take on more than merely the subject of relationships between women and men. Grounded in the critique of women's exclusion from full participation in religion and society, an emphasis on relationality has moved women to take on broader but interconnected concerns such as the vitality of their traditions' symbols and issues of religious pluralism and social justice. Although taken for granted as basic to the character of reality, inter-relatedness is not construed as simply a good upon which there need be no reflection. It has become, instead, a category of exploration. "Relationality" is not necessarily "right relation." As Marjorie Suchocki points out in her interpretation of original sin, the inter-relatedness of all can be as much a source of evil as of good.

The emphasis on relationality in women's religious thought is also a part of the ongoing American conversation about the one and the many, the parts and the whole. In a very short period of time women have moved away from regarding all women together as One. The "many" remain, but the idea of the One has given way to the more dynamic image of the whole that is a cosmic web of relationships. In women's religious thought this "whole" is understood as a reality out of which we live, but it is also depicted as a vision to be achieved. In the struggle to know whether to exercise theological creativity on behalf of the parts—that is, one's own community—or on behalf of the elusive and undefined whole, women find themselves at an in-between time, needing to go in many directions at once. Because women pledge their theological creativity to the cause of greater justice in the world, the questions of the one and the many, the parts and the whole, must go beyond aesthetic or linguistic considerations and take into account matters of ethics and morality as well. Much of women's religious thought demonstrates the desire and the effort to keep theology and ethics together and to make use of the benefits of the "linguistic turn" in religion and philosophy without losing sight of the goal of social transformation. Anne E. Patrick speaks of linguistics, in fact, as both "temptation and resource": "Whenever the linguistic turn leads to an obsession with language that is detached from the questions and struggles of ordinary life, there is danger of distraction and trivialization."[133]

Women of many traditions have discovered that to claim the inter-relatedness of all things is to compel participation in discussions of the theological and social issues that get in the way of constructing vital religious traditions and a just society. Women have found "relationality," as a religious idea with implied but not specific religious content, to have great evocative power and versatility; it functions to offer critique of existing symbols and systems and, in turn, to stir the creation of new constructions. The task of constructing just and fruitful relationships has led women, also, to turn to the concept of healing as one that conveys one of the particular intents of women's theological creativity.

6

Healing and Women's Theological Creativity

Strategies of Resistance,
Acceptance, and Hope

In her cross-cultural study of twelve women-dominated religions, anthropologist Susan Starr Sered did not find any healing techniques that are unique to women's religions, but she concluded that "[w]hat is striking about women's religions is the *accent* on healing and, in most cases, the *multiplicity* of healing procedures."[1] Sered's study confirms my own sense of how very often references to healing appear in American women's religious thought. However, it is not healing rituals and practices I am concerned with in this chapter other than indirectly. Instead, it is another matter: women's expansion of "healing" as a fruitful religious idea, as an ubiquitous, multivalent, powerful, and complex concept whose many meanings go far beyond the merely palliative. I see the subject of healing in women's religious thought as one more angle from which to explore women's search for intellectually and emotionally adequate ways, more theologically creative ways, to expand and transform traditional religious ideas—and healing itself is one of the ideas being expanded and transformed.

Over and over and in a variety of ways, women in many communities suggest that "healing" is one of the essential functions of theological creativity. Conversely, women hold both explicitly and implicitly that the most creative and compelling religious ideas—about the sacred, humankind, the world—are inevitably healing: that is, that however else they function, these ideas foster the possibilities of hope, persistence, and ultimate well-being for individuals and communities.

One approach to arguing this claim is to interpret the previously explored themes in this book in terms of healing. I think it is possible to do so without stretching the evidence. A cultivated ambivalence, for example, heals the pain of needing to accept a forced choice between two unappealing alternatives: over-acceptance of a religious tradition or rejection of it. An emphasis on the immanence of the divine heals the alienation and self-denigration of women who describe themselves as overwhelmed by, under-identified with, or indifferent to, a far-distant male deity or religious practices removed from the concerns of daily life. Elaboration of the sacredness of the ordinary and the ordinariness of the sacred heals the tendency of religious traditions to make universalizing claims that are disconnected from the lived realities of their members and to overlook the intellectual and devotional value of the details of daily life. Claiming that reality is radically relational heals the ultimate frustration of pursuing either the causes or the alleviation of suffering without recognizing that no one cause or cure can be extricated from the highly complex web of relationships that makes up the universe. Rather than re-visit these themes, I want their implications for the subject of healing in women's religious thought to serve as background and I want to move in several related but different directions that emphasize women's theological creativity with the subject of healing.

For the most part, I will not be talking directly about physical healing or curing in this chapter, even though it is often the case that women see a reciprocal relationship between physical well-being or the ability to come to terms with physical illness and the religious ideas they hold. In the metaphysical traditions, for example, physical healing often follows spiritual insight. But healing in women's religious thought is about more than making well or even making whole, although it is intimately related to both. It is this "more" and the different forms it takes that I am interested in.

Definitions of Healing

In my opinion, there is no one definition of healing that fits all the various examples I include in this chapter. The one that probably comes closest, at least in terms of frequency of use—healing as restoration to wholeness—doesn't offer much by way of actual content, since "wholeness" can mean so many different things that are certainly determined by context.[2] One thing it does *not* mean, however, is the achieving of perfection, as women of many different communities point out. It is, rather, as Buddhist Joan Tollifson puts it paradoxically, "enjoying the perfection of imperfection."[3] Seeking adequate definitions of healing in women's religious thought also requires acknowledgment that the subject of healing encompasses a double and also reciprocal dynamic: the quest for ongoing healing for oneself and one's community and the desire and obligation to offer healing to others. Thus, rather than to claim one definition of healing, it works better, I think, to use several.

In the realm of religious ideas, "healing" is often applied to efforts at forgiveness and reconciliation that emerge one way or another in almost all the communities I consider. Sometimes healing is equated with the naming and resisting of evil. It can also include radical changes in understanding about the nature of reality that are characteristic of the metaphysical traditions like Christian Science. Less radically, it may signal a shift in perspective, a new insight about a familiar teaching that has had negative consequences. In a memoir of her search for a Christianity that was not soul-deadening and debilitating for her as a woman, Protestant patristics scholar Roberta Bondi describes the insight that finally ended a nearly life-long depression not as an intellectual breakthrough but as an experience of healing.[4] In fact, the point of her book, according to Bondi, is to heal the split between "the universal and the individual, the public and the private" in theology. Bondi tells of awakening from a nearly stuporous episode of depression and hearing her own voice repeating the words from the Roman Catholic eucharistic prayers for Easter: "'The joy of the Resurrection renews the whole world,' I repeated to myself in wonder, and while I spoke, my long-broken heart was healed." Bondi asks herself, "How could I have been a church historian and a person of prayer who loved God and still not known that the most fundamental Christian reality is not the suffering of the cross but the life it brings."[5]

As a broad concept, healing takes form in women's religious thought as the bringing of greater wholeness (again) to that which has been fragmented; the restoration of balance to what has been distorted; clear sight to what has been obscured; and resistance to that which is considered destructive. Women invoke all these meanings in reference to a variety of theological projects: creating images for the sacred, developing new understandings of human nature and agency; distinguishing between unnecessary and inevitable suffering; working to make changes in the governance of their traditions.

Frequently, a definition of healing points to an overall stance toward life, a straightforward affirmation of the value of life that is also candid about the reality of suffering. In light of her experiences with both serious illness and Buddhist meditation, "the two things," she says "that have shaped my adult life more than anything else," Joan Iten Sutherland defines healing "not as the elimination of disease, but as falling in love with the poignancy of being alive."[6] In *Woman as Healer*, Jean Achterberg puts forth an eight-part definition of healing that includes the same kind of broad statement: "Healing is a lifelong journey toward wholeness," and "Healing is learning to trust life."[7]

My own candidate for an evocative if not completely adequate definition of healing in women's thought is related to the generation of hope: *to be healed is to have sufficient hope to proceed*, whatever that might mean in particular circumstances. And to offer healing to others *is to work at eliciting and acting on sources of hope in an individual or a community*. It seems to me that the most creative healing insights in women's religious thought are those that offer the peculiar combination of resistance and acceptance, struggle and persistence, critique of the status quo and intimations of vital possibility that are so frequently tangled together in women's writings. This, like healing as restoration of wholeness, is a broad definition, one that suggests that at some level most of us are being healed every day of our lives. But that is exactly the claim that turns up about healing, both explicitly and implicitly, in women's writings. "We do it with each other all the time," says Rachel Naomi Remen, "and we don't even know it."[8] This widespread perception is tied intimately to women's emphasis on the sacredness of the ordinary and the conviction that healing must not be a sometime thing in religious communities, reserved for occasions of crisis or unusual suffering, but a persistent and pervasive effort of the community, an everyday function.

The Complexities of Healing

Whatever definitions of healing one uses, the subject is a more complicated one in women's religious thought than one might expect. One reason is that women's ideas about healing have undergone significant modifications in emphasis and thus expanded over the last thirty years. References to healing have moved from an almost exclusive concentration on women's need for healing from the wounds of male-dominated culture and institutional religion[9] to a proliferation of ideas about various causes of suffering and sources of healing that are related to women's experiences in their traditions and society. Women now write not only about the need for healing from their traditions, but also about how they are working to heal their traditions and about how they find healing—often on their own terms—within them. And, as was evident in the previous chapter, women in different communities find that they have to generate creative ways to think about healing the suffering that women inflict on each other.

Further, the subject of healing gets one very quickly into deep theological waters and comparative worldviews. There is no way to isolate healing from questions about suffering, sin, and evil or how the sacred is related to all of these. Not only are these matters all intensely intertwined; they take varying shape and emphasis in different communities.

Finally, there is even the reality that "healing" has become such a taken-for-granted term in the popular lexicon. Like "relationality," the depth and possibilities of its meanings in various religious traditions and the kinds of theological inquiry and creativity it requires are sometimes concealed through casual use. "Heal us of our all-too-pat 'healing process,'" one writer pleads, and goes on to demand, "Starting immediately the words 'healing process' will be used only in reference to orthopedic injuries and surgical incisions."[10]

Why Healing?

In spite of the challenges of definition, diversity, and scope mentioned above, I have chosen to emphasize healing in this concluding chapter for two reasons. First of all, because, as I have already indicated, references to healing are found in abundance in the writings of women. By this I mean not only references to healing but also the extent to which women describe the theological work they do as healing in nature for themselves and for their communities.

Just as important, there is the reality that both historically and currently healing, physical and spiritual, has an intriguing and by now familiarly bifurcated lineage in American religious and cultural history. Women have traditionally found healing an arena in which they have been able to exercise creativity and authority. Even a small sample of resources available on women and healing in different racial and cultural communities points to how healing has functioned as a realm of multiple opportunities for women: to heal and to be healed; to earn an income; to be theologically creative and to take responsibility for traditional symbols and rituals; and to exercise religious authority in their communities.[11]

"Women have always been healers." This is the first sentence of Jeanne Achterberg's book, *Woman as Healer*, in which she makes a claim that is frequently repeated in women's religious thought.[12] But it doesn't take much research to uncover the familiar pattern of dissent and participation. Until recently women have tended to exercise healing authority—spiritual, emotional, medical—either privately (often domestically) in ways that do not obviously threaten clerical and medical authorities or by more public means that are alternatives to established practices within a given cultural context and that are considered dissenting and often threatening.[13] To remain aware of this history helps to make sense of the extent to which contemporary women's calls for healing in the realm of religious thought often exhibit a dynamic, sometimes volatile, tension between resistance and acceptance of a tradition.[14]

Further, healing in all its different meanings in women's thought brings us back in interesting ways to the subject of ambivalence. It offers a good perspective to explore from yet another angle American women's struggles to find a dynamic balance between life on the margins and life in the center of their traditions, and it moves women into the realm of world construction. Efforts to make sense of suffering and to find and use new sources of healing, as many scholars point out, are related to the construction of worldviews, to the making of meaning.[15] And such construction involves not only what is new but also the materials at hand. No one creates *ex nihilo*. No one steps completely out of the cultures they inhabit in order to build a completely new society.

Women ask, therefore, how much of life as it is now lived in their traditions and society to resist and how much to conserve. How much resistance is enough to be heard, to make a significant difference, to retain a critical edge, to sustain a feminist consciousness, to ensure that fuller participation of women persists and increases into succeeding generations? How much resistance is too much, misdirected, self-defeating? Women's experiences over the last thirty years have demonstrated that the early radical insights about the exclusion and suffering of women, however astute their diagnosis of the ills and excesses of male-dominated religion, cannot be lived out in their most absolute forms. Nor can they be totally abandoned.[16] "Healing" provides one good opening into the expression of ideas that women find most creative in the allocation of their energies toward resistance and acceptance, struggle and hope.

Finally, healing in women's religious thought demonstrates the increasing incorporation of healing into American religious thought in general, a subject that has tended to remain apart from the mainstream of theological creativity. Aside from those traditions that are perceived primarily as healing systems, healing has typically been allocated to the realm of the practical, the ameliorative, even the soothing, and is likely to be perceived as a separate topic from theology in general. The connotations of healing as more palliative than aggressive, more reactive than initiating, have muted the ways that healing as a multi-faceted idea (rather than a practice or ritual) demands movement into new and more prominent theological territory.

The three sections that follow in the rest of the chapter are efforts to explore some of the complexities that are a part of women's emphasis on healing and to illustrate from different angles the prominence of healing as a subject of significant concern in women's thought: the many forms and emphases it takes and its depth and versatility as a religious idea. The first section is an extended reference to two women, one from the nineteenth century and the other from the late twentieth: Mary Baker Eddy, founder of Christian Science, and Char Madigan, a Roman Catholic sister who founded St. Joseph's HOPE Community, a shelter for battered women and their children in Minneapolis. In their work and thought it is possible to bring together some persistent ideas about healing in American women's religious thought and several of the major divergences between women of the nineteenth and twentieth centuries. In Eddy we find historical evidence of the extent to which the quest for healing, in this case both physical and spiritual, serves as an entry into the construction of an entire religious worldview. Like the experiences of Sor Juana Inés de la Cruz recounted in Chapter 4, Eddy's life and work offer an example of some of the continuity of themes that continue to be prominent today in the theological work of women. From Madigan we learn something of a contemporary woman's questions about how best to understand evil and suffering in order to further her own search for the healing of an inner city neighborhood. The section that follows offers explorations of the focus and forms healing takes in five particular communities of women. The final section of the chapter explores efforts of women across several traditions to expand the meaning of healing—and being healed—to include resistance to suffering that is unnecessary and acceptance of the inevitable suffering that comes from being human.

155

Two Women Healers

MARY BAKER EDDY

On Thursday, February 1, 1866, Mary Baker Eddy (Patterson at the time) fell on the ice in Lynn, Massachusetts, and suffered serious injury. By Sunday she was healed physically. But hers was not only a physical healing. The healing occurred as Eddy was praying and reading a biblical account of one of Jesus' healings; she was not able to remember exactly which one. She experienced not only physical healing but a moment of insight into the nature of reality: that it is Spirit, not matter, that is ultimately real. Over the next forty years until her death in 1910, Eddy developed this insight into the foundational assumption for a new church, a new theology, and a new method of healing. Robert Peel, Eddy's foremost biographer, says that the significance of this experience lay in the change it brought about in Eddy's thinking and in the rest of her life: "Other people had had remarkable recoveries through prayer, but other people did not find the experience something on which to build a new church."[17]

Mary Baker Eddy's creative medium was religious thought, and it is possible to see in her writings and in the healing movement she founded the play of religious ideas. From an early age—at least as she saw it in retrospect—Eddy connected differing models of God with sickness and health. In *Retrospection and Introspection*, an autobiographical account published when she was seventy, Eddy told the story of being stricken by a fever brought on by her fear and doubt about the Calvinist doctrine of predestination. "I was unwilling to be saved," she said, "if my brothers and sisters were to be numbered among those who were doomed to perpetual banishment from God." She experienced her father's strict Calvinism and his attempts to persuade her from what he considered heresy, in great contrast to her mother's advice to her daughter to lean on God's love and seek guidance in prayer. She listened to her mother, and the fever was relieved. Furthermore, she said, the "'horrible decree' of predestination—as John Calvin rightly called his own tenet—forever lost its power over me."[18] What Eddy sought to convey, nearly sixty years after the event, was her experience that one way of understanding God made her sick and another made her well—in the broadest sense of both those experiences. Eddy spent the nine years after her healing working out the theological and ecclesiological implications of her insight into the unreality of matter. The first edition of *Science and Health*, Eddy's new scripture, which is used in conjunction with the King James version of the Bible in Christian Science churches, was published in October 1875.[19]

Eddy began her theological work with the intention of reforming rather than departing from the New England Calvinist tradition in which she had been raised. It was her hope to convince the churches that Christianity was essentially a healing religion. When it became clear that the established denominations were hostile to her message, she started a church of her own. *The Manual of the Mother Church*, the small book that elaborates the structure and governance of Christian Science, quotes Eddy's motion at the April 12, 1879, meeting of the Christian Science Association: "To organize a church designed to commemorate the word and works of our Master, which should reinstate primitive Christianity and its lost element of healing."[20] Eddy gradually realized that she would have to reconstruct all the elements of theology and "church" to be coherent with her claim that only Spirit, not matter, was ultimately real: everything from the creation story to church organization. At the same time she put forth a new understanding of God, she saw herself grounded in the Calvinist insistence on the sovereignty of God, and she insisted on the biblical integrity of her new healing religion.[21] On the other hand, Eddy was not so interested in creating a systematic theology as she was in healing as a demonstration (a word that is used with great frequency in Christian Science) of her understanding of God and reality. For Eddy there was a practical reciprocity between theology and healing: to know the true nature of God and reality was to be healed of both sin and suffering. Physical healing, although greatly to be desired, was considered a by-product of spiritual understanding. "People want healing," says Robert Peel in regard to Christian Science healing, "but even more they want the truth."[22]

Mary Baker Eddy is the most prominent of a number of nineteenth-century women healers who found outlets for theological creativity and opportunities for leadership in American religious history. Some of these women were, in fact, associated with Eddy and after various disputes with her left to start their own healing movements or join others.[23] She has many heirs, as well, although not always acknowledged, among contemporary women who understand themselves as healers in communities like the Unity School of Christianity or as New Age healers.[24] If they are not as absolute in their stance about the unreality of matter as Eddy, they nonetheless hold that change of consciousness can change physical circumstances, that thinking positive thoughts about who we are as human beings is more healing than thinking negative thoughts, that disease results from erroneous thinking about the nature of reality.

"Disease is loveless thinking materialized," says Marianne Williamson, although she points out that she does not intend by this statement to blame sufferers for their own illness: "The lovelessness that manufactures disease is systemic; it is laced throughout racial consciousness."[25] "We can promote the healing of others by healing our own consciousness in recognizing them as perfect expressions of God," according to C. Alan Anderson and Deborah G. Whitehouse, contemporary interpreters of New Thought.[26] For some metaphysical healers, detailed knowledge of what is causing suffering is not even necessary if the healer can foster a conviction of the sufferer's true and already-healed self. Linda Osborne, the former pastor of Lake Harriet Community Church (at one time the Church of Religious Science) in Minneapolis, says that she doesn't have any idea of what is wrong with people, spiritual or physical, when they come to her for healing, and she doesn't care. "If I care," she says, "then I get into controlling. What I care about is that people come to know their self-worth."[27] And here is New Age healer Barbara Brennen relating a healing understanding of the real person to the cultivation of love and hope: "The work of the healer is a work of love. The healer reaches into these painful areas of the soul and gently reawakens hope. S/he gently reawakens the ancient memory of who the soul is."[28]

There are innumerable ways that Mary Baker Eddy's radical ontology based on the sole reality of Spirit is distinct from—opposed to, actually—contemporary women's earth-oriented theologies. That is true as well of the world-views of the women mentioned above. But there are also instructive parallels in her life and thought for understanding contemporary women. Most obvious is the connection Eddy made and elaborated between spiritual and physical well-being and religious belief: if one does not have a true understanding of reality and of the nature of the holy, then one will be sick, both physically and spiritually, and so will society. There is also Eddy's emphasis on the pragmatic nature of religious thought. Its efficacy, its "truth," she claimed, must be demonstrated; it must have practical results, not just intellectual coherence. One hears echoes of Eddy's claim in contemporary women's insistence on a connection between theology and ethics. Even Eddy's breaking of the oppositional tension between spirit and matter in favor of spirit points to similarities to contemporary women's critique of opposing and hierarchical dualisms in religious thought—though contemporary women have mostly broken the tension by going the way of matter infused with spirit.

As a last point of comparison, we see in Eddy's theology an effort to formulate an understanding of human nature that she considered healing—"empowering," to use more contemporary language. Again, the comparison is not so much with the content of her thought. Very much unlike contemporary women, Eddy denied the ultimate reality of the body and insisted that reliance on "the corporeal senses" leads us astray spiritually. Rather the comparison points to an early effort in women's religious thought to formulate understandings of human nature that were more hopeful than pessimistic, and these, in turn, were used to foster the full participation of women. To empower women by giving them new thoughts to think about their very natures was also to ensure their spiritual and physical healing.

Eddy did not deny that men and women experienced themselves as finite creatures who sin and suffer and die, but this, she said, was due to a gross misunderstanding of the nature of reality. The task of true religion was to understand that "[m]an is spiritual and perfect; and because he is spiritual and perfect, he must be so understood in Christian Science."[29] To understand oneself as perfect—"true man" rather than "mortal man" in the language of Christian Science—was to be healed. This was much in contrast with many traditions' insistence on the deeply sinful nature of humankind, a doctrine from whose implications women understand themselves to suffer more than men. Where does hope for healing lie in Christian Science and other metaphysical traditions that have attracted so many women over the last century and a half? In the certainty that healing, both physical and spiritual, is available to those who understand that God intends only health and wholeness for human beings, who according to Christian Science are God's perfect reflection.

More than one hundred years after Mary Baker Eddy's experience of healing and her efforts to understand the meanings of good and evil, Char Madigan, another woman theologian, struggles with creative ways to understand them. She elicits hope and offers healing from within a very different philosophical and theological tradition from Eddy's.

CHAR MADIGAN, C.S.J.

St. Joseph's HOPE Community is centered in a big old house in inner-city Minneapolis. It offers emergency shelter to women and children seeking refuge from domestic violence. The work of the community has expanded to include rehabilitating "boarded and drug-infested buildings on our block and renting them to people who are committed to the health and vitality of themselves and the neighborhood."[30] St. Joe's HOPE was begun in 1977 by Char Madigan, who is also active in a large number of other social justice causes.

The community publishes a monthly newsletter that lists requests for specific kinds of help, letters from volunteers and former residents, news of goings-on at the house, and articles by people who are connected in some way with the work of the community.[31] Often there is a personal reflection by Madigan about her work, her theological convictions and questions, and her insider/outsider status in the Roman Catholic tradition.[32]

The June 1996 newsletter carries on the front cover a quote that one might interpret as having echoes of Eddy. It is from Macrina Wiederkehr, a Benedictine sister, who writes often about prayer: "Oh God help me to believe the truth about myself—no matter how beautiful it is!"[33] Given the neighborhood, the daily realities of the women and children who live at St. Joe's HOPE, and the continuing struggle of the staff and volunteers to keep the community going financially and spiritually, the admonition to women to believe the truth about themselves no matter how beautiful appears at first startling and incongruous. But it is very much in line historically with women's efforts to construct both hopeful and realistic theologies of human nature.[34]

In this same issue Char Madigan offers a meditation on evil that she wrote in both "anticipation and dread," she said, of a Twin Cities interfaith group's visit to the Holocaust Museum in Washington, D.C. "See," says Madigan, "I so much want human nature to be good, made in the divine image I know to be good. I do so want love to be stronger than hate. Yet I have a primal fear that the sky is falling in!" Madigan goes on with her questions about the nature of evil and her own dual confession of faith and of sin: "Prayer reminds me of my deepest foundations: God is love. What God creates is good. In God's

159

image, human nature is good. Whence then comes evil? freedom? I don't know. I resist an outside devil theory. Evil externalized would make freedom impossible. I know the possibilities of my own heart and mind." After listing many of the evils she has experienced during her lifetime, from the Holocaust to religious institutions' approval of homophobia, she continues with her thoughts about the nature of evil: "Evil, like beauty, are you in the eye of the beholder? always? sometimes? I think there are some things objective about you. You make people expendable to a cause or creed. You justify cruelty, horror, death. I stalk you. Trembling, yet I stalk you. I study how to resist you. More than love or beauty, you teach me how to pray."[35]

Char Madigan's meditation incorporates ancient questions in the history of religious thought and theology about the origins and naming and manifestations of evil. They emerge not out of a context in which abstract thought is uppermost but from her particular experiences as a life-long Catholic, a member of a religious order who is now in her sixties, and a woman whose work experience makes it impossible to ignore the relentlessness of violence against many in society and all the things that cause it. She sees the reality of lives transformed in a small and struggling community and the helplessness and oppression that drags some women down so deep that in a variety of ways they do not survive. Madigan ponders the imponderable natures of goodness and evil, speculates about what she has been taught and what she has experienced, what she hopes for and what she is afraid may be the case. Unlike Mary Baker Eddy, she comes to no absolute conclusions about the nature of reality other than that she will do what healing she can by taking action—she will stalk evil. The form her theological creativity takes is the shaping not of a healing worldview but of a healing and healed community.[36] The goal of her pondering and stalking is the possibility for healing of those who seek shelter at St. Joe's HOPE as well as for the health of the neighborhood. But her goal is also to keep thinking about how most authentically, how most pragmatically, to act on her questions about good and evil as they are embodied and intermingled at St. Joe's HOPE.

Women's Healing from Multiple Perspectives

In addition to constructing healing systems and communities, women's ways of appropriate healing in their theological work take other forms as well, based on the needs of their particular communities. To continue the exploration of how women find the concept of healing an expansive arena in which to exercise theological creativity, I have chosen several different communities to explore in terms of their approaches to healing: Mormons, Jews, African Americans, Muslims, and "white women." As in previous chapters, the selection is not meant to be exhaustive but rather illustrative of the particularity of forms healing takes given the histories and theologies of several different communities of women. For each, there are different issues at stake, a different kind of pain to be healed, and a strategy unique to the community for bringing about that healing. In all the examples there is also evident the two-way, reciprocal energy of the phenomenon of healing as women write about it. Women seek healing from various kinds of spiritual and physical suffering; in the process of discovering what will heal them, they find themselves offering healing as well to their communities and beyond.

MORMON WOMEN: LOST AUTHORITY

Mormon women use the term "healing" in much the same way as women of other traditions to refer to such aspects of theological creativity as finding new images for the divine. As just one example, Carol Lynn Pearson speaks of efforts to expand images of Heavenly Mother and devotion to her as "healing the motherless house."[37] But Mormon women also see healing—the bestowing of blessings and anointings that are now officially reserved to the male priesthood—as part of the loss of institutional authority that was once theirs in the early years of Mormonism's emergence as a new religious tradition. Historian Linda King Newell traces this circumscription of women's healing authority to early twentieth-century Mormonism, when Mormon women's healing authority was curbed by the institutional church due to concerns by the hierarchy that if women were given the opportunity to heal, they might think they also had the priesthood.[38]

Betina Lindsey reiterates this conviction in an essay on contemporary Mormon women's healing practices. She suggests that, in spite of being forbidden to do so officially, Mormon women have persisted in offering healing ordinances to other women and that especially in the last few years "there has been a resurgence of women discreetly exercising the gift of healing and blessing others."[39] She quotes a mother who blessed a son who was having difficulty breathing: "Suddenly in an [sic] natural instantaneous response I lay my hands on his head and said, 'As [your] mother I call on the power of [the] Melchizedek priesthood' and I blessed him." Although this mother had previously given blessings to other women for such things as infertility, alcoholism, and depression, she had never before invoked priesthood authority. Lindsey considers her "a pioneer" who "is rediscovering a vast landscape that was once the domain of Mormon women as healers—a territory from which three generations of Mormon women have been exiled."[40]

Terry Tempest Williams confirms Lindsey's thesis of a persisting tradition of healing among Mormon women who are well aware that they have "no outward authority . . . but with the secrecy of sisterhood we have always bestowed benisons upon our families." When Williams's mother, who is dying of cancer, asks her daughter for a blessing, Williams says, "I lay my hands upon her head and in the privacy of women, we pray."[41]

Lindsey makes a four-fold argument on behalf of reinstituting women's healing in the LDS church, which she sees as suffering at present from the loss of women's healing rituals. She maintains that there is scriptural and historical precedent; that healing is a gift that is ungendered; that participating in healing rituals would enhance the "spiritual empowerment" of women; and that the church itself would increase its spirituality.[42] It is Lindsey's hope to encourage women to seek and exercise the gift of healing immediately without fear that they are doing something wrong and without waiting for women's ordination. She does not seem to be suggesting that women act as secret and renegade healers. She advocates instead institutional changes to incorporate women as healers: by "setting women apart as healers as was done in the early church"; by allowing "for men and women within the church to hold common prayer circles together for healing"; or by providing ways for women to read about the healings of early church sisters.[43]

Lindsey's argument presents an interesting combination of resistance to the institution and its present practice of excluding women from official healing roles and a hope for a positive institutional response to women's healing powers and their desire to exercise them publicly.[44] Her essay illustrates as well how the subject of healing authority in Mormonism is related to gender issues and how it elicits women's theological responses beyond that specific issue to include broader matters of scripture and polity.

JEWISH WOMEN: HEALING FROM TRAUMATIC HISTORIES AND HEALING FOR THE WORLD

In some communities of women the emphasis is not so much on the authoritative exercise of women's healing powers as on the need for healing from the physical and spiritual devastation of specific historical events. For contemporary Jewish women the pain that needs to be healed is not only centuries of persecution as a minority people but the Holocaust in particular. One way for this suffering to be lessened, in the estimation of many Jewish women, is through Jewish efforts to respond to the suffering of others. Rabbi Lynn Gottlieb considers the work of healing from "the trauma of Jewish history" as multiple in its implications: "To become successful in our coalition with other peoples, Jews must grapple with the meaning of the Holocaust in our lives. How we respond to the Holocaust shapes our ability to relate to other people's suffering. It ultimately influences the direction of our time and energy toward our culture as Jews."[45]

Gottlieb thinks that Jewish healing must take place through efforts to work for justice on behalf of all people, including Palestinians, and that healing is more likely to come from insisting on strength than from dwelling on woundedness: "It is not our suffering that should distinguish us but the fruits of our religious life. Those who suffer need our courage, and we need our courage as well to overcome the temptation to dwell on our exile as a major theme." Gottlieb says, further, "We are not as vulnerable as we once were."[46] Part of her own work as a rabbi in Albuquerque to bring about Jewish healing has been to sponsor an art festival that "invited our friends to witness the creative fruits of our tradition." Another effort is involvement in local social justice issues: "We present a living tradition to the community as well as the memory of our greatest tragedy."[47]

Gottlieb is among many Jewish women who see the work of Judaism as intimately connected with the healing of the world's social structures. Another, Judith Plaskow, devotes the final chapter of *Standing Again at Sinai* to the connection between spirituality and politics that is part of Judaism and feminism: *tikkun olam*—the right ordering of society or "repair of the world."[48]

Jewish women are also concerned with theological questions about the common human experiences of pain—whether and how suffering might be transformative and what resources a Jewish worldview offers to those who suffer both physically and spiritually from illness or emotional traumas. "What can it mean to me to live *Jewishly* with my illness?" asks Tamara M. Green, who has lived for thirty years with a chronic illness.[49] In the familiar pattern of ambivalence toward her tradition, Green recounts the benefits she receives from "the Jewish embrace of my entire community" and the anger she feels at what some traditional Jewish texts have to say about "the causes and consequences" of illness, connecting it with punishment, isolation, and selective salvation. Green says she has made a list of various Jewish meanings of illness that she recites to herself when she is feeling trapped by her body and is despairing. She does not find any of them very satisfying. But she goes on to recount how she finds "solace in the pleasurable rhythms of a life lived Jewishly"—going to synagogue, praying, singing Sabbath songs.[50] It took Green a long time and a great deal of struggle, she says, "before it finally struck me that I was asking the wrong questions about being sick and being Jewish. The questions I really needed to ask were: Could I be spiritually healed even if I never got any better physically? And if I was not to be cured, what did *Adonai* expect of me?"[51]

Like Green, Marcia Cohn Spiegel looks to the Jewish tradition and her community for healing from yet another kind of pain: the failure of that same community to acknowledge that within it women and children suffer from domestic violence. Spiegel ties women's efforts to change Judaism in this respect—to both acknowledge and redress domestic violence—to the same broader task of Judaism that so many Jewish women cite as their framework for taking on issues of social justice, including feminism: *tikkun olam*, repair of the world. "Although I do not believe," says Spiegel, "that everyone who is struggling to change the patriarchy has been physically or sexually abused, I do believe that many women who have been abused are engaged in the struggle to reshape Judaism."[52]

Spiegel uses efforts to counter domestic abuse similar to those of women in other traditions, but she is also engaged in constructing a healing spirituality that is uniquely Jewish and includes new metaphors for God, the transformation of old rituals and creation of new ones, and recognition not only that domestic violence occurs in Jewish families but that "peace in the house, is a goal toward which we strive, not a measure of who we are." In Spiegel's understanding, many of the theological efforts of Jewish feminists to include women fully can be directed specifically toward the goal of healing. She speaks of this as the seeking of "*schlemut* (from the root of *shalom*), which means 'wholeness, harmony, completion."[53]

AFRICAN-AMERICAN WOMEN: BODILY SUFFERING

African-American women, not surprisingly, write about the need for healing from the endless and devastating effects of racism. A persistent theme in their work is that of "body"—the bodily suffering that black women experience. "Straight talk about the loves and troubles of our bodies is almost impossible," says Cheryl Townsend Gilkes, "because there is so much pain."[54] In an essay about the suffering of African-American women that is centered in their bodies, Gilkes points in two directions. She looks to white-dominated society and the cultural and physical humiliation racism has imposed on African Americans. She also addresses the black community and what Gilkes calls its "conflicted inner visions," its ambivalence, about the color spectrum and physical appearance in African-American communities. This includes black women's anger at one another. In this case, Gilkes sees ambivalence about the beauty and strength of black women's bodies not as catalyst to theological creativity but as a cause of community conflict and a barrier to the possibility of self-love.

Delores S. Williams's work on the surrogacy experiences of African-American women offers another source of understanding about the particular kinds of suffering of black women that are grounded in bodily experiences. Williams points to three areas of "coerced surrogacy" that have their origins in the antebellum South, in which "people and systems more powerful than black people forced black women to function in roles that ordinarily would have been filled by someone else": nurturance, field labor, and sexuality.[55] In all of these cases, says Williams, such antebellum realities fostered cultural stereotypes of black women that persist into the present and contribute to situations of "voluntary surrogacy." They exploit contemporary black women's sexuality and physical labor and undermine their authority in their own communities. Black women's surrogacy roles have had detrimental effects on African-American communities in general. One experience frequently cited by black women is that of missing the presence of their mothers, who had to expend their energies—their bodies—in the care of white people's children and homes.

In the work of these two womanist theologians, the need to acknowledge and heal physical and spiritual pain fosters theological creativity. It is not manifested in contorted explanations of how bodily suffering can be looked at positively but in new theological formulations, new claims, that work to diminish both the causes of pain and the chances that a community will see unnecessary suffering as acceptable. Tightly woven with analyses of particular kinds of bodily suffering and their causes in black women's religious thought are womanists' constructions of what they consider healing insights. These include the symbols and teachings of African-American Christianity interpreted in new ways that urge black women to reject suffering as their God-ordained lot and to cultivate self-love. One of the reasons, in fact, that Delores S. Williams so forcefully rejects traditional interpretations of the Atonement and Jesus' suffering in both black and white Christian theologies is because she see them promoting suffering as redemptive in itself. "As Christians," says Williams, "black women cannot forget the cross, but neither can they glorify it." She sees "nothing divine in the blood of the cross. God does not intend black women's surrogacy experience."[56] Related to Williams's rejection of the acceptance and even glorification of surrogacy roles is Jacquelyn Grant's critique of "the sin of servanthood," because for black women servanthood and servitude have too often been synonymous. She argues that, because "some folks are more servant than others," "servanthood" is a concept that has outlived its usefulness in Christian theology and needs to be replaced by "discipleship."[57]

Another source of healing insight is contemporary black women's literature, not only because black authors depict women's strength and survival and insist on the need for self-love, but because, as Katie Geneva Cannon puts it, "Black women novelists give me a way to look at AfroChristian thought outside of the institutional and traditionally articulated expressions of faith."[58] In her own work on Zora Neale Hurston, Cannon finds inspiration to reject traditional Christianity's "worries" about theodicy and how human suffering appears to undermine the goodness and omnipotence of God. Black women's literature, she says, does not begin with such questions and then move to justify God's goodness: "Rather, womanist protagonists contend that God's sustaining presence is known in the resistance to evil."[59]

Cheryl Townsend Gilkes uses Alice Walker's definition of "womanist" in her novel *The Color Purple* as a foundation for an ethical stance for black women, particularly Walker's emphasis on various "loves"—love of "the Folk," of Spirit, of "food and roundness." Most important to Gilkes is Walker's passionate call for black women to love themselves.[60] One of Walker's strengths, as Gilkes sees it, is offering "clarity" about the necessity of self-love as a way beyond the ambivalence created by the tension between the heroic and the pathetic.[61] For Gilkes the healing of African-American women requires the construction of hopeful worldviews. She refers to Walker's four womanist loves as the foundation for a cosmology, a healing vision of what the world might be like, that makes it possible for women to " 'live the loves' in a hateful and troubling world" and to participate in "healing, spiritual wholeness, celebration, and struggle."[62] In a variety of ways and sources, African-American women express the conviction that the ongoing healing required for any kind of decent life lived on this earth must be constructed on the basis of possibility rather than limit, on self-love rather than self-hatred.

BODY, SIN, AND THE VEIL AMONG ISLAMIC WOMEN

There are other traditions as well in which women insist that their communities' perceptions of women's bodies need healing. In her study of "corporal geographies" in contemporary Islam, Fedwa Malti-Douglas concludes that "[m]ore than simply a physical entity to be covered, woman's body, led by her face, becomes the locus for a kind of punitive Islamic religious discourse."[63] To make her point she excerpts the story, from a highly popular fifty-three-page pamphlet written by an Egyptian woman physician and feminist, of a woman with a toothache (punishment for the use of lipstick) and her subsequent repentance, healing, and veiling. "What a fascinating story!" she says. Malti-Douglas sees it not as a story of healing (even though the toothache goes away) but as one of bodily suffering inflicted as punishment. "From a mere tooth abstraction, the reader has been transported into the realm of female modesty, female covering, and a corporal discourse that recalls that of the punishments inflicted in the Muslim Hell. The female body—in its sexual and beautified nature—is mapped out as the locus of sin."[64] Malti-Douglas goes on to relate the story to controversies over women and the veil in Islam, and one can only assume that in her opinion removal of the veil would be a healing move for women, men, and Islam itself.

For some American Muslim women, the wearing of the veil can be a different source of punishment. In a strange reversal, they are foiled in their desire to wear it rather than forced to do so. They report experiences like public rudeness and job discrimination when they wear a veil or head scarf in public. "They think I'm a foreigner," said one woman, "and I've been here a long time. I wear American clothes, but I wear a scarf. The scarf changes everything."[65] Public commentators see reaction to the veil as one measure of tolerance of religious diversity in the United States, and stories such as these indicate that there is much work yet to be done. I emphasized distinctive clothing for Muslim women and issues of the sacredness of the ordinary in Chapter 4. In this chapter it is interesting to think about how Islamic women's wearing of the veil opens up different and contradictory ways to interpret what constitutes either healing or suffering for women within the context of a particular tradition and in relation to one powerfully symbolic article of clothing.[66]

WHITE WOMEN'S CYNICISM, DESPAIR, AND APOCALYPTIC SELF-RECRIMINATION

Although "white" needs to be qualified in a number of ways to reflect the realities of particular women's lives, most women maintain that there is nonetheless privilege afforded to whiteness that transcends a great number of other differences and makes possible some compelling generalizations. Many white women believe that racial privilege and blindness to disparities among different communities of women are among the wounds whose causes and effects need healing: undeserved privilege wounds those who exercise it as well as those upon whom it is exercised.

One of these wounds that Sharon D. Welch identifies is the temptation to cynicism and despair, "the death of the moral imagination," a "failure of nerve," that faces middle-class white feminists at this moment in history, particularly in response to nuclear threat. All of these add up to what Welch describes as "the inability to persist in resistance when problems are seen in their full magnitude."[67] Put another way, this is the temptation to do nothing if one discovers that it is impossible to do everything—what Welch refers to as espousing an ethic of control. She sees becoming easily discouraged as "the privilege of those accustomed to too much power": "To the extent that we will cling to the ideal of omnipotence—of a sovereign god or an all-wise, always successful father—we are trapped in our own role as oppressors, expecting a level of ease in action impossible in an interdependent world."[68]

Where will women of the white middle class find sources of healing from the wounds inflicted by privilege? Welch elicits them from the fiction of African-American women and their interpretations of what is required for the healing of individuals and communities: "Not written for us," she says, "but indicting us and our power, they offer the insight we need to stop our collective self-destruction, the abuse of power that threatens all life."[69] In Toni Cade Bambara's *The Salt-Eaters*, a novel about political and spiritual tensions and splits in the African-American community in the late 1970s, Welch finds, "One of the most salient lessons is discovering how to learn from pain without trying either to conquer it or to become immune to it." Another is that the possibility for collective and individual healing "lies in the recognition that although there is a way through, there is no way out."[70] A third is a description of "three aspects of persistent, joyful communal resistance to structural evil: an abiding love for other people, an acceptance of the need for taking risks in political action, and an active commitment to 'ancient covenants' with life."[71] Welch sees all of these insights—really articulations of stances toward life—as healing in nature. They promote theological creativity and, in her case, have contributed to her own construction of an ethic of risk that is more resistant to despair than an ethic of control.

Protestant theologian Catherine Keller takes on yet another phenomenon that imperils community and the world. She calls for healing from the destructive effects of a certain way of thinking that she identifies as "the habit" of apocalyptic, all-or-nothing, us-against-them, "end" discourse. In her historical and theological analysis of this phenomenon, *Apocalypse Now and Then: A Feminist Guide to the End of the World*, Keller asks, "When and where does our history as a whole—do our own individual and cultural stories in particular—re-enact apocalyptic strategies of transformative dissociation: a desire for justice braced with righteous moral dualism; an investiture with sacred meaning of the simple opposition of good and evil, of we and they, of now and then, of male and female?"[72] Keller refers to *apocalypse habit* in Western culture and "a broader, vaguer *apocalypse pattern*" whose traits she identifies as an inclination not only to think in polarities of good and evil, but to identify oneself with the good and to engage in purging the evil other.[73] She models her own method of resistance to apocalyptic thinking even in her attitude toward apocalypse itself: "Let me confess up front," she says, "that I find the apocalypse pattern neither good nor evil, sometimes very good and sometimes very evil."[74]

Her book is not addressed specifically to white women, but the impetus of its critique of apocalyptic discourse is directed toward Christian feminists rather than womanist or *mujerista* theologians, Jews, Buddhists, Goddess feminists, and the like. In the works of many Christian feminist theologians, Keller finds a troubling, anti-apocalyptic discourse that has been filtered and inscripted into Western culture through various interpretations of the final book of the Christian Scriptures, the Book of Revelation. One of the examples Keller offers is what she calls a "histrionic element" that has entered white women's discussions of racism, in which some of us women "make ourselves blameless and safe" by confessing our own racism and then going on to denounce it in others. This is particularly observable, Keller suggests, in efforts to put distance between oneself and the racism of past eras, at the same time suggesting that we would not have been so sinful had we lived in that age. Keller says that "while the self-unveiling of white feminist racism requires work in and upon every epoch, the accompanying implication that *I* would have proved morally superior, that *I* would have transcended the same circumstances, neatly reinvests the very neo-Victorian politics of purity under criticism."[75]

What is particularly interesting for the purposes of this chapter is Keller's description of "counter-apocalypse," the intellectual strategy she proposes to destabilize apocalyptic ways of thinking, as "healing." Keller is looking for a new theological insight, a more healing way of thinking that will be more creative in its response to the need for social transformation. "Resistance to either/or logic in assessing the habit of apocalypse," she says, "belongs to the present strategy for healing from the habit."[76] In fact, she insists, the overall "endless 'end'" of counter-apocalypse is "the healing of the *kosmos*, in its full etymological meaning of an aesthetic, social and natural order of relations."[77] For Keller healing involves the process of fostering hope, not by investing it in the cataclysmic end of whatever one considers evil but by luring the Spirit to a new way, "A way never known in advance, no matter how many names we give it. A way that appears only as we walk there."[78]

WOMEN'S HEALING IN THE NEW AGE MOVEMENT

There is a final category of examples I want to explore before going on to the third section of the chapter: the phenomenon of "women's healing" that has emerged from various sectors of the New Age movement.[79] Many of the women healers characterized as "New Age" attribute general kinds of illness and suffering to the separation of male and female principles of the cosmos and society's denigration or ignoring of the female principle. This is a very different kind of approach from that of most of the women cited in this study, who are not interested at all in talking about something as essentialist sounding as "the feminine principle." In many New Age writings, women's healing is thought to be of a different order from men's—more psychic, more tactile, more holistic. In these writings, allopathic (regular) medicine is often identified as male and holistic healing as female.

Diane Stein, author of *The Women's Book of Healing*, speaks of women's healing as psychic healing, based on intuition and aura awareness. She sees it as "an outgrowth of feminism and the radical women's movement, of the New Age and women's spirituality."[80] She bases her claim on the complex Theosophical understanding of the human person as made up of seven sheaths or bodies, an acknowledgment that we experience our lives physically, emotionally, mentally, and spiritually at all times and with many gradations between.[81] In Stein's opinion, women are particularly skilled at connecting the seen levels of existence with the unseen. For this reason their healing power goes deeper and is directed at all levels of existence, not just the physical. Stein also insists that women use their healing powers not just on behalf of individuals but in much broader arenas. In her description of the multiple roles women play in healing, Stein advances what theologians call a high doctrine of woman's nature: "Women are the healers of the universe and Earth, the positive civilizers, inventors, comforters and homebuilders of the planet, the guardians of peace and well-being, and the mothers, caregivers, listeners and priestesses of the life force."[82] Stein uses crystals, auras, the laying on of hands, chakras (considered the seven major energy sources of the body), and colors in her healing work, which is designed to address all aspects of the person.

New Age healers have other ways as well to refer to the need for women's healing in the world. Linda Osborne has her own healing practice and teaches courses as well. According to her understanding of healing, we are electromagnetic beings, and the qualities that we embody are reflections of the godhead. The electric center is male, and the magnetic center is female. Women, like men, in Osborne's opinion, draw their healing power from the godhead. If there is an overabundance of electric power in the godhead and an insufficiency of magnetic power, the power in the godhead is not enough to sustain women (who are 65 percent magnetic) in their healing work on earth. It is Osborne's understanding that we are moving into an era in which the magnetic power in the godhead is greater than the electric, thus signaling a time when women's healing will become more prominent. Women, Osborne claims, are closer to the earth and therefore are more natural healers.[83]

A third New Age healer, Demetra George, describes women's healing in Jungian terms in *Mysteries of the Dark Moon: The Healing Power of the Dark Goddess*.[84] She contends that the part that has been left out of contemporary culture is the dark phase of the moon, which symbolizes the realm of the psyche. The psyche in contemporary cultures is perceived as the underworld, a dwelling place for unclaimed fears and desires; therefore it is looked upon as a dangerous part of the person to probe. In reality, says George, this underworld is a place of healing and transformation: "As we become less fearful and allow ourselves to look at what we have hidden, we can begin to reclaim the dark feminine and heal our psyches."[85] This is certainly an echo of the theme in Chapter 3 that sees the prototypical spiritual journey as one to the interior of the psyche rather than up and out of the world; but in general women healers characterized as New Age, drawn as they are to assumptions about a feminine principle in the universe, sound a very different religious note from most of the other women I cite in this chapter.

Not all, not even most, New Age healers who are female are concerned exclusively with the healing of women. In *The Healing of America*, Marianne Williamson takes on the healing of the entire society. Her book, she says, "is about the yin and yang of American history, the Great Duality of our miraculous beginnings, the ultimate tearing apart of our vision from our politics, and an effort that can now begin in earnest to repair the resulting wounding of our collective soul."[86] This book might be seen as a metaphysical jeremiad, a metaphysically oriented rendering of the civil religion (Williamson includes the Declaration of Independence and the Constitution, including the Bill of Rights, in an appendix). Williamson urges her readers to repent of our departure from the vision of the Founders and its corruption by materialism. She asks citizens to awaken to the reality that all is not well in this country and to take action toward a renewal of the body politic based on a return to our first principles. These are four: (1) "All are Equal and Shall Be Treated Equally Before the Law"; (2) "Unity in Diversity"; (3) "The Federal Government Shall Secure the Collective Welfare, Yet with Enough Checks and Balances to Ensure Individual Liberty"; and (4) "All Americans Shall Be Free to Find God, or Not Find God, However Their Conscience Permits."[87]

The Healing of America is a lengthy book that covers a lot of territory, but throughout Williamson stresses the need for "inner work," which results in the creation of a force she calls "yin activism," made up of three elements: "the awakening of our minds, atonement for our errors, and the arousal of our spirits."[88] Williamson ties "yin activism" to the re-emergence of feminine consciousness in the world. She associates the feminine with the inner world and with "soul force" that "emanates subtle energies that invisibly move and heal the world." In the world of metaphysical healing that Williamson inhabits, the feminine force of soul consciousness is the healing principle, "the invisible womb out of which all manifest creation springs."[89] If it is at one level somewhat startling to see the feminine principle, "yin activism," juxtaposed with the Declaration of Independence and the Constitution as sources of healing in American culture, it is at the same time instructive to see how broadly and by what means healing is conceptualized by women in the New Age movement.

Resistance, Acceptance, Hope

HEALING AS A STANCE TOWARD LIFE

The several examples above demonstrate women's multiple approaches to what requires healing in their own communities. There are also broader themes emerging in regard to healing in women's religious thought. These themes are tightly tied to women's efforts to think creatively about what kinds of evil and suffering can be healed only by resistance, by fighting, by "stalking evil," to use Char Madigan's phrase, and what kinds of suffering in the experience of women can be healed only by acceptance of certain realities about who we are as human beings in the universe as it is constituted.

When to resist and when to accept are questions tightly tied to two strands of thought that Roman Catholic theologian Patricia L. Wismer has identified in women's theological writings. One is "suffering: never again," a stance that expresses indignation at all the injustices women have suffered and rejects the self-sacrifice of women as always inappropriate. The other is "suffering: part of the web of life," a stance that advocates acceptance of suffering that is deemed inevitable because it is part of nature. Wismer herself says that an adequate theology of suffering, and, I assume, of healing, advocates both these positions. "What I am suggesting," she says, "is that feminist theology should approach suffering within a framework created by the tension of affirming both these positions."[90]

A significant question emerges very quickly from what Wismer has to say: How do we tell the difference between suffering that is unjust and suffering that is natural and inevitable? One would think that this question would not be so terribly difficult to answer in any given situation. In reality, as women point out in many different ways, certainty about which kind of suffering is which is not a luxury we enjoy as individuals or as members of religious communities. And the complexity of discerning the difference—and knowing how to respond in either case—grows organically from the very themes that have been explored in this book.

Women convey from their own experiences that good and evil, suffering and joy, are inextricably mixed together in the world. Women's ambivalence toward their traditions has forced the recognition that women experience both suffering and healing in their traditions. An insistence on the immanence of the holy makes the sacred or the ultimate much more accessible through the world around us, but also harder to discern than in those traditional worldviews wherein sacred and secular, good and evil, are understood as more ontologically and obviously separated from each other. Attention to the mixed blessings of daily life reveals both the presence of the holy and the pervasiveness of evil, injustice, and suffering. The same can be said of relationships, which women claim as the inescapable stuff of reality. If reality is radically relational, it is also characterized by ambiguity and tragedy. Rita Nakashima Brock's insistence that relationships are both life-giving experiences and the way "we come to be damaged and damage others"[91] is echoed by women of many different traditions. Women are demonstrating an increasing awareness in their writings that absolutist, triumphalist, utopian, or apocalyptic approaches to questions of good and evil are not adequate to a world in which the two are so tangled up together.

In an effort to determine what kinds of suffering require resistance and what kinds necessitate acceptance, Wismer offers four questions that she is convinced can help make sense of both. She asks: "What are the causes of my suffering and how can they be eliminated? How can I find meaning in suffering and grow through it? When and how should I take on suffering I could avoid?" This third question breaks open new theological territory for women. It seeks to avoid traditional admonitions to women always to "sacrifice" for the good of others and at the same time works to acknowledge that the healing of individual and communal pain may require the taking on of suffering that might have been avoided.[92] Finally, Wismer asks, "Why am I suffering?" (a question she says must be asked but cannot be answered) and "Who suffers with me?" which is really a question about the relational nature of both suffering and healing.[93]

As women like Wismer raise new questions about suffering and healing, other questions drop out of women's religious thought. One of the most obviously missing is the issue of theodicy as it has been traditionally phrased, particularly among Jews and Christians: how can a good and omnipotent deity permit or cause suffering? Wismer states the conviction that appears often in women's religious thought: that this is no longer a fruitful question to ask. In her critique of several different responses to it she says, "We can only say that none of them completely answers the question and that even taken all together, they still fail to satisfy."[94] To reject the question of theodicy as it has been traditionally stated has had multiple implications for women's thought, among them re-evaluations of the meaning of Jesus' suffering and death for Christian women and the meaning—or lack thereof—of the suffering of the Holocaust for Jewish women. In many communities, "theodicy" takes a new turn, away from theological conundrums and toward statements of conviction and action, as in Cheryl Kirk-Duggan's womanist theodicy derived from her study of African-American Spirituals. As she understands them, "The Spirituals, from a perspective of theodicy, are always about naming evil and suffering, being hopeful for transformation, and doing what one can to effect that change, working in concert with a God who cares."[95]

In the remainder of the chapter I offer examples of women's insights about healing—first, as it demands resistance to certain kinds of suffering, and second, as it requires acceptance of other kinds.

TAKING THE CURE BY RESISTING AUTHORITY

I begin this section on resistance with a story told by Orthodox Jewish writer Vanessa Ochs that she calls "Taking the Cure." It is in many ways a funny story, and there is a wryness to the self-revelatory tale Ochs tells. It is also a healing narrative about resistance to the status quo and to the dictates of a worldview that is imposed rather than chosen—and resistance, also, to the kind of false consciousness that makes women forget that commitment to religious worldviews must arise out of awareness of their constructed nature.

Ochs begins the story of her healing experience with an anecdote about her deeply depressed, highly religiously observant oldest cousin, who was advised by her psychiatrist to engage in a therapeutic violation of the Sabbath by driving to Ochs's parents' home, drinking a cup of tea prepared on the stove, and driving home again. Ochs's family had multiple doubts about this advice but chose to cooperate for the sake of the suffering cousin. Thirteen years later, in the midst of a very demanding life compounded by friendship with a princess from a Middle Eastern country, Ochs needs a cure herself: "It was my seventh year of being a wife, my first year of being a mother, one of many difficult years of being a writer. And I was trying to hold it all together with a teaching schedule that had me scrambling here and there. Then the princess became suicidal. It was just one thing too much, much more than I could handle."[96]

At this moment, Ochs knows she herself needs an emergency cure, and her cousin's Sabbath-violation treatment is the only one she has observed firsthand. On her way to teach a class, Ochs decides to eat non-kosher food in a restaurant. After doing so, she declares, "I had eaten *traife*. I had violated the inviolable and nothing had happened. Good." Ochs says that, really, she knew nothing would happen, but the act of pushing against boundaries convinced her that "[t]o make it day to day, you had to call your own shots, invent and reinvent the terms of your own happiness."[97]

Ochs's entitling her essay "Taking the Cure" makes it reasonable, I think, to interpret her act of world deconstruction and reconstruction—on her own terms—as a healing enterprise and also as an act of moral agency. It enabled her to go on: "That was that. I bussed my tray. I taught a good class, drove home that night." It also gave her access to a healing strategy she could use again if she ever had to, "if ever I lost my center again, if I were constrained beyond my capacity, if all hopefulness and perspective ever leaked away."[98] But, Ochs concludes, "it would have to be a real emergency before I'd ever again resort to such a drastic measure." In a humorous story about what appears to be a small act of defiance, there is the healing act of accepting responsibility for one's religious commitments and one's religious worldview.

RESISTING HARMFUL IMAGES OF THE SACRED

A pivotal effort that women have found healing, beginning with the early years of this wave of feminism, is to resist the status quo of male images for the sacred and to construct new ones. These must demonstrate continuity with the tradition and at the same time break away from it. As Sallie McFague puts it in her description of metaphorical theological language, new images of the divine must be both shocking and recognizable.[99] This work has not been just a matter of rejecting male images and of making an extensive case for feminine imagery or using images from nature.[100] It has also come to involve the creation of images that are very particular to specific communities of people. Nancy L. Eiseland created an image of "God in a sip-puff wheel chair," the kind that many quadriplegics use, on behalf of her community of physically disabled people and as a member of the Christian tradition. In doing so she saw herself as taking on a double responsibility: resisting traditional images of an omnipotent, self-sufficient God and creating an image with which she felt an intimate connection, one that she felt had meaning for her own community of disabled people but also for the broader church: "God as a survivor, unpitying and forthright. I recognized the incarnate Christ in the image of those judged 'not feasible,' 'unemployable,' with 'questionable quality of life.' Here was God for me."[101] When Jacquelyn Grant shaped a new Christology based on the image of Jesus as a black woman she certainly had in mind resistance to insistently white depictions of God and Jesus. But her creative construction was also directed toward healing the self-perception of African-American women and contributing to the good of the entire black community and Christianity as a whole.[102]

These theologians claim that the manifestations of theological creativity that are healing for physically disabled people or black women are necessarily healing for others as well because of their continuity with the Christian tradition. Both instances demonstrate the healing properties of taking responsibility for a major symbol of the Christian tradition by expanding its images and by recognizing that reflection about "God" offers an arena of endless possibilities for theological creativity. To expand its images of God, these women imply, enhances the vitality of the tradition and its variously situated members. In this latter respect, pastoral theologian and United Methodist clergywoman Christie Cozad Neuger reports, "In the research I have done on women's images of God and the impact those images have on their lives, I have found that when one allows God to be experienced through a greater variety of images, (not concepts), then one's willingness to integrate spirituality with other aspects of life is greatly enhanced."[103] For these women healing lies also in resisting traditional fears that the meaning of religious symbols must be tightly controlled in order for its power to be retained.

Resistance can also take the form of revising the function of one of the traditional theological disciplines, for example homiletics. In a book about feminist preaching as "weeping, confession, and resistance," United Church of Christ clergywoman and preaching professor Christine M. Smith makes the claim that preaching itself is an act of resistance—both to old ways of preaching and to social injustice. Smith moves the act of preaching away from the impulse to simply give comfort either by conveying from the pulpit the certainties of the Christian tradition through the unquestioned authority of Scripture and tradition or by offering a primarily nurturing message aimed at furthering personal salvation. "Women," she says, "who preach from various feminist perspectives and men who embrace similar convictions and analysis share a belief that this approach to preaching is no longer adequate."[104] Smith's interpretation of preaching as resistance is related to her efforts to shape preaching as a form of "truth-telling," a stance that preachers must take, she holds, in order to "craft sermons that would passionately connect individuals and congregations to the pain and suffering of injustice and violence."[105] For Smith this act moves preaching into the realm of "weeping" and then "confession," both prerequisites for the kind of resistance that leads to the healing of social ills. Finally, though, says Smith, preaching as resistance fosters hope, because it gives rise to many voices that speak of "holy places of difference among us."[106] Healing from the status quo of traditional kinds of preaching requires new understandings of what preaching is for.

In addition to resisting social evil in its many manifestations, women also are resisting traditional definitions of sin and constructing new ones that seem more accurate and more fitting in light of the particular experiences of women. One example of this process is a widely cited essay by Mary Potter Engel about domestic and sexual violence against women and children, "Evil, Sin, and Violation of the Vulnerable."[107] Concerning traditional interpretations of sin as disobedience and pride, Engel sees resistance to them as necessary for constructing a theology that can liberate both victims and perpetrators from complying with what she calls the "evil structures" that perpetuate violence against the vulnerable. In reference to a reality that seems necessarily to call forth dichotomous definitions of sin and innocence, villain and victim, Engel is greatly concerned not to reduce the moral universe to a simple drama between heroes and villains, thereby contributing to "immobilizing guilt and resentment rather than heartfelt repentance and concrete change." She says she does not "want to suggest that the perpetrators (largely men) are wholly evil and that the victims (largely women) are wholly good. Women and other victims are no more or less pure than men."[108]

Engel sees her creative theological task, then, as one of constructing new understandings of sin that are versatile enough to cut both ways: to call both victim and victimizer to account. To that end she offers four definitions of sin that can be interpreted variously depending on the circumstances and the perspective of participants. These are (1) sin as a distortion of feeling, "a hardening of the heart," that takes for granted violence against the vulnerable and fosters a numbness to their suffering; (2) sin as "a betrayal of trust" rather than as disobedience; (3) sin as "lack of care" rather than sin as pride, a lack of care that takes the form of transgression by perpetrators and a diffusion of the boundaries of the self in victims; and (4) sin as "lack of consent to vulnerability," which Engel sees as a failure to maintain a dynamic tension between freedom and dependence, again on the part of both victims and victimizers, but taking different forms in each case.[109] For Engel this combination of resisting and constructing speaks to the complexity of the social and personal evil of violence against the vulnerable and the varieties of ways human beings are destructive to each other. It also fosters her conviction that "the capacity of human beings to do good and to repair the effects of evil by transforming them into good is co-original with this sinfulness."[110]

Healing as resistance has as its focus not only traditional understandings of sin, but also the rejection of traditionally prescribed virtues that women experience as having sacred status. These new definitions, poised between partial rejection of the old and construction of the new, advise their own kind of resistance. Maura A. Ryan suggests in her entry on "Virtue" in the *Dictionary of Feminist Theologies* that in order to be "truly transformative," a feminist ethic of virtue must "presuppose that questioning the virtue of whatever virtues women are asked to accept is a moral responsibility."[111] In the entry on "Virtue, Womanist," Katie Geneva Cannon says that for black women the concept of virtue cannot be separated from three principles: "invisibility [sic] dignity," "quiet grace," and "unshouted courage." "Quiet grace," says Cannon, "is the search for truth. It is defined as looking at the world with one's own eyes, forming judgments and demythologizing whole bodies of so-called social legitimacy."[112]

Both Ryan and Cannon express the conviction that women cannot be virtuous without questioning traditional meanings of virtue and constructing both new ideas of virtue and new virtues. Pastoral theologian Bonnie J. Miller-McLemore depicts her study of the theological dilemma of work and family in this light of redefining motherly virtue and as in part an act of defiance. "Ultimately," she says, "this book defies rules that a good person just does not go around defying lightly. It defies the virtue of never hurting another person, which defines the 'good girl,' and the virtue of unconditional love, which defines the 'good woman' and the 'good mother.' It defies the virtues of self-fulfillment and self-assertion, which define the 'good feminist'; the virtues of independence, self-reliance, and achievement which define the 'good man' and the 'good worker'; and ultimately, the virtues of objectivity and detachment which define the 'good scholar.'"[113]

Resistance to the demands of one set of virtues requires constructing others. Miller-McLemore resists taken-for-granted norms and virtues in every category that fits her life. This resistance is resonant with the framework of new understandings of virtue that are appearing in women's religious thought. That double task is what Miller-McLemore takes on in terms of both work and motherhood. She says that American society has thus far tended to address the mechanics of feminist protest in terms of some public policies and changes in the workplace. But, she contends, a theological perspective is needed as well, one that argues that "some forms of caring for human life can never be purchased and should never be quantified in material or product-oriented ways."[114] Miller-McLemore argues that a prophetic stance against present practices is required, not just a few changes, and that conviction would be a good one on which to end the book. "But the reality," she says, "is this: My life goes on amidst the ambiguities and mysteries of living, as do the lives of others who find themselves caught up in related or divergent dilemmas."[115]

Miller-McLemore's concluding confession of ambiguity is an indication of the extent to which women's religious thought, especially that which has emerged since the late 1980s, reveals an awareness that American culture and religion are in-between-times: past the early years of uncomplicated outrage on the part of women and well into a deep awareness of the precariousness and longevity of the struggle for full participation. If healing requires resistance of various kinds, it also requires acceptance of certain realities that women articulate as well in their religious thought.

HEALING AS ACCEPTANCE OF SUFFERING AND
THE INTERMINGLING OF GOOD AND EVIL

Women's theological creativity works to recognize, name, and resist evil, but also to acknowledge in ways that are not defeatist or fatalistic the continuing presence of suffering and evil in the world. In the writings of women from several different traditions, it becomes apparent how the acceptance of certain kinds of evil and tragedy functions as a healing insight, rather than, as one might assume, a cause for discouragement or even despair.

Discerning the difference between that which must be resisted and that which must be accepted requires ongoing theological effort of the kind Frida Kerner Furman demonstrates in *Facing the Mirror: Older Women and Beauty Shop Culture*.[116] In this ethnographic study, Furman, an ethicist, is interested not just in the quality of life of individual women, but in the social system that diminishes them and causes them pain. In keeping with the resistance/acceptance tension of women's thought, she characterizes her study of mostly Jewish women in the everyday world of a neighborhood beauty shop as one of resistance to the widespread cultural denigration of the "inner lives . . . experiences, observations, and reflections" of older people, especially women. Looked at the other way round, this is also an effort to recognize, accept, and empathize with the physical and psychic suffering that inevitably comes with aging. Furman concludes with an acknowledgment of "the knowledge and richness I have gained through my personal acquaintance with older women at Julie's International Salon. For me older women are no longer images on the screen or memories of my grandmother."[117]

ACCEPTANCE OF FINITUDE

Many women emphasize the inevitability of certain kinds of suffering in terms of the theological concept of "finitude." An acceptance of finitude moves us to assume that the world's goods and, thus, our goods are limited and that, because this world and our embodiment in it are all we have, religious worldviews must find their spiritual depth in this reality. Thus there will be no redress of injustice in other worlds; we must seek it for ourselves and for others here. Further, there are some kinds of suffering that cannot be avoided. The implications of an emphasis on finitude are apparent in Chapter 3, particularly in women's efforts to create meanings for traditional religious symbols such as "God" that can be at home on earth. In respect to ideas of finitude as they relate to healing, Rita Gross offers her perspective from the Buddhist tradition. She speaks of how essential it is to affirm "our limits and our embodied condition."[118] Gross acknowledges that Buddhism has strong anti-body and anti-world tendencies that may prompt practitioners to seek freedom from the world, but she finds in her feminist interpretation of Buddhism the wherewithal to seek freedom *within* the world.

Gross has also found in Buddhism a counter to what she has experienced as "aspects of feminist theology that did not fully realize that finitude and impermanence really are utterly basic" and "that even feminism will not cure some of life's hurts."[119] Like many Christian feminists, Gross refutes the notion that the limits of earthly life are a punishment for human sinfulness and that the spiritual life, therefore, must be directed toward escape from the world by means of death, another form of finitude, which in many traditional theologies is also regarded as punishment for the sin of being human. For Gross it does not heal life's hurts to view life as primarily a preparation for death. "Feminist Buddhism," according to Gross, "though not denying the possibility of rebirth, will emphasize that we know for sure that we are living *now* and that it is important to live this life well, wisely, and joyfully."[120]

FEMINISM, EVIL, AND TRAGEDY

Other women choose to write about human limitation in terms of the tragic element they see as part of the universe—that there is a certain amount of suffering and evil in the world that can never be obliterated. And, typically, they hold that accepting the inevitability of tragedy is a means to foster hope. In her book on women and evil, which is also an elaboration of a feminist ethics of care, educational philosopher Nell Noddings suggests that however much "evil" and "tragedy" are a profound part of life, they cannot be the last words about the human condition: "Perhaps we should now consider an education guided by a tragic sense of life, a view that cannot claim to overcome evil (any more than we can overcome dust) but claims only to live sensitively with as little of it as possible."[121]

Theologian Kathleen M. Sands argues that accepting tragedy as a part of reality is part of the feminist moral task of "making the world go on." She is also critical of feminist theology up to this point for its failure to incorporate a sufficient sense of the tragic, which she defines "not as meaningless suffering but the conflicted context where we must create what right and reason we can."[122] Sands uses such phrases as "irrecoverable loss" and "irresolvable contradiction" to indicate her conviction that we live in a world of "suffering and radical conflict" and that everything is not going to be all right in a finite universe with competing, plural goods.

As grounding for a feminist understanding of tragedy, Sands first rejects the Western liberal rationalist inclination to see evil as ultimately "nothing." Rationalism, in Sands's understanding, attempts to render evil impotent and tragedy nonexistent by either comprehending evil or rehabilitating it—in effect, by saying that it is nothing. She is no happier with the other strategy: a dualistic worldview that longs for a good that is unmixed with evil and based on claims to be able to distinguish the two—thereby seeing evil in the Other.[123] In each case, says Sands, the reality of tragedy is negated but only in theory. Evil continues to be a part of the lives of those who want and strive for goodness. We are inevitably involved in it, and to identify evil means to render "the negative moral judgments that set one's face against some part of life."[124]

What makes an insistence on the reality of tragedy, evil, and irreconcilable conflict a healing insight in women's thought rather than an overwhelming burden? In Sands's understanding, an acceptance of all three moves women's religious thought in new and more pragmatic directions. It gives rise to a tragic heuristic that requires theological wondering and questioning, rather than the kind of certainty theology has typically thought it needed. It encourages as well a move away from theodicies that repress rather than acknowledge and address the tragic. It moves theological conversation away from metaphysical speculation and into the arena of social action. Sands, like other feminist theologians already named, finds sources for accomplishing all three in literature written by women of many colors, particularly that which comes out of communities of color. Accepting the reality of tragedy, evil, and irreconcilable conflict is a way of acknowledging that "in a radically plural and often conflicted world, we cannot be for everything and what we are against has a cost."[125] Sands anticipates no perfect ending "out here, beyond the walls of paradise," but confesses herself content "with the daily proliferation of difference and the limping jig of grace."[126]

HEALING GENDER POLARIZATION: ACCEPTING WOMEN'S SINFULNESS

Marjorie Suchocki echoes Sands's acceptance of the idea that we are inevitably involved in evil and loss and reinforces Mary Potter Engel's contention that it is not theologically viable or politically helpful to construct a drama based on the interplay between heroes and villains. Suchocki says that "to break the world cleanly into victims and violators ignores the depths of each person's participation in cultural sin. There simply are no innocents."[127] Her interpretation of forgiveness, mentioned in the previous chapter, is "willing the well-being of those involved in violation," an act that "opens us to a new future, and therefore to time itself as healing and transformative."[128] What is important for the purposes of this chapter is Suchocki's emphasis on the power of forgiveness to bring about healing in the sufferer, because it releases the sufferer from the past and for the future by acceptance of what cannot be changed.

In their move away from futilely polarized depictions of victim and victimizer, male and female, through acceptance of the realities and complexities of certain kinds of suffering, women continue to seek new, more healing ways to talk about gender itself. After many years of writing about this subject Rosemary Radford Ruether finds herself still seeking ways to talk about what it means to be male or female without collapsing into categories of either normative male/deficient female or good female/bad male: "Is there sufficiently greater difference than similarity between human males and human females that we cannot construct a concept of a common 'species ideal' to which men and women can and should aspire 'equally'?"[129]

This is for Ruether a live, not a rhetorical, question. Asked by many women and men out of a desire for a never-quite-defined wholeness, one that is "not a known ideal, but goes ahead of us into an incomplete future," this question is prompting many varieties of theological work, some of them devoted to issues of suffering and masculinity from a feminist perspective. One such effort is *The Care of Men*, a collection of essays about pastoral care and counseling of men edited by Protestant theologians Christie Cozad Neuger and James Newton Poling. The editors asked the contributors to go beyond the typical issues of work, sexuality, marriage, and parenting by writing essays that assume "focusing on the care of men can be a creative way to approach the church's theology and practice in a time of transition and crisis in gender relationships."[130]

Additional efforts to move beyond polarized interpretations of gender differences focus on women's efforts to accept the realities of women's sinfulness and to reflect on them creatively without falling into some of the orgies of self-blame that have tended to characterize women's confessions of sinfulness in the past. This has been a self-blaming often coupled with a striving for perfection, a perfection that, it was hoped, would save one from suffering. How to be more theologically creative in naming "sin" in light of women's experience was one of the major issues of Valerie Saiving's 1960 essay, and her work prompted that of others, particularly Judith Plaskow. As related in the previous chapter, women's discoveries of their sinfulness toward other communities of women have also prompted new questions about how most fruitfully to accept the reality of women's capacities for sin and what actions to take in light of this knowledge.

In her construction of a feminist thealogy of pagan ritual, one of the missing elements for Wendy Hunter Roberts has been adequate language for expressing women's capacity for sin: "Having forsaken the traditional theological language of salvation, sin, and sacrifice, we too often find ourselves in the untenable position of trying to rewrite reality with only visualization and the barrenness of subjectivist psychological vocabulary and paradigm to help us."[131] In an intensely relational, ecologically oriented worldview that is in the main hopeful about human possibility and dedicated to the work of "fighting evil and healing our world," Roberts feels the lack of "a well-developed theology of good and evil, a common ground from which to speak and act." She speculates that one source would be the selective reclaiming of traditional theological language of sin and salvation.[132]

ACCEPTING SUFFERING AS WORTH
THE COST OF WHAT IT TEACHES

I conclude this section on healing and the acceptance of certain kinds of suffering with some excerpts from Nancy Mairs's memoir, *Ordinary Time*. She illustrates a theologically creative response to the purposeful taking on of suffering that she experiences as a feminist who chooses to remain within the Roman Catholic tradition, suffering she might certainly have avoided by leaving that tradition. "A Catholic feminist?" she asks. "Dear God," she responds, "couldn't I please be something else?"[133] Further, she has some things to say about the acceptance of the physical and emotional suffering that is part of her life because she has had multiple sclerosis for many years.

In the introduction to *Ordinary Time*, Mairs acknowledges that after more than a decade, being a Roman Catholic feminist hasn't gotten much easier. She confesses her compulsion to write about being a Catholic feminist when she'd rather be writing a novel she's started "about a woman who finds a skeleton walled up behind some shelves of old fruit preserves in her cellar," and her fear that because she is not an academic theologian she will not get things right in this spiritual autobiography. But here are many of the themes that characterize contemporary American women's religious thought: the ambivalence toward her tradition; commitment to reflection on the ordinary as revelatory of the sacred; an assumption of the relational nature of existence; and insistence that we "acknowledge personal responsibility for the God we choose and the ways in which we permit her into our lives."[134] Mairs makes it very clear that in her commitments she has taken on suffering she could avoid: "I'm smart enough to recognize without assistance the spiritual/social/intellectual dilemma I've skewered myself on. I may be foolhardy . . . but I'm not an utter fool."[135]

On the other hand, the suffering that has come to Mairs through multiple sclerosis is not one that she has chosen; it is simply part of the experience of human finitude. At the time of writing *Ordinary Time*, she is also experiencing her husband's serious cancer. She speculates whether she might commit suicide when her husband dies, having suffered from emotional illness and attempted it before. She does not fear that she will be damned for taking her own life—she doesn't believe in hell—but she doesn't think, finally, that she will do so. She tells her daughter, "who was present for my neurologist's life sentence," that she isn't sure: "But I think maybe I'm supposed to see this through to the end."[136] When her daughter asks Mairs in disapproval if she thinks somehow that she ought to suffer, Mairs says, "No, I don't. I may suffer, probably I will, but I don't think I'm *supposed* to. I'm just saying maybe I need to have the whole experience, not cut it off." "I am as afraid as ever," she says, "of loss and pain. Still, something tells me—I don't know what, I can't explain what, it's just a feeling I have in my bones—that I'm supposed to stay for it all."[137] If what Mairs has to say is not a closely argued treatise about the need to accept suffering in order to be healed, it is nonetheless a testimony with discernible theological underpinnings to this theme in the religious thought of many women.

Conclusion

For women, an emphasis on healing is a common and powerful way to talk about new ways of thinking about traditional religious ideas. "Healing" moves women quickly into the kinds of ontological and ultimate concerns that require seeking meaning at the deepest levels of human experience. The multiple narratives and perspectives in this chapter on healing and being healed, sinning and suffering, resisting and accepting, good and evil, offer evidence that "healing" as a broad concept is intellectually and spiritually provocative for women. It is also the very plurality of women's responses about what healing means in various communities that gives testimony to its power not only to stimulate theological creativity but to foster action on behalf of the community. Women seek to understand, as well, what evil means in particular communities and what forms healing must take in response to it. The more ideas about healing and sin and evil that emerge from different communities, women suggest, the more possibility of combating what Mary Potter Engel calls their "Hydra-headed nature." This is an image she uses to convey that understandings of sin and evil are simply not reducible to a single metaphor.[138]

"Healing" in women's religious thought continues to mean, as it did thirty years ago, alleviating the pain of women's exclusion from full participation in their traditions. To bring about healing, though, is not just a matter of imposing value on formerly denigrated, female-identified aspects of nature and culture. It is also looked upon as an ongoing, always needed activity of the theological imagination. It is not just a sometime-thing in women's religious thought. Given the realities and multiplicities of human suffering—much unnecessary, some inevitable—women insist that all religions must to a great extent be healing religions.

Chickasaw poet Linda Hogan calls one of her volumes of poetry *The Book of Medicines*, and in the poem "Sickness" she writes, "I saw disease./ . . . It went to work./ It tried to take my tongue./ But these words,/these words are proof/ there is healing."[139] In women's religious thought, ideas about healing have come to function as a call not for poetry, necessarily, but certainly for "words" that issue in theological creativity. It is a creativity that works toward the full participation of women in their religious communities; that pushes not only beyond intellectual and emotional impasses related to male and female but also past the ideological, social, and theoretical dead-ends that women of different communities have foundered on in their efforts to work together. The construction of healing ideas, as women are noting in a variety of ways, requires the ability to keep numerous, apparently contradictory ideas alive in the conversation and, at the same time, make decisions and take action. Healing ideas are those that foster hope without diminishing the complexities women experience. They are ideas that do not attempt either to falsely unify plural perspectives or to give up on the possibility that women of different communities can make claims together at this moment in history.

Epilogue

Après le déluge *What's Next?*

The question that has formed the foundation of this book—"When women write and speak publicly and as women about religious ideas, what do they have to say?"—could not have been answered in 1960 when Valerie Saiving speculated about how the distinctive experiences of women might call into question theological assumptions that religious traditions had always presented as universal. Forty years later women of many different communities have demonstrated the prescience of Saiving and of other early religious feminists like Mary Daly.

Daly recalls in her autobiography that several years before she began to publish her own feminist works, she had read an article by Rosemary Lauter in *Commonweal*, a Catholic periodical, arguing for the equality of women in the church. Daly responded with a letter to the editor confessing that she was ashamed of her own silence and that she should have published such an article herself. She predicted a "deluge" of such articles: "This much I know: the beginnings of these articles and these books (how badly we need these books especially!) are already in the minds and on the lips of many of us. And—this is both a prophecy and a promise—they will come." Daly recalls that "[t]hese words came out of my typewriter before I was even confident that I could write such a book. I did not even know that I knew such a thing until the words were right there before me."[1]

It was not only women like Daly, who came to be known as radical feminists, who were making such predictions. In 1979, in an article about new religious movements in America, religious historian Robert S. Ellwood mentioned the prominence of women in many of them. He concluded his article with his own speculation that "a possible American feminine religion has already been limned by certain common features of these movements, and that when its day comes it could break out of marginality with surprising speed."[2]

Whether the themes of this book already form the outline of a "women's religion" or have the potential to do so can only be a matter of speculation. After I have made the claim that there are common themes and even methods in women's religious thought that cut across traditions, and even, to an extent, centuries, is it a useful move to go one step further and think in terms of "women's religion"? By "useful," I mean will such a move have the effect of promoting the assumption that gender is a dimension of life and of religion to be consistently aware of and to explore rather than a problem to be solved?

I have given a great deal of thought to whether it is possible or wise or accurate or useful to talk about "women's religion" in America. Is one's interpretive energy likely to be exhausted by the preliminary task of pointing out all the things one doesn't mean by that phrase: separatism; some essential female nature that gives rise to similar ideas; women's ownership of particular ideas like immanence or relationality; gender-induced theological identity? Is the term "women's religion" intellectually usable? Does it offer the possibility of pulling together the insights and the theological constructions of disparate groups in order to reveal patterns that lead to provocative insights and new questions about American religious thought? Or does it mask important differences and close down avenues of further inquiry? Are the connotations of "women's" and "men's" currently so polarized in American culture and ordered in terms of inferior or superior (depending upon who is doing the ordering and why) that the term "women's religion" can only suggest either separatist or triumphalist connotations? The idea of "separate spheres" applied to women's cultural and religious history has sometimes opened up interpretive possibilities and insights in particular historical and cultural contexts, but it has also led to methodological and conceptual dead-ends. Is it possible or useful to talk about "women's religion" the same way one talks about liberal religion or evangelical religion or nature religion? I think that at this moment in history we simply do not yet know the answers to these questions. What we do know is that history does not give us much reason to be optimistic about the persistence of previous women's movements. But we have never before, either, seen the deluge of work in all aspects of religion and religions that the last thirty years have produced.[3]

It is not so very long ago that women discovered they had almost no written past—only the fragmentary and often imagined memory of generations of women's faithful support of their religious communities, based on their own experiences of circumscribed participation in the present. "Contemporaneity is not enough," Mary Pellauer concluded, when she worked in the 1970s on her study of the theologies of Elizabeth Cady Stanton, Susan B. Anthony, and Anna Howard Shaw: "'Behind' me—which is, after all, 'where' we in the West locate the past—was a great gaping emptiness." Pellauer said she felt as if she were sitting on a high kitchen stool with no back: "If I were to lean back, I would topple—topple into the abyss that lurked there just behind me, the darkness of centuries disappeared."[4] Several decades of work in religious history, textual interpretation, ritual formation, and theology have given women both a past and a present. Whether all this work can guarantee a future that sustains women's public presence in religious life is an open question. It may be that for the moment a phrase like" women's religion" can serve a necessary heuristic function: a reminder that we do not know enough about a religious tradition until we have asked, What do women say about what it means to be a woman, for better and for worse, in a particular tradition? What do women have to say about every aspect of their religious traditions: rituals, teachings, polity? What do they have to contribute? Perhaps it is enough for now simply to say that at this moment in history—for a great variety of reasons and in many different ways—women of different traditions have found certain ideas particularly stimulating to their religious imaginations.

In the meantime an exploration of women's religious thought has some insights to convey about religion in America that go beyond concerns with matters of gender. Women's simultaneous critique and continuing reinterpretation of the symbols and rituals and teachings of their particular traditions offer testimony to the power of these symbols at a time when there are widespread fears about growing cultural secularization and declining church membership (although one might well ask when, historically, this has not been the case). In fact, it is an interesting irony that women's critique of institutional religion has turned out to be so intensely conserving in many respects. Perhaps in our worries about secularization we have let ourselves be misled by the sociological dictum that a primary characteristic of religion in America is its voluntary nature. While the principle of voluntarism is considered the bedrock of a culture that separates religion from the state, its too-broad application may have promoted exaggerated fears about the ease with which people abandon or dilute their religious loyalties. Women's religious thought provides strong evidence that the power of religious symbols is ongoing and institution-transcending. Membership statistics might not always be the best source for understanding where religious vitality lies in a culture and what boundaries it crosses.

Related to the question of boundaries is the phenomenon of insiders and outsiders in American religious history. Women's self-described experience of being both insiders and outsiders in their traditions stirs up some interesting complexities in the ways these obvious-sounding categories are typically used to refer to established versus alternative religions. Women's religious thought speaks to the inside of their traditions from the outside, or at least from the far boundaries. It speaks from the inside outward as well to those, some feminists among them, who wonder why women continue to find religious communities meaningful.

186

This dual position helps to account for the intensity of both critique and construction in women's thought. It is a model that could go a long way toward helping religious traditions develop strategies for ongoing and rigorous self-critique with the confidence that self-critique and theological innovation are more likely to revitalize traditions than destroy them. It is my sense that because women have not been the custodians of theological boundaries within their institutions, they worry much less that theological experimentation and creativity will topple their traditions. Women testify from experience, and often ruefully, that traditions do not topple, or even wobble, very easily. Thus, who better than women to reassure institutions that all the ecclesiastical energy expended on guarding boundaries would be better spent on plumbing the depths of communities in search of wisdom and vitality? The boundaries are likely to take care of themselves.

There is also the matter of women's religious thought and the insights it provides into some of the dynamics of pluralism. Women's efforts to make claims about "women" in general have brought them very quickly into the arena of both religious and cultural pluralism in efforts to sort out in ways related to gender the never-ending drama of the one and the many in American culture. This has led women into some creative strategies concerned not so much with defending their traditions as trying to figure out how best to articulate and contribute their deepest meanings in conversation with women of different communities. The evidence of women's continuing desire to draw from and live out of the best of their own traditions and at the same time benefit from the collective vigor of other communities might also function to diminish the fears of relativism—usually defined as the inability or unwillingness to distinguish among multiple truths and values—that are so prevalent at the moment in American culture.

The idea of self-consciously constructing theologies is new to most American women. Nonetheless, women's efforts are very obviously a part of the American experiment in religion, with all its power to elicit and give voice and shape to the new and its simultaneous slowness in absorbing and integrating the theological fruits that emerge from experiences of embodied difference like gender and race. At the very least, an exploration of American women's religious thought reveals how much more there always is to be said about our religious traditions—they are, indeed, surprisingly inexhaustible when there is no bar on who can participate in their ongoing formation. More than that, the theological work of women may well be changing the contours of American religious thought.

Over the last several decades, women of many communities have demonstrated the significant, evocative power of gender as an interpretive and constructive category in religion and theology. They have offered publicly their experiences, their critiques, their commitments, and their creativity to the ongoing shaping of religious ideas in American history and culture. By their contributions, women have worked to broaden and deepen, reform and revitalize, the theological worldviews of their communities from both inside and outside those communities' boundaries. At the same time they have made it almost overwhelmingly possible to answer the question that only recently was not even asked: When women write and speak publicly—and self-consciously as women—about religious ideas, what do they have to say?

Notes

1. American Women as Religious Thinkers

1. I have always liked and found useful William Clebsch's contention in *American Religious Thought: A History* (Chicago: University of Chicago Press, 1973) that "Religious thought means something far broader than the denominational doctrines that theologians have certified, whether by appeal to traditional or to novel revelations, and also something more definite than personal opinions about things unexplained by accepted natural laws. Here religious thought means the reasoned, the cogent, and the evocative consideration of ways in which the human spirit of Americans seriously and strenuously relates itself to nature, to society, and to deity" (p. 2).

2. Nancy Frankenberry, "Classical Theism, Panentheism, and Pantheism: On the Relation between God Construction and Gender Construction," *Zygon: Journal of Religion and Science* 28, no. 1 (March 1993): p. 36.

3. "Womanist" is the term that African-American feminists have chosen to distinguish their work from that of white feminists, and *mujerista* is the name by which Latina women refer to their theologies. There will be more detail about both these communities in later chapters.

4. Recent studies show that even ordination to ministry, now available to women in many communities, is not an unambiguous gain for women. See Frederick W. Schmidt Jr., *A Still, Small Voice: Women, Ordination, and the Church* (Syracuse: Syracuse University Press, 1996); Barbara Brown Zikmund, Adair T. Lummis, and Patricia Mei Yin Chang, eds., *Clergy Women: An Uphill Calling* (Louisville, Ky.: Westminster/John Knox Press, 1998); and Mark Chaves, *Ordaining Women: Culture and Conflict in Religious Organizations* (Cambridge: Harvard University Press, 1997).

5. Judith Plaskow, "The Right Question Is Theological," in *On Being a Jewish Feminist: A Reader,* ed. with introd. and new preface by Susannah Heschel (New York: Schocken Books, 1983, 1995), pp. 223–233. This essay was written in response to another by Cynthia Ozick, originally printed in *Lilith* magazine in 1979 (and reprinted in this volume, pp. 120–151), suggesting that the "right question" was other than theological. Plaskow maintains that the view of women as Other is deeply rooted in Jewish theology, in fact in Torah itself.

6. See Gerda Lerner, *The Creation of Feminist Consciousness: From the Middle Ages to Eighteen-seventy* (New York: Oxford University Press, 1993). Or Ann Douglas's surprise in her study of nineteenth-century women writers (*The Feminization of American Culture,* Avon, 1977) that instead of discovering her grandmothers she had encountered her sisters—women whose issues sounded frighteningly familiar. Or Mary Pellauer's realization voiced in *Toward a Tradition of Feminist Theology: The Religious Social Thought of Elizabeth Cady Stanton, Susan B. Anthony, and Anna Howard Shaw* (Brooklyn: Carlson Publishing Inc., 1991) that the feminist theology of the 1970s she thought was so radical had already been articulated by Elizabeth Cady Stanton, Anna Howard Shaw, and Susan B. Anthony. "No one had told me," she said. "Indeed, it seemed as I went along that nobody knew it" (p. 309).

7. For an excellent survey of the history of evolving scholarship on feminism and religion see Rita M. Gross, *Feminism and Religion: An Introduction* (Boston: Beacon Press, 1996). Gross's concerns are broader than women in American religious history, but she catalogues and analyzes the major methodological issues that have concerned women theologians and religious scholars since the mid 1960s, describes major works and schools of thought, and also speculates about what's next.

8. I use the terms "community" and "tradition" somewhat interchangeably, but I think "community" has broader connotations in general and does a better job of signaling that I range beyond the boundaries of established denominations in this study.

9. Ann Braude, "Women's History *Is* American Religious History," in *Retelling U.S. Religious History*, ed. Thomas A. Tweed (Berkeley, Los Angeles, London: University of California Press, 1997), p. 102.

10. Jung Ha Kim, *Bridge-Makers and Cross-Bearers: Korean-American Women and the Church* (Atlanta: Scholars Press, 1997), p. 11.

11. Mary Farrell Bednarowski, "Outside the Mainstream: Women's Religion and Women Religious Leaders in Nineteenth-Century America," *Journal of the American Academy of Religion* 48 (Summer 1980): pp. 207–231.

12. In *Beyond Liberalism and Fundamentalism: How Modern and Postmodern Philosophy Set the Theological Agenda* (Valley Forge, Penn.: Trinity Press International, 1996), Nancey Murphy gives good descriptions of what she calls the "expressive" nature of liberal theology and the "descriptive" nature of conservative theology. See especially ch. 2, "Description or Expression: How Can We Speak About God?" and ch. 3, "Immanence or Intervention: How Does God Act in the World?" One of the examples Murphy gives of expressive theology is feminist theology (pp. 53–55).

13. For one example of this critique related specifically to women and religion, see Laura Levitt, *Jews and Feminism: The Ambivalent Search for Home* (New York: Routledge, 1997).

14. For feminist scholars, like me, who spend much of their time talking with and reading works generally characterized as liberal, it is highly instructive and very necessary, I am convinced, to be aware of feminist work among evangelical women. Conversations with Susan McCoubrie, former member services director of the feminist evangelical organization Christians for Biblical Equality, founded in St. Paul, Minnesota, in the late 1980s, made me aware of a whole realm of feminist inquiry and effort—authors I was unaware of, very popular books I had not heard of—that I would not have come across on my own. Two exceptions are Virginia Ramey Mollenkott and Mary Stewart Van Leeuwen, whose works are more widely known outside evangelical circles.

15. In 1989 Judith Plaskow and Carol P. Christ edited *Weaving the Visions: New Patterns in Feminist Spirituality* (San Francisco: Harper and Row), a well-known and highly regarded anthology of feminist theology and thealogy (the term used by many Goddess feminists as an alternative to the traditional "theology"). In the introduction they contrasted the process of selection with what had been the case more than ten years earlier when they had published another such anthology, *Womanspirit Rising; A Feminist Reader in Religion* (San Francisco: Harper and Row, 1979): "In 1978, there were only a small number of books and essays from which to choose chapters for our collection, and, rightly or wrongly, principles of organization seemed to leap out at us. This time, by way of contrast, we found ourselves confronted with hundreds of books and articles having strong claims on us, and with numerous possible structures into which they might fit. In weighing what to use, we found ourselves searching for balance on many different scales, and—despite the larger size of this book—feeling a much sharper sense of regret about what was excluded" (p. 1).

16. New volumes continue to emerge. It would not be difficult to offer a good-sized bibliography from 1998, the year during which I was making revisions in the original manuscript. Here are four examples of new works by authors whose earlier writ-

ings are cited in this study: Rachel Adler, *Engendering Judaism: An Inclusive Theology and Ethics* (Philadelphia, Jerusalem: Jewish Publication Society, 1998); Elizabeth A. Johnson, *Friends of God and Prophets: A Feminist Theological Reading of the Communion of Saints* (New York: Continuum, 1998); Wendy Hunter Roberts, *Celebrating Her: Feminist Ritualizing Comes of Age* (Cleveland, Ohio: Pilgrim Press, 1998); Rosemary Radford Ruether, *Women and Redemption: A Theological History* (Minneapolis: Fortress Press, 1998).

17. In the introduction to a collection of essays about gender, religion, and symbols, Caroline Walker Bynum makes the comment that "American feminism has tended to be empirical, inductive, and concerned with causal analysis, wrestling repeatedly with the question Why is the condition of women as it is today? whereas French feminism has been more literary and phenomenological, wrestling with the question How can we talk about women's experience?" "Introduction: The Complexity of Symbols," *Gender and Religion: On the Complexity of Symbols*, ed. Caroline Walker Bynum, Stevan Harrell, and Paula Richman (Boston: Beacon Press, 1986), p. 12. In more recent years American women's religious thought has turned more in the direction of how women's experience can transform religious symbols and doctrines.

18. Mary Daly, *Beyond God the Father: Toward a Philosophy of Women's Liberation* (Boston: Beacon Press, 1973), p. 98.

19. An exception to this pattern is William Clebsch's *American Religious Thought* (Chicago: University of Chicago Press, 1973), which looks at American religious thought in terms of three important figures: Jonathan Edwards, Ralph Waldo Emerson, and William James. In this book Clebsch argues for a movement over two centuries of American religious thought away from an emphasis on Puritan morality and toward an aesthetic stance grounded in being at home in the universe. There is no attention to issues of gender in this volume, nor to non-Protestant thought (using "Protestant" loosely in the case of Emerson and James). Amanda Porterfield, one of Clebsch's students, subsequently published a creative book on several prominent Protestant women from the eighteenth, nineteenth, and twentieth centuries that takes up the theme of "homemaking" as a spiritual pursuit likewise grounded in aesthetics. See Amanda Porterfield, *Feminine Spirituality in America: From Sarah Edwards to Martha Graham* (Philadelphia: Temple University Press, 1980).

20. For recent efforts in this area see Tweed, ed., *Retelling U.S. Religious History.*

21. David G. Hackett, "Gender and Religion in American Culture, 1870–1930," *Religion and American Culture* 5, no. 2 (Summer 1995): p. 127.

22. Gerda Lerner, *The Woman in American History* (Menlo Park, Calif.: Addison-Wesley Publishing Company, 1971), p. 22.

23. Ibid., pp. 146–149.

24. Ibid., p. 112.

25. Laurel Thatcher Ulrich, "Vertuous Women Found: New England Ministerial Literature, 1668–1735," *American Quarterly* 28 (1976): p. 20.

26. Re-Imagining was the primary North American event of the World Council of Churches' program The Ecumenical Decade: Churches in Solidarity with Women (1988–1998). It was sponsored by the Twin Cities Metropolitan Church Commission, the Greater Minneapolis Council of Churches, the St. Paul Area Council of Churches, and the Minnesota Council of Churches. As a member of one of the planning committees and as a presenter, I was dumbfounded by the reaction against Re-Imagining, although, given my knowledge of women in American religious history, I shouldn't have been. For a collection of essays of response to the first Re-Imagining conference — mostly positive, some negative—see *Re-Membering and Re-Imagining*, ed. Nancy Berneking and Pamela Carter Joern (Cleveland: Pilgrim Press, 1995).

27. Peter Steinfels, "Presbyterians Try to Resolve Long Dispute: Women's Gathering Prompts Peace Move," *New York Times*, June 17, 1994, p. A9.

28. It is not difficult to find very recent warnings from men of various traditions about the threat to a community's identity posed by women's call for ordination or for changes in liturgies. See Kenneth L. Woodward, "Gender and Religion: Who's Really Running the Show," *Commonweal* 123, no. 20 (November 22, 1996): pp. 9–14. Woodward is concerned, as many have been since the nineteenth century, that the feminization of Christianity is contributing to the decline of mainline denominations and "to the gradual disappearance of anything that might adequately be described as masculine, no matter who in the hierarchy is calling the shots." "Surely," he says, "there is need to incorporate, expand, and deepen what is feminine in religion. But there are limits. And as we can see in the exponents of post-Christian feminism, those limits have already been breached" (p. 14). In "God and Gender in Judaism," *First Things*, no. 64 (June/July 1996): pp. 33–38, Matthew Berke, a Reform Jew, expresses concerns about gender-inclusive liturgical changes in Reform Judaism, including his worry that "the introduction of feminized liturgies also reveals the Reform movement's continuing recklessness toward the principle of *Clal Yisrael*—the larger unity of the Jewish people. That sense of unity is now under heavy, almost unbearable stress" (p. 38). Neither of these articles is without subtlety or without issues that are worth discussion, but the fears expressed about "what is happening" to religious institutions because of feminism are typical in their call for limits and their emphasis on negative effects.

29. For a compelling elaboration on how women's numerical dominance in religious traditions has been perceived negatively, see Braude, "Women's History *Is* American Religious History," pp. 87–107. Braude contends that three influential narratives that have been used to structure American religious history—declension, feminization, and secularization—do not hold up well if one looks at them in terms of gender: "I believe that attention to gender helps to explain why these motifs, and the historical claims that ground them, have held such explanatory power for historians even though, from an empirical perspective, they never happened" (p. 87).

2. Ambivalence as a New Religious Virtue

1. Valerie Saiving, "The Human Situation: A Feminine View," in *Womanspirit Rising: A Feminist Reader in Religion*, ed. Carol P. Christ and Judith Plaskow (San Francisco: Harper and Row, 1979), pp. 25–42. First published in *The Journal of Religion* in 1960. For a good sense of how very fruitful and complex the category of women's experience has become since Saiving wrote her article see Serene Jones, "'Women's Experience' between a Rock and a Hard Place: Feminist, Womanist and *Mujerista* Theologies in North America," *Religious Studies Review* 21, no. 3 (July 1995): pp. 171–178.

2. Ibid., p. 25

3. "A Conversation with Valerie Saiving," *Journal of Feminist Studies in Religion*, 4, no. 2 (Fall 1988): p. 108. The conversation took place during a concluding session of Professor Mary Gerhart's senior seminar, Theology from a Feminist Perspective, for religious studies majors at Hobart and William Smith Colleges.

4. Ibid., 112.

5. Rebecca S. Chopp, *Saving Work: Feminist Practices of Theological Education* (Louisville, Ky.: Westminster/John Knox Press, 1995), p. 35. One of the earliest and best-known elaborations of Saiving's thesis appears in Judith Plaskow, *Sex, Sin and Grace: Women's Experience and the Theologies of Reinhold Niebuhr and Paul Tillich* (Lanham, Md.: University Press of America, 1980). Saiving's influence has not been confined to feminist theologians. Gordon Kaufman, now retired from the Divinity School at Harvard, says of Saiving's article that "her argument struck me as important and basically convincing—and I wrote her for an offprint, which she graciously sent me and which I still have." In Roundtable Discussion: "The Influence of Feminist Theory on My Theological Work," *Journal of Feminist Studies in Religion* 7, no. 1 (Spring

1991): p. 112. Other contributors were John B. Cobb Jr., Peter C. Hogdson, Wayne Proudfoot, Mark Kline Taylor, David Tracy, and Vincent L. Wimbush.

6. Jonathan Franzen, "Sifting the Ashes: Confessions of a Conscientious Objector in the Cigarette Wars," *New Yorker*, May 13, 1996, p. 48.

7. Gail Ramshaw, *God beyond Gender: Feminist Christian God-Language* (Minneapolis: Fortress Press, 1995), p. vii.

8. Ibid.

9. Rita Nakashima Brock, *Journeys by Heart: A Christology of Erotic Power* (New York: Crossroad, 1988).

10. Martha Sawyer Allen, "Faithful Iconoclast," Minneapolis *Star Tribune*, August 16, 1997, pp. B5, B8.

11. Judith Plaskow, *Standing Again at Sinai: Judaism from a Feminist Perspective* (New York: HarperSanFrancisco, 1990), p. 5.

12. Ibid., pp. xix–xx.

13. I was helped to clarify this distinction between affective and cognitive approaches, as I struggled to figure out whether I really did want to talk about ambiguity rather than ambivalence, by comments from John Barbour after a presentation I gave at St. Olaf College in Northfield, Minnesota, in March 1997.

14. Religious communities aren't the only institutions resisting. The spell-check feature on my word-processing program consistently changes "clergywomen" to "clergymen." "Ignore," I select in response.

15. Two terms have become heuristically indispensable in describing from women's perspective the "set of rules" that is in place in religious institutions: "patriarchy," which refers to male domination of institutions, and "androcentrism," the interpretation of a tradition's history and teachings from a male perspective that never asks, "What is it like to be a woman in this tradition?"

16. In *Your Daughters Shall Prophesy: Revivalism and Feminism in the Age of Finney*, preface by Jerald C. Brauer (Brooklyn: Carlson Publishing, 1991), Nancy A. Hardesty quotes the negative response of a clergyman to women in ministry: "Wailed one reverend gentleman (J. F. Stearnes): "The question is not in regard to *ability*, but to *decency*, to order, to Christian propriety" (p. 106).

17. Judith Plaskow, *Standing Again at Sinai*, p. 2.

18. Ibid., p. 95.

19. Anne E. Carr, *Transforming Grace: Christian Tradition and Women's Experience* (San Francisco: Harper and Row, 1988), p. 36.

20. Carolyn M. Wallace, "The Priesthood and Motherhood in the Church of Jesus Christ of Latter-day Saints," in *Gender and Religion: On the Complexity of Symbols*, ed. Caroline Walker Bynum, Stevan Harrell, and Paul Richman (Boston: Beacon Press, 1986), p. 117.

21. Catherine Mowry LaCugna, *God for Us: The Trinity and Christian Life* (New York: HarperSanFrancisco, 1991).

22. Catherine Mowry LaCugna, "Catholic Women as Ministers and Theologians," *America* 167, no. 10 (October 10, 1992): p. 239.

23. Ibid.

24. Rita M. Gross, *Buddhism after Patriarchy: A Feminist History, Analysis, and Reconstruction of Buddhism* (Albany: State University of New York Press, 1993), p. 23.

25. Kate Wheeler, "Bowing, Not Scraping," in *Buddhist Women on the Edge: Contemporary Perspectives from the Western Frontier*, ed. Marianne Dresser (Berkeley, Calif.: North Atlantic Books, 1996), p. 57.

26. Patricia Gundry, "Why We're Here," in *Women, Authority, and the Bible*, ed. Alvera Mickelsen (Downers Grove, Ill.: InterVarsity Press, 1986), p. 14.

27. Ibid.

28. Ibid., p. 15.

29. Diana Hochstedt Butler, "Between Two Worlds," *Christian Century* 110, no. 7 (March 3, 1993): p. 231.

30. Ibid., p. 232.

31. Of course, contemporary theistic theology, feminist and otherwise, is filled with controversy about whether characterizing the divine as Totally Other makes sense at the end of the twentieth century in view of what we know about the workings of the universe and whether it is conducive to fruitful theologies of human nature and creation.

32. Paul R. Sponheim, *Faith and the Other: A Relational Theology* (Minneapolis: Fortress Press, 1993), p. v.

33. Mary Daly, *Pure Lust: Elemental Feminist Philosophy* (Boston: Beacon Press, 1984), p. 395.

34. Paula M. Cooey, "Emptiness, Otherness, and Identity: A Feminist Perspective," *Journal of Feminist Studies in Religion* 6, no. 2 (Fall 1990): p. 11.

35. Ibid., p. 7.

36. Ibid., p. 19.

37. Janice Gould, "American Indian Women's Poetry: Strategies of Rage and Hope," *Signs* 20, no. 4 (Summer 1995): p. 797.

38. Laurel Thatcher Ulrich, "Border Crossings," *Dialogue: A Journal of Mormon Thought* 27, no. 2 (Summer 1994): p. 4. Much of this issue was devoted to the subject of women in Mormonism. Lavina Fielding Anderson is another Mormon woman who eloquently expresses her deeply felt religious identity in the face of official disapproval of both feminists and intellectuals. See "In the Garden God Hath Planted: Explorations toward a Maturing Faith," *Sunstone* 14 (October 1990): pp. 24–27, and "Modes of Revelation: A Personal Approach," *Sunstone* 16 (August 1992): pp. 34–38. Anderson, a sixth-generation Mormon, was excommunicated in 1993 along with several other Mormon intellectuals and feminists.

39. Ibid., p. 5.

40. Ibid., p. 6

41. Jan Shipps, "Dangerous History: Laurel Thatcher Ulrich and Her Mormon Sisters," *Christian Century* 110, no. 29 (October 20, 1993): p. 1015. Ulrich writes often about Mormonism, but not to my knowledge specifically about Mormon history. She is the author of two highly praised volumes about colonial women: *Good Wives: Image and Reality in the Lives of Women in New England 1650–1750* (New York: Knopf, 1982) and *A Mid-Wife's Tale: The Life of Martha Ballard, Based on Her Diary, 1785–1812* (New York: Knopf, 1990), which won a Pulitzer Prize, the Bancroft Prize, and two other prizes from the American Historical Association. She is also the winner of a MacArthur Foundation "genius" grant. She has contributed articles and editorials to and is a senior editor of *Exponent II*, a Mormon feminist publication that continues the efforts of *Women's Exponent*, published by Mormon women in the nineteenth century.

42. Ulrich, "Border Crossings," p. 7

43. Ibid.

44. "A Conversation on Feminism and Brethrenism," September 2, 1994. A student at United Theological Seminary of the Twin Cities offered me the transcript of this conversation and permission to use excerpts from it on condition that I keep the names of the participants confidential.

45. Ibid.

46. Ibid.

47. *A Time to Weep and a Time to Sing: Faith Journeys of Women Scholars in Religion*, ed. Mary Jo Meadow and Carole A. Rayburn (Minneapolis: Winston Press, 1985).

48. Mary Jo Meadow, "Scenes from a God-Search," in *A Time to Weep and a Time to Sing*, p. 233.

49. Sheila Graeve Davaney, "Journeys from the Heartland," in A *Time to Weep and a Time to Sing*, p. 119.
50. Chopp, *Saving Work*, pp. 85–86.
51. "Introduction," *Walking in Two Worlds: Women's Spiritual Paths*, ed. Kay Vander Vort, Joan H. Timmerman, Eleanor Lincoln (St. Cloud, Minn.: North Star Press, 1992), p. xi.
52. Elizabeth Dodson Gray, "Foreword," *Walking in Two Worlds*, p. x.
53. Miriam Therese Winter, Adair Lummis, and Allison Stokes, *Defecting in Place: Women Claiming Responsibility for Their Own Spiritual Lives* (New York: Crossroad, 1994), p. 197.
54. An illustration conveyed to me by a Benedictine sister at the College of St. Benedict, St. Joseph, Minnesota, gives some insight into how this stance might manifest itself. Linda Kulzer, O.S.B., told me about needing to clarify for a young man in her class that she had made her religious vows to God, not to the institutional church. The student had accused her of disloyalty to her vows and to the church when she criticized homophobia in the church. "As a loyal Roman Catholic, it is my obligation to say to the church, 'You can be better than that,'" she told him. Conversation with Linda Kulzer, O. S. B., March 19, 1997.
55. Winter, Lummis, and Stokes, *Defecting in Place*, p. 197. The authors mailed a total of seven thousand questionnaires across the United States in 1991, another one thousand in 1992 as a supplemental mailing to increase minority representation, and about two hundred to a sampling of men. They acknowledge that "[o]ur limited study consists primarily of white feminist groups in essentially white, fairly liberal denominations, and we have been exceedingly careful to interpret our findings within these limitations" (p. 274, n. 117). Several of the essays also provide a contrast with the overall findings. For example, Toinette Eugene, an African-American Catholic feminist who wrote one of ten essays in the volume contributed by scholars from different communities, described the black Catholic feminist experience as different from that in the overall study. She says that "spirituality of survival" more aptly describes their experience than does "defecting in place," and asks, "What is it that has allowed or persuaded a majority of black Catholic women *not* to 'defect in place,' as the findings of this report indicate as the choice of many women, but at the same time also to remain and to resist the negative, dehumanizing images that both the Roman Catholic Church and society in general have maintained of them?" In "No Defect Here: A Black Catholic Womanist Reflection on a Spirituality of Survival," pp. 217–220.
56. Delores S. Williams, *Sisters in the Wilderness: The Challenge of Womanist God-Talk* (Maryknoll, N.Y.: Orbis Books, 1993), p. xii. Like many black theologians, Williams identifies herself as a womanist theologian, that is, an African-American woman, in contrast with white feminists. For a historical study of a particular denomination that illustrates the kinds of conflicts Williams describes, see Evelyn Higginbotham, *Righteous Discontent: The Women's Movement in the Black Baptist Church, 1880–1920* (Cambridge, Mass.: Harvard University Press, 1992).
57. Ibid., p. xiii.
58. Ibid.
59. Katie Geneva Cannon, *Katie's Canon: Womanism and the Soul of the Black Community* (New York: Continuum, 1995), pp. 122–123. These excerpts come from ch. 10, "Hitting a Straight Lick with a Crooked Stick: The Womanist Dilemma in the Development of a Black Liberation Ethic," pp. 122–128.
60. Elisabeth Schüssler Fiorenza, *But She Said: Feminist Perspectives of Biblical Interpretation* (Boston: Beacon Press, 1992), p. 185.
61. Elisabeth Schüssler Fiorenza, *Jesus, Miriam's Child, Sophia's Prophet: Critical Issues in Feminist Theology* (New York: Continuum, 1994), pp. 11–12.
62. Chopp, *Saving Work*, p. 115.

63. Rita M. Gross, "Buddhism after Patriarchy?" in *After Patriarchy: Feminist Transformations of the World Religions*, ed. Paula M. Cooey, William R. Eakin, and Jay B. McDaniel (Maryknoll, N.Y.: Orbis Books, 1991), p. 66.

64. Marianne Dresser, "Editor's Introduction," *Buddhist Women on the Edge*, p. xvi.

65. Plaskow, *Standing Again at Sinai*, p. xiii.

66. Laura Levitt, *Jews and Feminism: The Ambivalent Search for Home* (New York: Routledge, 1997), p. 157.

67. Wheeler, "Bowing, Not Scraping," p. 59.

68. Ibid., p. 67.

69. Emily Culpepper, "The Spiritual, Political Journey of a Feminist Free-thinker," in *After Patriarchy*, pp. 162–163.

70. Elizabeth Bettenhausen, "Feminist Movement," in *Defecting in Place*, p. 207.

71. Ada María Isasi-Díaz and Yolanda Taranga, *Hispanic Women: Prophetic Voices in the Church* (Minneapolis: Fortress Press, 1988, 1992), p. x.

72. Ibid.

73. Jeanne McPhee, "Godly Rage: Feminism and Faith in the Roman Catholic Church" (D.Min. thesis, United Theological Seminary of the Twin Cities, 1995), p. 124.

74. Pythia Peay, "Making the Invisible Visible," *Common Boundary*, Nov./Dec. 1990, p. 20. This article is an interview with Meinrad Craighead.

75. Meinrad Craighead, *The Litany of the Great River* (Mahwah, N.J.: Paulist Press, 1991), pp. 9–10.

76. Ibid., p. 9. On the same theme of not being able to leave: In an article about the idea of God in feminist philosophy, Marjorie Hewitt Suchocki suggests that even Mary Daly's radical post-Christian statements about ultimate reality reflect her Catholic background. "Ironically," says Suchocki, "Daly may reflect her tradition more fully than she desires." In "The Idea of God in Feminist Philosophy," *Hypatia* 9, no. 4 (Fall 1994): p. 57.

77. Rita M. Gross, "The Dharma . . . Is Neither Male nor Female," in *Women's and Men's Liberation*, ed. Leonard Grob, Riffat Hassan, and Haim Gordon (Westport, Conn.: Greenwood Press, 1991), pp. 105–106.

78. Ibid.

79. Gross, *Buddhism after Patriarchy*, p. 130.

80. On the compelling nature of Buddhist practice for Buddhist women, see many of the essays in *Buddhist Women on the Edge* or those in *Buddhism through American Women's Eyes*, ed. Karma Lekshe Tsomo (Ithaca, N.Y.: Snow Lion Publications, 1995), which emphasize the pragmatic effects of Buddhist practice on American women's lives. See also Sandy Boucher, *Opening the Lotus: A Woman's Guide to Buddhism* (Boston: Beacon Press, 1997) and Joan Halifax, *A Buddhist Life in America: Simplicity in the Complex*, foreword by Thich Nhat Hanh (New York: Paulist Press, 1998). For a more indirect chronicling of Buddhist principles and practice in a particular woman's life, see Gretel Ehrlich, *A Match to the Heart: One Woman's Story of Being Struck by Lightning* (New York: Penguin Books, 1994).

81. Gloria Wade-Gayles, "Introduction," *My Soul Is a Witness: African-American Women's Spirituality*, ed. Gloria Wade Gayles (Boston: Beacon Press, 1995), p. 2.

82. Ibid., p. 3.

83. Ibid., p. 4.

84. Ibid., pp. 7–8.

85. Brock, *Journeys by Heart*, p. xv.

86. *Setting the Table: Women in Theological Conversation*, ed. Rita Nakashima Brock, Claudia Camp, Serene Jones (St. Louis, Mo.: Chalice Press, 1995), p. vii.

87. Ibid., p. viii.

88. Constance F. Parvey, "A Christian Feminist's Struggle with the Bible as Authority," in *Women's and Men's Liberation*, p. 52. For an interesting article from the perspective of discourse theory about the need to expand feminist understandings of "sexist texts" and the need to define more broadly what constitutes transformative communities of interpretation, see Mary McClintock Fulkerson, "Contesting Feminist Canons: Discourse and the Problem of Sexist Texts," *Journal of Feminist Studies in Religion* 7, no. 2 (Fall 1991): pp. 53–73.

89. Parvey, "A Christian Feminist's Struggle with the Bible as Authority," p. 52.

90. Ibid., pp. 53–55.

91. Riffat Hassan, "The Issue of Woman-Man Equality in the Islamic Tradition," in *Women's and Men's Liberation*, p. 65.

92. Ibid., p. 66.

93. Ibid., p. 69.

94. Ibid., p. 70.

95. Riffat Hassan, "Muslim Feminist Hermeneutics," in *In Our Own Voices: Four Centuries of American Women's Religious Writings*, ed. Rosemary Radford Ruether and Rosemary Skinner Keller (New York: HarperSanFrancisco, 1995), p. 456.

96. Riffat Hassan, "Muslim Women and Post-Patriarchal Islam," in *After Patriarchy*, p. 61.

97. Rachel Adler, "In Your Blood, Live: Re-Visions of a Theology of Purity," *Tikkun* 8, no. 1 (January/February 1993): pp. 38–41.

98. The earlier article is Rachel Adler, "Tumah and taharah-mikveh," *The Jewish Catalogue: A Do-It Yourself Kit*, compiled and edited by Richard Siegel, Michael Strassfeld, and Sharon Strassfeld (Philadelphia: Jewish Publication Society of America, 1973), pp. 167–172.

99. Adler, "In Your Blood, Live," p. 38.

100. Ibid., pp. 38–39.

101. Ibid., p. 41. Reactions to Adler's essay, ranging from adulation to outrage, and Adler's own theological response to them (she agreed with none) can be found in the letters to the editor, *Tikkun* 8, no. 2 (March/April 1993): pp. 4–5.

102. Adler, "In Your Blood, Live," p. 41.

103. Sheila Redmond, "'Remember the Good, Forget the Bad': Denial and Family Violence in a Christian Worship Service," in *Women at Worship: Interpretations of North American Diversity*, ed. Marjorie Procter-Smith and Janet R. Walton (Louisville, Ky.: Westminster/John Knox Press, 1993), pp. 80–81.

104. Tikvah Frymer-Kensky, "Women Jews," in *Women's and Men's Liberation*, pp. 38–39.

105. Catherine Keller, *Apocalypse Now and Then: A Feminist Guide to the End of the World* (Boston: Beacon Press, 1996).

106. Historical investigation into women's mistrust of religious institutions offers some insights into why earlier religious movements that promoted women's leadership have not prospered and grown. One good example is Ann Braude's analysis of nineteenth-century Spiritualism's antipathy to organization. See *Radical Spirits: Spiritualism and Women's Rights in Nineteenth-Century America* (Boston: Beacon Press, 1989), especially ch. 7, "'No Organization Can Hold Me,'" pp. 162–191. The chapter title is a quote from Lizzie Doten, a Boston trance medium about whom I wrote my M. A. thesis in English (Doten wrote poetry that she said came from the spirits of the dead, most frequently Edgar Allen Poe) and who early on stirred my interest in how women achieved leadership in alternative religions. Interestingly, a more recent study of nineteenth-century Spiritualism emphasizes its efforts at constructing cosmic order and community. See Brett R. Carroll, *Spiritualism in Antebellum America* (Bloomington: Indiana University Press, 1997).

107. Valuing ambivalence as a creative theoretical stance is, of course, a different

matter from living in a state that fosters the kind of constant ambivalence that is primarily painful. In a study of clergywomen who are thinking about leaving ministry, Karen Smith Sellers describes the nine women from several denominations she interviewed as beset by profound ambivalence: about the institutional church, about ordination, about conflicting loyalties, and about how much suffering is too much. Their ambivalence has led them not to theological creativity—at least not at the moment—but to a state of "feeling stuck" and seeing few appealing alternatives to the profession that is causing much more pain than joy. "Crossroads: Clergywomen Thinking Seriously about Leaving Church-Related Ministry" (Ph.D. diss., University of Minnesota, 1997).

3. The Immanence of the Sacred

1. Marsha Falk, "Introduction to New Blessings," in *Four Centuries of Jewish Women's Spirituality*, ed. and with introductions by Ellen M. Umansky and Dianne Ashton (Boston: Beacon Press, 1992), p. 241. Falk's more recent publication, *The Book of Blessings: New Jewish Prayers for Daily Life, the Sabbath, and the New Moon Festivals* (New York: HarperSanFrancisco, 1996) is a compendium of the blessings about which she was writing in this article.

2. Elizabeth A. Johnson, *Women, Earth, and Creator Spirit* (New York: Paulist Press, 1993), p. 58.

3. Suzanne Werner, from an excerpt in ch. 12, "Emerging Discourse on the Divine Feminine," *Women and Authority: Re-emerging Mormon Feminism* (Salt Lake City: Signature Books, 1992), p. 290.

4. Katie Geneva Cannon, *Katie's Canon: Womanism and the Soul of the Black Community* (New York: Continuum, 1995), p. 133. This quote comes from a response to a questionnaire that Cannon sent to fifty theologically trained African-American women in 1992.

5. Paula Gunn Allen, stanza from "The Text Is Flesh," in *Life Is a Fatal Disease: Collected Poems 1962–1995* (Albuquerque, N.M.: West End Press, 1997), p. 144.

6. Starhawk, *Truth or Dare: Encounters with Power, Authority, and Mystery* (San Francisco: Harper and Row, 1987), p. 21.

7. Sallie McFague, *Models of God: Theology for an Ecological, Nuclear Age* (Philadelphia: Fortress Press, 1987), p. 185.

8. Amina Wadud-Muhsin, "On Belonging as a Muslim Woman," in *My Soul Is a Witness: African-American Women's Spirituality*, ed. Gloria Wade-Gayles (Boston: Beacon Press, 1995), p. 263. Wadud-Muhsin grew up the daughter of a Methodist pastor.

9. Anne Carolyn Klein, *Meeting the Great Bliss Queen: Buddhists, Feminists, and the Art of Self* (Boston: Beacon Press, 1995), p. 72.

10. The emphasis on divine presence in the world rather than on divine action or intervention is a major subtext in women's religious thought, perhaps because immanental theologies tend to place greater stress on the need for human action, which, in turn, is empowered by divine presence or access to the ultimate in non-theistic traditions. There are exceptions to this pattern in the writings of more theologically conservative women. See, for example, Nancey Murphy, *Beyond Liberalism and Fundamentalism: How Modern and Postmodern Philosophy Set the Theological Agenda* (Valley Forge, Penn.: Trinity Press International, 1996). Murphy suggests in this book that there is a new Anglo-American postmodern worldview emerging that may heal the impasse between conservative and liberal Christian theologies that have up to now been based on incommensurate philosophical worldviews. Hers is not a work in feminist theology, and she mentions feminism only in terms of the issue over gender-inclusive language in a chapter about the differences between descriptive and expressive theologies. One

of her major concerns is how liberals and conservatives can talk to each other about God's action in the world without simply disagreeing over immanence or intervention as the only two possible—and contradictory—modes. In her concluding chapters Murphy makes suggestions that require "an emphasis on God's immanence at the quantum level" (p. 148, n. 22).

11. Carter Heyward, *Our Passion for Justice: Images of Power, Sexuality, and Liberation* (New York: Pilgrim Press, 1984), pp. 244–245.

12. Tamar Frankiel, *The Voice of Sarah: Feminine Spirituality and Traditional Judaism* (New York: HarperSanFrancisco, 1990), p. 118. I will return to Frankiel later in this chapter as an example of a Jewish feminist who bridges liberal and conservative views of women and Judaism and thereby complicates them in interesting ways.

13. Ibid., p. 117.

14. It is difficult to find a general term other than "sacred" or "holy" that can encompass both theistic and non-theistic traditions.

15. In *Amazing Grace: A Theological Vocabulary* (New York: Riverside Books, 1998), poet and memoirist Kathleen Norris offers an interesting discussion about the tensions between transcendence and immanence in a chapter entitled "God": "I take refuge in God's transcendence" she says, "continually giving thanks that God's ways are not my own. . . . I appreciate God's immanence as well, as expressed in the creation (including dogs) and the incarnation of Jesus Christ within it." Norris, who often calls herself a Benedictine Presbyterian, is concerned with too much emphasis on immanence and cites the writings of feminist Wiccan Starhawk as an example: "When I read the New Age author Starhawk, although I enjoy her very much as a writer—her piece on a snake shedding its skin in *Dreaming the Dark* is a small masterpiece—I ultimately grow bored. She is so insistent on living in a world in which holiness is all immanence, without the possibility of transcendence, that I feel flattened out and without hope" (p. 109). From my perspective this is a mis-reading of Starhawk, who has her own ways of defining transcendence, but Norris offers a good example, nonetheless, of a woman who desires to keep "transcendence" a powerful concept in her theological lexicon.

16. *The Random House Dictionary of the English Language*, College Edition (New York: Random House, 1969).

17. William A. Clebsch, *American Religious Thought: A History* (Chicago: University of Chicago Press, 1973). See ch. 2, "The Sensible Spirituality of Jonathan Edwards," pp. 11–56.

18. Catherine L. Albanese points out that the name for this movement emerged as a form of ridicule by critics like Octavius B. Frothingham, who claimed that these thinkers "walked with their heads in the clouds, out of touch with common ground." In Charles H. Lippy and Peter W. Williams, eds., *Encyclopedia of the American Religious Experience: Studies of Traditions and Movements* (New York: Charles Scribner's Sons, 1988), p. 1117. Yet their emphasis on inner knowledge of spiritual realities brought them to earth again in their reverence for nature.

19. The fifteen theological and philosophical themes J. Stillson Judah associates with metaphysical religions bear a significant resemblance to some of the major themes in women's religious thought, although these themes need to be qualified and contextualized for different traditions. J. Stillson Judah, *The History and Philosophy of the Metaphysical Movements in America* (Philadelphia: Westminster Press, 1967), pp. 12–19. Donald B. Meyer analyzes some of the same groups in *The Positive Thinkers*. In the first edition (1965) his assessment of women's participation in them is primarily negative, on the assumption that positive thinking was based on a theologically inadequate worldview. The most recent edition acknowledges more complexity in women's relationships to these religions. See *The Positive Thinkers: Popular Psychology from Mary Baker Eddy to Norman Vincent Peale and Ronald Reagan* (Middletown, Conn.:

Wesleyan University Press, 1988). In *The Varieties of Religious Experience* (New York: Modern Library, 1994), William James uses numerous examples of women's affiliation with mind-cure movements that he connects with his category of the religion of "healthy-mindedness," a worldview he finds wanting in its capacity to apprehend evil.

20. See William R. Hutchison, *The Modernist Impulse in American Protestantism* (Cambridge: Harvard University Press, 1976). Hutchison cites three characteristics of Protestant modernist thought: the need for adaption of religious ideas to modern culture; a conviction that society was moving toward a realization of the Kingdom of God; and "the idea that God is immanent in human cultural development and revealed through it" (p. 2).

21. A helpful elaboration of classical theism including an analysis of its theological difficulties appears in Ian Barbour, *Religion in an Age of Science* (San Francisco: Harper and Row, 1990), pp. 241–250. Another source is Charles Hartshorne, *Omnipotence and Other Theological Mistakes* (Albany: State University of New York Press, 1984). For a capsulized critique that includes feminist concerns and emerging women's definitions of "transcendence," see Fredrica Harris Thompsett, "Transcendence," in *Dictionary of Feminist Theologies*, ed. Letty M. Russell and J. Shannon Clarkson (Louisville, Ky.: Westminster/John Knox Press, 1996), pp. 302–303.

22. Among many other sources see Rosemary Radford Ruether, *Sexism and God-Talk: Toward a Feminist Theology*, with a new introd. (Boston: Beacon Press, 1993). First published in 1983 and often described in reviews as the "first feminist systematic theology."

23. Nell Noddings offers an overview of ways women have been perceived as evil in *Women and Evil* (Berkeley: University of California Press, 1989). See especially ch. 2, "The Devil's Gateway," pp. 35–58.

24. One particular American manifestation of assumptions about the purity of women emerged in the nineteenth century as what scholars have come to call the Cult of True Womanhood. First articulated by historian Barbara Welter, it is now widely acknowledged as a set of characteristics descriptive of and prescriptive for primarily upper- and middle-class white Protestant women. For an extended and helpful discussion of both the power and the limitations of the idea of "true womanhood" in American women's religious history, consult the several index entries in Susan Hill Lindley, *"You Have Stept Out of Your Place": A History of Women and Religion in America* (Louisville, Ky.: Westminster/John Knox Press, 1996). Lindley takes her title from the accusation leveled at Anne Hutchinson at her church trial at Boston in 1637.

25. *The Antinomian Controversy, 1636–1638: A Documentary History*, ed. David D. Hall (Middletown, Conn.: Wesleyan University Press, 1968), p. 337.

26. *Sisters of the Spirit: Three Black Women's Autobiographies of the Nineteenth Century*, ed. with intro. by William L. Andrews (Bloomington: Indiana University Press, 1986).

27. See Ann Braude, *Radical Spirits: Spiritualism and Women's Rights in Nineteenth-Century America* (Boston: Beacon Press, 1989).

28. Elaine J. Lawless, *Handmaidens of the Lord: Pentecostal Women Preachers and Traditional Religion* (Philadelphia: University of Pennsylvania Press and American Folklore Society, 1988). See by the same author "Rescripting Their Lives and Narratives: Spiritual Life Stories of Pentecostal Women Preachers," *Journal of Feminist Studies in Religion* 7, no. 1 (Spring 1991): pp. 53–71, and "Not So Different a Story after All: Pentecostal Women in the Pulpit," in *Women's Leadership in Marginal Religions: Explorations outside the Mainstream*, ed. Catherine Wessinger (Urbana: University of Illinois Press, 1993), pp. 41–52.

29. There is reason to cite Christian Science as an exception to this statement, since Mary Baker Eddy devoted the second half of her life to laying out the theological implications of her claim that "there is no reality in matter" and that a full understand-

ing of both God and reality as Spirit is exactly what made healing possible. But to speak of Christian Science's monistic theology in terms of "immanence" and "transcendence" requires nontraditional definitions of these terms not dependent upon accepting the reality of both spirit and matter. One could say the same, although to a lesser extent, of religions like the Unity School of Christianity, Religious Science, and Divine Science that have historical and theological connections with Christian Science.

30. Michael Novak, *Commonweal* 123, no. 2 (January 26, 1996): pp. 12–13.

31. Ibid.

32. Ibid. Ungrounded fears about what will happen to religious traditions if women are too numerous and influential in them are part of a pattern in American religious history. For a wider discussion of this subject, see Ann Braude, "Women's History *Is* American Religious History," in *Retelling U.S. Religious History*, ed. Thomas A. Tweed (Berkeley: University of California Press, 1997), pp. 87–107. One is reminded of John Cotton's remark to Anne Hutchinson at her church trial. Once her mentor, Cotton expressed his fear that, given her unorthodox religious beliefs, the next thing he expected to hear about Hutchinson was that she had been unfaithful to her husband. In Hall, *The Antinomian Controversy*, p. 372.

33. This generalization needs some qualification in regard to the writings of women in New Thought and New Age movements, a subject I take up toward the end of the chapter. It is not so much that these women, heirs of the metaphysical tradition in America, claim that life will be better "elsewhere," but that they insist on the need for different perceptions of what is ultimately "real."

34. Elizabeth A. Johnson, *Women, Earth, and Creator Spirit* (Mahwah, N.J.: Paulist Press, 1993), p. 61. This small volume is based on Johnson's lecture for the 1993 Madaleva Lecture in Spirituality, an annual event at St. Mary's College, Notre Dame, Indiana. Johnson is best known for *She Who Is: The Mystery of God in Feminist Theological Discourse* (New York: Crossroad, 1993). This idea of earth as home is by no means exclusive to women. In *American Religious Thought*, William Clebsch claims "being at home in the universe" as the central creative theme, however differently expressed, of Edwards, Emerson, and James, but he does not address issues of gender. In her first book on women's religious piety, *Feminine Spirituality in America: From Sarah Edwards to Martha Graham* (Philadelphia: Temple University Press, 1980), Amanda Porterfield uses the theme of "homemaking" to look at this theme in terms of selected women from Sarah Edwards to Martha Graham, all of them white Protestants. As compelling as I find both Clebsch and Porterfield, their emphasis, particularly Clebsch's, on the move in American religious thought from morality to aesthetics has limitations for contemporary women's thought, which is also highly concerned with ethics. See also Amanda Porterfield, *Female Piety in Puritan New England: The Emergence of Religious Humanism* (New York: Oxford University Press, 1992).

35. Ivone Gebara and Maria Clara Bingemer, *Mary: Mother of God, Mother of the Poor*, trans. from the Portuguese by Phillip Berrigan (Maryknoll, N.Y.: Orbis Books, 1989). Gebara, who was silenced by the Vatican in 1995 for supporting the legalization and regulation of abortion, is particularly well known. For an account of the incidents leading to her silencing, see Anne E. Patrick, *Liberating Conscience; Feminist Explorations in Catholic Moral Theology* (New York: Continuum, 1996), pp. 226–228. There are more and more feminist theologians, Roman Catholic and Protestant, emerging in South and Central America. For interpretations of the works of many of them, some, like Gebara, internationally known and others known more regionally, see Linda A. Moody, *Women Encounter God: Theology across the Boundaries of Difference* (Maryknoll, N.Y.: Orbis Books, 1996). Moody's is a comparative study of *mujerista*, womanist, and feminist theologies.

36. Gebara and Bingemer, *Mary, Mother of God*, p. 9.

37. Ibid., pp. 4–5.

38. Ibid., p. 17.

39. Ibid.

40. Ibid., p. 90.

41. Ibid., p. 126.

42. Ibid., p. 120.

43. Ibid., p, 170.

44. Sallie McFague, *The Body of God: An Ecological Theology* (Minneapolis: Fortress Press, 1993), p. 14.

45. Sallie McFague, *Metaphorical Theology: Models of God in Religious Language* (Philadelphia: Fortress Press, 1982).

46. Ibid., p. 41.

47. Sallie McFague, *Super, Natural Christians: How We Should Love Nature* (Minneapolis: Fortress Press, 1997).

48. Ibid., p. 1.

49. Ibid., p. 173.

50. Sallie McFague, *The Body of God*, p. vii. Actually, McFague is quoting herself here—from the conclusion of *Models of God*, in which she outlines the task she undertakes in *The Body of God*.

51. Ibid., p. 114.

52. Ibid., p. 208.

53. Ibid., pp. 208–209.

54. Ibid., p. 133.

55. McFague has a chapter on Christology in *The Body of God* (as would be necessary in a Christian systematic theology) that she concludes with some reflections on the Trinity. See pp. 158–195.

56. Marjorie Hewitt Suchocki, *The Fall to Violence: Original Sin in Relational Theology* (New York: Continuum, 1995). In this book Suchocki substitutes "relational theology" for "process theology," because she thinks that the foundational understanding of all forms of Whiteheadian theology as relational is not apparent with all that the term "process" implies.

57. Ibid., p. 11.

58. *The Fall to Violence* is not Suchocki's first book about sin and evil. See Marjorie Hewitt Suchocki, *The End of Evil* (Albany: State University of New York Press, 1988).

59. Suchocki, *The Fall to Violence*, p. 160.

60. Ibid., p. 18.

61. Ibid., p. 12.

62. Ibid., p. 34.

63. Ibid., p. 164.

64. Sharon D. Welch, *A Feminist Ethic of Risk* (Minneapolis: Fortress Press, 1990).

65. Ibid., p. 19.

66. Ibid., p. 70.

67. Ibid., p. 179.

68. Ibid., p. 178.

69. Ibid., p. 176. Welch points to some similarities between her feminist ethic of risk and work that is being done by deconstructionist male theologians like Thomas J. J. Altizer and Mark C. Taylor, and she identifies similar themes in the works of nineteenth-century theologian Ludwig Feuerbach, as well. Nonetheless she sees her own work as distinct: "In contrast to Taylor's valorization of sacrifice and Feuerbach's glorification of unlimited power, I celebrate a presence that is both healing and fragile, constitutive of life and unambiguously present in the human condition, as well as unam-

biguously absent in the atrocities of history and in humankind's despoliation of the earth" (p. 177).

70. Rita M. Gross, *Buddhism after Patriarchy: A Feminist History, Analysis, and Reconstruction of Buddhism* (Albany: State University of New York Press, 1993), pp. 137, 141.

71. Sandy Boucher, *Opening the Lotus: A Woman's Guide to Buddhism* (Boston: Beacon Press, 1997), p. 42. This book includes a Directory of Women Teachers in the United States and a directory of publications that are helpful to women.

72. Ibid., pp. 47–51.

73. Jan Willis, "Buddhism and Race: An African American Baptist-Buddhist Perspective," in *Buddhist Women on the Edge: Contemporary Perspectives from the Western Frontier*, ed. Marianne Dresser (Berkeley: North Atlantic Books, 1996), p. 87. Emphasis in the text. In this same essay Willis acknowledges the question that people often ask her, implicitly or explicitly, "What does Buddhism offer to *any* African American," but she turns it around, as well, and suggests that a better question might be what African Americans and other people of color might have to offer to Buddhism on the way toward helping a truly "American" Buddhism to emerge (p. 88).

74. Sandy Boucher, *Turning the Wheel: American Women Creating the New Buddhism*, updated and expanded ed. (Boston: Beacon Press, 1993), pp. 76–77. The first edition was published in 1988.

75. Miranda Shaw, "Wild, Wise, Passionate: Dakinis in America," in *Buddhist Women on the Edge*, p. 9. "Dakinis" are female embodiments of divine consciousness. As one example of the influence of Kuan Yin on the spiritual development of a Buddhist woman, see Sandy Boucher's story of her first encounter with Kuan Yin in the form of a wooden statue in the Nelson-Atkins Art Museum in Kansas City in *Opening the Lotus*, pp. 57–59.

76. Shaw, "Wild, Wise, Passionate," p. 9.

77. Gross, *Buddhism after Patriarchy*, p. 285.

78. Ibid.

79. Ibid.

80. Ibid., p. 288.

81. Charlotte Joko Beck with Steve Smith, *Nothing Special: Living Zen* (New York: HarperSanFrancisco, 1993), p. 272.

82. Mary Catherine Hilkert, "Cry Beloved Image: Rethinking the Image of God," in *In the Embrace of God: Feminist Approaches to Theological Anthropology*, ed. Ann O'Hara Graff (Maryknoll, N.Y.: Orbis Books, 1995), p. 194.

83. I think we greatly underestimate the power of traditional religious symbols to hold traditions together in the midst of efforts toward theological innovation. There is certainly testimony to this in the stories women tell in Chapter 2 about their attachments to their traditions. Reference to major religious symbols can evoke centuries and lifetimes of meaning. One example: For the 1993 Re-Imagining conference in Minneapolis, Pamela Carter Joern, an American Baptist clergywoman and playwright, wrote a play, "Simple Gifts." Set in a nineteenth-century Shaker village, the play spoke to numerous issues of exclusion women encounter in their religious traditions. During a childbirth scene, one of the characters spoke the words from the Christian communion service, "This is my body, broken for you." There was a gasp of recognition from the—admittedly select—audience, demonstrating in my opinion a marked ability to draw upon multiple levels of meaning and history to make sense of a very different context from a communion service. Another good example is a work like Rebecca S. Chopp's *The Power to Speak: Feminism, Language, God* (New York: Crossroad, 1992), in which she equates the symbol "God," the "proclaimed Word," with the "perfectly open sign that funds multiplicity and otherness in and through feminist discourses" (p.

7). On the surface it would appear that cutting "God" loose from the moorings of metaphysical claims and setting "God" adrift in a sea of language is to invite confusion at best and chaos at worst—with no safeguards at all to halt a slide into the eventual meaninglessness of all God-talk. But no matter how radical Chopp's suggestion, the language she uses evokes the whole weight of meaning present in traditional Christian concepts of "Word" that are all there to draw on. What is at stake for women is just what Chopp suggests in the title: the power to speak. Chopp seems to me to be demonstrating exactly what she is calling for: a conserving of the tradition by means of a radical claim about its ongoing possibilities for depth of meaning.

84. Judith Plaskow, *Standing Again at Sinai: Judaism from a Feminist Perspective* (New York: HarperSanFrancisco, 1990).

85. Judith Plaskow, "Transforming the Nature of Community: Toward a Feminist People of Israel," in *After Patriarchy: Feminist Transformations of the World Religions*, ed. Paula M. Cooey, William R. Eakin, and Jay B. McDaniel (Maryknoll, N.Y.: Orbis Books, 1991), p. 87.

86. Ibid., p. 91.

87. Ibid., pp. 101–102.

88. Plaskow, *Standing Again at Sinai*, p. 159.

89. Ibid., p. 135.

90. Ibid., pp. 134–135.

91. Ibid., p. 138.

92. Ibid., p. 152.

93. Judith Plaskow, "Telling Stories about Faith and Unfaith," review of *The Spirit of Renewal: Crisis and Response in Jewish Life*, by Edward Feld (Jewish Lights Publishing Company, 1991), in *Tikkun* 8, no. 1 (January/February 1993): p. 67. For an interesting contrast to this contention by Plaskow and a good reminder that women of the same tradition, however immanental their theologies, do not offer identical insights about God and God-language, see Marcia Cohn Spiegel, "Spirituality for Survival: Jewish Women Healing Themselves," *Journal of Feminist Studies in Religion* 12, no. 2 (Fall 1996): p. 26.

94. Judith Plaskow, "Facing the Ambiguity of God," *Tikkun* 6, no. 5 (September/October 1991): pp. 70, 96.

95. Judith Plaskow, "'It Is Not in Heaven': Feminism and Religious Authority," *Tikkun* 5, no. 2 (March/April 1990): p. 39.

96. Ibid., p. 40.

97. Ibid.

98. Plaskow, *Standing Again at Sinai*, p. 155–156.

99. Marcia Falk, "Introduction to New Blessings," in *Four Centuries of Jewish Women's Spirituality*, p. 241.

100. Ibid.

101. Falk, *The Book of Blessings*, p. 3.

102. Ibid.

103. Ibid., p. xix.

104. Plaskow, *Standing Again at Sinai*, pp. 139-40.

105. Lynn Gottlieb, *She Who Dwells Within: A Feminist Vision of a Renewed Judaism* (New York: HarperSanFrancisco, 1995). Foreword by Ellen Umansky, another Jewish feminist, who points favorably to the eclecticism of Gottlieb's sources: "Drawing on such diverse sources as classical rabbinic texts, including mystical Jewish writings, ancient Near Eastern myths, Native American rituals, and feminist appropriation of the Goddess, Lynn has attempted not only to tap the spiritual potential of American Jews but also to create a nonsexist, ecologically responsible Jewish peace culture that welcomes into its midst all who seek to become members" (p. xv). Jewish theologians are

by no means the only women who speak about Shekhinah. See Kristin Johnson Ingram, "Shekinah: The Glory of God," *Daughters of Sarah* 20, no. 1 (Winter 1994): pp. 32–34. *Daughters of Sarah* was a journal with a feminist evangelical emphasis that ceased publication in 1996 after more than fifteen years in existence. There will be more about this article below.

106. Ibid., p. 20.

107. Ibid., pp. 16–17. There is a very well known essay by Carol P. Christ, "Why Women Need the Goddess: Phenomenological, Psychological, and Political Reflection," that appeared first in a short-lived journal called *Heresies* and was later reprinted in *Womanspirit Rising*, ed. Carol P. Christ and Judith Plaskow (New York: Harper and Row, 1979), pp. 273–287. For an essay that includes discussions and disagreements about the Goddess among Roman Catholic feminists see Mary Jo Weaver, *New Catholic Women: A Contemporary Challenge to Traditional Religious Authority* (San Francisco: Harper and Row, 1986), ch. 6, "Affirming the Connections: Roman Catholic Feminist Spirituality," pp. 180–213.

108. Ibid., p. 20.

109. Ibid., p. 22.

110. Frankiel, *The Voice of Sarah*, p. 61.

111. Ibid., p. 121.

112. Ibid.

113. Ibid., p. xiii.

114. Ibid., p. xii.

115. Ibid., p. 121.

116. A word of qualification is needed here. However much traditional Judaism and a great deal of Jewish feminist theology are grounded in monotheism, the issue of whether Judaism and monotheism are inextricably linked is not as settled as one might think. In *Jews and Feminism: The Ambivalent Search for Home* (New York: Routledge, 1997), Laura Levitt suggests that Plaskow's "liberal monotheism" does not sufficiently acknowledge the theological diversity among Jewish feminists. She notes her agreement in this matter with questions raised by Ellen Umansky in a review of *Standing Again at Sinai* in *Sh'ma, a Journal of Jewish Responsibility* 20, no. 390 (March 16, 1990): pp. 78–79. See Levitt, *Jews and Feminism*, p. 195, n. 7. Some of that diversity is discussed in Melissa Raphael, "Goddess Religion, Postmodern Jewish Feminism, and the Complexity of Alternative Religious Identities," *Nova Religio: The Journal of Alternative and Emergent Religions* 1, no. 2 (April 1998): pp. 198–215.

117. Terry Tempest Williams, *Refuge: An Unnatural History of Family and Place* (New York: Random House, 1991), p. 241.

118. See, for example, Linda P. Wilcox, "The Mormon Concept of a Mother in Heaven," in *Women and Authority: Re-Emerging Mormon Feminism*, ed. Maxine Hanks (Salt Lake City: Signature Books, 1992), pp. 3–21. It appears also in *Sisters in Spirit: Mormon Women in Cultural and Theological Perspective*, ed. Maureen Ursenbach Beecher and Lavina Fielding Anderson (Urbana: University of Illinois Press, 1987), along with other essays that seek to recover Mormon women's history. See also Carol Lynn Pearson, "Healing the Motherless House," pp. 231–245, Martha Pierce, "Personal Discourse on God the Mother," pp. 247–256, and "Emerging Discourse on the Divine Feminine," pp. 257–296, all in *Women and Authority*. And Janice Allred, "Toward a Mormon Theology of God the Mother," *Dialogue; A Journal of Mormon Thought* 27, no. 2 (Summer 1994): pp. 15–39.

119. Margaret Merrill Toscano, "Put on Your Strength O Daughters of Zion: Claiming Priesthood and Knowing the Mother," in *Women and Authority*, p. 411. Toscano and her husband Paul Toscano have also written a book together, *Strangers in Paradox: Explorations in Mormon Theology* (Salt Lake City: Signature Books, 1990), in

which they argue for a priesthood that is both male and female, a full theological development of Heavenly Mother, and development as well of a female counterpart of Jesus. All of these they see as already inherent in Mormon doctrine, however undeveloped at present. They also have some very interesting things to say about immanence and transcendence in Mormonism, particularly in ch. 4, "The God of Flesh and Glory," pp. 37–46. They also offer speculations about how to expand the concept of God the Mother so that characteristics in addition to the traditional one of "nurturing" are present—the Goddess, possibly, or the Great High Priestess. Toscano herself points out in "Put on Your Strength" that in some interpretations of Mormonism, three figures—Eve, Mary, and the Holy Spirit—have been seen as both female and divine, and she wonders, "Could these three persons form a trinity of female divinities: the Mother, Daughter, and Holy Spirit? Do they parallel the male trinity of Creator, Redeemer, and Nurturer?" (pp. 426–427). The Toscanos and also Maxine Hanks have been excommunicated.

120. Janice Allred, "Toward an Emerging Theology of God the Mother," in *Women and Authority*, p. 39. On the subject of personal revelation in Mormonism, Lavina Fielding Anderson has an interesting essay about what she sees as the narrowing of possibilities for varieties of spiritual experience in Mormonism. She says that she has been struck not by the fact that nineteenth-century Mormons reported many spiritual experiences but by the fact that were so many different kinds: "Divine messengers appeared in night visions, people spoke in new tongues or interpreted them, broken bodies healed, departed loved ones or individuals who were far away came with messages and reassurance." It is her sense that now such possibilities for "respectable" spiritual experiences are much more limited: "answered prayers, healings, and feelings of enlightenment about the scriptures." In "Modes of Revelation: A Personal Approach," *Sunstone* 16 (August 1992): p. 34.

121. An excerpt from Connie Disney in "Emerging Discourse on the Divine Feminine," *Women and Authority*, p. 295.

122. For an example of an article by a male author defending ordained ministry for women, see Ralph A. Kee, "Revelation, Proclamation and Women's Responsibility (A Systematic Theology in Two or Three Pages)," *Priscilla Papers* 6, no. 4 (Fall 1992): pp. 10–11. Kee is identified as a career missionary with the Conservative Baptist Home Missionary Society.

123. Tina J. Ostrander, "Who Is Sophia," *Priscilla Papers* 8, no. 2 (Spring 1994): p. 2.

124. Here, for example, is the blessing proclaimed over each speaker before her address: "Now [Bless] Sophia, dream the vision, share the wisdom dwelling deep within." Hawaiian chant, p. 11 of Re-Imagining Booklet, Nov. 4–7, 1993.

125. Ostrander, "Who Is Sophia," p. 3.

126. Aida Besançon Spencer, "Avoiding the Either-Or Trap," *Priscilla Papers* 8, no. 2 (Spring 1994): p. 4. Regarding her concern about a litany that called for participants to say, "I reverence the Presence within you," Spencer has this to say: "If every participant at the conference were a Christian this might be satisfactory. However, if God's presence is present in *every* human being that would be universalism. The apostle Paul instead explains that humans live and move within God's presence, not necessarily that God is present within all humans (Acts 17:28)," p. 4.

127. Ibid., p. 5. There may be more latitude, however, for evangelical women to identify with Jesus. In "Mystical Masculinity: The New Question Facing Women," Faith Martin concludes her argument against male-exclusive language for God with an anecdote about a little girl who asked to play the part of Jesus in a Sunday school class and was told by a boy that a girl could not be Jesus: "Before the teachers could intervene the girl shot back, 'A girl can be Jesus, a girl can be Jesus!' She wasn't exactly crying but her rising voice managed to convey such emotion that the noisy room fell silent and all eyes focused on her. This little girl and her adversary are not fictional characters

dreamed up for illustration, but real children who for one moment crystallize a profound theological debate going on in the church. Consider for one moment: If you had been the teacher, would you have had any hesitation in awarding the role of Jesus to that little girl?" *Priscilla Papers* 6, no. 4 (Fall 1992): p. 7.

128. Aida Besançon Spencer, "Power Play," *Christian Century* 114, no. 20 (July 2–9, 1997): pp. 618–619.

129. Kristin Johnson Ingram, "Shekinah—The Glory of God," *Daughters of Sarah* 20, no. 1 (Winter 1994): pp. 32, 33.

130. Ibid., p. 32. For even more complexity emerging from the writings of evangelical women see Virginia Ramey Mollenkott, *Sensuous Spirituality: Out from Fundamentalism* (New York: Crossroad Publishing Company, 1993). In this theological autobiography, Mollenkott, a lesbian, opens the story of her spiritual journey by asking, "So how does a fundamentalist who believes she is essentially and totally depraved become transformed into a person who knows she is an innocent spiritual being who is temporarily having human experiences?" (p. 16). Her book-long reply outlines the variety of sources from which her theology is constructed and has a strongly immanentist flavor.

131. Elizabeth A. Johnson, *She Who Is: The Mystery of God in Feminist Theological Discourse* (New York: Crossroad, 1993), p. 19.

132. Ibid., p. 51.

133. Ibid., p. 124.

134. Elizabeth A. Johnson, "A Theological Case for God-She: Expanding the Treasury of Metaphor," *Commonweal* 120, no. 2 (January 29, 1993): p. 12.

135. Johnson, *She Who Is*, p. 231.

136. Cynthia Eller, *Living in the Lap of the Goddess: The Feminist Spirituality Movement in America* (New York: Crossroad, 1993), pp. 136–138. At the November 1993 meeting of the American Academy of Religion, Eller delivered a paper about significant signs of transcendence in women's spirituality.

137. Carol P. Christ, *Rebirth of the Goddess: Finding Meaning in Feminist Spirituality* (Reading, Mass.: Addison-Wesley Publishing Company), p. 104.

138. Ibid., p. 106.

139. Nancy Frankenberry, "Classical Theism, Panentheism, and Pantheism: On the Relation between God Construction and Gender Construction," *Zygon* 28, no. 1 (March 1993): p. 39.

140. Ibid., p. 33.

141. Ibid., pp. 36–37.

142. Ibid., p. 44. In her mention of the way women generate religious symbols, Frankenberry is referring to Caroline Walker Bynum's introduction to *Gender and Religion: On the Complexity of Symbols*, ed. Caroline Walker Bynum, Stevan Harrell, and Paula Richman (Boston: Beacon Press, 1986), pp. 1–20.

143. Ibid., pp. 44–45. One wonders why this would be the case any more so than with constructions of language or political or economic systems—all of whose human origins are acknowledged with little psychic difficulty.

144. Ibid., p. 38.

145. Ada María Isasi-Díaz, *En la lucha: A Hispanic Women's Liberation Theology* (Minneapolis: Fortress Press, 1993), p. 17.

146. Ibid.

147. Ibid., p. 16.

148. Ibid., pp. 155–156.

149. Ibid., p. 156.

150. Delores S. Williams, *Sisters in the Wilderness: The Challenge of Womanist God-Talk* (Maryknoll, N.Y.: Orbis Books, 1993).

151. Ibid., p. 60.

152. Ibid., p. 175.

153. Ibid., pp. 144, 146.

154. Ibid., p. 167. Williams's presentation at the first Re-Imagining conference in 1993 emphasized this contention. Several of her comments about the unnecessary bloodshed of the cross were taken out of context and used as a basis for the claim that the women at Re-Imagining were ridiculing Christian doctrine, particularly the atonement. For example, see Carlton Elliott Smith, "Charges of Pagan Acts Hit Ecumenical Event," *Chicago Tribune,* January 14, 1994, section 2, p. 7. Smith included in a list of happenings that caused controversy a reference to Williams: "A panel on Jesus, in which seminary professor Delores Williams was quoted as saying, I don't think we need folks hanging on crosses and blood dripping and weird stuff. . . . We just need to listen to the God within." Within the context of Williams's entire presentation, this comment sounded much less sensational.

155. Ibid., p. 56.

156. This phrase comes from a review by Luke Timothy Johnson of Elizabeth A. Johnson's *She Who Is: The Mystery of God in Feminist Discourse* in *Commonweal* 120, no. 2 (January 29, 1993): p. 22. It is a phrase that gives some insights, I think, into one of the reasons women's religious thought is construed as so much more dissenting than, in my opinion, it actually is: critics do not see beyond the daring expression to the orthodoxy.

157. Ibid., pp. 238–39.

158. In *The History and Philosophy of the Metaphysical Movements in America,* J. Stillson Judah includes chapters on Spiritualism, Theosophy and Its Allies, New Thought, the Divine Science Church, the Church of Religious Science, the Unity School of Christianity, Christian Science, and two nineteenth-century healers, Phineas Parkhurst Quimby and Warren Felt Evans.

159. In *New Thought: A Practical American Theology* (New York: Crossroad, 1995), C. Alan Anderson and Deborah G. Whitehouse devote a chapter to similarities and differences (pp. 80–82) between New Thought and New Age. See ch. 5, "New Thought and New Age," pp. 66–84. It is not my intent to conflate New Thought and New Age even though I point to some similarities. A cultural phenomenon with boundaries as fluid as those of the New Age movement presents ongoing challenges in definition and categorization. For an attempt to address some of those challenges, see Mary Farrell Bednarowski, "Literature of the New Age: A Review of Representative Sources," *Religious Studies Review* 17, no. 3 (July 1991): pp. 209–216.

160. For a lesson in New Thought perceptions of God, see Ernest Holmes, *A Dictionary of New Thought Terms: The Words and Phrases Commonly Used in Metaphysics* (Marina del Rey, Calif.: DeVorss and Company, 1991). First published in a longer form as *New Thought Terms and Their Meanings: A Dictionary of the Terms and Phrases Commonly Used in Metaphysical and Psychological Study* (New York: Dodd, Mead and Co., 1942). There are forty-five entries of various kinds that include "God" and many cross-references. Holmes (1887–1960), who studied with well-known New Thought teacher Emma Curtis Hopkins (who herself had studied with Mary Baker Eddy), is the founder of Religious Science, also known as Science of Mind.

161. An adequate survey and interpretation of metaphysical religions requires making distinctions among them in regard to their beliefs about the relative reality of spirit and matter. Christian Science, for example, makes more radical statements about reality as "spirit" than do some of the other traditions like Unity. In *New Thought: A Practical American Christianity,* Anderson and Whitehouse point to differences they see between Christian Science and New Thought (p. 23).

162. Marianne Williamson, *A Return to Love: Reflections on the Principles of A Course in Miracles* (New York: HarperCollins Publishers, 1992). *A Course in Miracles* is a set of three books "channeled" by Helen Schucman, a Jewish clinical and research

psychologist, and first published in 1975 by the Foundation for Inner Peace of Mill Valley, California. Schucman claimed that the voice she was channeling identified itself as that of Jesus. The Course uses Christian terminology but, its promoters and interpreters say, in non-traditional, psychologically oriented ways. Set within a metaphysical worldview, the basic theme of the course is "forgiveness."

163. Ibid., p. 258.

164. Williamson includes "Endnotes" that offer references to her citations from the three volumes of *A Course in Miracles.*

165. Ibid., pp. 247–248.

166. Marianne Williamson, *A Woman's Worth,* (New York: Random House, 1993; reprint, Hampton, N.H.: Contemporary Large Print, 1994), p. 2.

167. Ibid.

168. Ibid.

169. Ibid., p. 6.

170. Williamson says in The Preface to *A Woman's Worth* that she has no other purpose in writing the book than "a creative spill of my own guts. But that in itself is a passionate purpose, and I have seen how like my guts are those of other women" (p. viii).

171. For example, one suggestion Williamson gives for deepening spiritual practice and healing in the 1990s is "Go talk to Mary. . . . Talking to Mary doesn't make you a Catholic, nor does being a Catholic give you a special 'in.' If Mary doesn't feel comfortable for you, that's OK too. Find a Greek goddess or a female Indian avatar you can relate to, or any other symbol of feminine divinity, and begin a relationship with her" (p. 20).

172. Gordon Kaufman has been working on these ideas for many years and has reflected on them in many publications. See especially *In Face of Mystery: A Constructive Theology* (Cambridge: Harvard University Press, 1993).

173. In *The Modernist Impulse in American Protestantism,* William R. Hutchison points to both these themes—universal beliefs underlying religious pluralism and a faith in human progress—as marks of the immanentalism of Protestant liberalism that flourished for 120 years from the middle of the nineteenth century through the 1930s.

4. The Revelatory Power of the Ordinary and the Ordinariness of the Sacred

1. Sor Juana Inés de la Cruz, "La Respuesta a Sor Filotea," in *A Woman of Genius,* trans. Margaret Sayers Peden (Salisbury, Conn.: Lime Rock Press, 1982). This is a complicated and somewhat bizarre story. Sor Juana put in writing the critique that had originated, she said, in the "patter of conversation" with friends. The document came to the attention of the Bishop of Puebla (he and Sor Juana were also friends), and he published it at his own expense as "Carta Atenagorica." But he also sent Sor Juana a letter signed "Sor Filotea" (lover of God) and criticized her for public teaching, suggesting that women should be content to study for the love of learning. Not long afterward Sor Juana, widely acknowledged as "the most learned woman in Mexico" and author of many volumes of sacred and secular poetry and drama, retired from public life; she died four years later of the plague while nursing others, at approximately forty-four (the date of her birth is not certain). Scholars debate as to whether her decision to withdraw from the intellectual life, to give away her books and mathematical instruments, signaled surrender to episcopal power, depression, or a move authentic to what she felt called to do at that time in her life. For an elaboration of this story see Octavio Paz, *Sor Juana Or, The Traps of Faith,* trans. Margaret Sayers Peden (Cambridge: Harvard University Press, 1988), especially chs. 25 and 26, "An Ill-Fated Letter" and "The *Response,* pp. 389–424. I first encountered Sor Juana's "Respuesta" in the early 1960s in an un-

dergraduate Spanish literature course. This was long before she became what one scholar has called an "icon" of feminism, and I did not think of her then as "a woman in American religious history." But I did remember "La Respuesta" as a powerful piece of literature and later worked on a comparison of her with Anne Bradstreet (like Sor Juana referred to as the "tenth muse" in America) for a graduate course in colonial American literature. Now I always use "La Respuesta" in courses on women in American religious history, and students continue to be surprised at how greatly Sor Juana's feminist issues parallel their own.

2. Ibid., pp. 103–105.

3. Ibid., pp. 111–113.

4. Ibid.

5. Barbara Myerhoff, *Number Our Days: A Triumph of Continuity and Culture among Jewish Old People in an Urban Ghetto* (New York: Simon and Schuster, 1978), p. 234.

6. Ibid. That many women long for intellectual as well as domestic religion is evident in stories like one that appeared in the Minneapolis *Star Tribune* about elderly Jewish women in a nursing home having Bat Mitzvahs. In anticipation of the ritual Sylvia Fink, 87, said, "I am a little bit excited. I always felt something was missing. I was always an observant Jew. I kept a kosher house. But something didn't feel complete. This feels like it" (Saturday, April 12, 1997, p. B5).

7. Rita M. Gross, *Buddhism after Patriarchy: A Feminist History, Analysis, and Reconstruction of Buddhism* (Albany: State University of New York Press, 1993), p. 269.

8. Ada María Isasi-Díaz, "Elements of *Mujerista* Anthropology," in *The Embrace of God: Feminist Approaches to Theological Anthropology*, ed. Ann O'Hara Graff (Maryknoll, N.Y.: Orbis Books, 1995), p. 98.

9. Laurie Zoloth-Dorfman, "Traveling with Children: Mothering and the Ethics of the Ordinary World," *Tikkun* 10, no. 4 (July/August 1995): p. 26. It is obvious from the title that Zoloth-Dorfman is making this statement within the particular context of caring for children, but what she says has wider implications as well. See in addition Bonnie J. Miller-McLemore, *Also a Mother: Work and Family as Theological Dilemma* (Nashville: Abingdon Press, 1994).

10. Nancy L. Eiesland, *The Disabled God: Toward a Liberatory Theology of Disability*, foreword by Rebecca S. Chopp (Nashville: Abingdon Press, 1994), p. 14.

11. Ibid., p. 13.

12. Ibid., pp. 31–32.

13. Ibid., p. 31.

14. Ibid., pp. 13–14.

15. Ibid., p. 47.

16. Ibid., pp. 70–71.

17. Melanie A. May, *A Body Knows: A Theopoetics of Death and Resurrection* (New York: Continuum, 1995).

18. Melanie A. May, "'A Body Knows': Writing Resurrection," *Cross Currents* 46, no. 3 (Fall 1994): p. 344.

19. Ibid., p. 346.

20. Ibid., p. 347.

21. Ibid.

22. Adele B. McCollum, Roundtable Discussion: "Women with Disabilities," *Journal of Feminist Studies in Religion* 10, no. 2 (Fall 1994): p. 127.

23. Ibid., p. 126.

24. Ibid., p. 128. Not all the women in this roundtable discussion have the same things to say about "body" or even how to refer to themselves. Some choose "disabled" and reject "physically challenged" as a euphemism; others prefer the latter term. As to the tension over where to place one's emphasis—on body or spirit—Carol R. Fontaine

suggests that placing the stories of people with disabilities as central in an interpretation of the Bible can reveal new readings: that in contrast with feminism's rejection of the hierarchy of spirit over body, "For disabled women, . . . the New Testament's preference for 'spirit' as the defining construct of human anthropology actually *works*. We know better than to identify fully with bodies that are so patently unable to give shape and structure to the yearnings of our spirits" ("Women with Disabilities," p. 113, emphasis in the text). But there are many women with disabilities who claim that traditional emphasis on "spirit" is exactly what has kept religious traditions from responding to the different realities of "bodies."

25. Ibid., p. 128.
26. Ibid., p. 127.
27. Ibid.
28. Dorothee Wilhelm, "Women with Disabilities," p. 106.
29. Valerie C. Saiving, "Reflections on Sickness, Aging, and Death," *Journal of Feminist Studies in Religion* 4, no. 2 (Fall 1988): p. 117.
30. Ibid., p. 118. Saiving originally wrote this paper for a workshop on embodiment in 1976. When it was published in 1988, an editorial note made the case that the women's movement has still not addressed the issues she raises. And I know from my own experience that it is very difficult to find feminist interpretations of death and dying, although there is obviously more attention being paid to disability and illness. There is also more to be found if one looks at materials on "healing."
31. Ibid., p. 119. Emphasis in the text.
32. Ibid., p. 122.
33. Ibid., p. 123. Emphasis in the text.
34. Ibid.
35. Ibid.
36. Ibid., p. 125.
37. Kay Miller, "Bridging the Cultural Divide: Heavy Runner Helping Indians within Traditions," Minneapolis *Star Tribune*, July 12, 1993, pp. 1E, 3E. In an essay called "A Stranger in My Own Life: Alienation in American Indian Poetry and Prose," Paula Gunn Allen points to many variations on this theme of Indian identity. In *The Sacred Hoop: Recovering the Feminine in American Indian Traditions* (Boston: Beacon Press, 1986), pp. 127–146.
38. Miller, "Bridging the Cultural Divide," p. 3E.
39. Allen, *The Sacred Hoop*, p. 2.
40. Miller, "Bridging the Cultural Divide," p. 3E.
41. Ibid.
42. Diane Glancy, *Claiming Breath* (Lincoln: University of Nebraska Press, 1992), unnumbered page. The untitled poem-like paragraph from which the quote is taken is on a page preceding the first poem of the volume. Many other poems in the volume speak to the same everyday experience of living and writing between two cultures, among them, "Ethnic Arts: The Cultural Bridge" (pp. 59–65) and "The Nail-down of Oral Tradition" (pp. 103–115). Mary C. Churchill refers to the poetry of Diane Glancy and to that of other Cherokee women poets as well, particularly Joan Shaddox Isom, Maggie Culver Fry, Marilou Awiatka, and Gladys Cardiff, in "Walking the 'White Path': Toward a Cherokee-Centric Hermeneutic for Interpreting Cherokee Literature" (Ph.D. diss., University of California Santa Barbara, 1997).
43. Diane Glancy, "A Confession or Apology for Christian Faith," in *Claiming Breath*, pp. 94, 96, 98. The last reference, to Indian tradition as another Old Testament of Christianity, sounds to me like a reference to Steve Charleston's essay, "The Old Testament of Native America," in *Lift Every Voice: Constructing Christian Theologies from the Underside*, ed. Susan Brooks Thistlethwaite and Mary Potter Engel (San Francisco: Harper and Row Publishers, 1990), pp. 49–61. Charleston was on the faculty

of Luther Northwestern (now Luther) Theological Seminary in St. Paul, Minnesota, when he wrote this essay.

44. Janice Gould, "American Indian Women's Poetry: Strategies of Rage and Hope," *Signs: Journal of Women in Culture and Society* 20, no. 4 (Summer 1995): p. 797.

45. Ibid., pp. 805–806. "Workday" comes from Hogan's collection, *Savings* (Minneapolis: Coffee House Press, 1988), p. 43.

46. Ibid., p. 82.

47. Linda Hogan, "Gate," in *The Book of Medicines* (Minneapolis: Coffee House Press, 1993), pp. 79–80.

48. Joy Harjo, *The Woman Who Fell from the Sky* (New York: W.W. Norton and Company, 1994), p. 68.

49. Roberta J. Hill, "Immersed in Words," in *Speaking for the Generations: Native Writers on Writing*, ed. Simon Ortiz (Tucson: The University of Arizona Press, 1998), p. 73. Hill is well known for her first collection of poetry, published under the name Roberta Hill Whiteman, *Star Quilt* (Minneapolis: Holy Cow! Press, 1984).

50. Gould, "American Indian Women's Poetry," pp. 806–807.

51. Katie Geneva Cannon, *Katie's Canon: Womanism and the Soul of the Black Community* (New York: Continuum, 1995), pp. 133–134. This is a quote from one of the interviewees who responded to a questionnaire Cannon sent out asking about "Epistemological Sources for Critical Womanist Scholarship."

52. Ibid., p. 137.

53. Ibid., p. 134. Cannon wrote her own Ph.D. dissertation on ethics and the fiction of Zora Neale Hurston.

54. Cheryl A. Kirk-Duggan, *Exorcizing Evil: A Womanist Perspective on the Spirituals* (Maryknoll, N.Y.: Orbis Books, 1997), p. xiii.

55. Ibid., p. xiv.

56. Ibid., p. 59.

57. Ibid., p. xviii.

58. Ibid., p. 330.

59. Ibid., p. 332.

60. Cannon, *Katie's Canon*, p. 24.

61. Carol Ochs, "Miriam's Way," *Cross Currents* 45, no. 4 (Winter 1995): p. 493.

62. Ibid.

63. Ibid., p. 496.

64. There are several variations of the spelling of this word in Jewish and Christian writings.

65. Tikva Frymer-Kensky, "Toward a Liberal Theory of Halakha," *Tikkun* 10, no. 4 (July/August 1995): pp. 44–45.

66. Ibid., p. 45.

67. Ibid.

68. Ibid., p. 47.

69. Ibid.

70. Ibid., pp. 47–48, 77. Emphasis in the text.

71. Ibid., p. 77.

72. Zoloth-Dorfman, "Traveling with Children," p. 25. See also "What Kind of Society Nurtures the Soul," *Tikkun* 11, no. 5 (September/October 1996): 33–35.

73. Zoloth-Dorfman, "Traveling with Children," p. 25.

74. Ibid., pp. 26–27.

75. Ibid., p. 27.

76. Ibid., p. 26.

77. Ibid., p. 27.

78. Ibid.

79. Bonnie J. Miller-McLemore, *Also a Mother: Work and Family as Theological Dilemma* (Nashville: Abingdon Press, 1994), p. 22. See particularly ch. 7, "According to the Pace of Children: Generative Acts of Faith, Discipline, and Parental Inclination," pp. 152–174.

80. Ibid., p. 23.

81. Ibid., p. 15.

82. Ibid., p. 31.

83. Kathleen Norris, *Dakota: A Spiritual Geography* (New York: Ticknor and Fields, 1993), p. 154.

84. Zoloth-Dorfman, "Traveling with Children," p. 27.

85. Leslie A. Northrup, "Claiming Horizontal Space: Women's Religious Rituals," *Studia Liturgica: An Ecumenical Review for Liturgical Research and Renewal* 25, no. 1 (1995): p. 94. My thanks to Denise Dijk, a liturgical theologian at *Theologische Universiteit Kampen* in the Netherlands, for sending me a copy of this article.

86. Hallie Iglehart Austen, "Women's Spirituality from the Roots to the Heart," in *The Womanspirit Sourcebook* (San Francisco: Harper and Row, 1988), p. 107.

87. Penina V. Adelman, "A Drink from Miriam's Cup: Invention of Tradition among Jewish Women," *Journal of Feminist Studies in Religion* 10, no. 2 (Fall 1994): pp. 151–166. Adelman analyzes the major symbols of *Kos Miriam*, "a drink from Miriam's cup," and the legend on which it is based. The ritual is based on a text she had previously written about Jewish women's rituals and legends of Miriam, the sister of Moses and Aaron, a woman often neglected in Jewish tradition. She also provides an extended discussion of what "tradition" means for Jewish women, how its boundaries are determined, in the context of creating rituals that are accessible to those beyond their own group—families for example—and that can include men. She quotes the unpublished material of Rabbi Laura Geller of Los Angeles, who maintains that "for new ritual to work, it must include elements of the Creation, the Exodus, or the Redemption stories" (p. 162). See also Adelman's book, *Miriam's Well: Rituals for Jewish Women around the Year* (New York: Biblio Press, 1986; new ed. 1994).

88. Lynn Gottlieb, *She Who Dwells Within: A Feminist Vision of a Renewed Judaism* (New York: HarperSanFrancisco, 1995), pp. 205–206.

89. Ibid. One of the best discussions I'm aware of about improvised ritual and the extent to which it is or is not compelling is Barbara Myerhoff's *Number Our Days*. Myerhoff draws on the work of Victor Turner and her own experiences with the "made-up" rituals of the elderly Jews she studied in the Aliyah Community Center in Venice, California. In conjunction with Adelman, it is very illuminating about Jewish women's ideas on the meaning of tradition.

90. Ada María Isasi-Díaz, "On the Birthing Stool: Mujerista Liturgy," in *Women at Worship: Interpretations of North American Diversity*, ed. Marjorie Procter-Smith and Janet R. Walton (Louisville, Ky.: Westminster/John Knox Press, 1993), p. 192.

91. Ibid., pp. 195, 196, 207.

92. Miriam Therese Winter, *Woman Word: A Feminist Lectionary and Psalter: Women of the New Testament*, illus. Meinrad Craighead (New York: Crossroad, 1990), p. ix.

93. Ibid.

94. Paula Gunn Allen, "Paula Gunn Allen and the Ritual Tradition," interview by Julie Fretzin, *Creation Spirituality* 8, no. 2 (March/April 1992): p. 19.

95. Ibid.

96. Ibid., p. 20.

97. Ibid.

98. Ibid., p. 21.

99. Susan A. Ross, "God's Embodiment and Women," in *Freeing Theology: The Essentials of Theology in Feminist Perspective*, ed. Catherine Mowry LaCugna (New York: HarperSanFrancisco, 1993), p. 193. The article from which Ross draws is Christine Gudorf, "The Power to Create: Sacraments and Men's Need to Birth," *Horizons* 14 (1987): pp. 296–309.

100. Ibid., pp. 204–205.

101. Ibid., p. 205.

102. *Setting the Table: Women in Theological Conversation*, ed. Rita Nakashima Brock, Claudia Camp, and Serene Jones (St. Louis: Chalice Press, 1995), p. 251.

103. Ibid.

104. Ibid., pp. 249, 268.

105. Gross, *Buddhism after Patriarchy*, p. 269. Emphasis in the text.

106. Ibid., p. 288.

107. Ibid.

108. Ibid., p. 286.

109. Kay Bessler Northcutt, "August in Her Breast: Prayer as Embodiment," in *Setting the Table*, p. 207.

110. Ibid., p. 206.

111. Ibid.

112. Ibid., p. 217.

113. Marcia K. Hermansen, "Two-Way Acculturation: Muslim Women in America between Individual Choice (Liminality) and Community Affiliation (Communitas)," in *The Muslims of America*, ed. Yvonne Yazbeck Haddad (New York: Oxford University Press, 1991), p. 192. Two other issues related to identity that Hermansen discusses in this article are women's religious meetings and marriage.

114. Ibid., p. 193.

115. Ibid., p. 200.

116. Helen Beach Cannon, "Sacred Clothing: An Inside/Outside Perspective," *Dialogue* 25, no. 3 (Fall 1992): pp. 138–148. McDannell's research formed the basis for one chapter of her book *Material Christianity: Religion and Popular Culture in America* (New Haven: Yale University Press, 1995). See ch.7, "Mormon Garments: Sacred Clothing and the Body," pp. 198–221. McDannell offers a history of this special kind of undergarment, sometimes described as like a "union suit," and an interpretation of its religious meanings for Mormons, including their stories about their reasons for the wearing and discarding of garments.

117. Ibid., p. 139.

118. Ibid., p. 143.

119. Terry Tempest Williams offers an interesting interpretation of controversies over folk magic in Mormonism. Many Mormons are angry and defensive in their denial of Joseph Smith's apparent knowledge and use of folk magic and are hostile toward historians like Michael Quinn who have written about it. And obviously his use of folk magic has discredited Smith even further among those who are skeptical of the authenticity of his revelations and of Mormon theology and history. Still others see Smith's use of folk magic as evidence of his shamanistic gifts. Williams has yet another response: "For me, it renders my religion human. I love knowing that Joseph Smith was a mystic who ascribed magical properties to animals and married his wives according to the astrological 'mansions of the moon.' To acknowledge that which we cannot see, to give definition to that which we do not know, to create divine order out of chaos, is the religious dance." *Refuge: An Unnatural History of Family and Place* (New York: Vintage Books, 1991), pp. 196–197.

120. Cannon, "Sacred Clothing," p. 141.

121. Ibid., p. 140.

122. Ibid., p. 146.

123. Ibid., p. 147. Cannon is quoting Jewish anthropologist Barbara Myerhoff, who referred to this saying in a film, "In Her Own Time," made by her students while Myerhoff was dying of cancer and at the same time studying an ultraorthodox Jewish community in Los Angeles, a community that offered Myerhoff healing in a variety of ways. This film is one of the best studies I've ever seen of creative ambivalence (Myerhoff's) about both the restrictions a religious community imposes on women and the liberation and community it offers.

124. Judith N. Scoville, "Toward a Theological Ethic of the Land: Environmental Ethics in the Context of American Agriculture" (Ph.D. diss., Graduate Theological Union, Berkeley, California, 1995), p. 263.

125. Ibid., p. 264.

126. Ibid., p. 324. When I asked Judith Scoville whether she ever did buy the pork chops, she was unable to remember, but said that whether she bought them in the future depended on where they had come from.

127. Pamela A. Smith, "The Ecotheology of Annie Dillard: A Study in Ambivalence," *CrossCurrents* 45, no. 3 (Fall 1995): p. 351.

128. Ada Maria Isasi-Díaz, *Mujerista Theology: Theology for the Twenty-First Century* (Maryknoll, N.Y.: Orbis Books, 1996), pp. 66–67. Isasi-Díaz draws these categories from her own experience with Latina women and from the work of Daniel H. Levine, *Popular Voices in Latin American Catholicism* (Princeton, N.J.: Princeton University Press, 1992).

129. Isasi-Díaz, p. 67.

130. Ibid., p. 69. Some of this is a quote from Ivone Gebara. See n. 22.

131. Ibid.

132. Ibid., pp. 71–72.

133. Ibid., p. 72.

134. Ibid.

135. Joanna B. Gillespie, "Gender and Generations in Congregations," in *Episcopal Women*, ed. Catherine Prelinger (New York: Oxford University Press), pp. 209–210. For a similar study based on the life of one woman, "Mrs. Langlois," see in the same volume, Irene Q. Brown, "Feasts, Fairs, and Festivities," pp. 239–262. For other examples see Mary McClintock Fulkerson's study of Pentecostal and Presbyterian women, *Changing the Subject: Women's Discourse and Feminist Theology* (Minneapolis: Fortress Press, 1994); Susan Starr Sered, "Childbirth as a Religious Experience? Voices from an Israeli Hospital," *Journal of Feminist Studies in Religion* 7, no. 2 (Fall 1991): pp. 7–18.

5. "Relationship" and Its Complexities

1. Beverly Wildung Harrison, "The Power of Anger in the Work of Love: Christian Ethics for Women and Other Strangers," in *Making the Connections: Essays in Feminist Social Ethics*, ed. Carol S. Robb (Boston: Beacon Press, 1985), pp. 8–16.

2. Margaret A. Farley, "New Patterns of Relationship: Beginnings of a Moral Revolution," *Theological Studies* 36 (1975): pp. 627–646. See also Farley's entry, "Relationships," in *Dictionary of Feminist Theologies*, ed. Letty M. Russell and J. Shannon Clarkson (Louisville, Ky.: Westminster/John Knox Press, 1996), pp. 238–239.

3. Letty M. Russell, *The Future of Partnership* (Philadelphia: Westminster Press, 1979) and *Growth in Partnership* (Philadelphia: Westminster Press, 1981).

4. Carol Gilligan, *In a Different Voice: Psychological Theory and Women's Development* (Cambridge: Harvard University Press, 1982). Gilligan put forth her thesis with more caution and subtlety than more recent summaries of it typically suggest. She

claimed that the "different voice" she detected in her research on how people talk about moral issues "is characterized not by gender but theme," although she certainly acknowledges that "it is primarily through women's voices that I trace its development" (p. 2). Gilligan's thesis has generated an immense amount of positive and negative response. Part of Gilligan's case is to refute the assumption in much psychological and ethical literature that women's capacity to reflect ethically is less well-developed than men's. Some of the negative response to her thesis is based on a fear that assuming women are by nature more oriented toward relationships than men, even if true, makes it even more difficult for women to develop and be perceived as moral agents whose reflections are just as sophisticated as—but different from—men's. For a study that surveys the literature, acknowledges the negatives, and then makes a case for her own development of an ethic of care, see Rita C. Manning, *Speaking from the Heart: A Feminist Perspective on Ethics* (Lanham, Md.: Rowman and Littlefield Publishers, 1992). Manning is a moral philosopher, not a theologian.

5. Carter Heyward, *The Redemption of God: A Theology of Mutual Relation* (Lanham, Md.: University Press of America, 1982).

6. Kate O'Neill, "Sounds of Silence," in *Buddhist Women on the Edge: Contemporary Perspectives from the Western Frontier*, ed. Marianne Dresser (Berkeley: North Atlantic Books, 1996), p. 21.

7. Judith Plaskow, "Transforming the Nature of Community: Toward a Feminist People of Israel," in *After Patriarchy: Feminist Transformations of the World Religions*, ed. Paula M. Cooey, William R. Eakin, and Jay B. McDaniel (Maryknoll, N.Y.: Orbis Books, 1991; reprint, 1997).

8. Catherine Mowry LaCugna, *God for Us: The Trinity and Christian Life* (New York: HarperSanFrancisco, 1991), p. 344.

9. Joy Harjo, "Reconciliation: A Prayer," in *The Woman Who Fell from the Sky* (New York: W. W. Norton and Company, 1994), n.p. This is a poem written for the Audre Lord memorial in 1993.

10. Ada Maria Isasi-Díaz, "Un Poquito de Justicia: A Little Bit of Justice," in *Mujerista Theology: A Theology for the Twenty-First Century* (Maryknoll, N.Y.: Orbis Books), p. 119.

11. Marjorie Hewitt Suchocki, *The Fall to Violence: Original Sin in Relational Theology* (New York: Continuum, 1995).

12. Paula M. Cooey, *Religious Imagination and the Body: A Feminist Analysis* (New York: Oxford University Press, 1994), p. 109.

13. Mary Grey, "Claiming Power-in-Relation: Exploring the Ethics of Connection," *Journal of Feminist Studies in Religion* 7, no. 1 (Spring 1991): pp. 13–14.

14. Carol J. Adams, "Introduction," *Ecofeminism and the Sacred*, ed. Carol J. Adams (New York: Continuum, 1993), pp. 4–5.

15. Carol P. Christ, *Rebirth of the Goddess: Finding Meaning in Feminist Spirituality* (Reading, Mass.: Addison-Wesley Publishing Company, 1997), p. 160.

16. Cooey, *Religious Imagination and the Body*, p. 126. One of the best-known essays questioning too much reliance on women's experience as an ontological or epistemological category is Sheila Greeve Davaney, "The Limits of Appeal to Women's Experience," in *Shaping New Vision: Gender and Values in American Culture*, ed. Clarissa W. Atkinson, Constance H. Buchanan, and Margaret Miles (Ann Arbor: UMI Research Press, 1987), pp. 31–50.

17. Mary E. Hunt, "Shifting Spiritual Authorities for Feminist Ethics," *Annual of the Society of Christian Ethics*, 1994 (Lexington, Va.: Society of Christian Ethics, 1994), p. 267.

18. For an analysis of this dilemma and an acknowledgment of how it has influenced his own theology, see David Tracy, Roundtable Discussion: "The Influence of

Feminist Theory on My Theological Work," *Journal of Feminist Studies in Religion* 7, no 1 (Spring 1991): 122–124.

19. There are other directions to go in as well in order to see what uses Buddhist women make of the concept of relationality. For example, Rita M. Gross offers an extensive discussion of *sangha*, or community, in Buddhism and the role she sees relationship playing in the process of enlightenment in post-patriarchal Buddhism. *Sangha* is one of the Three Jewels in Buddhism to which Buddhists go for refuge, the others being the Buddha and the teachings. Gross contends that feminist Buddhism has much more to say about supportive community than patriarchal Buddhism, and she interprets *sangha* as "the companionship and feedback of fellow travelers on the path to freedom." See especially pp. 258–269 in *Buddhism after Patriarchy: A Feminist History, Analysis, and Reconstruction of Buddhism* (Albany: State University of New York Press, 1993). See, also, "I Go for Refuge to the Sangha: A Feminist Buddhist Response to Rosemary Radford Ruether," *Buddhist-Christian Studies Journal* 11 (1991): pp. 230–239, and "Community, Work, Relationship, and Family: Renunciation and Balance in American Buddhist Practice," in *Buddhist Women on the Edge: Contemporary Perspectives from the Western Frontier*, ed. Marianne Dresser (Berkeley: North Atlantic Books, 1996), pp. 133–150.

20. Anne Carolyn Klein, *Meeting the Great Bliss Queen: Buddhists, Feminists, and the Art of the Self* (Boston: Beacon Press, 1995). For an essay-length discussion of Buddhist and feminist understandings of "self," see Anne C. Klein, "Persons and Possibilities," in *Buddhist Women on the Edge*, pp. 39–43.

21. Klein, *Meeting the Great Bliss Queen*, p. 12.

22. Ibid., pp. xv–xvi.

23. Ibid., p. 89.

24. Ibid., p. 117.

25. Ibid., p. 118.

26. Ibid., p. 119.

27. Quoted in Sandy Boucher, *Turning the Wheel: American Women Creating the New Buddhism*, updated and expanded ed. (Boston: Beacon Press, 1993), p. 274.

28. Joanna Macy, *World as Lover, World as Self*, foreword by Thich Nhat Hanh (Berkeley: Parallax Press, 1991), p. 86. This is a book of essays about many different aspects of Macy's work and thought.

29. Ibid., p. 238.

30. Ibid., p. 89. For an extended discussion see ch. 8, "Karma: The Co-Arising of Doer and Deed," pp. 85–94.

31. Ibid., p. 203.

32. Ibid., p. 217.

33. Ibid., p. 222.

34. Ibid., p. 241.

35. Boucher, *Turning the Wheel*, p. 274.

36. Judith Plaskow, "Transforming the Nature of Community: Toward a Feminist People of Israel," in *After Patriarchy: Feminist Transformations of the World Religions*, ed. Paula M. Cooey, William R. Eakin, and Jay McDaniel (Maryknoll, N.Y.: Orbis Books, 1997). See Ellen M. Umansky, "Creating a Jewish Feminist Theology: Possibilities and Problems," in *Weaving the Visions: New Patterns in Feminist Spirituality*, ed. Judith Plaskow and Carol P. Christ (San Francisco: Harper and Row, 1989), pp. 187–198, for an approach that emphasizes relationship in terms of Jewish women's connection with their tradition.

37. Plaskow, "Transforming the Nature of Community," p. 89.

38. Ibid., p. 92.

39. Ibid., p. 93.

40. Ibid., p. 98.

41. Judith Plaskow, *Standing Again at Sinai: Judaism from a Feminist Perspective* (New York: HarperSanFrancisco, 1990), pp. 105–106.

42. Ibid. p. 103.

43. Ibid., p. 109.

44. Anne E. Patrick, *Liberating Conscience: Feminist Explorations in Catholic Moral Theology* (New York: Continuum, 1996).

45. Ibid. pp. 40–41.

46. Ibid., pp. 78–79.

47. Ibid., p. 23.

48. Ibid., p. 35.

49. Ibid., p. 36.

50. Ibid., p. 100.

51. Ibid., p. 163.

52. Ibid. For an elaboration on the last question, see Mary E. Hunt, *Fierce Tenderness: A Feminist Theology of Friendship* (New York: Crossroad, 1991). Hunt points to the need for ethical norms to guide lesbian/gay relationships: "It is not enough to say that all is now permissible where nothing used to be allowed. . . . But neither is it fair to leave a large segment of the population without moral anchors, indeed to leave everyone with the impression that there are no lesbian/gay sexual ethical parameters. That there are, and that they may differ from and influence the existing ones based on heterosexual relationships, is something that will come about only by trying on or experimenting with various approaches" (p. 89).

53. Patrick, *Liberating Conscience*, p. 173. "Conscience" has a very long history in Roman Catholicism. Ada María Isasi-Díaz is another Roman Catholic theologian who has devoted extensive attention to the matter of conscience, particularly among Latina women, as was discussed, also, in Chapter 3. One of her primary theological and social goals is for Latina women to develop as moral agents and move away from the "authoritarian conscience" that promotes obedience and dependence as major virtues. This is a distortion, as Isasi-Díaz sees it, of traditional Roman Catholic teaching about the *sensus fidelium*, the ideas and ideals of the whole community about moral matters.

54. Catherine Mowry LaCugna, *God for Us: The Trinity and Christian Life* (New York: HarperSanFrancisco, 1991).

55. Ibid., p. ix.

56. Ibid.

57. Ibid., p. 6.

58. Ibid., p. 1.

59. Ibid., p. 269.

60. In a review of the works of several feminist theologians, Serene Jones is mostly positive about the accomplishments of LaCugna's work, but also points to LaCugna's insistence on relational ontology as "the locus of a *new essence*, a new point around which the structural coherence of the subject (albeit a new subject-self-person) is secured" (emphasis in text). This, as Jones sees it, is an invitation to a new essentialism, one that thinks of women's experience in more open-ended and historicized ways than the kind that posits some kind of static woman's nature and to which many kinds of feminism are opposed, but essentialism nonetheless. Serene Jones, "'Women's Experience' between a Rock and a Hard Place: Feminist, Womanist and *Mujerista* Theologies in North America," *Religious Studies Review* 21, no. 3 (July 1995): p. 173.

61. Marjorie Hewitt Suchocki, *The Fall to Violence: Original Sin in Relational Theology* (New York: Continuum, 1995), p. 48.

62. In a study of four alternative religions of the nineteenth century that women

founded or were drawn to in great numbers, one of the primary common themes I discovered was a rejection of the assumption that we are by nature sinful. See Mary Farrell Bednarowski, "Outside the Mainstream: Women's Religion and Women Religious Leaders in Nineteenth-Century America," *Journal of the American Academy of Religion* 48 (June 1980): pp. 207–231.

63. Suchocki, *The Fall to Violence*, p. 82.

64. Ibid., p. 103.

65. Ibid., p. 113. Suchocki acknowledges debts to the theologies of Walter Rauschenbusch and Reinhold Niebuhr for these perceptions of the institutional nature of sin.

66. Ibid., p. 129.

67. Ibid., p. 145.

68. Ibid., pp. 145–146.

69. Christ, *Rebirth of the Goddess: Finding Meaning in Feminist Spirituality*. "Thealogy" is a term first used by religious studies scholar Naomi Goldenberg. It is generally used to refer to Goddess (*thea*) theology as an enterprise set apart from traditional theology.

70. Ibid., p. xv.

71. Ibid., p. 156.

72. Ibid., pp. 157–158.

73. Ibid., p. 159.

74. Elaine J. Lawless, *Holy Women, Wholly Women: Sharing Ministries through Life Stories and Reciprocal Ethnography* (Philadelphia: University of Pennsylvania Press, 1993).

75. Ibid., p. 61.

76. Ibid., p. 287.

77. Ibid., p. 62.

78. Ibid., p. 79.

79. Ibid., p. 71.

80. Ibid., p. 129. Emphasis in text.

81. Ibid., p. 286.

82. See Audre Lord, "Open Letter to Mary Daly," in *This Bridge Called My Back: Writings by Radical Women of Color*, ed. Cherrie Moraga and Gloria Anzaldua (New York: Kitchen Table Press, 1983), pp. 94–97; Delores S. Williams, "The Color of Feminism," *Christianity and Crisis* 45, no. 7 (April 29, 1985): pp. 164, 165; Judith Plaskow, "Christian Feminism and Anti-Judaism," *CrossCurrents* 28 (1978): pp. 306–309; and Annette Daum, "Blaming Jews for the Death of the Goddess," *Lilith* 7 (1980): pp. 12–13. See also Susannah Heschel, "Anti-Judaism in Christian Feminist Theology," *Tikkun* 5, no. 3 (May/June 1990): pp. 25–28, 95–97. Heschel sums up three themes in Christian feminist theology negative to Judaism: scapegoating Judaism as the originator of patriarchy, the murderer of the Goddess, and the destroyer of the Goddess's peace-loving culture; putting forth Christianity as the answer to all feminists' problems, no matter what religion they are; and affirming first-century Christianity's liberation of women by contrast with Judaism's negative treatment—the "Jesus was a feminist" approach that ignores the fact that what has come to be seen as early Christianity was a Jewish movement. For a response to this issue by one of the best-known Christian feminist biblical scholars, see Elisabeth Schüssler Fiorenza, *Jesus: Miriam's Child, Sophia's Prophet* (New York: Continuum, 1994), particularly ch. 3, "The Power of Naming: Jesus, Women, and Christian Anti-Judaism." Schüssler Fiorenza asks complicated questions in this chapter, among them, "Why are Jewish feminist scholars compelled to hear any positive Christian feminist reconstruction of the Jesus movement in exclusivist and absolutist terms even when such a reconstruction seeks to underline in feminist terms

the emancipatory elements of first-century Judaism? Why is it that Christian feminists, despite their expressed intention to the contrary, end up reinscribing anti-Jewish arguments?" (p. 72). Judith Plaskow and Schüssler Fiorenza founded and edit together the *Journal of Feminist Studies in Religion.*

83. Barbara Hilkert Andolsen, *Daughters of Jefferson, Daughters of Bootblacks: Racism and American Feminism* (Macon, Ga.: Mercer University Press, 1986).

84. Delores S. Williams, *Sisters in the Wilderness: The Challenge of Womanist God-Talk* (Maryknoll, N.Y.: Orbis Books, 1993), p. xii.

85. Rebecca Alpert, *Like Bread on the Seder Plate: Jewish Lesbians and the Transformation of Tradition* (New York: Columbia University Press, 1997), p. vii. "Bread on the Seder plate" refers to the Jewish tradition of eating only unleavened bread at the Seder meal. Thus to have leavened bread on the Seder plate is a transgression of what traditionally has been acceptable. Alpert relates a story that was told among Jewish lesbians during the 1980s of a male rabbi who apparently declared that "there is as much place for lesbians in Judaism as for leavened bread at the Seder table." Alpert tells, also, of ritual responses to this story among Jewish lesbians that ranged from actually putting bread on the Seder plate to leaving a space on the plate to represent lesbians and others who felt alienated to substituting an orange (for those who felt uncomfortable with the bread) to represent Jewish lesbians and gay men. These various rituals and the stories about them gave rise to what Alpert calls a "contemporary legend," one that is evocative and seldom told the same way twice (pp. 1-3).

86. Ibid., pp. 165-166.

87. Katharina von Kellenbach, *Anti-Judaism in Feminist Religious Writings* (Atlanta: Scholars Press, 1994), p. 1. Von Kellenbach is a German theologian who received a Ph.D. in religion from Temple University; this manuscript had its beginnings in her dissertation.

88. Constance F. Parvey, "A Christian Feminist's Struggle with the Bible as Authority," in *Women's and Men's Liberation: Testimonies of Spirit*, ed. Leonard Grob, Riffat Hassan, and Haim Gordon (Westport, Conn.: Greenwood Press, 1991), pp. 58-59.

89. Diana Eck, *Encountering God: A Spiritual Journey from Bozeman to Banaras* (Boston: Beacon Press, 1993), p. 222.

90. Ibid., p. 223.

91. Susan Stanford Friedman, "Beyond White and Other: Relationality and Narratives of Race in Feminist Discourse," *Signs* 21, no. 1 (Autumn 1995): 1-49. In her discussion of race among feminists, Friedman suggests three scripts—denial, accusation, and confession—as forms that feminist discourse has taken in response to the prevalence of white/other binary opposition. She suggests a fourth, "relational positionality," that is more creative because of its potential for "resisting and dissolving the fixities of the white/other binary." She holds that "[w]ithin a relational framework, identities shift with a changing context, dependent always upon the point of reference," but she doesn't want "relational positionality" confused with pluralism, which, she thinks, tends to suppress analyses of power arrangements.

92. See for example "The Questions That Won't Go Away: A Dialogue about Women in Buddhism and Christianity," *Journal of Feminist Studies in Religion* 6, no. 2 (Fall 1990): pp. 87-120; Mary E. Hunt, "Feminist Ecumenism: Models for the Mainstream," *Christian Century* 108, no. 31 (Oct. 30, 1991): pp. 1000-1002; Virginia Ramey Mollenkott, "Interreligious Dialogue: A Pilgrimage," *Daughters of Sarah* 21, no. 2 (Spring 1994): pp. 11-13; Mary C. Boys, *Jewish-Christian Dialogue: One Woman's Experience*, (New York: Paulist Press, 1997).

93. Cooey, *Religious Imagination and the Body*, p. ix.

94. Ibid., pp. 9-10.

95. Ibid., pp. 126-127.

96. Ibid., p. 7.

97. Ibid., p. 6.
98. Ibid., p. 116.
99. Ibid., p. 128.
100. Lisa Sowle Cahill, *Sex, Gender and Christian Ethics* (Cambridge: Cambridge University Press, 1996). This quote comes from an abstract that precedes the actual text (n.p.).
101. Ibid., pp. 254–255.
102. Ibid., p. 255.
103. Ibid.
104. Ibid., p. 67.
105. Ibid., p. 69. For an interesting article about feminism and sexuality from a related but distinct perspective, see Kathleen M. Sands, "Uses of the Thea(o)logian: Sex and Theodicy in Religious Feminism," *Journal of Feminist Studies in Religion* 8, no. 1 (Spring, 1992): pp. 7–33. Sands says, "What women really need from feminist thea(o)logians, I believe, is assistance in cultivating a practical sexual wisdom" (p. 8).
106. Ibid., p. 108.
107. For two other sources that are illuminating on the subject of natural law and its potential for defusing rather than promoting ethical absolutes, see Patrick, *Liberating Conscience*, and Cristina L. H. Traina, "Oh, Susanna: The New Absolutism and Natural Law," *Journal of the American Academy of Religion* 65, no. 2 (Summer 1997): pp. 371–401.
108. Frida Kerner Furman, "Women, Aging, and Ethics: Reflections on Bodily Experience," *Annual of the Society of Christian Ethics*, p. 231. My first encounter with Furman's work was this article. She has since published a book-length study of Julie's International Salon: *Facing the Mirror: Older Women and Beauty Shop Culture* (New York: Routledge, 1977). It includes chapters on community, beauty, aging, work and family, and resistance.
109. Ibid.
110. Ibid., p. 240.
111. Ibid., pp. 253–254.
112. Ibid., p. 244.
113. Marianne Williamson, *A Return to Love: Reflections on the Principles of A Course in Miracles* (New York: HarperCollins Publishers, 1992). Williamson devotes chapter 6 to "Relationships," in which she discusses not so much "relationship" in general but specific kinds of relationships, and chapter 8 to "The Body."
114. Ibid., p. 216.
115. Ibid., pp. 28–29.
116. Mary McClintock Fulkerson, *Changing the Subject: Women's Discourses and Feminist Theology* (Minneapolis: Fortress Press, 1994), p. 182.
117. Ibid., pp. x–ix.
118. Ibid., p. 183.
119. Ibid., p. 284.
120. Ibid., p. 384.
121. Karen McCarthy Brown, *Mama Lola: A Vodou Priestess in Brooklyn* (Berkeley: University of California Press, 1991), p. 7.
122. Ibid., pp. 13–14.
123. Ibid., p. 15.
124. Ibid., p. 20.
125. Ibid., p. 8.
126. Ibid., p. 11.
127. Ibid.
128. Ibid., pp. 380–381.
129. Cahill, *Sex, Gender, and Ethics*, p. 33.

130. Alpert, *Like Bread on the Seder Plate*, p. 97. Alpert takes issue with both Carol Gilligan and Carter Heyward for, in her opinion, placing justice and love in opposition to each other (p. 98).

131. Ibid., p. 98.

132. It is not impossible to find suggestions among feminist theologians that women's emphasis on relationality emerges from patriarchal assumptions about women's nature. For references to this issue, see Schüssler Fiorenza, *Jesus: Miriam's Child, Sophia's Prophet*, p. 55.

133. Patrick, *Liberating Conscience*, p. 56.

6. Healing and Women's Theological Creativity

1. Susan Starr Sered, *Priestess, Mother, Sacred Sister: Religions Dominated by Women* (New York: Oxford University Press, 1994), p. 103. Emphasis in original. See especially ch. 3, "Misfortune, Suffering, and Healing," pp. 103–118.

2. Rachel Naomi Remen offers this definition of healing as related to wholeness: "Healing is the very ground of being. Everyone is moving toward wholeness. And that's all healing is, that movement." Remen also considers healing an "ordinary" and ongoing process, not something magical or mystical, but something natural to everyone: "Our task is not to make something happen but to uncover what is already happening in us and in others, and to recognize and foster those conditions that nurture it. That's all." "The Search for Healing," in *Healers on Healing*, ed. Richard Carlson and Benjamin Shield (Los Angeles: Jeremy P. Tarcher, 1989), p. 96.

3. Joan Tollifson, "Enjoying the Perfection of Imperfection," in *Being Bodies: Buddhist Women on the Paradox of Embodiment*, ed. Lenore Friedman and Susan Moon (Boston: Shambhala, 1997), p. 18. In this essay, Tollifson, who was born without a right hand, describes what she means by her paradoxical claim about life and living with a disability with a series of adjectives that echoes much of the spirit of Chapter 4: "Asymmetrical. Messy. Unresolved. Out of Control. Imperfect. Terrible. And miraculous" (p. 23).

4. Roberta C. Bondi, *Memories of God: Theological Reflections on a Life* (Nashville: Abingdon Press, 1995).

5. Ibid., p. 170.

6. Joan Iten Sutherland, "Body of Radiant Knots: Healing as Remembering," in *Being Bodies*, p. 3.

7. Jeanne Achterberg, *Woman as Healer: A Panoramic Survey of the Healing Activities of Women from Prehistoric Times to the Present* (Boston: Shambhala Publications, 1990), p. 194.

8. Remen, "The Search for Healing," p. 96.

9. Mary Daly's work represents some of the most graphic descriptions of women's suffering from patriarchy, most famously in *Gyn/Ecology: The Metaethics of Radical Feminism* (Boston: Beacon Press, 1978). But it is possible to open most of the early volumes of feminist theology and find that very prominent theme. It is also not rare in contemporary works to find statements such as the following: "A way of conceptualizing the distinctiveness of feminist therapy (and feminist pedagogy) is that its purpose is to heal the last 2500 years' of wounding of the feminine principle," in Ellen B. Kimmel and Barbara W. Kazanis, "Exploration of the Unrecognized Spirituality of Women's Communion," in *Women's Spirituality, Women's Lives*, ed. Judith Ochshorn and Ellen Cole (New York: Harrington Park Press, 1995), pp. 215–216. Kimmel and Kazanis cite two sources for this statement: Charles Simpkinson and Anne Simpkinson, *Sacred Stones: A Celebration of the Power of Stories to Transform and Heal* (San Francisco: Harper, 1992), and Marion Woodman, *Leaving My Father's House* (Boston: Shambhala Press, 1992). In the introduction to *Women at Worship: Interpretations of North American*

Diversity, ed. Marjorie Procter-Smith and Janet R. Walton (Louisville, Ky.: Westminster/John Knox Press, 1993), Procter-Smith says, "The development of feminist liturgies and rituals is often motivated as much by women's need to recover from deep hurt as by anything. Many of the earliest feminist liturgies were healing rituals. So perhaps this book is best understood as a kind of healing ritual itself, in the naming of pain and the claiming of ritual authority" (p. 3). And all the narratives in the first part of Chapter 2 can certainly be taken as evidence of what women describe as the need for healing.

10. Elizabeth Kastor, "Heal Us of Our All-Too-Pat 'Healing Process,'" Minneapolis *Star Tribune*, July 21, 1997, p. 6A. Kastor quotes several theologians in her article to the effect that there are some things that can't be fixed and concludes by saying, "To insist on healing before the wound has been tended, before the pain has been understood, is to end the process too soon." This is obviously a stance prevalent in women's thought about the need to end male domination of church and society.

11. See Helen Jakoski, "'My Heart Will Go Out': Healing Songs of Native American Women," *International Journal of Women's Studies* 4 (1981): pp. 118–134; Olivia M. Espin, "Spiritual Power and the Mundane World: Hispanic Female Healers in Urban U.S. Communities," *Women's Studies Quarterly* 16, nos. 3 and 4 (Fall 1988): pp. 33–47; Ana Mariella Bacigalupo, "Mapuche Women's Empowerment as Shaman-Healers (*Machis*) in Chile," in *The Annual Review of Women in World Religions*, ed. Arvind Sharma and Katherine K. Young (Albany: State University Press, Albany, 1996), pp. 57–129; Karen McCarthy Brown, *Mama Lola: A Vodou Priestess in Brooklyn* (Berkeley: University of California Press, 1991). There are other sources that point to opportunities for women in alternative forms of medicine. See Theresa Gromala, "Women in Chiropractic: Exploring a Tradition of Equity in Healing," *Chiropractic History* 3, no. 1 (1983): pp. 59–63; Naomi Rogers, "Women and Sectarian Medicine," in *Women, Health, and Medicine in America: A Historical Handbook*, ed. Rima D. Apple (New York: Garland Publishing, 1990), pp. 281–310. Also there is the whole phenomenon of women in metaphysical religious traditions that I will consider in this chapter's discussion of Mary Baker Eddy.

12. Jeanne Achterberg, *Woman as Healer: A Panoramic Survey of the Healing Activities of Women from Prehistoric Times to the Present* (Boston: Shambhala, 1991), p. 1. Achterberg describes her book as examining "the role of the feminine in the Western healing traditions" (p. 1) and thus provides a good example of a whole category of works that can be called "women's healing." Although this is not a category I explore in this chapter, it is nonetheless one that deserves acknowledgment, in part because it offers another manifestation of the essentialist/constructionist controversy in women's thought. Achterberg speaks in terms of the "feminine myth" and attributes to women's healing "intuition, nurturance, and compassion." Translated into professional practice, says Achterberg, these attributes support "the virtues of nature as healing resources, and the curative aspects of caring," and they can be embodied in men or women. For many feminists this argument for a feminine healing myth would suggest a false and dangerous essentialism, but Achterberg takes a pragmatic view about its origins: "Whether the myth originates in culture or biology is debatable and somewhat irrelevant—it simply is" (p. 3).

13. One of my favorite quotes on this subject, encountered during dissertation days, is in reference to the Spiritualist medium Cora L. V. Scott Richmond, who began her healing career as a girl of eleven in Lake Mills, Wisconsin. Cora apparently developed the ability to diagnose illnesses while in trance, and, in doing so, according to her biographer, "aroused the antagonism of the regular physicians and clergymen in the neighborhood. The former were without patients and the latter lacked audiences. . . . That village in Wisconsin soon became the center of a spiritual circle that had greater power than all the professionals taken together." In Harrison D. Barrett, *Life Work of Mrs. Cora L. V. Richmond* (Chicago: Hack and Anderson, 1895), pp. 8–9.

14. In an essay about women and patent medicine, Susan E. Cayleff describes the preparation and administration of medicine as "a vital component of women's central function in the domestic economy, as well as an extension of her caretaking role." This was the case, says Cayleff, for a variety of cultural and economic conditions. See Susan E. Cayleff, "Self-Help and the Patent Medicine Business," in *Women, Health, and Medicine in America*, p. 312. There are also very helpful recent ethnographic studies in American religion, among them Karen McCarthy Brown's *Mama Lola* (n. 11 above) and Elaine Lawless's *Holy Women, Wholly Women* (cited in previous chapters). Two other studies that particularly emphasize healing among women who are not feminists but who find ways to achieve healing and liberation in traditions that prescribe women's roles very traditionally are Robert A. Orsi, *Thank You, St. Jude: Women's Devotion to the Patron Saint of Hopeless Causes* (New Haven: Yale University Press, 1996), and R. Marie Griffith, *God's Daughters: Evangelical Women and the Power of Submission* (Berkeley, Los Angeles, London: University of California Press, 1997).

15. Some of the sources I find most helpful for thinking about relationships between healing and the construction of worldviews are concerned with various kinds of alternative healing, even though gender issues are not at all their main focus. Among them are Fred M. Frohock, *Healing Powers: Alternative Medicine, Spiritual Communities, and the State* (Chicago: University of Chicago Press, 1992); Robert Fuller, *Alternative Medicine and American Religious Life* (New York: Oxford University Press, 1992); and Meredith B. McGuire with the assistance of Debra Kantor, *Ritual Healing in Suburban America* (New Brunswick, N.J.: Rutgers University Press, 1988). Another especially good resource is the series on healing, Health/Medicine and the Faith Traditions, edited by James P. Wind and published by the Park Ridge Center of Chicago, part of the Lutheran General Health Care System. Among the traditions included are Anglicanism, Christian Science, Evangelicalism, Hinduism, Islam, Judaism, Lutheranism, Mormonism, Native North American traditions, Orthodoxy, and Roman Catholicism. These studies offer compelling evidence that "healing" is an excellent entry point for learning about a religious tradition. Some sample titles are *Health and Medicine in the Catholic Tradition* by Richard McCormick, *Health and Medicine in the Islamic Tradition* by Fazlur Rahman, and *Health and Medicine in the Christian Science Tradition* by Robert Peel.

16. Lutheran theologian Gail Ramshaw concludes *God beyond Gender: Feminist Christian God-Language* (Minneapolis: Fortress Press, 1995) with a Hasidic tale told by Martin Buber about a famous rabbi who went to the pond every day at dawn and stayed awhile. Asked after his death why he had done so, another rabbi explained that he was attempting to learn the song with which frogs praise God: "It takes a very long time to learn that song." Ramshaw compares his efforts to the feminist reform of liturgical language, and says, "We can concede that this will be a hundred-year project, but only if the church is zealously engaged in the endless and exacting tasks of reform today" (p. 135). Ramshaw excerpted the Hasidic tale from Martin Buber, *Tales of the Hasidim: The Early Masters* (New York: Schocken, 1947), p. 111. In *A Feminist Ethic of Risk* (Minneapolis: Fortress Press, 1990), Sharon D. Welch calls for "an ethic of risk that begins with the recognition that we cannot guarantee decisive changes in the near future or even in our lifetime. The ethic of risk is propelled by the equally vital recognition that to stop resisting, even when success is unimaginable, is to die" (p. 20).

17. Robert Peel, *Mary Baker Eddy: The Years of Discovery* (New York: Holt, Rinehart and Winston, 1966), p. 197. Published since 1972 by The Christian Science Publishing Company. This is the first volume of Peel's three-volume biography of Eddy, based on access to the documents in the Archives of the Mother Church of Christian Science in Boston. Peel chronicles the emotional and physical illnesses, the financial dependence on relatives, the inability to care for her child, and the long, unhappy sec-

ond marriage to Daniel Patterson after an early widowhood that were part of Eddy's bleak history up to this point. Peel is a Christian Scientist whose work on Eddy has been assessed as both sympathetic and critical, and he includes in the account of her healing some of the controversy around the extent of her injuries. Eddy's life and work, in fact, do not constitute an uncomplicated narrative. She was a controversial figure during life, and the sources of her theological ideas continue to be questioned. She and her church, her teachings, and her healing method have been subject to both caricature and over-adulation, as is often the case with founders of new religious movements, but she is also a fruitful figure to study as a woman in American religious history. It is generally agreed that she was not a feminist in the contemporary meaning of that term, but neither was she unaware of restrictions on women's roles in both church and society in nineteenth-century America. For several essays that emphasize Eddy as a woman, see Mary Farrell Bednarowski, "Mary Baker Eddy and Theological Reform," in *American Reform and Reformers: A Biographical Dictionary*, ed. Randall M. Miller and Paul A. Cimbala (Westport, Conn.: Greenwood Press, 1996), pp. 187–202; Jean A. McDonald, "Mary Baker Eddy and the Nineteenth-Century 'Public' Woman: A Feminist Appraisal," *Journal of Feminist Studies in Religion* 2, no. 1 (Spring 1986): pp. 89–111; and Susan Hill Lindley, "The Ambiguous Feminism of Mary Baker Eddy," *Journal of Religion*, no. 64 (1984): pp. 318–331. Susan Starr Sered also includes Eddy and Christian Science in *Priestess, Mother, Sacred Sister*.

18. Mary Baker Eddy, *Retrospection and Introspection* (1891), in *Prose Works Other Than Science and Health* (Boston: Christian Science Publishing Company, 1925), pp. 13–14.

19. There is no ordained clergy in Christian Science. When she retired as pastor of the Mother Church in Boston, Eddy named not another person to succeed her but the Bible and *Science and Health* to function as the pastor of the Church. In the *Manual of the Mother Church* (Boston: First Church of Christ Scientist, 1895), it is stated under "Ordination" that "I, Mary Baker Eddy, ordain the *Bible* and *Science and Health with Key to the Scriptures*, Pastor over The Mother Church, — The First Church of Christ, Scientist, in Boston, Mass., and they will continue to preach for this Church and the world" (p. 58). Readers elected by each branch church read from these sources during services. There is a Lesson-Sermon published by the Mother Church but no preached sermon, thus safeguarding against a distortion of Eddy's teachings.

20. Mary Baker Eddy, *Manual of the Mother Church* (Boston: Christian Science Publishing Company, 1980).

21. Stephen A. Gottschalk, *The Emergence of Christian Science in American Religious Life* (Berkeley: University of California Press, 1973), offers a compelling interpretation of Eddy as a Calvinist.

22. Robert Peel, *Health and Medicine in the Christian Science Tradition* (New York: Crossroad, 1988), p. 54.

23. Among them were Augusta Stetson, a one-time favorite who was eventually excommunicated and founded her own version of Christian Science; and Ursula N. Gestefeld and Emma Curtis Hopkins, both of whom became well known New Thought teachers and healers. Myrtle Fillmore, who, along with her husband Charles, founded the Unity School of Christianity, was influenced, in turn, by Hopkins. Another New Thought healing church, Divine Science, had several founders, all of them women. However, one does not have to stay with Christian Science and its offshoots to find women healers. There are Ellen G. White of Seventh Day Adventism, Pentecostal Aimee Semple McPherson of the Foursquare Gospel Church, and healing evangelist Kathryn Kuhlman. More recently there are large numbers of New Age healers, among them Louise L. Hay and Marianne Williamson.

24. A well-known author/healer in the Unity School of Christianity is Catherine Ponder, one of whose best-selling books is *The Dynamic Laws of Healing* (Marina del

Rey, Calif.: DeVorss and Company, 1966). Her writings were recommended to me by Anne McGrath, who works in the bookstore at the Unity Church in Golden Valley, Minnesota, and is a former Christian Scientist.

25. Marianne Williamson, *A Return to Love: Reflections on the Principles of a Course in Miracles* (New York: HarperCollins Publishers, 1992), p. 197.

26. C. Alan Anderson and Deborah G. Whitehouse, *New Thought: A Practical American Spirituality* (New York: Crossroad, 1995), p. 107.

27. Interview with Linda Osborne, January 15, 1993.

28. Barbara Brennan, *Hands of Light* (New York: Pleiades, 1987), p. 132. In addition to the work she does with healing, Brennan is also an atmospheric physicist and an expert on weather satellites.

29. Mary Baker Eddy, *Science and Health with Key to the Scriptures* (Boston: Christian Science Publishing Company, 1934), p. 475. First published in final form in 1910.

30. *St. Joseph's HOPE Community News* 10, no. 5 (June 1996): p. 2.

31. The March 1997 issue (vol. 11, no. 2) has an article about the twenty-year history of the community: Mary Vincent, "Spirited Weavers: A Tribute to the Love Woven through Twenty Years of St. Joe's HOPE," pp. 13–15. In 1998, St. Joseph's HOPE Community became known simply as HOPE Community.

32. Madigan, who remains a Sister of St. Joseph of Carondolet, says, "I tremble a little to describe ourselves in 'religious' ways, because we are of so many different religions; and many have been more hurt than enlivened by official religion. Of course, though, our roots are spiritual, because we are all 'of God' whose will is simply: life in abundance. That is at once very good news and a great challenge for followers of God. Talk is cheap. As I heard in church last Sunday, Jesus said to preach the good news. Use words if necessary." In "Impulse from Char Madigan," *St. Joseph's HOPE Community News* 11, no. 2 (March 1997): pp. 6–7.

33. Front cover, *St. Joseph's HOPE Community News* 10, no 5 (June 1996). For an example of Wiederkehr's writing see Macrina Wiederkehr, *A Tree Full of Angels: Seeing the Holy in the Ordinary* (New York: HarperSanFrancisco, 1988).

34. The frequency with which women in various traditions tend to construct theologies of human nature that are more hopeful than pessimistic has always intrigued me. This is due in part, certainly, to the critique on the part of both nineteenth and twentieth-century women that theologies of human depravity are likely to be more spiritually harmful to women than to men. There is also a long-standing inclination on the part of theologians and historians to assess more hopeful theologies of human nature as inadequate in their attention to evil. I think that that assessment is often made too quickly without adequate interpretation of these theologies, a tendency I find in sources as varied as William James's *The Varieties of Religious Experience* and Ann Douglas's *The Feminization of American Culture*. For an investigation of hopeful theologies constructed by nineteenth-century women, see Mary Farrell Bednarowski, "Outside the Mainstream: Women's Religion and Women Religious Leaders in Nineteenth-Century America," *Journal of the American Academy of Religion* 48, no. 2 (Summer 1980): pp. 207–231. For just one of many contemporary critiques of how doctrines of human depravity and original sin are considered harmful to women see Rosemary Radford Ruether, *Sexism and God-Talk: Toward a Feminist Theology*, 10th anniversary ed. (Boston: Beacon Press, 1993).

35. Char Madigan, "Impulse from Char Madigan," *St. Joseph's HOPE Community News* 10, no. 5 (June 1996): pp. 10–11.

36. The September 1998 newsletter, now called *HOPE Community News*, is full of photographs: members of the community, picnic celebrations of the community and National Night Out, remodeled homes in the neighborhood that house multiple fami-

lies, gardens on "the Hope block," playgrounds, and an empty lot where a new duplex will soon be built.

37. Carol Lynn Pearson, "Healing the Motherless House," in *Women and Authority: Re-Emerging Mormon Feminism*, ed. Maxine Hanks (Salt Lake City: Signature Books, 1992), pp. 231–245.

38. Linda King Newell, "Gifts of the Spirit: Women's Share," in *Sisters in Spirit: Mormon Women in Historical and Cultural Perspective*, ed. Maureen Ursenbach Beecher and Lavina Fielding Anderson, foreword by Jan Shipps (Urbana: University of Illinois Press, 1987), pp. 111–150. In the same volume in "Mormon Women and the Temple: Toward a New Understanding," Carol Cornwall Madsen recounts many instances of women's engagement in temple ordinances: "baptisms and washings and anointings [that] were administered not just as saving ordinances but also as healing ordinances" (p. 91).

39. Betina Lindsey, "Women as Healers in the Modern Church," in *Women and Authority*, p. 440.

40. Ibid., p. 439.

41. Terry Tempest Williams, *Refuge: An Unnatural History of Family and Place* (New York: Vintage Books, 1991), p. 158.

42. Lindsey, "Women as Healers in the Modern Church," p. 440.

43. Ibid., p. 454.

44. Mormon women also use the concept of healing to refer to efforts to expand images of Heavenly Mother and devotion to her. See Carol Lynn Pearson, "Healing the Motherless House," in *Women and Authority*, pp. 231–245.

45. Lynn Gottlieb, *She Who Dwells Within: A Feminist Vision of a Renewed Judaism* (New York: HarperSanFrancisco, 1995), p. 195.

46. Ibid., pp. 199–200. Jewish women are not alone in this conviction. See, for example, Marc H. Ellis, *Ending Auschwitz: The Future of Jewish and Christian Life* (Louisville, Ky.: Westminster/John Knox Press, 1994).

47. Ibid., p. 201.

48. Judith Plaskow, *Standing Again at Sinai: Judaism from a Feminist Perspective* (New York: HarperSanFrancisco, 1990). See ch. 6, "Feminist Judaism and Repair of the World," pp. 211–238.

49. Tamara M. Green, "Broken Tablets/Scattered Light," *Lilith* 21, no. 4 (Winter 1996): p. 14. This issue of *Lilith*, a Jewish feminist publication, devotes a special section to healing: "Is Our Suffering Transformative?"

50. Ibid., pp. 15–16. Nancy L. Eiseland makes some of the same accusations against Christianity—that its teachings about illness are debilitating rather than healing—in *The Disabled God: Toward a Liberatory Theology of Disability*, foreword by Rebecca S. Chopp (Nashville: Abingdon Press, 1994). See especially ch. 4, "Carnal Sins" (pp. 69–87).

51. Ibid., p. 17.

52. Marcia Cohn Spiegel, "Spirituality for Survival: Jewish Women Healing Themselves," *Journal of Feminist Studies in Religion* 12, no. 2 (Fall 1996): p. 125.

53. Ibid., p. 137.

54. Cheryl Townsend Gilkes, "The 'Loves' and 'Troubles' of African-American Women's Bodies: The Womanist Challenge to Cultural Humiliation and Community Ambivalence," in *A Troubling in My Soul: Womanist Perspectives on Evil and Suffering*, ed. Emilie M. Townes (Maryknoll, N.Y.: Orbis Books, 1993), p. 240.

55. Delores S. Williams, *Sisters in the Wilderness: The Challenge of Womanist God-Talk* (Maryknoll, N.Y.: Orbis Books, 1993), p. 60. See, in fact, all of ch. 3, "Social-Role Surrogacy: Naming Black Women's Oppression," pp. 60–83.

56. Ibid., p. 167.

57. Jacquelyn Grant, "The Sin of Servanthood and the Deliverance of Discipleship," in Townes, *A Troubling in My Soul*, pp. 199–218.

58. Katie Geneva Cannon, "'The Wounds of Jesus': Justification of Goodness in the Face of Manifold Evil," in *A Troubling in My Soul*, p. 226.

59. Ibid., p. 229.

60. Gilkes, "The 'Loves' and 'Troubles' of African-American Women's Bodies," p. 239.

61. Ibid., p. 238.

62. Ibid., p. 245.

63. Fedwa Malti-Douglas, "Faces of Sin: Corporal Geographies in Contemporary Islamist Discourse," in *Religious Reflections on the Human Body*, ed. Jane Marie Law (Bloomington: Indiana University Press, 1995), p. 67.

64. Ibid., pp. 67–69.

65. "Muslim Head Covering Is a Lightning Rod for Prejudice," Minneapolis *Star Tribune*, November 14, 1997, p. A29.

66. I also find it fruitful to interpret efforts by scholars like Riffat Hassan and Amina Wadud-Muhsin to argue for the Qu'ranic support of women's complete equality in Islam as healing in nature. Likewise a recent work by Annemarie Schimmel, long time professor of Indo-Muslim culture at Harvard, even though it is not set in the American context: *My Soul Is a Woman: The Feminine in Islam* (New York: Continuum, 1997).

67. Sharon D. Welch, *A Feminist Ethic of Risk* (Minneapolis: Fortress Press, 1990), pp. 14–15.

68. Ibid., p. 15.

69. Ibid., pp. 18–19.

70. Ibid., p. 93.

71. Ibid., p. 95.

72. Catherine Keller, *Apocalypse Now and Then: A Feminist Guide to the End of the World* (Boston: Beacon Press, 1996), p. xii.

73. Ibid., p. 11.

74. Ibid.

75. Ibid., p. 259. R. Marie Griffith's study of the Women's Aglow Fellowship also fits well as another example of where women need to engage in counter-apocalyptic thinking. In her concluding chapter Griffith calls for conservative and feminist women to stop vilifying each other, a frequent practice in both camps, and holds particularly that "[f]eminists who desire respectful treatment toward women in all spheres of life ought especially to employ such respect when journeying into the religious worlds of nonfeminist women." *God's Daughters*, p. 201.

76. Ibid., p. 11.

77. Ibid., p. 31.

78. Ibid., p. 276. In "Pro-life, Pro-choice: Can We Talk?" *Christian Century* 113, no. 1 (January 3–10, 1996), Frederica Mathewes-Green writes of one such way appearing in the formation of Common Ground Network by B. J. Isaacson-Jones, a pro-choice activist and at one time the director of a large abortion clinic. Common Ground Network does not attempt to solve the abortion issue but asks pro-choice and pro-life participants to visualize common ground as the area shared by two overlapping circles and to join each other in that space, "instead of staying in their own circles glaring at each other." Isaacson-Jones attributes the founding of the organization to her friendship with pro-life activist Loretto Wagner, who had picketed the abortion clinic, and "to a personal healing within myself" (p. 15).

79. Much of this section appeared in Mary Farrell Bednarowski, "Holistic Healing in the New Age," *Second Opinion* 19, no. 3 (January 1994): pp. 72–74.

80. Diane Stein, *The Women's Book of Healing* (St. Paul, Minn.: Llewellyn Publishers, 1987), p. xxii.

81. A very clear explanation of the seven sheaths appears in Robert S. Ellwood, *Theosophy: A Modern Expression of the Wisdom of the Ages* (Wheaton, Ill.: Theosophical Publishing House, 1986), pp. 102–106.

82. Ibid., p. 5

83. Personal interview with Linda Osborne, January 15, 1993. Osborne recommended to me a set of five books that she draws from in her healing practice. "Received" by Ceanne DeRohan and published by Four Winds Publications of Santa Fe, N. M., they are *Original Cause: The Unseen Role of Denial* (1986); *Right Use of Will: Healing and Evolving the Emotional Body* (1984, 1986); *Original Cause: The Reflection Lost Will Has to Give* (1987); *Earth Spell: The Loss of Consciousness on Earth* (1989); and *Heart Song: Vibrating Heartlessness to Let Heart In* (1992).

84. Demetra George, *Mysteries of the Dark Moon: The Healing Power of the Dark Goddess* (San Francisco: HarperSanFrancisco, 1992).

85. Ibid., p. 55.

86. Marianne Williamson, *The Healing of America* (New York: Simon and Schuster, 1997), p. 22.

87. Ibid., ch. 2, pp. 61–89.

88. Ibid., p. 177.

89. Ibid., pp. 228–229.

90. Patricia L. Wismer, "For Women in Pain: A Feminist Theology of Suffering," in *In the Embrace of God: Feminist Approaches to Theological Anthropology*, ed. Ann O'Hara Graff (Maryknoll, N.Y.: Orbis Books, 1995), pp. 146–148. Joan Griscom's essay, "On Healing the Nature/History Split in Feminist Thought," in *Feminist Theological Ethics*, ed. Lois K. Daly (Louisville, Ky.: Westminster/John Knox Press, 1994), pp. 271–281, distinguishes between what she calls "nature feminists" and "social feminists," categories that do not exactly duplicate Wismer's but overlap in many ways. Griscom laments what she sees as the split between these two groups (note "healing" in the title) and the either/or choices they seem to force: "When nature feminists assert that women are biologically superior to men, I think they are setting up a false split between men and women. When social feminists say that nature feminists are siphoning energy away from direct action if they choose to work on transforming consciousness, I think they are setting up a false either/or" (p. 280). Griscom's conclusion, like Wismer's, is to choose both: "Suddenly it becomes clear that our history is inseparably part of our nature, our social structures are inseparably part of our biology" (p. 279).

91. Rita Nakashima Brock, *Journeys by Heart: A Christology of Erotic Power* (New York: Crossroad, 1988), p. 7.

92. In her entry on "Suffering" in the *Dictionary of Feminist Theologies*, ed. Letty M. Russell and J. Shannon Clarkson (Louisville, Ky.: Westminster/John Knox Press, 1996), Flora A. Keshgegian mentions several such possibilities: "Yet another kind of suffering which ought to be considered is that which may result from choices made by a person who is trying to change or right a situation of abuse or oppression: e.g., the process of recovery from an abusive situation may entail a certain amount of pain; action against an oppressive government may result in torture or assassination; entering into solidarity with those who suffer or are oppressed may entail painful challenges and changes in one's own life" (p. 279). Robert Orsi's *Thank You, St. Jude* offers a creative interpretation of some of the differences between suffering inflicted and suffering taken on voluntarily in a very particular historical and cultural context among "daughters of immigrants" in mid-twentieth-century Chicago. In "Crossroads: Clergywomen Thinking Seriously about Leaving Church-Related Ministry" (Ph.D. diss., University of Minnesota, 1997), her study of women thinking about leaving ordained ministry and asking

themselves how much suffering is enough or too much, Karen Smith Sellers offers another angle from which to understand this tension.

93. Wismer, ""For Women in Pain," pp. 148–150.

94. Ibid., p. 142.

95. Cheryl Kirk-Duggan, *Exorcizing Evil: A Womanist Perspective on the Spirituals* (Maryknoll, N.Y.: Orbis Books, 1997), p. 74.

96. Vanessa L. Ochs, "Taking the Cure," *Tikkun* 10, no. 2 (March/April 1995): pp. 47–49.

97. Ibid.

98. Ibid.

99. Sallie McFague, *Models of God: Theology for an Ecological Nuclear Age* (Philadelphia: Fortress Press, 1987), p. 35.

100. McFague, who is particularly well known for her creation of new metaphors for God, suggests, also, that Christians go beyond human imagery: "If we now accept that language about God can result in "She who is" as well as "He who is," ought it not also, on the basis of the same reasoning, include "Nature which is?" *Super, Natural Christians: How We Should Love Nature* (Minneapolis: Fortress Press, 1997), p. 173.

101. Eiseland, *The Disabled God: Toward a Liberatory Theology of Disability*, p. 89.

102. Jacquelyn Grant, *White Women's Christ and Black Women's Jesus: Feminist Christology and Womanist Response* (Atlanta: Scholars Press, 1989), pp. 216–217.

103. Christie Cozad Neuger, "Feminist Pastoral Theology and Pastoral Counseling: A Work in Progress," *Journal of Pastoral Theology* 2 (1992): p. 53.

104. Christine M. Smith, "Preaching as an Art of Resistance," in *The Arts of Ministry: Feminist-Womanist Approaches*, ed. Christie Cozad Neuger (Louisville, Ky.: Westminster/John Knox Press), p. 39. See also Smith's *Preaching as Weeping, Confession, and Resistance: Radical Responses to Radical Evil* (Louisville, Ky.: Westminster/John Knox Press, 1992).

105. Smith, "Preaching as an Art of Resistance," p. 45.

106. Ibid., p. 56.

107. Mary Potter Engel, "Evil, Sin, and Violation of the Vulnerable," *Lift Every Voice: Constructing Christian Theologies from the Underside*, ed. Susan Brooks Thistlethwaite and Mary Potter Engel (San Francisco: Harper and Row, Publishers, 1990). Engel was a Christian theologian when she wrote this essay but has since converted to Judaism.

108. Ibid., pp. 155–156.

109. Ibid., pp. 156–164.

110. Ibid., p. 164.

111. Maura A. Ryan, "Virtue," *Dictionary of Feminist Theologies*, ed. Letty M. Russell and J. Shannon Clarkson (Louisville, Ky.: Westminster/John Knox Press, 1996), pp. 312–313.

112. Ibid., p. 313.

113. Bonnie J. Miller-McLemore, *Also A Mother: Work and Family as Theological Dilemma* (Nashville: Abingdon Press, 1994), p. 13.

114. Ibid., p. 195.

115. Ibid.

116. Frida Kerner Furman, *Facing the Mirror: Older Women and Beauty Shop Culture* (New York: Routledge, 1997).

117. Ibid., p. 184.

118. Rita M. Gross, *Feminism and Religion: An Introduction* (Boston: Beacon Press, 1996), pp. 237–238.

119. Ibid., p. 238.

120. Ibid., p. 239. As examples of women from other traditions who also take this

stance, Gross mentions Christian theologian Rosemary Radford Ruether and Goddess feminist Carol P. Christ, "who often disagree with each other quite sharply on many issues, [but] have written very similar statements about the importance of affirming finitude" (p. 239). Gross particularly mentions Ruether's *Gaia and God: An Ecofeminist Theology of Earth Healing* (New York: HarperSanFrancisco, 1992), one of many examples of women's work in what has come to be called "eco-feminism," a broad and rapidly growing area of inquiry in women's religious thought that is closely related to the subject of women and healing and links theologically the exploitation of nature and the oppression of women.

121. Nell Noddings, *Women and Evil* (Berkeley: University of California Press, 1989), p. 244.

122. Kathleen M. Sands, *Escape from Paradise: Evil and Tragedy in Feminist Theology* (Minneapolis: Fortress Press, 1994), p. xi.

123. Ibid., pp. 2–8. Sands does not see either of these strategies as reflecting "the attitudes or practices of Christian women and nonelite Christian men" (p. 2). Her critique includes specifically the writings of Rosemary Radford Ruether and Carol Christ, in whose work she finds much to praise but an inadequate acceptance of the tragic nature of human existence.

124. Ibid., p. 9.

125. Ibid.

126. Ibid., p. 168. In her concluding chapter, "A World of Color," Sands interweaves her own story with those of characters in novels by Toni Morrison, Dorothy Allison, Louise Erdrich, and Marilynne Robinson. Here, again, then, is the use of literature, in this case by both women of color and white women, to ground and illuminate theological claims.

127. Marjorie Hewitt Suchocki, *The Fall to Violence: Original Sin in Relational Theology* (New York: Continuum, 1995), p. 149.

128. Ibid., p. 153.

129. Rosemary Radford Ruether, "Christian Understandings of Human Nature and Gender," in *Religion, Feminism, and the Family*, ed. Anne Carr and Mary Stewart Van Leeuwen (Louisville, Ky.: Westminster/John Knox Press, 1996), p. 100. It is interesting to note that one of the critiques made by feminist evangelicals against the Promise Keepers movement is that it equates the characteristics of "godliness" with those of a redeemed masculinity. See Rebecca Merrill Groothius and Douglas Groothius, "Women Keep Promises, Too!: Or, The Christian Life Is for Both Men and Women," *Priscilla Papers* 11, no. 2 (Spring 1997): pp. 1–9.

130. Christie Cozad Neuger and James Newton Poling, "Introduction," *The Care of Men*, ed. Christie Cozad Neuger and James Newton Poling (Nashville: Abingdon Press, 1997), p. 22.

131. Wendy Hunter Roberts, "In Her Name: Toward a Feminist Thealogy of Pagan Ritual," in *Women at Worship: Interpretations of North American Diversity*, ed. Marjorie Procter-Smith and Janet R. Walton (Louisville, Ky.: Westminster/John Knox Press, 1993), p. 155.

132. Ibid., p. 156.

133. Nancy Mairs, *Ordinary Time: Cycles in Marriage, Faith, and Renewal* (Boston: Beacon Press, 1993), p. 3.

134. Ibid., pp. 7–9.

135. Ibid., p. 2.

136. Ibid., p. 228.

137. Ibid., pp. 228–229. A book that relates many of these themes, particularly that of deriving meaning from suffering, from the perspective of a doctor is Rachel Naomi Remen's best-selling *Kitchen Table Wisdom: Stories That Heal* (New York: Riverhead Books, 1996). Another is Margaret E. Mohrman, *Medicine as Ministry: Reflec-*

tions on Suffering, Ethics, and Hope (Cleveland: Pilgrim Press, 1995), a demonstration of theological creativity devoted to explicating how the practice of medicine itself can be understood as ministry, in part because of its highly relational nature. See especially ch. 3, "God Is Three: "Metaphors of Relation," pp. 34–50.

138. Engel, "Evil, Sin, and Violation of the Vulnerable," pp. 163–164.

139. Linda Hogan, "Sickness," in *The Book of Medicines* (Minneapolis: Coffee House Press, 1993), p. 63.

Epilogue

1. Mary Daly, *Outercourse: The Be-Dazzling Voyage* (New York: HarperSanFrancisco, 1992), p.77.

2. Robert S. Ellwood Jr., "The Study of New Religious Movements in America," *Bulletin, The Council on the Study of Religion* 10 (1979): p. 72.

3. While making the final revisions on this manuscript, I have been reading Cullen Murphy's study of feminist biblical scholarship, *The Word According to Eve: Women and the Bible in Ancient Times and Our Own* (New York: Houghton Mifflin Company, 1998). In the foreword, Murphy cites a conversation with Roman Catholic theologian David Tracy in which Murphy asked, "what he thought would be the result of feminism's encounter with religion, and he said simply, 'The next intellectual revolution.'" Murphy goes on to recount what he considers the Bible's implication in four previous intellectual revolutions, from the formation of the people of Israel through the search for new ways to interpret traditional biblical authority motivated by the Enlightenment. "Is feminism truly the Bible's fifth intellectual revolution?" asks Murphy. "That assessment may sound overblown," he says in response, "but in all likelihood it is not. Feminism's larger conversation with religion, brought about both by issues of faith and by issues that know no faith, touches every aspect of it, leaves no subject off the table" (p. xi).

4. Mary D. Pellauer, *Toward a Tradition of Feminist Theology: The Religious Social Thought of Elizabeth Cady Stanton, Susan B. Anthony, and Anna Howard Shaw* (Brooklyn: Carlson Publishing, 1991), p. 308.

Index

acceptance of finitude, 177–178
Achterberg, Jeanne, 152, 154
Adams, Carol J., 122
Adelman, Penina V., 106
Adler, Rachel, 39–41, 76
affinity, 146
African-American churches, 31
African-American women: ethic of control in literature of, 60–61; on God-language of, 80–81; healing by, 164–165; healing through literature by, 165; ministries claimed by, 51; text, oral culture, ordinary reality of, 98–101; ties to community of, 36; "two-edged sword" experience of, 30–31; who become Muslims, 112
aging experiences, 92–95, 143–144, 177
ahadith, 38–39
alienation experiences, 21–25
Allen, Paula Gunn, 96, 108–109
Allred, Janice, 72
Alourdes (Haitian woman), 147
Alpert, Rebecca, 139, 148
ambivalence: awareness of, 176–177; engendered by ordinary life, 89, 91–92; healing and, 154–155; toward sacred clothing, 113–114; value as theoretical stance, 197n.107; within traditional theology, 29; within women's religious thought, 17–21
American Muslim women, 112–114, 165–166
American religious thought: immanence in, 49–50; place of gender in, 11–14
American women's religious thought: accent on healing in, 150–151; ambivalence of, 17–21; author's views on, 14–15; catalysts for, 4–7, 16–17; developing framework for, 1–2; during feminism's second wave, 3–7; emphasis of relationality on, 148–149; ethics of ordinary life and, 116–117 (*see also* the ordinary); five themes of, 1, 2–3, 7; focus in study of, 7–9; generations engaged in, 10; importance of healing to, 182–183 (*see also* healing); intellectual revolution through, 232n.3; rationale for focus of study on, 10–14; regarding God, 54; resemblance to metaphysical religions, 199n.19; transvaluation of otherness and, 25–26, 41–

42, 84. *See also* immanence; transcendence; women's experiences
Anderson, C. Alan, 157
Andolsen, Barbara, 138
Anthony, Susan B., 185
Anti-Judaism in Feminist Religious Writings (von Kellenbach), 139
Apocalypse Now and Then: A Feminist Guide to the End of the World (Keller), 167
Aquinas, Thomas, 100
Augustine, 100
Austen, Hallie Iglehart, 106

Bambara, Toni Cade, 60, 167
Barstow, Ann, 69
Barth, Karl, 100
Beauvoir, Simone de, 22
Beck, Charlotte Joko, 64
Bettenhausen, Elizabeth, 34
Beyond God the Father (Daly), 10
Bible, 55
bimah, 106–107
Bingemer, Sister Maria Clara, 54, 55, 56, 57
the body, 141–145, 165–166. *See also* disabilities
body knowledge, 92–95
A Body Knows: A Theopoetics of Death and Resurrection (May), 92
The Body of God: An Ecological Theology (McFague), 57, 58
Bondi, Roberta, 152
The Book of Blessings (Falk), 68
The Book of Medicines (Hogan), 98, 182
Book of Revelation, 168
Book of Ruth, 103
Boucher, Sandy, 62, 128
"Bowing, Not Scraping" (Wheeler), 23
Braude, Ann, 7
Brennen, Barbara, 158
Brock, Rita Nakashima, 18–19, 28, 36–37, 171
Brown, Antoinette, 12
Brown, Karen McCarthy, 146–148
Buddhism: acceptance of finitude in, 178; earthly goals of spiritual practice, 61–64;

Dresser, Marianne, 32
Dyer, Mary, 12

Eastern religious thought, 49
Eck, Diana, 140
Eddy, Mary Baker, 12, 155, 156–159, 160, 224n.17, 225n.19. *See also* Christian Science
Edwards, Jonathan, 49
Eiesland, Nancy L., 91, 95, 173
Eller, Cynthia, 76
Ellwood, Robert S., 184–185
Encountering God: A Spiritual Journey from Bozeman to Banaras (Eck), 140
end of the world perception, 82
Engel, Mary Potter, 175, 179, 182
Episcopal Church, 53
Erickson, Kai, 104
ethic of control, 60–61
ethic of risk, 60–61
ethics of ordinary life, 114–117
Eucharist, 107, 108, 110
evangelical feminism: awareness of, 190n.14; experienced by Protestant women, 24–25; God-language constructed by, 73, 206n.127; immanence of the divine and, 73–75; writings of, 207n.130
Evangelical Lutheran Church, 37
Evangelical Protestant women, 24–25
Eve, 51
evil, 158–159, 160, 167, 171, 177, 178–179, 226n.34. *See also* good; sin
"Evil, Sin, and Violation of the Vulnerable" (Engel), 175
exclusion feelings, 21–25
Exorcizing Evil: A Womanist Perspective on the Spirituals (Kirk-Duggan), 99–100

Facing the Mirror: Older Women and Beauty Shop Culture (Furman), 177
"Faithful Iconoclast" (Brock), 19
The Fall to Violence: Original Sin in Relational Theology (Suchocki), 59
Farley, Margaret A., 120
feelings of exclusion, 21–25
female intelligence, 109
feminism's second wave movement: dualistic thinking of, 83–84; on the sacred, 90; women's religious thought during, 3–7
feminist movements: conflict between traditional theology and, 27–28; disabilities neglected by, 94; of Evangelical Protestant women, 24–25; evil, tragedy and, 178–179; experience of Jewish feminist, 19; nature vs. social, 229n.90; three generations engaged in, 10
feminist theology: anti-Judaism and Christian, 219n.82; evangelical, 73–75, 190n.14; immanence of the divine and

evangelical, 73–75; intellectual revolution and, 232n.3; Jewish, 19, 69–71; on Mary, Mother of God, 54–57; Mormon, 22–23, 27, 71–73, 161, 205n.119; panentheism/pantheism and, 75–78; relationship as central to, 120–124; Sophia link between Christianity and, 73–74; the transcendent and, 46–47; Trinity and, 132–133; Western Buddhist, 126. *See also* traditional theology
Fiorenza, Elisabeth Schüssler, 7, 31, 73
Five Books of Moses, 101
folk magic, 214n.119
forgiveness, 134
Frankenberry, Nancy, 2, 77–78, 121
Frankiel, Tamar, 46, 70–71
freedom, 25–26
Frymer-Kensky, Tikva, 42, 101–102
Fulkerson, Mary McClintock, 145–146
Furman, Frida Kerner, 143–144, 177

"Gate" (Hogan), 98
Gebara, Sister Ivone, 54, 55, 56, 57
Gede, or St. Gerard (Vodou saint), 147
Gedelia (feminine Gede), 148
gender: American religious thought and, 11–14; compassionate self and, 127; healing polarization of, 179–181; Jewish experience and, 87–88. *See also* women
George, Demetra, 169
Gilkes, Cheryl Townsend, 164, 165
Gillespie, Joanna B., 118
Gilligan, Carol, 120, 126, 128
Glancy, Diane, 96–97
gnosticism, 53
God: Bible as human word about, 55; conceptualized in Judaism/Christianity, 50; doctrines that depersonalize, 81–82; Jewish women's imagery of, 66–71; moral ambiguity of, 67; nature and, 76–78; panentheism/pantheism and, 75–78; relational metaphors for, 57; relationship of Latina women to, 79–81; women's religious thought on, 54; world as body of, 58. *See also* Trinity (Godhead)
"God Is in the Details" (Norris), 104
God-language: of African-American women, 80–81; evangelical feminist constructions of, 73, 206n.127; Jewish feminist revision of, 67; panentheism and, 78; on Shekinah, 70; survival and, 78–81; women and creation of, 65, 75
Goddess: Buddhist figures of, 63, 203n.75; Jewish feminism on the, 69–70; nature and, 76–77; Shekhinah as, 68–69, 70, 71, 74–75; Sophia imagery of the, 73–74. *See also* Heavenly Mother
Goddess theology, 134–136
Godhead (Trinity), 72, 132–133, 169

Mary Farrell Bednarowski is Professor of Religious Studies at United Theological Seminary of the Twin Cities, where she is a founding participant of the Women's Studies Program. She is the author of *American Religion: A Cultural Perspective* and *New Religions and the Theological Imagination in America,* as well as other articles and essays on women in American religious history and new religions in American culture.